Sabers through the Reich

Battles and Campaigns

The Battles and Campaigns series examines the military and strategic results of particular combat techniques, strategies, and methods used by soldiers, sailors, and airmen throughout history. Focusing on different nations and branches of the armed services, this series aims to educate readers by detailed analysis of military engagements.

Series Editor: Joseph Craig

An AUSA Book

SABERS THROUGH THE REICH

WORLD WAR II CORPS CAVALRY FROM NORMANDY TO THE ELBE

WILLIAM STUART NANCE

Foreword by Robert M. Citino

UNIVERSITY PRESS OF KENTUCKY

Paperback edition 2019

Scholarly publisher for the Commonwealth,
serving Bellarmine University, Berea College, Centre College of Kentucky, Eastern Kentucky University, The Filson Historical Society, Georgetown College, Kentucky Historical Society, Kentucky State University, Morehead State University, Murray State University, Northern Kentucky University, Transylvania University, University of Kentucky, University of Louisville, and Western Kentucky University.

Editorial and Sales Offices: The University Press of Kentucky
663 South Limestone Street, Lexington, Kentucky 40508-4008
www.kentuckypress.com

Maps and figure by Mariann K. Nance. Photographs from the WWII Signal Corps Photo Collection, U.S. Army Heritage and Education Center, Carlisle, Pennsylvania.

Library of Congress Cataloging-in-Publication Data

Names: Nance, William Stuart, author.
Title: Sabers through the Reich : World War II Corps Cavalry from Normandy to the Elbe / William Stuart Nance ; foreword by Robert M. Citino.
Description: Lexington, Kentucky : The University Press of Kentucky, 2017. | Series: Battles and campaigns | Includes bibliographical references and index.
Identifiers: LCCN 2017003552| ISBN 9780813169606 (hardcover : alk. paper) | ISBN 9780813169613 (pdf) | ISBN 9780813169620 (epub)
Subjects: LCSH: World War, 1939–1945—Cavalry operations. | World War, 1939–1945—Tank warfare. | United States. Army—Armored troops—History—20th century. | United States. Army. Cavalry—History—20th century.
Classification: LCC D769.32 .N36 2017 | DDC 940.54/1343—dc23

ISBN 978-0-8131-7753-3 (pbk. : alk. paper)

This book is printed on acid-free paper meeting the requirements of the American National Standard for Permanence in Paper for Printed Library Materials.

Manufactured in the United States of America.

Member of the Association
of University Presses

Fiddlers' Green

Halfway down the trail to Hell,
In a shady meadow green
Are the Souls of all dead troopers camped,
Near a good old-time canteen.
And this eternal resting place
Is known as Fiddlers' Green.

Marching past, straight through to Hell
The Infantry are seen.
Accompanied by the Engineers,
Artillery and Marines,
For none but the shades of Cavalrymen
Dismount at Fiddlers' Green.

Though some go curving down the trail
To seek a warmer scene.
No trooper ever gets to Hell
Ere he's emptied his canteen.
And so rides back to drink again
With friends at Fiddlers' Green.

And so when man and horse go down
Beneath a saber keen,
Or in a roaring charge of fierce melee
You stop a bullet clean,
And the hostiles come to get your scalp,
Just empty your canteen,
And put your pistol to your head
And go to Fiddlers' Green.

—Traditional American cavalry poem/song.
First appeared in print in the *Cavalry Journal* in 1923, though tradition has it that the words existed long before.

Contents

Illustrations

Maps

Photographs

Figure

Foreword

Bill Nance begins with a bold statement: "Much of what we know about American operational art in the Second World War is incomplete or wrong." It is hard not to smile when reading that line: a bold declaration of independence and purpose by a younger scholar. For someone who has been in the field for a while, such a sentence invariably provokes a defensive reaction. After all, Nance is challenging those of us who have been researching and writing on this topic for decades. Can he back it up?

The answer is yes. *Sabers through the Reich* deals with a well-defined and circumscribed topic: the operations of U.S. mechanized cavalry groups (MCGs) in the European theater in World War II. Nance is an active duty officer in the army, a cavalryman through and through. Indeed, when he studied under me as a graduate student at the University of North Texas, I occasionally had to remind him that the U.S. Army no longer has a cavalry branch! He knows cavalry—the men, the mission, and the equipment—as well as anyone in the world. The result is a highly detailed account of the MCG in Europe that is unlikely to be superseded anytime soon, if ever.

But at the same time, Nance goes well beyond a mere descriptive account and makes a point that is worth pondering about the nature of the U.S. Army, about its wartime operations, and about the true character of its doctrine. Think of the stereotypes that still pervade the literature. The Germans invented Blitzkrieg, wedding new machines to a traditionally mobile vision of war to produce lightning victories. The Red Army had "deep battle"—wave after wave (or perhaps echelon after echelon) of men and tanks attacking along the same axis, breaking through the defenders and striking hundreds of miles into the depth of the enemy position.

And the U.S. Army? Well, here we are stuck with a decidedly un-glamorous "broad front advance"—divisions, armies, and corps advancing in lockstep, carefully staying aligned with friendly forces on both flanks, grinding ahead inexorably due to the overwhelming dominance of the hyper-efficient U.S. industrial complex. Think of Courtney Hodges and the operations of the U.S. 1st Army. They got the job done in the European theater, but no one's ever going to make a movie about Hodges's "art of war." Or think of Eisenhower's generalship. Few list him among the great operators of military history or even World War II. In fact, the kudos he receives are usually those which accrue to the successful CEO or personnel manager. You can imagine him running IBM and reliably turning an annual profit.

The stereotype of the broad front advance has never been completely true, of course, but every stereotype grows from a seed of truth. Our view of the U.S. Army in World War II arose from a number of sources: the memoirs of the German officer corps, who tended to sniff at their American counterparts as being more concerned with security than with seizing opportunities in battle; the later, distasteful wars in Korea and Vietnam, in which U.S. operations were often clumsy and muscle-bound. But the truth is there. Eisenhower really did employ a broad-front strategy—armies moving forward from horizon to horizon across the countryside, and it was arguably just the ticket to beating the Wehrmacht in 1944 and 1945 with minimal friendly casualties.

But at the operational level, especially at the level of the corps, the picture was very different. As Nance shows chapter and verse, U.S. commanders employed their MCG's in an extremely innovative manner, using them to hold vast stretches of front so that the actual fighting divisions could bulk up on narrow sectors and concentrate overwhelming power against designated portions of the German defenses. The Wehrmacht could rarely draw a bead on just where the Americans were about to attack, and indeed, the U.S. Army could shift its point of main effort (its *Schwerpunkt*) literally overnight. The Germans were manpower- and division-poor, and the only way they could mount an effective defense was to anticipate the specific location of an Allied attack and assemble reserve forces to counter it. Going "Schwerpunkt to Schwerpunkt," German planners called it. Trying to do so against the Americans proved impossible, and that was in no small part due to the mechanized cavalry groups' holding thirty, forty, or fifty miles of front on either flank of the main body. Nance's focused case study, in other words, forces us to ask a big question. How and how well did this army fight? The big green machine didn't just lumber forward and blow up everything in its path (although it could do precisely that when it needed to). Rather, its corps were as mobile, as innovative, and as effective as any other force in the field.

Finally, let me offer a word of praise for the book's balance. Nance loves the cavalry, and one suspects he would have been perfectly at home on a nineteenth-century battlefield. But *Sabers through the Reich* has a good, cold eye when necessary. Having a light MCG hold the long strategic flank of a field army is a marvelous way to concentrate your forces, as long as you have the initiative. But if the enemy momentarily seizes the initiative and launches a great offensive, you suddenly have an MCG standing in the path of a large, mech-heavy attacking force. And then things do not go well. Just ask Colonel Mark Devine and the 14th MCG holding the Losheim Gap in December 1944. War is the domain of uncertainty, as Clausewitz wrote, and no matter how well trained or skilled the force, the potential for disaster is always there. But the MCGs got it right far more often than they failed. Nance is correct in pointing out that they did so "while being the smallest operational formations on the battlefield"—Davids in a land of Goliaths.

Robert M. Citino
Samuel Zemurray Stone Senior Historian
The National World War II Museum
New Orleans, Louisiana

1

Introduction

Much of what we know about American operational art in the Second World War is incomplete or wrong.[1] While the actions of divisions, corps, and field armies have been chronicled extensively throughout the past seventy years, the contributions of the corps cavalry have largely been forgotten. American corps cavalry filled their long-held doctrinal niches of reconnaissance, security, economy of force, and coordination/liaison on the operational battlefield, allowing their corps and field armies to achieve success. Although these roles proved absolutely vital to the ability of the U.S. Army to succeed, they have generally been overlooked or marginalized in campaign and battle histories. This omission is serious and dramatically affects our understanding of how the U.S. Army fought in the Second World War and beyond. While the cavalry were always in a supporting role, and never the main effort, without them the American army would have struggled to succeed.

The combat history of the cavalry groups is impressive. Participating in every American campaign but Operation MARKET-GARDEN in the European Theater of Operations (ETO), the cavalry had substantive and direct impacts on the success of the army. Cavalry led the exploitation of Operation COBRA and provided offensive guards for their parent organizations across France. Cavalry conducted economy of force missions, security missions, prisoner of war rescue missions, and by the end of the war had even participated in a daring rescue of the Lipizzaner breeding herd. These groups all contributed significantly to the overall operational success of the U.S. Army in northwestern Europe by performing the traditional cavalry missions as well as a host of other missions. Although corps cavalry did not win the war by themselves, they certainly played a major role well above that of other regiment-size formations. In fact, these groups, arguably, were the most operationally significant formations of their size in the army.

The traditional American cavalry tasks of reconnaissance, security, and economy of force are absolutely critical to the success of a military operation. However, these missions are also some of the least understood in the military lexicon, often being completely ignored or, at best, barely mentioned in military histories (official and otherwise). Perhaps the reason for this neglect is that these operations, almost by definition, occur on the fringes of, or prior to, the main action. However, reconnaissance, security, and economy of force operations can dramatically affect how a commander sees, understands, and shapes the battlefield. Without a proper understanding of how these actions occurred, historians and military practitioners can potentially gain an inaccurate understanding of the combat operation that they are studying.

Current army doctrine defines reconnaissance as "a mission undertaken to obtain, by visual observation or other detection methods, information about the activities and resources of an enemy . . . or to secure data concerning the meteorological, hydrographic, or geographic characteristics of a particular area."[2] This function has long been the province of cavalrymen, and is vital to the success of any operational maneuver. J. E. B. Stuart's cavalry's successes in the Second Bull Run campaign allowed Robert E. Lee to gain superiority in situational awareness and set the conditions for a major Confederate victory. Conversely, Lee's lack of cavalry blinded him to the locations and movements of the Army of the Potomac during the Gettysburg campaign, allowing him to blunder into battle under unfavorable circumstances.

Security operations are less well known than reconnaissance. In fact, many times the two are confused by historians and military personnel alike. The problem lies in the fact that a unit conducting security operations often, almost by definition, is also conducting reconnaissance. However, security operations are "those operations undertaken by a commander to provide early and accurate warning of enemy operations, to provide the force being protected with time and maneuver space within which to react to the enemy, and to develop the situation to allow the commander to effectively use the protected force."[3]

Security operations are further divided into screen (protection against observation); guard (protection against direct fire); and cover (protection against indirect fire). Note how reconnaissance can be included in these doctrinal tasks, but the primary mission under security operations is protecting the main body, not finding the enemy, although success in the former often requires the latter. Therefore, success in these tasks is measured by the impact on the protected force, and not necessarily on anything else. A unit conducting a security mission might be driven back ten miles, but so long as the force the unit is protecting is safe, the loss of ground does not matter.

A useful way of thinking about security forces is that they serve as the main body's crumple zone. In offensive security operations, the cavalry makes contact with enemy forces first, develops the fight, finds centers of resistance, and passes this information back to the main body. Thus, the main body is able to commit its strength where it is most needed, and not haphazardly as it would in a meeting engagement, as occurred for the Confederacy on the first day of Gettysburg or the Prussians at the battle of Auerstädt. In defensive operations, unless a unit has absolutely perfect intelligence (a near impossibility), it generally has no way of knowing exactly where an enemy will commit his main effort, and thus the choice of where to commit strength is an educated guessing game. A defensive security zone helps solve this problem by absorbing the initial attack, identifying axes of advance, potentially defeating the enemy's offensive security, inflicting casualties, and hopefully forcing the enemy to fully deploy before reaching the main defensive belt. These actions allow the defender the luxury of choosing how to strike back even when it does not initially possess the initiative.

Economy of force is defined as "the allocation of minimal combat power to secondary efforts."[4] While this is a fairly obvious concept, the application becomes much more difficult in combat. An area that is secondary to the friendly force might not be so to the enemy. The Ardennes Forest in 1940 and in 1944 is a perfect example. While the French and Americans both considered the forest a place to conserve combat power, the Germans chose that ground to mass their main efforts in both *FALL GELB* (1940) and *WACHT AM RHEIN* (1944). Therefore, a unit conducting an economy of force mission should be robust enough to handle unexpected circumstances, but not so large as to defeat the point of economizing combat power. The inherent mobility and combat power of American cavalry from the Civil War forward has made it particularly qualified to fulfill such a role.

In addition to reconnaissance, security, and economy of force operations, cavalry excels at liaison and coordination duties. These tasks are frequently overlooked by historians and military writers, but they are critical, particularly in large unit operations. When multiple formations are moving across the battlefield, their perimeters are areas of particular danger. Friendly units could engage one another, entangle their formations due to lack of traffic control, or leave gaps in the line while assuming the other unit has taken responsibility. Some of these problems can be ameliorated through proper staff work and coordination. However, things can still go wrong on the ground. The military solution to this problem is for adjacent units to talk directly to one another and establish physical coordination at what are called contact points.

However, at the operational level this solution becomes more challenging. Oftentimes an entire unit will be given responsibility to accomplish it. This organization must be able to keep pace with both its parent and the unit with which it is trying to coordinate. Additionally, although this is an important task, it is rarely one that justifies committing line infantry or armor formations. What is needed is a light, mobile formation with enough radios and combat power to talk, keep up, and take care of itself without distracting from the main effort—in short, cavalry.

Cavalry has long held these particular niches in American operational doctrine, albeit mostly in the theoretical realm. The Second World War would really be the first time since the Civil War that American forces would be maneuvering at the operational level. Interestingly enough, despite the vast plethora of theaters in this war, the U.S. Army would only conduct operational maneuvers (at the corps level) in three of them—North Africa, Italy, and northwestern Europe.[5] The campaigns in North Africa and Italy (including Sicily) provided some limited operational experience for the army, but no corps cavalry existed at that time. There were some independent squadrons operating, but most cavalry fought as part of divisional fights. Not until the campaigns in northwestern Europe would the army really have the opportunity to come into its own at the operational level of war. With this chance, the U.S. cavalry would also get its moment to shine.

Three types of cavalry formations fought in Europe from 1944 to 1945, all fulfilling the cavalry missions mentioned earlier at various levels of command. The smallest of these, cavalry reconnaissance troops, were assigned individually to each infantry division to serve as the divisional commander's personal reconnaissance formation. Progressing in size, armored reconnaissance battalions (later renamed squadrons) performed much the same role in the armored divisions, but they possessed greater capabilities due to their increased size as well as supporting elements, including light tanks and assault guns. Finally, the mechanized cavalry groups were regiment-size formations, generally consisting of two squadrons equipped similarly to the armored reconnaissance battalions and assigned to corps or armies to provide operation-level reconnaissance. These groups will be the focus of this study. The cavalry reconnaissance troops and the armored reconnaissance battalions performed admirably, but their contributions were generally limited to the tactical level. The mechanized cavalry groups, however, contributed to the operational success of the U.S. Army in the ETO.

Studies of the U.S. cavalry in the Second World War are few and far between. In fact, for a number of years there was no significant scholarship on the topic at all. Even the U.S. Army "Green Book" series, so comprehensive in so many areas, barely recorded the achievements of most of the mechanized cavalry. All that remained to recall the cavalry's accomplishments were a small number of histories published at the close of the war by the veterans of these groups.

In the mid-1990s, a small group of army officers (specifically cavalrymen and tankers) began to address this oversight. John Tully conducted perhaps the first study of this new renaissance in his very personal master's thesis recounting the deeds of the 4th Cavalry Group, commanded by Tully's grandfather. Dean A. Nowowiejski followed shortly thereafter with a monograph arguing that the cavalry branch failed to adapt to the changing nature of warfare and that this failure led to battlefield difficulties. Louis DiMarco then wrote his master's thesis on the failed doctrine of the mechanized cavalry, and argued that the cavalry's success hinged on ignoring the new doctrine while retaining the best of the old procedures of the horse cavalry. Matthew Dooley then followed DiMarco's thesis with his own, in which he railed against separating reconnaissance and security into different formations, using the mechanized cavalry as his first exhibit.[6]

Despite this small surge in scholarly work, it was not until 2006 that the first book on mechanized cavalry in over a generation arrived, George F. Hofmann's *Through Mobility We Conquer.* Creating the seminal background work on the topic, Hofmann nevertheless steered away from controversy in his book. Additionally, Hofmann only devoted a small portion of his piece to actual combat operations, and then further subdivided it into discussions of all the different forms of cavalry. Harry Yeide followed two years later with his *Steeds of Steel,* a general study of all American cavalry operations in the Second World War. It had much less detail than Hofmann, though Yeide did include information on cavalry operations in the Pacific. Matthew Morton's recent work, *Men on Iron Ponies,* presents a narrower but more tightly focused work on the cavalry, and is currently the best work on the subject, except for Hofmann's overarching work. Robert Cameron (best known for his synthesis on the history of the armor branch, *Mobility, Shock, and Firepower*) in his 2010 work, *To Fight or Not to Fight?,* addresses many of the same issues of mechanized cavalry as the others, but continues the story of Hofmann's work that ends in 1950 by recounting the history of cavalry and reconnaissance forces to the present day. In a 2011 dissertation, Christopher Prigge touches on the mechanized cavalry in his sweeping narrative of American cavalry doctrine development. Finally, Gary Palmer's *The United States Cavalry: Time of Transition* provides a fascinating insight into the mechanization of the cavalry branch, predominately through the eyes of the troopers of the 106th Cavalry Regiment (soon to be the 106th Mechanized Cavalry Group).[7]

While the recent growth in scholarship of American cavalry in the World War II era is heartening, the overwhelming emphasis has been on either the reformed cavalry doctrine of the 1940s or the mechanization debate that consumed much of the 1930s and early 1940s. So far, historians have placed very little emphasis on the actual combat history of the cavalry groups. Harry Yeide stands as the exception to this rule, but his work, while exceptional, makes no effort to present a comprehensive operational analysis.

The reason behind this trend in cavalry scholarship is that much of it was inspired by doctrinal debates on the structure and organization of how the army will field its mounted forces in the twenty-first century. As such, the authors' assessments are heavily weighted to support arguments in this current debate. The battle analyses presented by these authors have been excellent, but also episodic—jumping from one group to the next—without a great deal of continuity for any unit. Additionally, most of these authors rarely spend much time assessing the cavalry's role in the corps battle. Finally, these works often make little distinction between the different kinds of cavalry available to the army. This trend is acceptable in these works, as they are making generalized statements about the mechanized cavalry and doctrine to support a current argument and are not focused on the achievements of a specific formation. Tully stands alone in presenting in great detail the achievements of the 4th Group, but he does not assess its sister groups in the First Army and their cumulative effect on that formation.

Moreover, while the preceding scholarship in this field has been excellent, its overemphasis on doctrine and organization has tended to overshadow the actual accomplishments of the corps cavalry, which are numerous and deserving of notice. Additionally, doctrine only gets an army so far. By all accounts of the mechanized cavalry, the new doctrine of the 1940s that has been so roundly criticized in the historiography was barely used. While the new theory of "reconnaissance only" (to be discussed in the next chapter) did shape tables of organization, all commentators agree that the cavalry and the army at large found ways around this new doctrine's structural flaws. Thus, too tight a focus on published doctrine detracts from an understanding of how the army actually fought in World War II. Finally, while this scholarship has provided insight into doctrinal and organizational development for the U.S. Army during a period of intense turmoil, it has also pulled attention away from introducing serious study of security operations during the war. This is a deficiency that this work attempts to resolve. Therefore, a complete study into the battlefield contributions of U.S. corps cavalry in the ETO is long overdue.

In his 2013 article "The U.S. Mechanized Cavalry's Critical Contribution to Allied Victory in Europe, 1944–1945," Lou DiMarco begins to address the obvious shortcomings in the historiography. He addresses the full range of missions that cavalry performed. However, he asserts that the primary contributions of the mechanized cavalry lay in its ability to dismount to fight as infantry as well as its capacity to perform economy of force missions. These two capabilities allowed the rest of the army to concentrate its forces for the decisive blows in the campaigns in northwestern Europe.[8] While DiMarco is absolutely correct in his assertions, he does not go far enough. The cavalry were not simply important to individual corps battles—they were vital to the success of the ETO. Furthermore, while economy of force missions were certainly a huge part of the cavalry's contributions, reconnaissance, security, and coordination/liaison missions require the same emphasis. Finally, although DiMarco's work is a solid start in this field, a subject involving thirteen regiment-size formations fighting over a span of eleven months cannot fully be addressed by a single article.

My intent is to follow in DiMarco's footsteps and complete the work he started. Contained in the following pages is the most complete operational history of American corps cavalry to date. While the work is heavily based on American sources, its intent is not to provide detailed campaign analyses, but rather to provide a basic construct of what happened in Europe. Therefore, I have leaned heavily on the American official histories, the "Green Books," as well as the vast plethora of excellent campaign studies available to provide the larger operational narrative. These works have already provided the story. I have simply placed the corps cavalry into this framework, demonstrating how these formations proved vital to the overall success of the army. Additionally, I have shied away from addressing the great controversies of the war. Whether or not a campaign could have been fought more efficiently is not important here, but rather how the cavalry enabled its parent organizations to fight once the strategic and operational decisions had been made. My hope is that the reader leaves this work with an understanding of how cavalry contributed to victory in the ETO, and also an appreciation for the role of security operations on the operational battlefield.

2

Background

The American cavalry groups of the European Theater of Operations, as opposed to the new armor divisions, were not new organizations.[1] Rather, they were heirs of a unique and proud heritage and tradition that the army leadership had subjected to massive revision in a very short period of time. The history of how the army viewed cavalry and the horribly confusing doctrinal shift concerning cavalry in the early 1940s sheds a great deal of light onto the challenges of corps cavalry during World War II. Significantly, commanders from the regimental level to the army groups grew up with one form of cavalry and were suddenly presented with a new table of equipment and with a new, experimental doctrine immediately prior to entering combat. This shift explains why, even as late as 1945, senior leaders, to include Lucian Truscott and John Wainwright, advocated for the retention of at least limited horse cavalry.[2] It also explains the dramatic revisions of cavalry doctrine over the next fifty years, away from strictly reconnaissance and back to the more traditional cavalry missions, as commanders essentially ignored the changes of the early 1940s and used their cavalry as they had been trained to use it.[3]

The U.S. cavalry has long been different than its European counterparts. During the Napoleonic era, when vast cavalry corps participated in titanic battles, the fledgling United States possessed a single regiment of mounted soldiers.[4] The nation did not raise its first two permanently established regiments of cavalry until the 1830s.[5] These regiments were dragoons, a form of light cavalry armed with short-range carbines and often associated with dismounted fighting. A regiment of mounted riflemen, essentially mobile infantry, augmented the two regiments of dragoons in 1846.[6] These early cavalry regiments served on the frontier, fighting in small detachments, to secure the population from hostile Native Americans. This style of combat did not often allow for the massed saber and lance charges of the European continent. Thus, the Americans became more dependent on their horses for transportation than as battle platforms. Ambushes, distant reconnaissance, and small firefights (often dismounted) became the currency of the American cavalier.[7]

The American style of mounted combat would continue to evolve throughout the Mexican War and Civil War. In both conflicts there remained a decided lack of actual mounted (horse-on-horse) combat. More commonly, both sides used their cavalry as reconnaissance and security formations and not as active participants on the main field of battle. After the Civil War, mounted action for the American cavalry consisted of small unit actions against Native Americans. Once again, the dragoon style of fighting proved to be the most effective means of combat. Finally, the experience of the U.S. cavalry in both the Spanish-American War and the Philippine Insurrection saw mounted formations constantly fighting on foot. In fact, the famous charge up San Juan Hill (and Kettle Hill) by the 10th U.S. Cavalry and the 1st U.S. Volunteer Cavalry Regiment was conducted entirely on foot, under the cover of Gatling guns, in an assault that bore a striking resemblance to some infantry actions in the First World War.[8]

From the preceding examples, it becomes obvious that the American cavalry had a long tradition of fighting both mounted and dismounted, utilizing fire and maneuver as much as their brethren in the infantry. The earliest available American cavalry manual, *Drill Regulations for Cavalry, United States Army,* first published in 1896, codified much of the experience gained in the previous century and emphasized these points. This manual was updated in 1902 and again in 1909, with final pre–Great War corrections and revisions coming in 1911 (*DRC 1911*).[9]

A huge portion of *DRC 1911* is committed to basic soldier tasks, including how to march, salute, stack arms, etc. However, even in the section entitled "School of the Soldier," some conclusions can be drawn as to how the cavalry expected to fight. From the illustrations and attention given to the concept of firing both the rifle and pistol (fully one-third of this section), it is apparent that the U.S. cavalry viewed the firearm as an essential part of the trooper's gear.[10] Furthermore, the manual instructs new troopers in the art of firing either prone or kneeling, essential to any soldier expecting to fight dismounted. It then spends a full nine paragraphs detailing how to carry and fire the rifle and pistol from the horse, including such admonishments as "aim well to the left of the horse's head."[11] In contrast, saber movements are covered in two short paragraphs. Further reinforcing this idea of the essential nature of the firearm to cavalry, the manual specifies: "In the charge in close order and in the melee, the saber is habitually used, but under favorable conditions the pistol may be used in the charge in close order. The pistol should habitually be used in the pursuit or retreat following the charge, and in the charge as foragers."[12] This section outlines some interesting doctrinal thoughts. Perhaps the most obvious point is that the American cavalry still believed in the efficacy of a mounted assault. However, the cavalry also seemed to believe the pistol to be the most effective weapon while mounted, not the saber. In fact, as the manual clearly asserts, the saber was expected to be used only in a massed, tight formation charge, or a horse-on-horse melee, something with which American cavalry did not have much experience.[13] Despite the continued presence of the saber, the rest of the paragraph clearly demonstrates that the American cavalry viewed firepower as more important than simple shock action on the battlefield.

In concluding its remarks on basic soldier and trooper tasks, *DRC 1911* commits a substantial amount of effort to the concept of extended order, wherein each trooper moves independently as part of a larger mass. Included in this section is a large amount of direction on how to fight on foot, and it generally matches what would be seen for infantry training. Although this portion and the preceding sections are all individual- or squad-level tasks, and not doctrine per se, they do show the basic skills that the cavalry branch expected of the units that would carry out their operational doctrine. Thus, these sections clearly demonstrate that the American cavalry of the pre–First World War era expected the modern trooper to be equally familiar in combat off his horse as he was upon it. Additionally, these sections prove that the use of cover, fire, and maneuver were also important to American cavaliers, perhaps even more so than the cherished ancient cavalry ideal of shock.

DRC 1911 also demonstrates that the early twentieth-century American cavalry had a full appreciation of the dangers of the modern battlefield, and retained a practical view of the horse in combat. In fact, the duties of the cavalry during a general engagement are explicitly detailed in the manual as:

> Preliminary to the general engagement, the cavalry divisions that have been scouting and reconnoitering remain in front of the main body to harass the enemy and mask their own troops. When the engagement has begun, they clear the front and take position on a flank. While conforming to general instructions, the commander of the cavalry should not neglect to act efficiently in any way that chance may offer. He may, with his horse artillery, gain the flank or rear of the enemy; aid and support a flanking force of infantry; oppose a flanking movement on the part of the enemy; oppose every offensive movement of the enemy's cavalry; fill up, provisionally, gaps made in the line of battle; meet and delay bodies of the enemy endeavoring to join in the battle; in defeat, retard the enemy's pursuit; when victorious, pursue the enemy.[14]

As can be seen, the cavalry branch expected to operate aggressively against enemy cavalry in the security fight, but was circumspect about attacking infantry as early as 1911. A list of occasions when infantry may be charged by cavalry is given, but they all resolve down to advising commanders to never charge infantry unless the enemy is seriously inhibited in some manner. In fact, the manual specifies that "unbroken infantry may be charged by cavalry to accomplish some special end; it can be useful only to the extent of its influence in causing delay or drawing fire, which is taken advantage of by other troops."[15] These paragraphs speak to an understanding of the firepower of unbroken infantry, with the branch installing safeguards into its doctrine to prevent needless loss of life. This doctrine is echoed in the army's official capstone doctrinal statement of the pre–First World War era, *Field Service Regulations 1913* (*FSR 1913*), which assigned cavalry the reconnaissance and security missions but kept it from the general battle, except as flank protection and a mobile reserve.[16]

Thus, far from being a branch stubbornly clinging to its mounts for the sake of tradition in the face of changing technology, American cavalry demonstrated a workable (although not perfect) understanding of the flexible role of mounted troops in contemporary combat. While the days of massed cavalry charges were certainly numbered even before the First World War, this development meant little to the American cavalry, as their key missions remained reconnaissance, security, economy of force, and liaison/coordination.[17] These missions require a specialized unit that is, at its heart, a compromise between agility and robust combat power.

This compromise often resulted in fundamental misunderstandings of how to use cavalry, and therefore how to equip them. At the core of the problem was the tension between two of the basic missions of cavalry: reconnaissance and security. The two are very similar in how they are conducted, but there are substantial differences—the most important of which is the amount of combat expected. Reconnaissance simply requires locating the enemy and procuring information on him. Security missions, on the other hand, demand the defeat of enemy reconnaissance or security forces in order to allow the friendly main body time and space in which to maneuver.

The idea that a unit can always conduct reconnaissance and avoid fighting for information through either stealth or technology is seductive. These units can be smaller and less heavily equipped than those built for security operations. Unfortunately, neither stealth nor technology are panaceas in the brutally chaotic and unpredictable environment of war. Units designed solely for reconnaissance will often find that in order to accomplish this mission they will have to engage in combat, sometimes merely to survive long enough to report. The American cavalry branch prior to 1940 had long understood this issue, as noted previously, and emphasized robust combat formations that were capable of conducting security operations, fighting dismounted, and moving mounted, all the while retaining the ability to conduct reconnaissance.

The First World War began what many in the American cavalry viewed as a struggle for no less than the survival of their profession. The Western Front demonstrated the futility of horses in modern positional warfare. Although the British kept large mounted reserves to exploit a breakthrough, this was impractical considering the extreme vulnerability of horse-mounted troops to machine guns and artillery, as well as the broken nature of the trench battlefield. Additionally, the invention and use of tanks and armored cars promised a new form of warfare that pointed away from the use of the horse. However, despite the difficulties of open maneuver throughout the First World War, U.S. military leaders still believed in the concept and the inherent superiority of this type of warfare. This conviction resulted from the successes of such operations at the end of the war.[18]

The U.S. Army's capstone doctrinal statement, *Field Service Regulations 1923* (*FSR 1923*), reflected the American military leadership's trust in movement over positional warfare. In this document, which would stand until 1939, cavalry is noted as a highly mobile force that "executes the missions of reconnaissance, counter-reconnaissance, and security in the service of large units and delivers combat in the execution of these missions and in combination with the operations of other elements of the large units to which it is assigned."[19] Furthermore, the authors of *FSR 1923* argue that cavalry screening operations are "most effective when the cavalry is employed as a mass to engage and defeat the hostile cavalry."[20] Note how the army expected its cavalry not only to find the enemy, but also to fight in order to gain information and prevent enemy reconnaissance efforts. Finally, cavalry was expected to conduct offensive operations against targets of opportunity, as seen from the following excerpt from *FSR 1923*: "Cavalry constitutes a mobile fire element in the hands of higher commanders. It is especially adapted to combat missions requiring rapidity of attack and delaying action. Rapidity of movement enables cavalry to take advantage of opportunities to strike a sudden blow at weak points in the hostile dispositions. It may thus be employed to attack hostile forces in process of concentration, to operate against exposed enemy flanks or rear, and to exploit by pursuit the successes obtained by other arms. Its rapidity of movement enables cavalry to meet critical situations arising in the course of operations."[21]

Nowhere throughout the entire portion on cavalry does *FSR 1923* insist that horses are the only means for cavalry to accomplish its mission. The inclusion of horses was probably assumed, especially since cavalry troopers were still to be armed with sabers and there were few alternatives to horses in 1923. However, the descriptions of what the cavalry was intended to accomplish in *FSR 1923* do not limit them merely to equine transportation. In fact, when viewing the topic utterly dispassionately, any platform that offered cavalry the same mobility and combat capabilities would suffice. Moreover, cavalry already assumed the use of limited numbers of armored cars in larger formations, such as at the regimental and divisional level. Thus, the great debate over retention of the horse throughout the 1920s and 1930s would center on what platform, or combinations of platforms, would provide the most efficient means of accomplishing the cavalry's mission.

The army began the 1920s with the National Defense Act of 1920 abolishing the Tank Corps and placing all tank development under the auspices of the infantry branch.[22] Under this organization, senior leaders gave the armored forces two doctrinal missions. The first was to penetrate enemy lines, and the second was to accompany infantry forces in order to prevent a reversion to positional warfare. Both of these tasks are a direct reflection of the standard view of tanks held across Europe. Neither task called for a fast tank capable of quick maneuver—an absolute requirement for cavalry formations. Brigadier General Samuel Rockenbach, the first commander of the Tank Corps and the first commandant of the Tank School, insisted on the development of armored vehicles that would serve multiple roles. While still acknowledging the tank as a support weapon, Rockenbach started the drive for a reliable medium tank that could perform these two doctrinal roles and thereby reduce the economic cost of maintaining the Tank Corps.[23]

Early in the 1920s, army officers continued to debate the appropriate role for mechanization. Although official doctrine tied the tank to the infantry branch, cavalry officers viewed the tank and other mechanized vehicles as an appropriate platform to enhance the abilities of the cavalry. Major Bradford Chynoweth published an article extolling the virtues of cavalry tanks.[24] These views were reinforced by British experiences in Palestine during the First World War, when United Kingdom cavalry forces equipped with armored cars assisted Field Marshal Edmund Allenby in defeating superior Turkish forces.

British experimentation with medium tanks in 1925 also sparked cavalry branch interest, as the branch had always been more concerned with the marriage of firepower and mobility than the infantry. The cavalry branch's desire for fast "cavalry tanks" inspired a decade-long army association with the inventor J. Walter Christie to create such a vehicle. Christie produced a number of very fast prototypes, but their failure to meet army specifications meant that none of them ever went into production in the United States.[25] These failures would help retard American tank development as the army committed time and resources to an ultimately flawed designer.[26]

In April 1930, Colonel James Parsons, commandant of the U.S. Tank School (an infantry branch organization), argued for the establishment of six tank divisions, one assigned to each field army. These tank divisions would essentially replace the role of cavalry in many respects, as Parsons argued that these formations could "[cover] the advance and flank of the main force, [exploit] a breakthrough . . . , [seizing] strategical positions and filling gaps in the line."[27] This proposal was a significant affront to the cavalry branch, as the infantry branch controlled all the tanks in the army—and thus the new tank divisions. Therefore, these new divisions would place most of the cavalry's functions under the purview of the infantry. While this argument seems parochial (and is to a degree), it actually made sense at the time. The two branches possessed very different ideas over the employment of combat power. The cavalry generally focused heavily upon maneuver, while the infantry were more firepower oriented. Thus, for the cavalry branch to cede missions to the infantry branch would essentially concede doctrinal debates on the use of mechanized vehicles and the place of cavalry on the battlefield, while admitting complete irrelevance. Due to resistance from the cavalry branch, as well as many of the other branch chiefs, Parson's idea was defeated and promptly ignored.[28]

In 1931, the chief of staff of the army, General Douglas MacArthur, ordered that the army would not have a single unified mechanization doctrine, but rather that the branches would study the problem independently and create their own unique solutions to the issue. At this juncture, the cavalry branch did not view mechanization as a full-bore threat to the use of the horse. Rather, as seen by its interest in cavalry tanks (known as combat cars to get around the legal restrictions keeping tanks in the infantry), the branch viewed these vehicles as a way to augment their combat power. As noted in the *Cavalry Journal,* motorized vehicles would allow the cavalry to carry more firepower and equipment while simultaneously reducing the load on packhorses.[29]

The chief arguments against the full-scale mechanization of the U.S. cavalry revolved primarily on the alleged superior mobility, sustainability, and reliability of the horse. Bernard Lentz, an infantryman writing in the *Cavalry Journal,* summarized these arguments neatly in an article in which he challenged the reader to imagine the battle of Eylau fought with motorized vehicles. He asked, "Would the engines have started on this bleak February morning, and if so would they have any place to go?"[30] He additionally noted the large amount of rough terrain abounding in the world and how current vehicles were unsuited to traverse them, while horsed cavalry could manage these challenges. Furthermore, the unique challenges and vast distances of the North American continent presented difficulties for a mechanized or even partially mechanized force. Allenby's assault to Damascus, which included extensive use of armored cars and was often noted as an example of a long-range mechanized mission, covered a distance equal to only two-thirds of the Texas border with Mexico. Therefore, any use of mechanized vehicles in the American Southwest (the most likely deployment area for American cavalry) would face dramatic logistical issues in terms of fuel, spare parts, and vehicle recovery. Horses could subsist off the land for short periods, vehicles could not. Despite these difficulties, the cavalry decided on a limited test for mechanized formations.

In 1933 the cavalry branch formed the 7th Cavalry Brigade (Mechanized), with a combination of light tanks and armored cars. This brigade served as a test bed for cavalry mechanization. Due to legal restrictions emplaced by the 1920 National Defense Act, restricting tank development to the infantry branch, cavalry tanks could not be designated as "tanks," but rather were referred to as "combat cars." However, at this particular stage in their development cavalry combat cars differed little from the infantry branch's experimental light and medium tanks.[31] While the sleight of hand in names did trend toward the absurd, it also speaks to the ingenuity of some officers in the cavalry branch and the army in general to overcome bureaucratic obstacles.

By 1934, the cavalry branch had decided scout cars were of enough utility to provide an armored car platoon to each horse cavalry regiment.[32] These cars would serve as highly mobile forward scouts for the horsed elements of the regiment, which would still provide the main combat power of the formation. Additionally, as noted above, the branch decided to motorize the logistics elements of the horse cavalry regiments. Cavalry officers viewed the mechanized (more appropriately motorized) elements within the horse regiments as force multipliers, but not necessarily as vital to the overall success of the mission.[33]

The 7th Cavalry Brigade faced significant hurdles to its development, including lackluster support from its own branch as well as a lack of vehicles with which to train. However, it did accomplish a significant amount of doctrinal progress, drawing on lessons learned primarily from German sources. In 1935 a small number of American officers, including a limited number of cavalrymen, were allowed to attend the German *Kriegsakademie*.[34] This helped to greatly increase American understanding of new German doctrinal trends and development. Moreover, one only has to look at the performance and organization of the 7th Cavalry Brigade in maneuvers to note the German influence, as it emphasized rapid, violent, decentralized execution at the small unit level. The brigade's tactics essentially involved the armored car elements conducting reconnaissance that would then pull the heavier combat cars to the decisive point.[35] The armored cars were very firmly fixed to the principle of stealth reconnaissance, "[attacking] by fire only and [seeking] concealed positions."[36] The reason behind this approach was that the armored cars lacked the ability to drop dismounts and thus could not protect themselves in restricted terrain. Additionally, the vehicles lacked the necessary armor to protect them from heavy machine guns or anti-tank guns. Therefore, while useful, the armored cars were fragile creatures.

The armored reconnaissance car proved successful in the 7th Cavalry Brigade's tests and the vehicles were soon firmly established in the table of organization and equipment of the horse cavalry regiments. However, formations built for stealth-only reconnaissance require a nearby combat formation for battlefield survival. Basically, the scouts would find the enemy, then bring forward the killers to finish the fight. In the case of the 7th Cavalry Brigade, this combat formation was near at hand in the form of combat cars (tanks) organic to the formation. In the case of armored cars assigned to horse cavalry regiments, the line squadrons provided that combat power.

In August 1939, the 7th Cavalry Brigade performed so well in the First Army maneuvers in New York that they had to be stopped by the exercise controllers before they prematurely ended the exercise by crushing the opposing forces' rear areas and supply lines.[37] The brigade operated as a concentrated mechanized force, utilizing its speed and mobility to pierce the enemy's line and then completely disrupt its rear areas, in a textbook example of U.S. horse cavalry doctrine. The speed and firepower of the 7th Cavalry Brigade was unlike anything previously created by the army.

However, the U.S. mechanized cavalry (the 7th Cavalry Brigade and the armored cars assigned to the horse regiments) had a crucial lack of infantry or dismounted personnel in the organization. This issue was particularly problematic, as it was still expected to conduct traditional cavalry missions—which for the American cavalry arm had always meant dismounted combat in conjunction with mounted maneuver. The 1941 field service regulations (*FM 100-5*), making no differentiation between horse and mechanized cavalry, lists cavalry missions as: "Cavalry is capable of offensive combat; exploitation and pursuit; seizing and holding important terrain . . . ; ground reconnaissance; screening; security for the front, flanks, and rear of other forces on the march, at the halt, and in battle; delaying action; covering the retrograde action of other forces; combat liaison between large units; acting as a mobile reserve for other forces; harassing action; and surprise action against designated objectives deep in hostile rear areas."[38]

The army generally understood the concept of the cavalry's need to fight both mounted and dismounted, as evidenced in the 1941 version of *FM 100-5,* in which it clearly states that "large bodies of horse cavalry usually maneuver mounted and fight dismounted."[39] This doctrine allowed the cavalry to use its horses for rapid maneuver, then dismount to take full advantage of stabilized firepower (as opposed to shooting from a horse) and the ability to take cover and fight in rough terrain. However, working from vehicles meant that mechanized cavalrymen needed to stay near their vehicles to maximize the combat enablers that came with vehicles (radios, mounted machine guns, mortars, etc.), thereby limiting the amount of troopers available for action on the ground. The cavalry branch had accepted the fact that the mechanized cavalry would be undermanned in dismounted combat, and so it provided these formations with an abundance of firepower, more than for a normal horse cavalry regiment, in order to compensate for fewer riflemen.[40]

Additionally, acknowledging the fact that full combat operations require many more men on the ground than a mechanized cavalry formation could muster, the branch emphasized the mission of reconnaissance for the mechanized formations of horse regiments, leaving the primary fighting to the horse cavalry, as noted earlier. The problem of fighting for information was "solved" by keeping mechanized formations close to larger combat formations—either horsed or line infantry formations. The 7th Cavalry Brigade, as the only completely mechanized formation, provided the branch with an interesting quandary on this issue. It had done well in tests using its mobility, but still suffered from a lack of dismounts. The cavalry branch never did solve this problem to anyone's satisfaction. Unfortunately, since outside of the cavalry branch mechanized cavalry was assumed to be merely a cavalry on a different platform, the lack of dismounted troopers in mechanized formations, either in the armored car formations or the 7th Cavalry Brigade, was not something that was studied in great detail at the army level until the outbreak of the Second World War.

Despite growing evidence that mechanized formations were improving in terms of reliability and mobility, the cavalry branch still persisted in its belief that the horse should remain its dominant platform. As late as 1939, cavalry officers were still insisting that although mechanized cavalry was important, it simply could not fulfill all the mission requirements of the cavalry branch.[41] These officers argued that the future of the cavalry lay in the cooperation of horse and machine, with each element complementing the other. Considering the actual limitations of mechanized cavalry equipment at the time, this argument made some sense. Cavalry officers understood the dangers of enemy aircraft to mechanized columns and realized that horse formations possessed greater stealth than these units, although at the cost of heavy firepower. However, this cost was acceptable because, although horse units had fewer heavy weapons, they had more dismounts, and thus were considered more suitable for combat operations across multiple terrain types. Moreover, horses could operate across muddy or extremely broken terrain much more effectively than the wheel-borne forces of the mechanized forces.

Reports from the Spanish Civil War also suggested that mechanized forces were not as effective as theorized. Even the highly influential mechanized cavalryman Brigadier General Van Voorhis described the failings of mechanization in that war, acknowledging that mechanical unreliability played a large part in these failures.[42] But cavalry branch leaders also appreciated that the increased lethality of the modern battlefield made the man on a horse a tremendous target, and thus insisted on cooperation between horse and mechanized formations in the attack. Mechanized cavalry would serve to suppress the enemy with its greater firepower, while the horse cavalry would seize and hold terrain. However, despite this concession to the growing utility of mechanized vehicles, the cavalry branch still considered them an auxiliary arm, albeit a useful one, and still continued to relegate these formations mostly to reconnaissance.

In May 1940 the U.S. Third Army conducted a series of exercises to test the various mobile elements of the army in the first ever army-level exercises.[43] The horse-mounted 1st Cavalry Division, the mixed motorized and horse corps reconnaissance 6th Cavalry Regiment, the 7th Cavalry Brigade (Mechanized), and a provisional tank brigade comprised of infantry tank battalions all participated in the exercise. The 7th Cavalry Brigade and the provisional tank brigade performed well and stimulated more intense interest in forming a tank board separate from the infantry. Moreover, the ad hoc arrangement of the two brigades into a mechanized division proved to be a powerful force. This provisional division still had serious flaws, most notably the lack of a coherent staff organization and the lack of dedicated infantry or artillery support. Unfortunately for proponents of the horse cavalry, the performance of both their pure and mixed horse formations proved disappointing.[44]

At the completion of the exercise, Brigadier General Frank Andrews, the army G3 (operations), conducted an after action review with the members of the 7th Cavalry Brigade. His conclusions, endorsed by General Marshall, recommended the establishment of an independent armored force with responsibility for all mechanized forces in the army. With support from General George C. Marshall, the Armor Force was established on 10 July 1940. Both Major General George Lynch and Major General John Herr, the current chiefs of infantry and cavalry, respectively, opposed this move. Lynch argued that the German panzer divisions were simply "armored cavalry."[45] Herr opposed the new branch because he also saw it duplicating many of the same roles as cavalry. It could also be pointed out that both branch chiefs stood to lose substantial parts of their organizations, and the substantial funding that came with them, to a new branch.

The creation of the Armor Force and the resulting loss of all cavalry combat cars (as well as the 7th Cavalry Brigade) would prove disastrous for mechanized cavalry doctrine. The slowly emerging doctrine of reconnaissance units closely linked to combat formations immediately began to unravel with the departure of the cavalry tanks. This close relationship (and proximity) between hunters and killers was what had allowed the light combat cars to survive and succeed in tests. Thus, stealth reconnaissance worked, but generally only when immediately (in the same formation) backed by combat forces strong enough to fight and win against most security zone adversaries. Although the horse cavalry regiments still maintained their armored cars, mechanized cavalry doctrine was frozen into stealth reconnaissance only, as the only formations that had been fully equipped with vehicles were now part of a new branch. The cavalry branch, relieved from the pressure of needing to advance mechanized doctrine beyond this point due to the lack of this kind of unit, simply chose not to continue experimentation along this line. It retained its horse regiments and, under the prevailing orthodoxy of the branch, continued to believe that they would be sufficient to meet the doctrinal requirements as laid out in *FSR 1923* and its revision in 1939 (almost a complete reprint of the earlier manual).[46]

In April of 1941, the cavalry branch published *FM 2-10: Cavalry Field Manual: Mechanized Elements* for its remaining mechanized formations, the scout cars attached to horse formations. This manual emphasized the need for mechanized cavalry to conduct stealth reconnaissance, speaking only of aggressive action against enemy scouts in the counter-reconnaissance role.[47] Combat is mentioned in the manual, but it specifies that the mechanized cavalry should avoid fighting if at all possible, and that it should be reinforced prior to engaging anything more than minor enemy forces. The extremely limited roles given to mechanized cavalry in this manual speaks to the branch's insistence on the prevalence of its horse formations.

The 1941 version of *FM 100-5* still noted the unique role that cavalry played on the modern battlefield. It stated that the armored division's "primary role is in offensive operations against hostile rear areas."[48] Cavalry divisions still retained their roles from *FSR 1923* of reconnaissance, counter-reconnaissance (essentially security), and economy of force.[49] Thus, as late as 1941 the U.S. Army still viewed cavalry as a vital member of the total strength on the battlefield. The Armor Force had consumed some of the cavalry's missions, the two performed in different manners, doing very different things against the enemy. While not the subject of this work, the armor branch's mission reflected confusion within the army over the best utilization of this new unit. Unfortunately for the cavalry branch, many senior officers, notably General Leslie McNair, viewed armor as simply cavalry on tanks instead of horses. Although this comparison could hold true (as evidenced by the presence of tanks in modern cavalry formations), it depends greatly on how these units are used on the battlefield. The mount matters less than the mission. In the case of the armor division, massed tanks in combined arms formations would prove to be that rarest of military items—an entirely new kind of formation. However, McNair's mind-set would lead to further army-level neglect of cavalry formations. Finally, the 1941 Louisiana maneuvers demonstrated to McNair the growing obsolescence of horse cavalry on the modern battlefield, despite the introduction of innovations like the horse-*portee* regiment.[50]

In 1942, responding to the increasingly bitter debates between the branch chiefs, General Marshall abolished the entire branch chief system, placing all ground forces under the newly organized Army Ground Forces commanded by McNair in an attempt to streamline the creation of a modern military force.[51] This move led to the loss of the cavalry's chief advocate at a time of doctrinal debate and confusion. In 1943, at the direction of McNair, the 1st Cavalry Division, the principal unit of the cavalry branch, was sent to the Pacific as an infantry division, and the army transitioned all the corps horse cavalry regiments to mechanized formations.

This shift placed cavalry doctrine in a quandary. There had been little thought of how to conduct the traditional cavalry missions with just mechanized forces outside of the 7th Cavalry Brigade, which was now in the new Armor Force. Additionally, the latest doctrine coming from Army Ground Forces seemed to imply that divisions and corps could provide their own operational level security, thereby requiring the corps cavalry regiments to only provide operational reconnaissance.

In a step toward a solution, as part of the overall modularization of the army, McNair redesignated the cavalry regiments as cavalry groups. Although the actual organization changed very little, this move allowed for the rapid attachment and detachment of various combat enablers. Furthermore, the army designated that each infantry division would receive a single troop and each armored division would get a squadron (or battalion) of mechanized cavalry to conduct tactical reconnaissance. These formations would be the first cavalry formations to see combat in North Africa, with the recon squadrons of the 1st and 2nd Armored Divisions gaining particularly valuable experience.

Training Circular 107, published in September 1943, specified that mechanized cavalry units were "organized, equipped, and trained to perform reconnaissance missions employing infiltration tactics, fire, and maneuver. They engage in combat only to the extent necessary to accomplish the assigned missions."[52] Moreover, the mechanized cavalry units were trained to "employ infiltration tactics rather than combat to gain information."[53] *Training Circular 107* became the primary basis for American mechanized cavalry doctrine for the rest of the war, with its statements reappearing almost verbatim in the 1944 edition of *FM 100-5.*[54] This doctrine would help shape the table of organization and equipment of the mechanized cavalry.

A mechanized cavalry group consisted of no more than two mechanized cavalry reconnaissance squadrons with a headquarters element. This organization basically set up a headquarters that could take care of the administration for the two attached squadrons.[55] Moreover, these squadrons were not organic to the group, allowing for rapid detachment to other units or missions, including independent assignments.

Each squadron consisted of three reconnaissance troops, a light tank company, and an assault gun company. The reconnaissance troops were made up of three platoons of three M8 Greyhounds (see photograph 1) and six quarter-ton jeeps each.[56] The Greyhound was a six-wheeled armored car, armed with a 37mm cannon and a .50-caliber machine gun. Its armor was very light, and the open topped turret

Photograph 1. M8 Greyhound.

proved unpopular with many soldiers, particularly in bad weather or under shell fire. Each reconnaissance troop also had twenty-seven riflemen for dismounted use.[57] The reconnaissance troops were heavily armed with machine guns and mortars, with each troop possessing nine 60mm mortars and multiple .30-caliber machine guns. In fact, the cavalry squadron possessed more machine guns than an infantry battalion.[58]

The light tank company consisted of seventeen M5 Stuarts equipped with 37mm cannons (see photograph 2).[59] The M5 was the premier light tank of the army. It was fast, but very lightly armored. Its gun, considered adequate in 1939, would prove to be completely inadequate against German armor by 1944. The assault gun company had six 75mm Howitzer Motor Carriage M8 Scott self-propelled guns organized into two platoons (see photograph 3).[60] The M8 Scott was a 75mm howitzer placed on an M5 chassis. The howitzer gave it some punch, but the round's relatively low velocity made the M8 a very poor anti-armor weapon.

Photograph 2. M5 Stuart.

Photograph 3. M8 Scott.

Each squadron also possessed a headquarters troop that ran the administrative and control functions for the other troops. Combined with the tank company, assault gun troop, and reconnaissance troops, each squadron consisted of approximately thirty-one officers, two warrant officers, and 721 enlisted men, although the numbers fluctuated constantly due to casualties and the ebb and flow of replacements (see figure 1).[61]

As can be seen by the above organization, the mechanized cavalry groups were not organized for heavy combat at all. With only twenty-seven dismounts in a reconnaissance troop, as compared to over one hundred in a rifle company, the cavalry was not very suited to dismounted infantry-type combat in which numbers were significant.[62] Moreover, with the heaviest vehicles in the squadron being light tanks, and the rest of the force equipped with quarter-ton jeeps and armored cars, the cavalry was not suited for armored combat either. These deficiencies were acceptable to the Army Ground Forces though, as they saw the cavalry as not engaging in serious combat, either mounted or dismounted, as per the doctrine discussed earlier.

In contrast to the lightly equipped and manned cavalry, the line infantry and armor formations of the U.S. Army proved fairly robust. The standard armor divisions contained three battalions of tanks, dominated by the M4 Sherman medium tank, and three battalions of armored infantry mounted in half-tracks.[63] While certainly not the best tank of the war, the M4 had heavier armor and a bigger gun than the cavalry's light tanks, giving it a much better chance against German panzers. The infantry divisions had three regiments of infantry, each with over three thousand personnel, not counting the supporting artillery, engineer, and independent tank battalions that almost always accompanied the infantry into battle.[64]

By mid-war, the U.S. Army took some steps to fix the worst of the cavalry's equipment deficiencies. The M5 Stuart would be replaced by the M24 Chaffee with a 75mm cannon. The Chaffee had come as a result of the 37mm cannon proving nearly useless against mid- to late war German armor. While the 37mm had been perfectly acceptable in 1939 and 1940 (when the decision to buy the Stuart had been made), by 1943 it was woefully underpowered. However, the lead time to design, mass produce, and then field a new tank in the midst of a huge

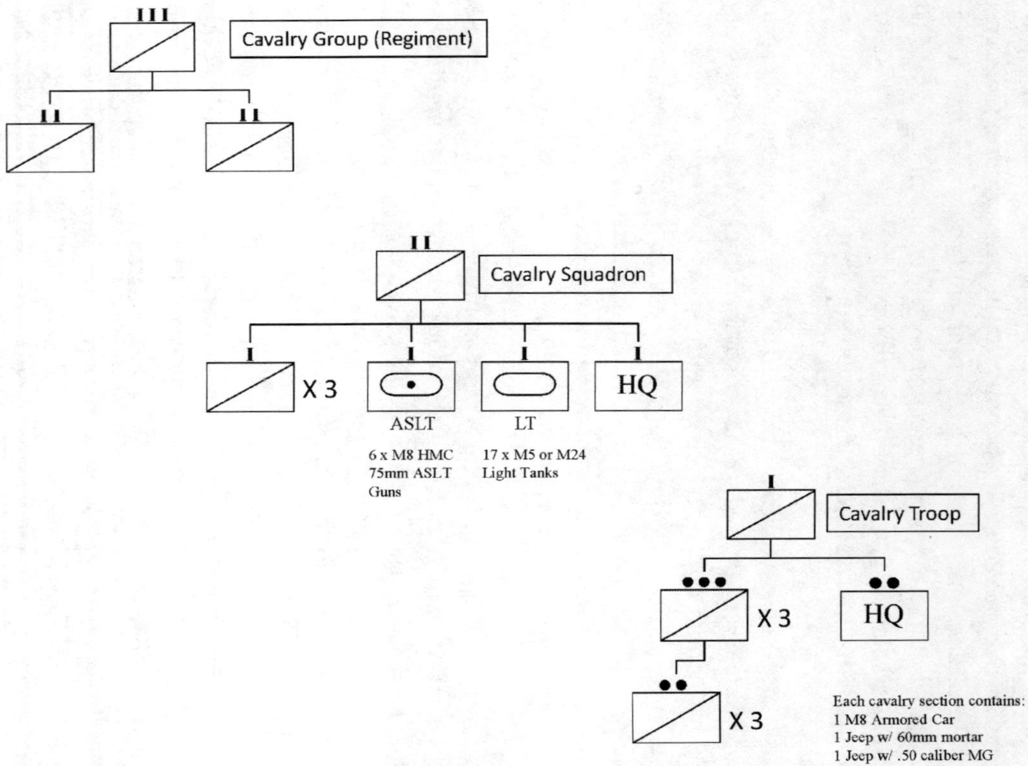

Figure 1. Standard Organization of a Mechanized Cavalry Group.

number of competing priorities meant that the new tanks would not see combat until late 1944. Interestingly, the same paradigm applied to the Sherman. When the tank was being developed and first fielded, the armor and the 75mm cannon of the M4 were more than sufficient to face the Panzer I, II, and III models, as well as the early model Panzer IVs. However, by late 1943 the newer German models easily outmatched the Sherman.

Further complicating the training of the cavalry groups was the nature of their raising and manning. Much like the rest of the army, by 1944 organizations bore little resemblance to their 1940 selves, if they had even been active at that time. While this massive personnel turbulence hit all organizations in the army, the cavalry were particularly affected, as they were attempting to fundamentally change doctrine and tables of organization and equipment at the same time.

The 2nd (Dragoons), 3rd (Brave Rifles), and 11th (Blackhorse) Cavalry Groups were all preexisting Regular Army formations prior to 1940. However, in 1942 the personnel and equipment of these units were redesignated as armor regiments, and in 1943 the Army Ground Forces raised new formations with the old traditions from a mix of regular army soldiers and draftees. In the case of the 3rd Cavalry Group, the old honor guard at Fort Myer had been replaced by draftees from New York, including large numbers of Polish immigrants.[65] The 14th, 15th, and 16th Cavalry Groups were raised in much the same manner, but they had been inactive prior to 1942 and had no long and storied traditions to draw upon, unlike their lower-numbered counterparts. In fact, of the eight Regular Army cavalry units, only the 4th and 6th Cavalry Groups retained the majority of their prewar personnel, and the 6th was the sole group to not lose large numbers of soldiers to form other cadres.[66] In other words, the experience of the Regular cavalry proved to be no different than their peers across the army.

The remaining six cavalry groups all hark back to the National Guard. The 101st Group was drawn from New York, with its greatest distinction prior to 1940 having been a short term of service on the Mexican border during the Punitive Expedition. The 113th Group, the Redhorse, came from the Iowa Guard, while the 115th Cavalry came from Wyoming.[67] The 106th Group, with no real battle history of its own, combined squadrons from Illinois and Michigan. However, this organization would shift, with the original 2nd Squadron being separated from the group, redesignated the 27th and then the 32nd Cavalry Squadron, and moving first to Panama, and then joining the 14th Cavalry Group and fighting with that organization throughout the war. Army Ground Forces then created a new 2nd Squadron from available cadre and new draftees.[68]

The 102nd Group proved an interesting mixture of New Jersey Guard, elements of other guard formations, and Regular Army soldiers. The group headquarters and one squadron (the 102nd) were pure Jersey Guard. The other original squadron had been pulled from the group early in 1942 to participate in Operation TORCH as the security for the Allied Forces Headquarters. This squadron, eventually relabeled as the 117th Cavalry Reconnaissance Squadron, would serve in an independent role in the Mediterranean Theater until it entered France as part of Operation DRAGOON in the summer of 1944 as part of VI Corps, an association that would remain throughout the war.[69] The replacement squadron became known as the 38th Cavalry Reconnaissance Squadron. It had been formed from a mixture of Regular Army (from the 1st Cavalry Division, the 2nd Armored Division, and Cavalry School cadre) and members of the 113th Cavalry, itself a National Guard unit, but from Iowa.[70]

While the nature of the National Guard allowed for these six groups to maintain a larger degree of stability than the newly forming Regular formations, they experienced their own degree of turmoil as well. All of the groups received mass infusions of draftees, diluting their original characters. Additionally, as was the case in at least two groups, entire squadrons were moved out of the organization and replaced by entirely newly formed units. Moreover, the tension between the Regular Army and the National Guard extended to the cavalry as well. In the case of the 106th Cavalry Group, Army Ground Forces relieved both Guard squadron commanders, the Guard group commander, and the Guard group executive officer, replacing them with Regulars. The incoming executive officer, Major James H. Polk, noted the immense amount of tension between the new command teams and their soldiers, as the Regulars were "getting tough with them."[71] While the tension between the Guard soldiers and their new leadership certainly produced problems, an influx of new draftees and soldiers from other units, as well as understanding that training meant self-preservation, led to some mitigation of the stress. Finally, despite the challenges of mixing Guard with Regular, all of the Guard groups emerged with solid combat records.

In January 1944, Army Ground Forces published *FM 2-20: Cavalry Reconnaissance Troop: Mechanized.* This document was the distillation of nearly eighteen months of cavalry combat experience in the Mediterranean Theater, predominantly from the recon squadrons of the 1st and 2nd Armored Divisions. It acknowledged the combat missions that the mechanized cavalry formations could face, but still emphasized reconnaissance as the primary mission of cavalry. It stated: "The cavalry reconnaissance troop, mechanized, is organized, equipped, and trained to perform reconnaissance missions. Other types of missions are given only in the furtherance of a reconnaissance mission of the troop or the squadron of which the troop is a part, unless no other troops are available for other types of operations for the division or other larger units. Reconnaissance missions are performed by employment of infiltration tactics, fire, and maneuver. Combat is engaged in only to the extent necessary to accomplish the assigned mission."[72] The same statement appears nearly verbatim in the August 1944 version of *FM 2-30: Cavalry Mechanized Reconnaissance Squadron.* Note the obvious deletions of several traditional functions of cavalry in this doctrine. Although additional missions, including security, are mentioned, the manuals immediately qualify this statement with the addition that the cavalry would only perform these missions if no other units were available. Thus, as late as 1944, cavalry doctrine still had not recovered from the transition to a fully mechanized force. A horse cavalryman of the early 1930s would have been horrified to hear tasks that he considered part of his overall mission described in this manner. He would have understood that cavalry is the dedicated force for the army to accomplish security functions. Other elements may be able to do cavalry-type missions, but at the expense of their own important roles. Unfortunately, Army Ground Forces did not see things as clearly.

Additionally, the U.S. Army as a whole had not created an organization capable of replacing the cavalry branch in the niche that it had occupied from the Civil War to 1942 because, in the imaginations of many, as mentioned earlier, the Armor Force was supposed to supplant the cavalry in their traditional roles. The 1944 *FM 100-5: Field Service Operations* made greater progress in assigning cavalry-type missions to the armored divisions. While still insisting that armor's primary role was to attack enemy rear areas, the manual additionally listed such missions as: "Break through an enemy protective screen and establish early contact with hostile forces . . . Seize ground essential to the development of the higher commander's plan . . . exploit a success . . . and pursue a defeated enemy."[73]

The 1944 *FM 100-5 Operations* does demonstrate that the army realized it had a doctrinal gap, and the manual attempts to make a 1944 armor division sound like a 1941 cavalry division. Unfortunately, the 1944 armored division in the context of the standard corps of 1944–1945 was intended more for high-intensity combat than the specialized security, reconnaissance, and economy of force missions traditional to cavalry. Additionally, in actual practice, armored divisions in the army were generally used to spearhead offensives but otherwise occupied a portion on the broad front, like every other division in the army. In short, the armored division was a highly mobile main body division with a lot of firepower, not a cavalry formation performing roles for the corps at an operational level. A corps commander would never place his primary armored element in an economy of force role, or even in a security screen. Rather, he needed the armored division as his exploitation/counterattack force or to hold portions of an increasingly widening front.

In a further dose of irony, the 1944 *FM 100-5 Operations* still provided for cavalry divisions conducting operational counter-reconnaissance and security of corps-level organizations. It notes: "A Cavalry Division protects the disposition and other ground forces by counter-reconnaissance or screening, which may be conducted either offensively or defensively. In executing a counter-reconnaissance mission, the division seeks to defeat or neutralize enemy ground reconnaissance forces."[74]

However, by June 1944 (the publication date of the manual) the only division designated as cavalry was the 1st Cavalry Division, which was dismounted and fighting as infantry in the South Pacific. Thus, doctrinally, the army understood the need for cavalry to perform security as well as reconnaissance. Unfortunately, the reality was that Army

Ground Force leaders merely paid lip service to the idea, continuing with their basic (albeit flawed) assumptions of how mechanized combat would proceed.

Despite these immense doctrinal problems, there remained a silver lining. That is, the old joke that Americans never read their doctrine or feel compelled to follow it has a fairly large grain of truth to it. The old doctrines of how to use horse cavalry had been in the army school system for decades, and the shift to a reconnaissance-only formation was still a new phenomenon when the cavalry groups went to war in 1944. The traditions of American cavalry doing much more than reconnaissance were taught in the Command and General Staff School at Fort Leavenworth as well as the cavalry schools at Fort Riley up until the Second World War. This schooling would be important: of the twenty corps commanders who served in the ETO, nineteen attended Leavenworth. Additionally, half of the commanders of the cavalry groups also attended a cavalry school prior to the war.[75] Thus, it is not a stretch to conclude that when the generals saw a cavalry group in their order of battle, they were trained to use it for much more than what the new doctrine intended. Additionally, the group commanders themselves, also by training or inclination, ignored a large part of the new doctrine, as evidenced by their actions and how they fought their formations in combat. Perhaps with too many changes happening too quickly, most cavalrymen or their superiors simply reverted to type or experience rather than attempt an untried way of doing things.

The cavalry branch failed to properly prepare its forces for war in Europe. The reconnaissance-only mechanized cavalry doctrine remained virtually unchanged from the mid-1930s through 1945, with minor adjustments made after combat experiences in 1943. However, this doctrinal inertia was not the product of blind adherence to dogma. Cavalry leaders understood that they had a large number of specific tasks to perform for the larger army. While infantry or artillery could concentrate on a focused group of skills, the cavalry had to be proficient at a number of missions, ranging from stealth reconnaissance to outright battle in an economy of force role. Moreover, the army expected the cavalry to be an all-terrain, all-weather organization. Mechanized (or motorized) vehicles throughout the 1920s and 1930s were not very reliable and certainly not as mobile as a horse across most types of terrain. In fact, to the modern day, there are certain terrain types where vehicles simply will not go, whereas horses can.

The experiments of the 7th Cavalry Brigade demonstrated the potential of mechanization, but also its limitations. In a time of extreme budget shortages, the cavalry branch was faced with the option to place its faith in vehicles that showed promise but were as yet unproven, or to rely on horses, a platform that had proven successful in campaigns for more than a hundred years. Unfortunately, this focus on immediate mission success blinded many cavalry officers to the possibilities of the future, allowing them to fixate on the horse rather than to start thinking how they could accomplish the mission with another platform. The leaders of the branch chose poorly, but had solid professional reasons for their decision. The decision to mechanize the cavalry came at the same time that the army removed the branch system, and shortly after a large number of cavalry officers had transitioned to the new Armor Force. Thus, the cavalry branch was thrown into turmoil at precisely the same time that it needed to create an entirely new doctrine to perform traditional cavalry tasks with equipment and an organization that had never been intended to perform these roles. The result of this situation was a compromise that was not ideal, though it would serve in combat.

Army Ground Forces (AGF) and its commander must also bear a portion of the blame. General McNair made a conscious decision to strip away capabilities that had existed for over a century and replace them with a new doctrine. The army often blindly mimicked the early German organizations that achieved their initial battlefield successes. The early war German reconnaissance forces looked much the same as the U.S. mechanized cavalry, using light vehicles (often motorcycles and small cars) to conduct stealthy reconnaissance.[76] These formations were brutalized in France as well as the early stages of BARBAROSSA, with casualties so heavy that entire formations were disbanded.[77] By 1943 the Germans had learned from their earlier losses and created robust mechanized cavalry formations capable of fulfilling all of the traditional cavalry roles.[78] The Germans' early failings, and that of the AGF, can be traced to confusion over the role of the tank. While the creation of the Armor Force was a tremendous advancement for the army, AGF leaders failed to understand that the armor division was a completely new addition to the battlefield and did not replace the role of cavalry. Rather, armored divisions had their own unique role to play on the modern battlefield. This failure to understand that there still existed a need for a dedicated force to perform cavalry missions hampered American doctrine and tables of organization and equipment for the rest of the war.

Thus, both the cavalry branch and the larger army lost sight of the greater goal of fielding a fully capable force, but for different reasons. The branch failed to see the promise of mechanization technology, whereas the AGF overstated the impact and capabilities of the new Armor Force. Combined, these issues produced a muddled doctrine and organization that would hamper American cavalry forces throughout the war. The troopers of the mechanized cavalry groups would have to become very adept at creative solutions to tactical problems.

However, these problems should be viewed in light of the times. The Second World War was the first heavily mechanized conflict in history. Many technologies employed in it were seeing their first widescale use. With new technologies come new ideas. Some of these are good and some are not. The cavalry branch was certainly not alone in having ideas that proved unworkable in combat. The tank destroyer concept and doctrine proved an evolutionary dead end. The Sherman tank remains a highly controversial vehicle. Nor were the Americans alone in having problems. England's concept of cruiser and infantry tanks proved problematic. Germany's quest for the perfect tank proved fatal, producing lethal but seriously flawed vehicles. In the end, every army in the Second World War had its share of problems that it had to either overcome or accommodate. How they succeeded or failed in surmounting their challenges were significant in the difference between victory and defeat.

Therefore, although an understanding of doctrine and organization are important, they are only part of the puzzle of military success. These elements can provide insight into how a formation trained and why it possessed the tools it had. However, units are much more than simple line diagrams in a manual. People within that organization adapt, improvise, and innovate. In the case of American corps cavalry in the ETO, despite a flawed doctrine and less than ideal organization, the end result was a successful cavalry force, thanks to the innovation, courage, and adaptability of the cavalrymen and their leaders.

3

Cavalry in the Bocage

The Normandy campaign provided the mechanized cavalry groups (MCGs) of the U.S. Army with their first test of combat. While some individuals may have possessed combat experience, an overwhelming majority of the cavalrymen arriving in France were green, much like most of the rest of the army in Normandy. This uniform inexperience contrasted sharply with some of the polyglot German forces in France, which consisted of everything from war-weary but veteran formations to raw recruits.[1] Both sides quickly gained the measure of the other in the ensuing two months of combat.

The U.S. sector in Normandy proved to be a challenging battlefield for the lightly armored and manpower-poor cavalry groups. Marshes as well as deliberately flooded lowlands dominated the region around Carentan (in the southeast corner of the Cotentin Peninsula) all the way north to the vicinity of Saint Mère Église. This terrain limited any force, particularly if vehicle-mounted, to a relatively small number of clear causeways and routes. Farther south, the infamous hedgerow country surrounded the city of Saint Lô. Here the compartmentalized terrain again restricted attacking forces into a few relatively easy-to-identify avenues of approach. Moreover, the hedgerows were perfect for a stubborn defense. Thus, the nature of the fighting in Normandy would, of necessity, be close infantry engagements entailing very little maneuver. Therefore, the problem of the cavalry for the first two months of action in northwestern Europe would be to find utility in an environment almost custom-designed against the type of fighting for which they had been built.

The two assault corps of General Omar Bradley's First Army, the V and VII, both had cavalry groups attached (the 102nd and 4th MCGs, respectively), although only the VII Corps used its cavalry on D-Day. This difference in use resulted less from the preferences of the corps commanders and more from the unique circumstances presented to each organization. While the V Corps faced a fairly direct assault across Omaha Beach, followed by a planned exploitation inland, the VII Corps faced two situations that called for the application of corps cavalry on D-Day.

The first challenge facing the VII Corps came in the form of the Îles Saint Marcouf, a pair of islands approximately four miles east of the Cotentin Peninsula. These islands lay nearly astride the route that the 4th Infantry Division (ID) would be taking to Utah Beach. Additionally, initial aerial reconnaissance had discovered signs of potential German defenses on both islands.[2] If German forces were present on these islands, they could not only disrupt the landing force with direct fire, but they could also call down artillery fire against forces afloat in the naval staging areas as well as on the beaches. Therefore, Major General Joseph Collins, the corps commander, needed to confirm the presence or absence of German forces on these islands as well as secure this key terrain to protect his assault force. The 82nd and 101st Airborne Divisions could not attack these tiny islands (the larger of the two is less than a quarter mile long), as the risk of dumping the paratroopers into the sea instead of on the objective was unacceptably high. Any element sliced from the 4th ID would detract from that division's combat power on the beach and might encounter difficulties linking up with the division through the stream of corps units landing on Utah after D-Day. The corps cavalry group, Colonel Joseph Tully's 4th MCG, proved to be the perfect solution, as they had been organized and trained for conducting reconnaissance, and these tiny islands were well within their capabilities.

At 0430, two hours prior to H-Hour on Utah Beach, detachments from Troop A, 4th Cavalry Reconnaissance Squadron (CRS), and Troop B, 24th CRS, landed simultaneously on both islands in the Îles Saint Marcouf. Both formations quickly discovered the islands were unoccupied but heavily mined. Despite delays imposed by moving through minefields, the 4th MCG detachments reported the islands cleared one hour before the 4th ID landed on Utah Beach. The cavalry suffered nineteen casualties from mines and enemy artillery out of a combined force of 132 troopers. These two formations continued to secure the islands until 7 June, when an air defense unit relieved them.[3] Although somewhat anti-climactic, this operation is a perfect example of corps cavalry performing reconnaissance against a potential threat to the operational success of the corps.

The second issue facing the VII Corps on D-Day involved making contact with and conducting resupply and support operations for the widely scattered airborne formations that had landed behind Utah Beach. The 4th ID did not have the inherent mobility for the task, so the corps established a small task force consisting of a platoon of the 4th CRS, a medium tank company, a battalion of armored artillery, some glider infantry, and a truck company that would immediately proceed from the beach to the vicinity of Saint Mère Église to assist the 82nd Airborne Division.[4] The cavalry used their mobility to find clear routes for the rest of the column. Although German resistance proved scattered and confused, it was enough to prevent this ad hoc formation from reaching its objective on 6 June 1944. Following this check, the commander of the detachment used the cavalry's mobility to aid wounded glider infantrymen, who were strewn across the region from the night's airborne assault. The cavalry did make contact with the 82nd Airborne's headquarters the following day. The platoon of cavalry, reinforced by the rest of its troop on 10 June, spent the rest of the month conducting tactical reconnaissance and fire support missions, first for the 82nd Airborne Division and later for the 90th ID.[5]

Although in this instance the cavalry were not able to immediately finish their mission, they did complete the task the following day. Moreover, although most of the impact of this particular cavalry formation occurred at the tactical (or micro-tactical) level, the reconnaissance provided by these units allowed the 82nd Airborne and 90th ID to focus combat power where needed. This assistance proved particularly important during the early days of the fighting in Normandy, when the situation was still very fluid and the divisions in question did not have the organic mobility to conduct these missions themselves.

Although the V Corps had no occasion to use its corps cavalry, the 102nd MCG of the New Jersey Guard, it quickly found work for them on D-Day. The restricted nature of the terrain led to the corps' detailing out its cavalry in squadron or smaller formations. On 10 June, Major General Leonard T. Gerow, commander of the V Corps, ordered the 102nd CRS to clear the town of Isigny. This critical town, approximately six miles to the east of Carentan, dominated the coastal road leading west from the V Corps' sector to the VII Corps' sector. Although the town had been bypassed by elements of the 29th ID, the Corps needed it cleared of enemy resistance in order to facilitate cross-corps communications. The cavalry accomplished this mission within the day, capturing seventy-four prisoners.[6] Although the 29th ID's 175th Infantry Regiment had the capacity to clear Isigny, to do so would have drawn off combat power from the vital drives to expand the bridgehead and link with the VII Corps at Carentan. Thus, the heavily armed but numerically small corps cavalry filled this requirement perfectly in a textbook example of an economy of force mission.

Immediately following this mission, on 11 June 1944 Gerow attached the 102nd CRS to the 1st ID. This division was in the process of conducting an attack south through the town of Balleroy to Caumont.[7] This drive would accomplish two purposes. The first was to begin the isolation of the critical town of Saint Lô. Caumont, approximately eleven miles to the east of Saint Lô, controlled one of the major routes into the city. The second reason behind the offensive was to flank German resistance that had stymied the British Second Army, which occupied positions immediately east of the V Corps. The cavalry would conduct an offensive screen in front of the 1st ID, identifying enemy positions as well as attempting to destroy enemy outposts and security posts.

Although the 1st ID possessed their own reconnaissance troop, the scale of the attack (two full regiments—the 26th and 18th Infantry) as well as the constricted nature of the terrain meant that a more robust cavalry presence would be required. The 102nd CRS, later reinforced with elements of the 38th CRS, aided the 1st ID in the successful capture of Caumont by 12 June.[8] For the rest of the month, the V Corps employed the 102nd Group largely in an economy of force role. The cavalry screened gaps between battalions, regiments, and the 1st and 2nd IDs. These efforts allowed the corps to concentrate its infantry strength around critical areas of the front.[9] Considering the brutal nature of the fighting in the *bocage,* concentrating combat power was not simply a good idea, it was absolutely imperative if the V Corps was to achieve any forward progress.

While the 102nd Group slogged forward in the hedgerow country east of Saint Lô, the 4th MCG participated in a slightly more open style of battle on the Cotentin Peninsula. Although minor elements of the group participated in the drive across the peninsula, the VII Corps did not use its corps cavalry in anything larger than troop strength until nearly a week after D-Day. Just like the experience of the V Corps, the nature of the terrain and fighting in the Cotentin forced the VII Corps to break apart the 4th MCG and use its squadrons independently of each other.

The 24th CRS entered the fight first, relieving the 22nd Infantry Regiment of the 4th ID on a two-mile front along the coast.[10] This move allowed the 4th ID to concentrate an entire infantry regiment in reserve for its assault north. The ability to keep a third of the division's combat power in reserve became a powerful tool for the division commander in the ensuing attack.

The VII Corps attack to seize Cherbourg began on 19 June. The 24th CRS protected the right flank of the 4th ID, the easternmost division, preventing the bypassed German defensive positions along the coast from interfering with the division's attack. The 4th CRS (under the control of the group headquarters) protected the juncture of the 9th and 79th IDs.[11] The attack went well, as German resistance had already begun to crumble. Still, the 4th CRS encountered stiff resistance at the town of Rocheville, approximately eight miles south of Cherbourg. The fighting grew intense, requiring the cavalry to fight dismounted from house to house.[12] Despite their difficulties, the cavalry still managed to accomplish their purpose of allowing the corps to concentrate its infantry regiments along its main axis of attack.

After the seizure of Cherbourg, the VII Corps used one squadron of the group, the 24th, to shield the supply routes of the 4th ID from roving bands of Germans, and the other squadron, the 4th, to clear the Cap de la Hague, the northwest tip of the Cotentin Peninsula.[13] While the 24th Squadron's mission took full advantage of the cavalry's mobility and firepower, the 4th Squadron's fight was the exact opposite. The 9th ID gave this squadron a series of sixteen objectives that all required dismounted combat to achieve. The purpose throughout the attack was to protect the flank of the division's main effort as it cleared the Cape.[14] Thus, although some authors may have declared this action to be a straightforward infantry mission, the truth is that, yet again, the VII Corps was using its cavalry in a security role.[15] Once again, the mount matters less than the mission.

After the conclusion of the fighting in the north of the Cotentin Peninsula, the corps held the 4th MCG behind the lines in preparation for operations in support of a breakout from Normandy. During this time, the group conducted rear area security as well as occasional missions along the front to screen gaps between regiments and divisions as the VII Corps fought its way to Saint Lô.[16]

In late June and early July 1944, the First Army added two more corps to its line in Normandy, the VIII and XIX Corps (see map 1). These corps arrived with their own corps cavalry, the 106th and 113th MCGs. However, due to the differing situations facing each corps and the choices of the corps commanders, these two groups would be used very differently.

Colonel Vennard Wilson's 106th MCG would be introduced to combat in early July by Major General Troy Middleton's VIII Corps. However, the group spent the entire month until Operation COBRA screening the gap between the west coast of the Cotentin Peninsula and the 79th ID, the rightmost division of the corps. It also conducted rear area security missions for the corps.[17] These missions allowed VIII Corps to concentrate its infantry combat power into the grueling slugfest of the assault south to arrive at assault positions designated for Operation COBRA.

Major General Charles Corlett's XIX Corps would be much more aggressive in its use of cavalry. In one of the first major actions for the corps, the 30th ID conducted an attack to cross the Taute-Vire Canal as part of its drive to reach Saint Lô. The 117th Infantry Regiment would be the main effort for the operation. It would cross the canal and drive south toward Pont Hébert, a major crossroad a little over three miles northwest of Saint Lô. Corlett tasked Colonel William Biddle's 113th MCG to cross behind the 117th Infantry and move west, establishing a protective screen along the infantry's right flank, with the intention of eventually tying in with the VII Corps' 9th ID.[18]

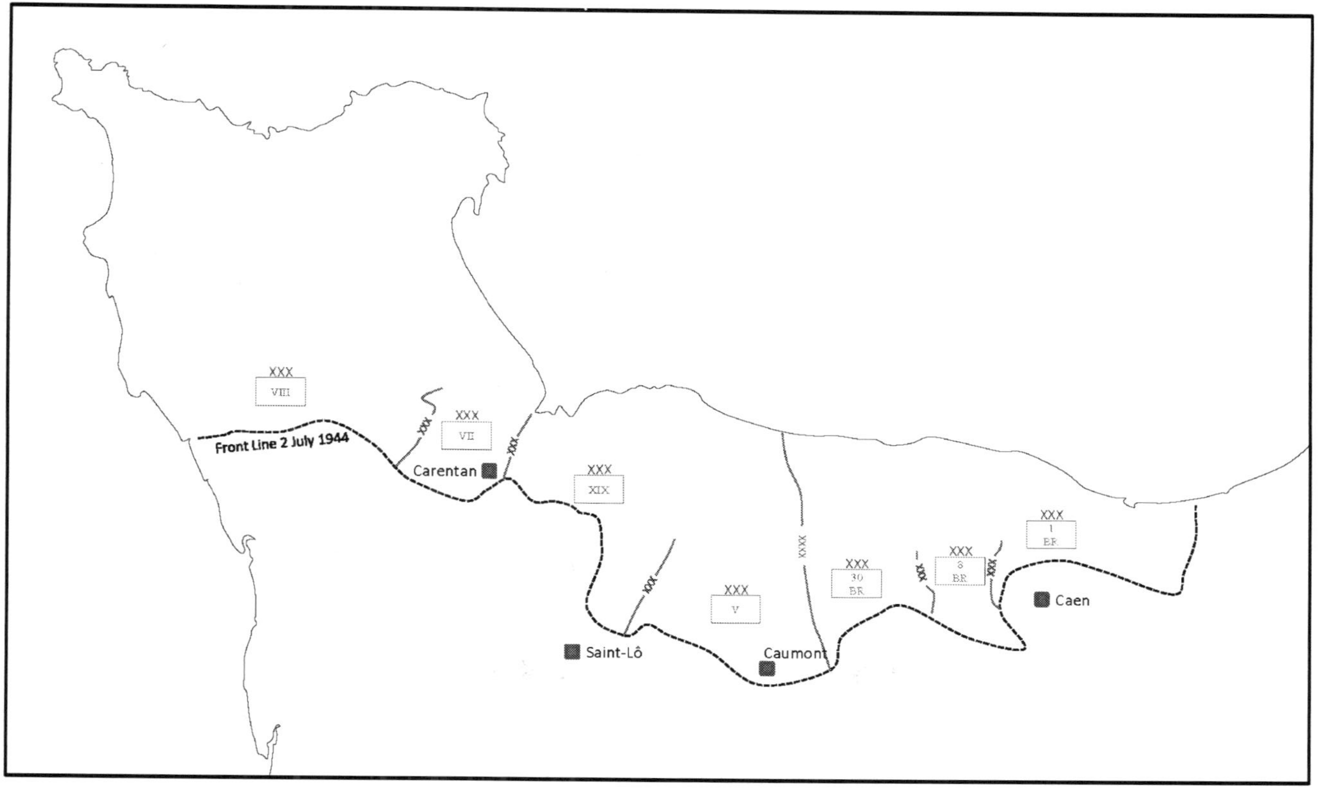

Map 1. Allied Front Line, 2 July 1944.

The attack started on 7 July. Due to heavy German resistance and traffic jams at the crossing point, the Redhorse did not cross until very early in the morning of 8 July. Despite the delay in crossing the canal, the group quickly seized a front approximately one mile long facing west, stretching from the town of La Groucherie in the north to Le Mesnil-Venéron in the south.[19] These towns dominated the corps' right (western) flank and would become useful strongpoints in later fighting. Although the attack of the 30th ID fell short of its intended objective, the flank protection of the 113th MCG helped prevent the Germans from counterattacking the vulnerable beachhead across the canal from that direction. The Germans did attack on the morning of 9 July against the front of the 30th ID, causing a minor panic. If the flanks had been less secure, this panic might have become a general rout.[20] Moreover, the ground gained by the 30th ID persuaded Bradley to commit the 3rd Armored Division (AD) to the XIX Corps in the hope that this additional combat power would lead to a more decisive breakthrough.

As part of the reorganization of the battlefield, Corlett attached the 113th MCG to the 3rd AD. The division ordered the cavalry to attack on the night of 9 July in conjunction with elements of its Combat Command A (CCA). The intent behind this assault was to seize the high ground to the west of the bridgehead along the major north-south highway in the area. This ground also overlooked the original crossing point and broadened the base of the bridgehead.[21] With this high ground in friendly hands, the Germans would have a much harder time interdicting friendly forces crossing the canal, allowing for the unimpeded commitment of the 9th ID south of the canal. The attack met heavy resistance, and although the cavalry and portions of the 3rd AD's CCA seized their objectives, German pressure forced them to withdraw back to their original positions.[22] Corlett pulled the 113th MCG back into reserve on the morning of 11 July, just as the Panzer Lehr Division counterattacked from the south and southwest. Despite some initial German gains, the XIX Corps defeated the counterattack, destroying approximately 25 percent of the enemy division.[23]

While some authors have claimed that the 113th MCG's failure to gain its objectives on the night of 9 July set the conditions for a spoiling attack by the Panzer Lehr Division on 11 July, the actual circumstances are somewhat more ambiguous.[24] While the Panzer Lehr Division did indeed use that same ground to cover a portion of their initial advance, the fact remains that the German resistance in that region had been fierce across the board. The 113th MCG's attack had failed on 10 July, but an ad hoc combat team of the 3rd AD had also failed to achieve their objectives.[25] Although the cavalry might not have had the combat power to fully succeed, neither did any other force on that flank of the battlefield. Instead of a clear failure of the cavalry to achieve depth, what instead emerges is an image of a hard-fought battle wherein the cavalry did not achieve full success, but did help in establishing a line that would bend but not break against the Panzer Lehr. Moreover, although the attack may indeed have cost the XIX Corps "a day of planned advance," it is hard to imagine how else the corps would have been able to respond to the commitment of a panzer division. Finally, wrecking a quarter of a German panzer division would seem a fair use of the corps' time.[26]

Thus the first battle of the 113th MCG produced mixed results. The corps had achieved its bridgehead and gotten substantial combat power across and the cavalry had performed reasonably well. Although it proved unable to seize the high ground overlooking the crossing site, the 113th MCG had taken their initial positions and done a credible job in protecting the corps' flank. Finally, Corlett proved satisfied enough with the group to issue a letter of commendation to them.[27]

After a period of respite for the 113th MCG, the XIX Corps recalled them to the front to participate in the battle for Saint Lô proper. The corps attached the cavalry to the 29th ID for the purposes of the operation. The 113th MCG aided the division by conducting reconnaissance into and around the city. As German resistance stiffened on the south side of Saint Lô, the fight transferred to the 35th ID, but the 113th MCG remained in the line. For over a week the cavalry continued to aid the infantry through a series of raids and reconnaissance patrols. The relatively static nature of the battle meant that they did most of their fighting dismounted.[28] Although the cavalry were not the main effort in this fighting, they did contribute by gaining and maintaining contact with the enemy as well as assisting in probing the German defenses.

Throughout the latter half of July, American forces fought to establish the conditions necessary for a breakout from the Normandy region. Numerous British assaults on the Allied left, Operation GOODWOOD perhaps being the most famous, had drawn substantial German reserves and attention away from the American portion of the front. The seizure of Saint Lô by the XIX Corps signaled that the First Army was ready to commence its attack, codenamed Operation COBRA. The planned assault would be conducted by the right two corps of the American line, Middleton's VIII Corps and Collins's VII Corps. Preceded by a massive aerial bombardment, the VII Corps initiated the attack on 25 July, followed a couple of days later by the VIII Corps. The oversized VII Corps (two armored divisions and four infantry divisions) ground its way through German defenses all day on 25 July with three infantry divisions, and by 26 July it managed to create the beginnings of a breakthrough. Collins committed the 1st ID, 2nd AD, and 3rd AD that day to break the last German resistance and to cement the American penetration through the German lines.

In an effort to strengthen the 1st ID, Collins attached the 4th CRS to it in order to give that division a more robust mechanized reconnaissance force than its organic cavalry reconnaissance troop. This division also had Combat Command B (CCB) of the 3rd AD attached for the initial phase of the exploitation. He then ordered the 24th CRS to be split between different portions of the 2nd AD in order to augment their reconnaissance capabilities as well. Although the armored division possessed its own armored reconnaissance squadron, perhaps the corps headquarters envisioned a scenario wherein the division would be forced to attack in multiple directions, necessitating even more reconnaissance capability than it ordinarily had.[29]

On 26 July, the 4th CRS followed the 1st ID's attached armored combat command toward the important crossroads of Marigny, five miles west of Saint Lô. Heavy German resistance in the town stalled the attack. As a column of motorized troops like the truck-mounted 1st ID is most vulnerable when stationary, the 4th CRS moved to establish flank security to the west of the road, and northwest of Marigny. There, the squadron encountered a large German force, which, although almost certainly out of touch with its higher headquarters and suffering from some disorganization due to the effects of COBRA, could have constituted a major threat to the truck-mounted infantry of the 1st ID strung out along the road. The cavalry attacked and fixed the German force, although it required reinforcements from the column to finish the fight.[30] This action has received little mention in the histories of COBRA, but it stands as a good example of cavalry conducting a security mission. The actions of the 4th MCG protected the 1st ID from suffering unnecessary casualties and allowed the division to keep most of its forces mounted and capable of moving at a more rapid pace. If the infantry had been forced to dismount and defend themselves, the resulting confusion that always accompanies battle would have dramatically slowed their ability to continue the advance.

As the 1st ID cleared Marigny and linked up with the VIII Corps around Coutances, nine miles to the southwest, the 4th CRS continued its reconnaissance south in support of the 4th ID. The squadron determined that the Germans were attempting to make a stand along the Sienne River, approximately ten miles south of Marigny. The VII Corps exploited this information as it continued the attack to the south and east by shifting combat power to envelop the emerging strongpoints or apply significant combat power against them in frontal assaults. After completing this mission, the 4th ID pulled the cavalry back, using it to connect the division with the 1st ID as it attacked south.[31]

As Tully's 4th MCG participated in a variety of mainly reconnaissance missions for the VII Corps during COBRA, Wilson's 106th MCG maintained a purely security function, screening the western flank of the VIII Corps, connecting it to the coast as it attacked south. While both groups fought in very different fashions, their contributions were important to the success of the operation. The 4th MCG protected the 1st ID's column from attack and conducted reconnaissance that helped enable the success of follow-on attacks. The 106th MCG filled a role that would have otherwise occupied a line infantry formation at a time when all of those needed to be pressed into the assault.

While the 4th and 106th MCGs actively participated in the breakthrough phase of COBRA, the 102nd and 113th MCGs participated in vital operations that fixed German forces east of Saint Lô, as well as holding the shoulder of the penetration. Both endured significant contact, particularly the 102nd MCG, in fighting that was very different from what their counterparts in the VII and VIII Corps experienced.

During its downtime in the relatively quiet period after the V

Corps had reached the Saint Lô line in mid-July, the 102nd MCG hit upon a novel manner with which to breach the ubiquitous hedgerows. Sergeant Curtis Culin of the 102nd CRS welded discarded German beach fortifications to the front of his light tank, in effect creating a bulldozer plow that could cut through the thick dirt berms and heavy hedges of the bocage. The cavalrymen showed off their invention to their commander, Gerow. He was so impressed by the device that he invited Bradley and Lieutenant General Courtney Hodges, the present and future commanders of the First Army, to a demonstration. Bradley proved to be so taken with the device that he immediately ordered it classified and directed production of it across the army for use in Operation COBRA.[32] In a dose of irony that rings familiar to all who have served in the military, army fabrication resources for the "Culin Cutter" would be so consumed with outfitting tanks in units designated for COBRA that the troopers of the 102nd MCG, the inventors of the device, would be left to equip their vehicles with only the materials and support that they could scrape up themselves.[33] Although this invention's use was not strictly for cavalry missions, its impact directly supported the 102nd MCG's higher headquarters, and thus deserves special mention.

While the VII and VIII Corps conducted the primary attacks of Operation COBRA to the west of Saint Lô, Gerow's V Corps, at the far left of the American line at the juncture between the British Second Army and the U.S. First Army, also went on the offensive. The corps' attack, approximately two miles east of Saint Lô, would fulfill two functions. The first would be to fix the German forces in the corps' sector, preventing them from displacing and interfering with the breakout operations. The second purpose essentially was to pinch the XIX Corps (in between the VII and V corps) out of the line, allowing for its use in further exploitation.[34] The 102nd MCG's role in this attack was to assault forward and establish a defensive screen to protect the western flank of the 2nd ID as it attacked into the German 3rd Parachute Division, as well as to maintain contact with the easternmost element of the XIX Corps, the 35th ID.[35]

The cavalry initiated their attack on 26 July with the 38th CRS. The light tanks of the squadron's F Company, equipped with "Culin Cutters," led the assault, followed by dismounted troopers from two other troops. After initial success penetrating three hedgerows, a German counterattack nearly drove the cavalry back to their line of departure. The 102nd MCG reinforced the 38th CRS with elements of the 102nd CRS, and after heavy fighting they regained the positions seized earlier in the day. The fighting had been brutal, with the 38th CRS taking 108 casualties, including the wounded squadron commander, and losing thirteen of seventeen tanks in its light tank company.[36] However, despite the cavalry's losses, they had secured the 2nd ID's flank so well that it advanced nearly a mile before it had to halt due to increasing German resistance and having outrun the cavalry's flank protection. Although the cavalry's inability to advance quickly is cited as a reason for the eventual halt of the attack on 26 July, an advance of one mile through the bocage is not inconsequential.[37] Moreover, considering the ferocity of the German defense, the cavalry's actions protected the 2nd ID's infantry regiments from even more resistance. However, Gerow was so unimpressed with the group's performance that he fired the group commander during the battle, leaving the group XO to lead the formation through the remainder of the action.[38]

The 102nd CRS continued the attack until 28 July, advancing another 1.5 miles south past the town of Cotigny, in the process losing both its commander and XO to wounds.[39] The 2nd ID attack advanced another half-mile from its positions gained on 26 July. However, problems with the green units of the 5th ID on the corps' left prevented further exploitation of the gains made on 26 and 27 July.[40] Despite the overall lack of progress after the promising start on 26 July, the V Corps' attack should be considered a success. It fixed the German forces to its front during the critical first day of Operation COBRA The actions of the 102nd MCG had contributed substantively to this fight.[41] By the end of 27 July, the First Army situation had changed dramatically and the V Corps' private action was halted in preparation for follow-on operations against a now retreating enemy.

While the 102nd MCG smashed its way through the hedgerows east of Saint Lô, the XIX Corps' 113th MCG moved from its positions south of the city and headed west to link up with the CCA of the 2nd AD. The corps had received control of that division as it pivoted to protect the eastern shoulder of the COBRA penetration. Corlett attached the 113th MCG to the CCA in the expectation that the cavalry would be able to move forward of the armored division's forces as they reached their objectives around Villebaudon, approximately eleven miles south-southwest of Saint Lô. Unfortunately, the 113th MCG never made it in front of the 2nd AD's forces, as first German resistance and then German counterattacks slowed and then stopped the division's advance. However, the cavalry still provided value to the tankers by conducting route reconnaissance, clearing bypassed pockets of German resistance, and fighting alongside the division as it fought off the attack of the 116th Panzer Division.[42]

The Normandy campaign saw corps cavalry participate in a variety of different roles. However, throughout the two months of the fighting to break out of the beachhead, the primary missions of cavalry shone through clearly. Sometimes the cavalry were able to conduct security missions in relative safety from defensive positions. At other times they had to fight their way into German defensive positions to accomplish their tasks. Reconnaissance missions ranged from the relatively anti-climatic, like the Île Saint Marcouf, to the harrowing reconnaissance of German positions south of Saint Lô. Economy of force missions allowed the cavalry's parent corps to concentrate combat power where necessary, as seen by the 106th Cavalry's operations along the flank of the VIII Corps.

All of these missions contributed to the success of the army in Normandy. Although the cavalry were not the main effort at any point during the campaign, they enabled successes for the units that were in that position. With the cavalry doing their job, the infantry, armor, and engineers of the line divisions could focus on theirs, making the total effort of the army more effective than merely the sum of its parts. After Normandy, the cavalry would have the opportunity to fully come into their own in the free-wheeling but still dangerous fighting that would erupt as the Allies swept across France.

4

Race to Glory

The campaign that encompassed the Allied advance across northwestern France proved to be very different from the fighting in Normandy. Whereas the Norman battlefields had been typified by nearly static, claustrophobic fighting with little chance for maneuver, the fighting across northern France became almost the polar opposite. The broad, sweeping countryside of the western end of the North European Plain is the dominant terrain feature. Several large rivers cross the area, but they can only be considered barriers if their long banks can be properly defended. The major cities are well spaced out and connected by an extensive network of roads. In short, this region is nearly ideal cavalry or tank country.

The mechanized cavalry groups were fully in their element during this campaign, using their mobility to advance rapidly across the battlefield, identifying German positions, outflanking their security forces, and bypassing enemy forces that they were unable to defeat. Moreover, the cavalry groups' unique radio sets (for units of their size) allowed them to communicate over larger distances than other regiments or even divisions in the army.[1] These capabilities of the corps cavalry groups stood the cavalrymen and their supported headquarters in good stead over the months of August and September 1944.

August opened with the activation of Lieutenant General George S. Patton's U.S. Third Army and the creation of the 12th Army Group under newly promoted General Omar Bradley. This new army group allowed the American forces to take full advantage of the operational level of war by expanding the ability of their headquarters to control the growing battle. In fact, the battle for France would offer something rarely witnessed in American military history: the sight of two or more armies fighting in concert toward the same operational objective. The First Army, under the command of Lieutenant General Courtney Hodges and still in heavy contact with German forces in southern Normandy, would bear the brunt of the fighting as it fixed the German Seventh Army, while the Third Army exploded out into the open fields of Brittany and northern France in a massive envelopment.

First Army

As the First Army continued its exploitation from Operation COBRA, Major General Joseph Collins's VII Corps continued to expand the neck of the penetration to the east of the Coutances–Avranches corridor being used by Major General Troy Middleton's VIII Corps and the rest of the newly developed Third Army (VIII, XII, XV, XX Corps). With three corps stacked up behind the VII and VIII Corps, the Americans needed every highway they could take to expedite their attack. Two north-south roads were already coming under control of the Third Army's VIII Corps to the west, but the highway running north to south from Saint Lô through Villedieu-les-Poêles to Avranches was needed as well to get both the Third and First Armies moving. The northern end of the highway fell into the zone of the XIX Corps. However, the southern end, starting around the town of Percy (thirteen miles south of Saint Lô and seventeen miles northeast of Avranches) belonged to the VII Corps. The corps was approaching the highway from the northwest, swinging south around the XIX Corps.[2]

The key to seizure of this highway was the town of Villedieu-les-Poêles. Control of the town would give the Americans access to all of the major routes in the eastern portion of the expanding corridor. Elements of Collins's 1st ID had already bypassed the area, but if the Americans wanted to use the road, the town itself would have to be taken. The 4th ID's initial attempts to seize the town had been stymied to the west by stiff German resistance. The 4th ID then assigned the task to Colonel Tully's 4th MCG because the cavalry had the mobility and firepower (as long as they did not encounter enemy armor) to slip around the enemy defenses and seize the town before the Germans could consolidate and reorient. To assist in this action, the corps attached the 759th Light Tank Battalion to the group, an attachment that would last most of the war. The 4th MCG quickly took control of the town by the evening of 1 August by side-stepping German strongpoints and defeating the light enemy forces physically occupying the objective, as well as repulsing a counterattack that night. The cavalry held until midnight, when a regiment of the 4th ID relieved them.[3] This attack enabled the 4th ID to continue its movement forward without becoming ensnared in a tough fight for control of a key town. The 4th ID would reach the town of Saint Pois, nine miles southeast of Villedieu-les-Poêles, by the end of 1 August partly as a result of the cavalry's actions.[4] This success demonstrates the utility of the cavalry in the attack, as they had the mobility to shift around German positions, were light enough to use stealth to move past other defenses, and possessed enough firepower to handle minor forces. No other formation in the army possessed this unique blend.

After their success on 1 August, the VII Corps transferred the 4th MCG from the 4th ID to the 1st ID, then attacking toward Mortain. While that division seized this critical road junction, which dominated yet another north-south route out of Normandy, the 4th MCG seized towns to the west and south, providing a security zone within which the division could operate.[5] Over the next several days, as the 1st ID and VII Corps consolidated their positions, the cavalry kept busy. One squadron, the 24th CRS, conducted reconnaissance operations nearly all the way to Mayenne (twenty-six miles south of Mortain), while the 4th CRS maintained a screen to the east of Mortain.[6]

On 7 August, elements of the 4th CRS met the first waves of the massive German armored counterattack toward Mortain. The German attack, Operation LÜTTICH, was the last German attempt to prevent the Allied breakout from Normandy. Consisting of four panzer divisions, it represented a serious threat. If the Germans could penetrate the American line past Mortain, they could cut the roads feeding the Third Army's drive and potentially defeat that army in detail.[7] With only two major roads south for the Third Army, the German plan seemed relatively feasible, although the ability of their forces to maintain their positions astride the Third Army's rear was perhaps questionable.

The VII Corps was then transitioning control of Mortain from the 1st ID to the 30th ID. Although unable to halt the attack, the 4th MCG did provide early warning and inflicted some casualties on the Germans before being forced to withdraw. The group continued to resist the German penetration, even sending cooks and members of the group band into the line in order to prevent further intrusions. Although the 4th MCG could not keep the Germans out of Mortain (which had never been their mission), it did manage, initially by itself and later with some help from the 1st ID, to prevent any German movement south of the road connecting Milly to Saint Jean-du-Corail, approximately two and a half miles south of Mortain (this road is now the D481). This containment proved absolutely critical, as American resistance to the east of the town stymied further German advances. In fact, a battalion of American infantry on high ground to the west used their positions to call down very accurate and heavy artillery fire upon the Germans. With the cavalry and other forces preventing them from maneuvering, the panzers found themselves caught in a trap that cost them thousands of casualties and almost a hundred tanks.[8]

While the VII Corps continued to stabilize its line and prepare for a counterattack, reconnaissance patrols from the 4th MCG provided critical information to the 1st and 30th IDs that facilitated the rescue of 30th ID forces cut off around Mortain.[9] Upon the rescue of the infantry, the group continued to provide reconnaissance on the southern flank of the battle as well as assisting in the containment of the Germans in that area. The actions of the 4th MCG at Mortain are a series of textbook examples of corps cavalry in action. The 4th MCG initially screened a divisional battle handover, provided early warning of a German attack, participated in containing the battle, and then conducted reconnaissance that aided in the execution of the corps battle.

While the 4th MCG fought around Mortain, the 113th MCG screened the flanks of the 2nd AD and the XIX Corps as they fought around the town of Gathemo, eight miles north of Mortain. The German Mortain offensive lengthened this fighting, with the corps wrapping up that battle around 12 August. The next day, Major General Charles Corlett attached Colonel Biddle's 113th MCG to the 30th ID, which had just come under control of the corps at the completion of the Mortain battle. After the success of Collins's VII Corps in defeating the German counterattack, the XIX Corps attacked across the front of the VII Corps and engaged German forces to the east of Mortain. The Redhorse led the 30th ID in a thirteen-mile dash east to the region around the city of Domfront. Seizure of this town helped solidify the inside corner of the American penetration, as Bradley continued to rotate his army south and east around the point of the German salient forming east of Mortain. As the 30th ID fought for Domfront, the 113th MCG established a security screen to the north to protect it against German forces engaged with, and retreating from, Allied forces advancing south.[10]

The fighting by the VII and XIX Corps around Mortain not only stopped a potential disaster for the Third Army; it also fixed a huge portion of the mobile German forces in France inside a growing pocket. While these forces had attempted to break through at Mortain, the Third Army and elements of the First Army had swept around the southern flank of the Germans and were now attacking east and north in a giant attempt to encircle the German Seventh Army and Fifth Panzer Army in what would become known as the Falaise Pocket. While the Germans would ultimately be successful in withdrawing significant units (mostly headquarters elements) from the pocket, the end result would still cripple German efforts to stand anywhere before their own border.

On 18 August, the First Army continued to sideslip east to facilitate the Third Army's attack around the German Seventh Army's flank. In support of this effort, the XIX corps ordered the 113th MCG to move to the vicinity of Bezolles, more than seventy miles to the east of their current positions around Domfront, to protect the truck-mounted 30th ID as it moved to participate in entrapping German forces trying to escape from the remains of the Falaise Pocket. After completion of this mission, Corlett ordered the group to screen a frontage of approximately thirty-five miles from Sées to Verneuil-sur-Avre on 20 August as part of the general containment of the pocket.[11]

As the Mortain battle concluded and passed into the battle for the Falaise Pocket, the 4th MCG spent its time conducting reconnaissance on the flanks of the VII Corps and maintaining contact with the XIX Corps through their brethren in the 113th MCG. On 19 August, Collins ordered the 4th MCG to move approximately fifty miles to the east—to the city of La Loupe, approximately fourteen miles east of Chartres—to make contact with the Third Army. Patton's forces were heavily engaged in this area, but with the Falaise Pocket collapsing, the First Army would soon take responsibility for the region. This would allow the Third Army to continue its attack to the east, oriented on Chartres and aiming for the Seine River south of Paris. The left flank would rest along the remnants of the Falaise Pocket, and the right flank would be secured by the Third Army to the south. The 4th MCG would screen the thirty-five miles of front along the collapsing Falaise Pocket east of Sées, covering the deployment of the 9th ID into the VII Corps' new zone and replacing the 113th MCG, who shifted their responsibility farther east.[12]

The screen by both the 113th and 4th MCGs proved particularly important as the Falaise Pocket closed on 19 August at Chambois, twenty miles north of Sées and the western extent of the two groups' screen.[13] German forces to the east of Chambois were streaming east in an attempt to escape. The cavalry helped canalize the enemy away from the First Army's axis of advance, allowing the Americans to move more rapidly to the Seine and Paris.

The 4th MCG completed their screening mission on 23 August as the corps completed its arrival in its new zone. The cavalry then screened the VII Corps' flank as it advanced to and across the Seine south of Paris, near the city of Melun. Meanwhile, their fellow cavalrymen in the 113th MCG advanced approximately six miles to the north after the fall of Verneuil-sur-Avre on 22 August, eventually making contact with forces of the British Second Army around Breteuil. This town, sixty-two miles west of Paris, marked the closure of another pocket, as the American First Army and British Second Army attempted yet again to trap more German forces. However, despite the Allies' inflicting heavy casualties on the enemy, the German Seventh Army escaped yet again from complete destruction.[14] After being relieved by the British forces, the 113th MCG shifted their efforts east, aiding the XIX Corps' movement across the Seine by conducting reconnaissance along the river north of Paris, as well as making contact with elements of the XV and V Corps.[15]

While the VII and XIX Corps, with the 4th and 113th MCGs, helped widen the penetration made by COBRA and turn the U.S. First Army east, Major General Leonard Gerow's V Corps and its attached

102nd MCG served as the pivot for the entire army. The corps attacked directly into the face of weakening but still strong German defenses east and southeast of Saint Lô in early August while maintaining contact with the British Second Army. This corps had not yet experienced the rapid advances of its sisters, but its task was still important. While British and American forces crushed the German forces on the flanks from the north and south, the V Corps pushed the balloon in from the front.

The New Jersey cavalry of the 102nd CRS led the 2nd ID east to the Vire River, north of Mortain, and on 1 August identified crossing points as well as German defenses south of the river. The guardsmen attacked the German forces occupying high ground dominating the crossing point. A fierce battle ensued, costing the squadron thirty-three casualties and vehicle losses so heavy that entire platoons had to be reequipped. However, the squadron was successful in its efforts and drove the Germans out of their defensive positions.[16] The casualties taken by the 102nd caused the group commander to pass the 38th CRS through the 102nd to continue the offensive guard for the 2nd ID. On 3 August, the 38th CRS moved farther down the Campeaux–Vire highway until it hit the next line of German defenses, which proved somewhat tougher than that experienced by the 102nd. Rather than risk more casualties to the cavalry, the commander of the 2nd ID ordered a regular infantry regiment supported by medium armor to penetrate the German defenses.[17] These actions are highly typical of an offensive security mission, as the cavalry found the enemy, developed the situation, and then passed the main body forward. Additionally, the cavalry were able to protect the infantry until they were needed, rather than allow the main body of the corps to be eaten away in small actions.

Following the fighting around Vire, the squadrons of the 102nd MCG moved to the flanks of the V Corps, maintaining contact with the XIX Corps on the west flank and the British Second Army on the east flank. These efforts allowed the V Corps to concentrate its forces against the weakening German resistance at the western tip of the Falaise Pocket. However, by the middle of August the V Corps had been pinched out of the line by the XIX Corps and the British forces as these units advanced north and south across the V Corps' front. From 16 to 22 August 1944, Eisenhower's Supreme Headquarters Allied Expeditionary Force (SHAEF) ordered most of the divisions assigned to the V Corps west to besiege the city of Brest under the direction of the Third Army's VIII Corps. The V Corps headquarters along with its corps troops, including the 102nd MCG, moved east to take command of the French 2nd Armored Division and the 4th ID then preparing to take Paris.[18]

Once the group established itself in its new positions southwest of Paris with the V Corps, the corps detached Troop B, 102nd CRS, from the group and attached it to the French 2nd Armored Division to augment that division's reconnaissance formations prior to its "thunder run" into Paris. The V Corps then attached the rest of the group to the 4th ID as it attacked into the southern suburbs of the French capital.[19] On 25 August, the group led the 4th ID and the French 2nd Armored Division into Paris. As the 4th ID was the only American division in the corps, a full cavalry squadron led each of its two forward regimental combat teams.[20] The group entered Paris by mid-morning, aiming for the Seine River crossings in southern Paris. This concentration of power allowed the cavalry to fight their way past most opposition, although a troop of the 102nd fell into an ambush that cost it the better part of a platoon before the rest of the squadron could support it.[21] Meanwhile, the troop attached to the French met with spectacular success in its advance and by 1530 of that day was fully assembled at the Arc de Triomphe.[22]

The actions of the 102nd MCG in the advance into Paris are a perfect example of cavalry in an advance guard role. The cavalry identified enemy positions, defeated the German security zone (such as it was), and permitted the main body to advance and put its full weight into the main effort. The success of the group helped speed the liberation of Paris and facilitated the V Corps' quick movement through the city.

By late August the First Army had liberated Paris and was driving at full speed toward the Belgian border. The XIX Corps held the left flank, having passed north of Paris while maintaining contact with the British Second Army. Gerow's V Corps held the center, having passed straight through Paris. And the VII Corps, having crossed the Seine south of Paris, held the right flank, maintaining a very tenuous link with the Third Army to the south.

The XIX Corps' 113th MCG crossed the Seine River at Saint Germain-en-Laye (seven miles west of Paris) on 28 August, reinforced with a company of tank destroyers and a company of combat engineers. After spending the end of August clearing the triangle formed by the Oise and Seine Rivers, the group crossed the Oise River on 1 September 1944.[23] Bradley had directed the XIX Corps to reach Tournai, Belgium, as rapidly as possible. Corlett chose to do this by placing two of the 79th ID's regiments and one of the 30th ID's regiments onto trucks. To protect these highly vulnerable motorized formations, he instructed the 2nd AD to lead the corps, with the 113th MCG attached to and leading the 79th ID.[24] The corps would move to the north of Paris, aiming for the Belgian border. With two regiments motorized, the 79th ID moved faster than the 30th ID, leading to half of the corps moving at a faster rate than the other half. The result was that instead of the 113th MCG being behind the 2nd AD, it often was in front of the armored division, or intermingled with it.

The 113th MCG reached the Somme River by the evening of 1 September, having moved over sixty miles in a day. The troopers identified a useable highway bridge near Péronne, twenty-five miles east of Amiens. Additionally, the cavalry identified additional sites where the 79th and 30th IDs could build more bridges.[25] The advance continued on 2 September, with the Redhorse reaching its objective eight miles south of Tournai, Belgium, that night, having traversed at least an additional forty-two miles despite encountering stiff resistance from German rear guards. The cavalry simply used their mobility to bypass these formations, marking them for the follow-on infantry divisions and airpower.[26] The cavalry's reconnaissance allowed the corps to overcome obstacles rapidly by finding crossing points and identifying (and occasionally destroying) enemy strongpoints. The security mission also conducted by the cavalry protected the vulnerable truck-mounted elements of the 79th ID, preventing them from being ambushed by fire from those same strongpoints.

As gas shortages threatened the advance of the entire 12th Army Group, the XIX Corps could not move as quickly after the seizure of Tournai. However, Corlett gave the 113th MCG the mission to reconnoiter to the Albert Canal on the opposite side of Belgium in order to maintain contact with the retreating German forces and keep some form of momentum going for the corps. On 5 September the group began its march, and three days and 130 miles later it arrived on the Albert Canal across from Maastricht, the Netherlands.[27] This advance, averaging over forty-two miles a day, stands as a spectacular achievement, even among the rapid advances so common in the France campaign. Compared to the advances of a couple of miles or hundreds of yards that the 113th MCG had experienced in Normandy, the attack across Belgium is unbelievable.

The 30th ID relieved the 113th MCG on 11 September, having benefitted from the cavalry's reconnaissance as well as crumbling German resistance. Although the Germans were already in full retreat, the cavalry's actions certainly prevented any chance of German forces taking advantage of the respite that the fuel shortage had imposed on the rest of the XIX Corps and coalescing in central Belgium.

As the VII Corps progressed past the Seine River, south and then east of Paris, in late August it left behind the 4th MCG to defeat enemy pockets that had been bypassed by the main units of the corps. The cavalry engaged in a particularly heavy fight with the remains of an entire German infantry regiment. Despite the fact that the Germans were in full retreat, they were still capable of putting up a fight, particularly since the cavalry stood between them and the relative safety of Germany. After a couple days of vicious fighting, however, the cavalry nearly destroyed the German 128th Infantry Regiment, inflicting large numbers of killed and wounded while taking just under five hundred prisoners.[28]

On 28 August, the 4th MCG crossed the Marne River and moved to the front of the VII Corps, where it conducted reconnaissance in front of and with the 3rd AD. This reconnaissance would prove highly useful on 29 August, when patrols of the 4th CRS discovered three German artillery batteries supporting the defense of Soissons against the 3rd AD. The destruction of these batteries substantially helped in the defeat of the Germans holding the city.[29] Two days later, the 4th MCG provided security to the 3rd AD as it fought around the city of Laon, with the 24th CRS establishing a blocking position in Marle, twelve miles to the north. The cavalrymen not only prevented German forces from reinforcing their comrades in Laon, but the 24th CRS also destroyed a combined German force of infantry, anti-tank guns, and armor in Marle itself.[30] Once again, the 4th MCG demonstrated a textbook security operation, protecting the corps' main effort in battle.

At the beginning of September, the First Army ordered Collins's VII Corps, the rightmost corps in the army line, to attack north toward the Belgian city of Mons. This move was yet another attempt to destroy the remaining German forces in France before they could reach the relative safety of the Siegfried Line. The forces of the V and XIX Corps as well as the British would drive the enemy forward, into the arms of the VII Corps. However, this neat operational maneuver would create a nearly one hundred-mile gap between the main elements of the First and Third Armies, practically inviting a counterstroke into the flank of the corps.[31] Collins had to reduce some of this gap, retain some security on his right flank, and still keep his primary combat power focused on the expected fighting around Mons. Thus, he decided to create a combined arms task force built around the 4th MCG.[32] On 1 September, the VII Corps attached the 85th Tank Destroyer Battalion (Towed) and the 87th Armored Field Artillery Battalion (105mm, Self-Propelled) to the group in addition to allowing them to retain the 759th Light Tank Battalion. The next day the corps also attached the 1st Battalion, 60th Infantry Regiment, to the burgeoning task force.[33]

As the VII Corps continued its fight around Mons on 2 September, Tully's 4th MCG (reinforced) guarded the corps' flank along a frontage of nearly twenty-nine miles, from just south of the Belgian border to the town of Amagne, twenty-six miles northeast of Reims (see map 2).[34] The group kept a tenuous contact with the Third Army's 90th ID to the south while maintaining their screen to the east. However, the cavalry did not simply remain static. The group continued its advance to the east on 3 September, seizing the towns of Charleville and Mézières along the Meuse River. Although the Germans had destroyed all vehicular bridges along the river in the region, the group still established a small bridgehead on the east bank with its attached infantry battalion. The group also seized the town of Rocroi, four miles west of the Meuse River, and just south of the Belgian border.[35]

Shortly after the 4th MCG's successes in Charleville and Rocroi, the First Army conducted a dramatic reorganization of its line. Gerow's V Corps, having been pinched out by the advance of the XIX and VII Corps, was moved to the southern end of the army line to cover the

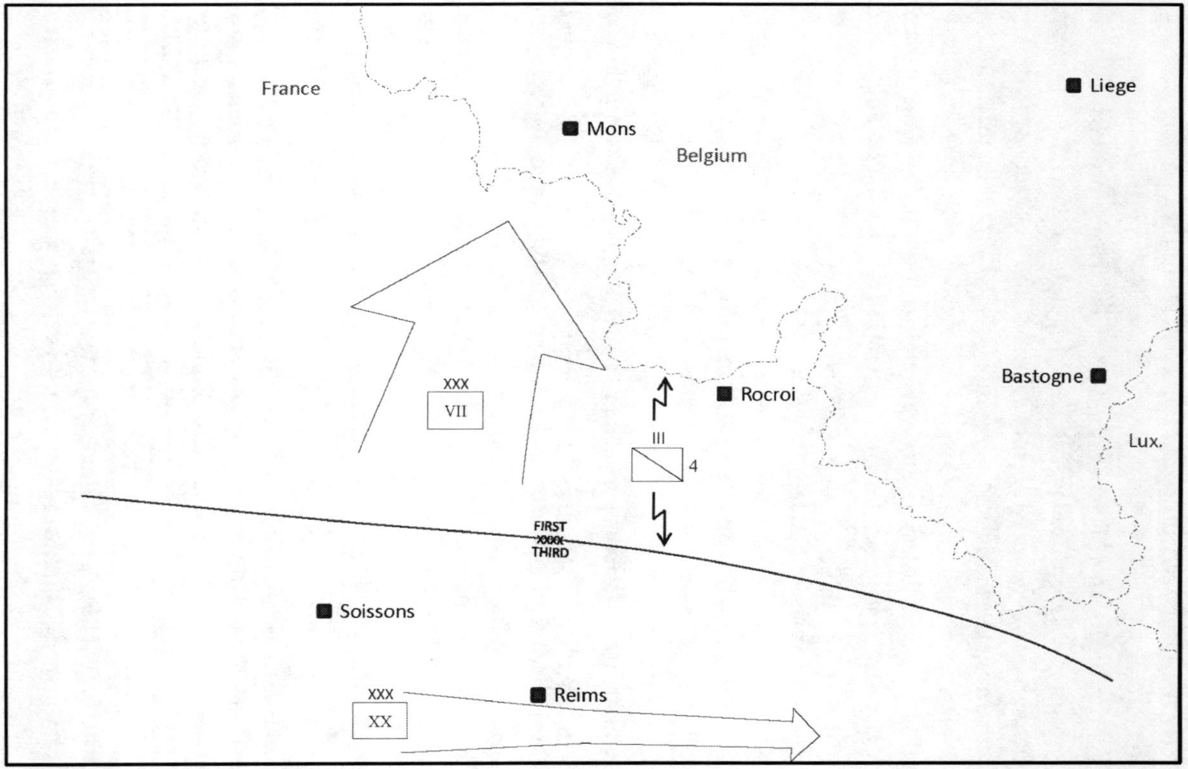

Map 2. 4th MCG Holds the Flank, September 1944.

gap between the VII Corps and the Third Army—the same ground a single reinforced cavalry group was holding in conjunction with minor elements of the Third Army's 90th ID. The actions of the 4th MCG materially aided not only the VII Corps, but the V Corps as well. They had advanced the front line to the banks of the Meuse River, speeding the commitment of the V Corps into Belgium. Additionally, the group had provided Collins with peace of mind about his right flank while the corps fought a meeting engagement with fleeing German forces around Mons. The actions of the 4th MCG allowed the VII Corps to concentrate three divisions for the corps fight, resulting in the seizure of nearly twenty-five thousand prisoners.[36] This action stands as a perfect example of cavalry acting not only as security, but also as an economy of force in a larger corps action, allowing the commander to focus his main combat power at the decisive point.

While the V Corps and the rest of the First Army advanced north and east of Paris, the 102nd MCG had enjoyed a respite the last week of August, with the 102nd CRS in corps reserve and the 38th CRS conducting local security in the city. The soldiers of the 38th CRS greatly enjoyed their time guarding Paris, with the squadron history stating that "guard duty was declared a pleasure with so much cheerful company." Truly any assignment where soldiers look forward to such a mundane task must have been memorable.[37] This short vacation ended in early September when the group found itself back in front of the corps as it passed through the 4th MCG and drove toward the Belgian border between Reims and Saint Quentin.

On 3 September, the 38th CRS conducted an assault crossing of the Meuse River near Fumay, Belgium. Despite heavy resistance, the troopers conducted their mounted attack across a ford site, forcing the German defenders back. The cavalry used the comparatively stronger engines of their armored cars to literally drag their jeeps across the swiftly moving river. The 102nd CRS conducted similar duty to the south of the 38th Squadron. The two squadrons combined led the 4th ID east, conducting an advance guard for the division, while the 5th AD acted in much the same fashion for the 28th ID.[38] Both squadrons fought a number of minor engagements with elements of German rear guards and security forces.

The fighting encountered by the 102nd CRS from 6 September

to 7 September in the vicinity of Vivy and Paliseul, Belgium, is typical of these actions. Over the course of these two days the 102nd CRS defeated a number of delaying German forces and beat back a local counterattack by two companies of German infantry. In the process they destroyed a Tiger tank, two assault guns, four half-tracks, an antitank gun, and multiple trucks.[39] These actions, though minor in scope, were typical of a security fight, as the New Jersey cavalry fought to protect the advancing elements of the 4th ID from small—but still deadly—encounters.

Although resistance began to stiffen as the corps approached the German border, both wings continued to advance. This is particularly impressive for the cavalry, as they were keeping pace with a full armored division to their south despite their lesser numbers and firepower.[40] On 10 September, a detachment from the 102nd CRS escorted Prince Felix of Luxembourg back to his capital in Luxembourg City.[41] By 13 September, elements of the 102nd CRS had made contact with the Siegfried Line.[42]

From Operation COBRA to the increasingly fierce fighting along the German border, the corps cavalry of the First Army had proven their worth time and again. The cavalry conducted reconnaissance, provided security, and acted in economy of force roles. Corps cavalry screened the fighting around the Falaise Pocket, protected truck-mounted infantry divisions moving rapidly in pursuit of fleeing German forces, led the way into Paris, and were the first units to make contact with the Siegfried Line.

The First Army's cavalry made an immediate impact on the success of that army. Without the protection offered by their screening operations, Hodges would have been forced to move much more deliberately as individual divisions groped their way forward or cautiously looked over their shoulders into open flanks. Furthermore, the cavalry allowed the army's corps to mass against German forces time and again by covering these open areas. German positions that may have held against battalions or regiments were instead confronted with overwhelming force, preventing them from establishing a secure line any place before the German border. Debating whether to call these missions reconnaissance, security, or economy of force would be to miss the point that the cavalry did all three simultaneously, allowing the First Army to fight a smashing battle of materiel against opponents who could not match such a concentration of resources. While the encirclement battles of Falaise and Mons may not have produced the decisive results for which some may have hoped, they might not have happened at all without the actions of the First Army's corps cavalry.

Third Army

While Hodges's First Army engaged German forces continuously from Operation COBRA to the German border, Patton's Third Army truly experienced the full benefits of the breakout from Normandy. With the bulk of German forces in France engaged with the First Army and Field Marshal Bernard Law Montgomery's 21st Army Group, Patton was free to assault across France in one of the most famous drives in U.S. military history. Just as the First Army used its corps cavalry to great effect in its actions across northwestern France, so too did the Third Army.

On 1 August 1944, the Third Army became operational under Patton. The army's initial task as part of the COBRA plan called for the seizure of the Brittany Peninsula and its valuable ports. Patton would be the right man for this task, as it called for aggressive maneuver in open space—Patton's specialty.[43] To facilitate its movement through the First Army, Middleton's VIII Corps, the westernmost formation of the First Army, moved to the Third. Three additional corps—XII, XX, and XV—stacked up in column behind the VIII. Middleton was to help the VII Corps create the breakout and then immediately turn west into Brittany. The rest of the army would make a wide turn to the east in order to outflank and perhaps encircle the German positions still holding in Normandy. Major General Manton Eddy's XII Corps would follow the VIII Corps out of Normandy, then take the outside track of the turn, protecting the southern flank of the Third Army as it assaulted toward Paris. Major General Walton Walker's XX Corps would turn inside of the XII Corps, holding the army center. Major General Wade Haislip's XV Corps would follow the XX Corps, taking the inside track of the turn and maintaining contact with the First Army.[44]

On 31 July, the day before the Third Army became operational, the Army Communications Zone that had controlled the 2nd and 15th MCGs for use in rear area security released both groups to the Third Army, which promptly attached them to the VIII Corps, then in the process of conducting and exploiting Operation COBRA. This corps was leading the entire Third Army in the breakout from the Normandy beachhead, and it had the mission of isolating and seizing the Brittany Peninsula with its ports of Brest and Saint Nazaire. This mission would require the corps to attack in two directions at once—south to Saint Nazaire, and west to Brest—hence the requirement for three cavalry groups (the 2nd, 15th, and 106th MCGs).

In order to assist the VIII Corps as it attacked south toward Nantes (4th AD) and west toward Brest (6th AD), the Third Army created an ad hoc brigade-size combined arms task force to seize a series of bridges to secure the rail line from Brest to Normandy, which could then be used for supply of the Allied armies after the seizure of Brest.[45] Task Force A consisted of: Headquarters, 1st Tank Destroyer (TD) Brigade; Colonel John Reybold's 15th MCG; the 705th TD Battalion (Self-Propelled); Headquarters, 6th TD Destroyer Group; the 509th Engineer Light Pontoon Company; and the 159th Combat Engineer Battalion.[46]

Middleton had originally planned on using the 2nd MCG (Dragoons) as part of Task Force A. However, the rapid success of the 4th AD in its drive to the south to isolate the Brittany Peninsula prompted him to reassign it to that division for flank security, since the following infantry divisions were too slow to keep pace with the armor. Thus, rather than participate in Task Force A's charge west into Brittany, the group raced south in an attempt to link up with its new senior command.[47]

By the evening of 2 August, the 2nd MCG had made contact with the 4th AD and were ordered to conduct a reconnaissance and screening mission to the southeast of the division to protect its flank. While the 8th ID contained the city of Rennes, the 4th AD continued the attack south along a broad front from Saint Nazaire to Lorient. The Dragoons used one squadron (the 42nd) to screen along the eastern flank of the division and corps for approximately a week, allowing the main effort (the 4th AD) to concentrate all available forces for the drive south to isolate the Brittany Peninsula. The unit's remaining squadron (the 2nd) conducted route security along the division's supply lines.[48] This period saw minor contact for the group, with the majority of the Wehrmacht in this particular region being in a state of disarray. However, the Germans still possessed the ability to interdict lightly defended supply columns along the Americans' wide-open flanks. Momentum in combat can be easily lost if the main effort is constantly distracted by threats to its flanks and rear, thus making the cavalry's mission essential to allowing the VIII Corps to maintain its drive to the south. There were several short, sharp engagements between the group and scattered German resistance around the towns of Vitre and Segre, but they were generally resolved with little effort by the individual troops involved in these actions.[49] Through these actions, the 2nd MCG performed a traditional cavalry security mission.

On 2 August, as Task Force A prepared to assault into the Brittany Peninsula, and the 2nd MCG drove south, the VIII Corps ordered the 106th MCG to protect the corps' eastern (left) flank. The group moved with alacrity, seizing the town of Fougères, twenty-four miles south of Avranches, ahead of the 79th ID, a XV Corps division.[50] This town controlled access to the main road network running south to the city of Rennes, one of the primary objectives of the VIII Corps in the first stages of the breakout. Additionally, Fougères was to be in the vicinity of the pivot point for the XV Corps' attack to the southeast. Thus, the 106th MCG's rapid seizure of this key road intersection allowed the Third Army to "set the corner" for the XV Corps to run around as well as have the cavalry protect the key roads needed for the VIII Corps' drive to the south, without requiring the 79th ID to fight for this location (see map 3). The following day, the Third Army transferred the 106th MCG to the XV Corps to provide it with cavalry support, as the VIII Corps had at the time both the 2nd and 15th MCGs working for it.[51]

While the 2nd MCG aided the southern element of the VIII Corps' drive, Task Force A and the 15th MCG prepared for action. Middleton's original intent had been for the 6th AD to clear Saint Malo, thirty miles to the west of the key city of Avranches, prior to continuing to their primary objective, the port of Brest. However, as this task would slow the division considerably, General Patton, bypassing Middleton, directed the 6th AD to "take Brest."[52] Therefore Task Force A received

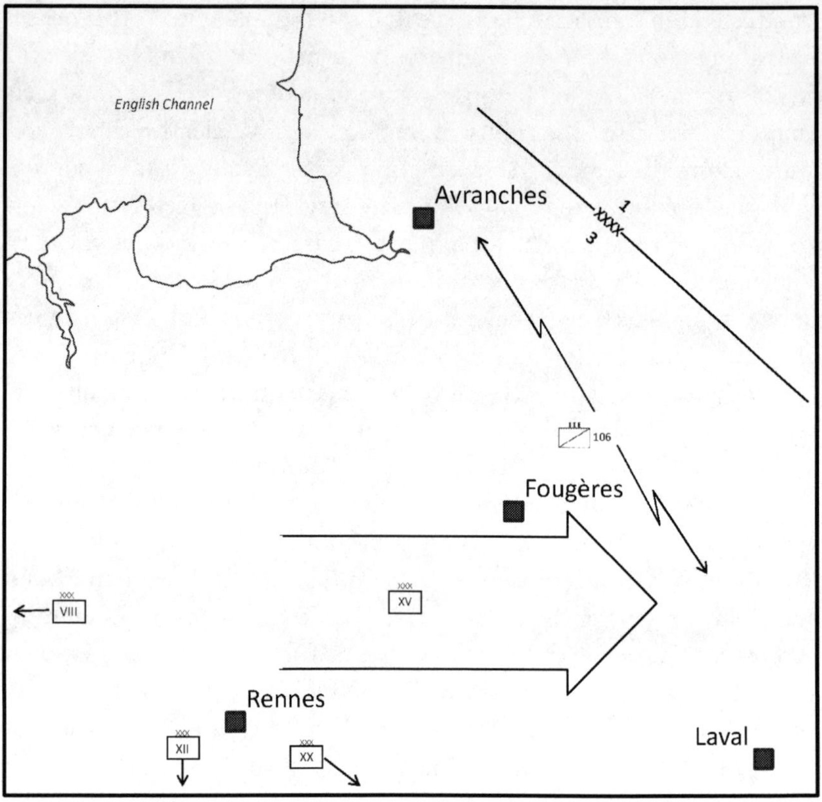

Map 3. 106th MCG Sets the Inside Corner.

the additional mission of assisting in the clearance of Saint Malo in addition to its primary role of the seizure of vital bridges in the Brittany Peninsula (see map 4).[53]

At 0100 hours on 3 August, the 15th MCG led Task Force A out of its assembly areas around Coutances as they sped toward Saint Malo. The task force crossed the line of departure around Avranches at 0500, having covered twenty-five miles in two hours.[54] Although elements of the 6th AD were to the front of the task force, the situation was so fluid that the concepts of a "front" or "rear" were entirely inappropriate. By 0700, the cavalry were a few miles east of the town of Dol-de-Bretagne (thirteen miles southeast of Saint Malo) when the lead platoon of the 15th Squadron hit a German ambush. Surprise was complete, as the element was moving at over forty miles an hour. Nearly the entire pla-

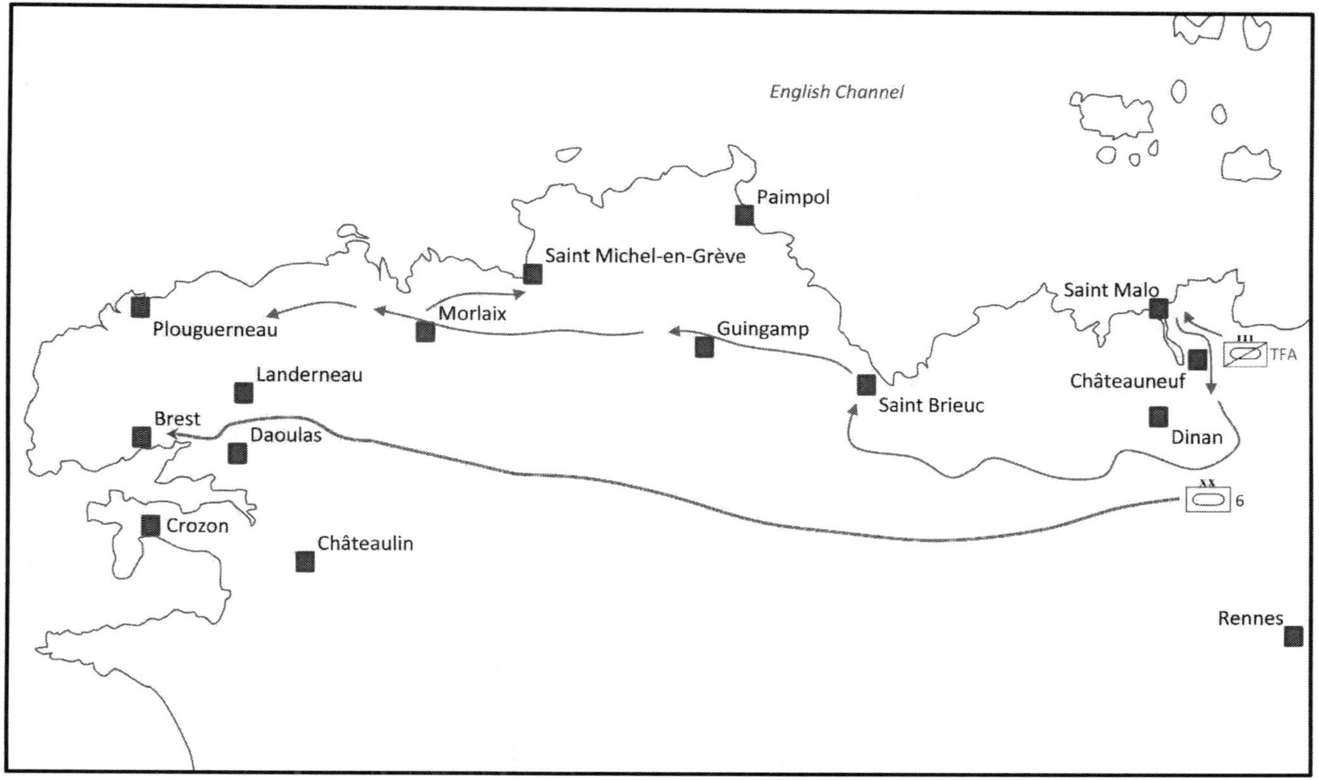

Map 4. Task Force A in Brittany.

toon was captured or killed. Only three men escaped. The most serious effect of this ambush was that the group commander, Colonel Reybold, had been traveling with this platoon, leading them in the attack, and he was now missing in action.[55]

Although this incident highlights the fragile nature of the cavalry's survivability in combat, it also stands as the perfect example of how not to conduct a movement to contact. This platoon had been moving far too fast to do any real reconnaissance of the route. Moving at forty miles per hour means that a particular observer is looking at any given piece of ground for mere seconds, if that. Any German that did not wish to be seen by this group could have simply laid low and let the column pass. Additionally, moving so quickly gave the unit very little time to respond to any obstacles in the road, particularly surface-laid mines or even road spikes. Essentially, the platoon in question impaled itself on the German defenses. This is only reconnaissance in the sense that follow-on units know something bad happened ahead.

Furthermore, a group commander being in the lead platoon means that he does not have the distance or perspective necessary to control the battle. When the shooting started, this colonel with decades of experience became as useful as a rifleman with one year in the army. Although leading charges is fun, every soldier has a part to play, and they must be where they can do it most effectively. The group commander had no business being this far forward.

Despite the loss of their group commander, the cavalrymen continued their advance around 1800 on 3 August to assembly areas five miles southeast of Saint Malo. The new group commander, Colonel Logan Berry, ordered an immediate reconnaissance by both squadrons north to Saint Malo in order to determine the strength of the city's defenses. However, a combination of heavy German artillery, small arms fire, and darkness forced the lightly armored cavalrymen to halt well short of their objective. The next day, 4 August, the cavalrymen, supported by the task force's tank destroyers and engineers, conducted a deliberate attack, seizing a foothold in the German defenses by the end of the day.[56] The group resumed their attack, now in conjunction with the 330th Infantry Regiment of the 83rd ID, on 5 August. Although this attack made some headway, it quickly became apparent to Middleton that Saint Malo would be a protracted battle. He therefore relieved

Task Force A of its responsibility for the city, turning the fight entirely over to the 83rd ID.[57]

This decision demonstrated that Middleton understood that the cavalry's strength lay in their mobility and that they did not have the dismounted combat power for extended positional warfare. The 15th MCG had made contact with the enemy, removed his security belt, developed the situation, and then passed the fight on to main body formations. These actions would aid the rest of the VIII Corps as it settled into the tough fight for the main defenses of Saint Malo without the extra stress of having to perform these functions.

On 5 August, well to the east of Brittany, Haislip ordered the 106th MCG to conduct a zone reconnaissance in front of the XV Corps as it attacked east to the Mayenne River, twenty-five miles to the east of Fougères, which was itself twenty-three miles south of Mortain.[58] His intention was to continue to sweep around the First Army's southern flank and get into the rear of the German Seventh Army. The cavalry successfully reached the river, crossing it at two locations on the night of 5–6 August.[59]

After the crossing of the Mayenne River, the group moved to the northern flank of the corps (and the army) and continued to drive toward Le Mans, forty-five miles away. The group reached it on 8 August and participated in its capture by screening the northern suburbs and roads as the 79th and 90th IDs took the bulk of the city.[60] This action by the 106th MCG allowed the infantry divisions to concentrate their strength in the effort to cut off the German forces to their north without having to devote forces to protecting their northern flanks.

Meanwhile, in Brittany, Task Force A resumed its attack to the west on 6 August accompanied by a battalion of infantry from the 83rd ID, with its primary objective being the rail bridges in the town of Saint Brieuc, a port on the north Brittany coast. The 15th MCG made the move in a single day, bypassing strong German defenses around the city of Dinan. Free French forces met the 15th MCG in the outskirts of Saint Brieuc and reported that they had seized the town.[61]

The cavalry continued the task force's advance on 7 August, clearing the seventeen miles from Saint Brieuc to the major crossroads town of Guingamp to the west. This day saw serious action as the 15th

MCG, supported by the rest of Task Force A, fought against a force of over one thousand Germans who were in blocking positions to the west of Saint Brieuc.[62] The cavalrymen quickly established a technique that would stand them in good stead throughout the rest of the Brittany campaign. The reconnaissance troops made direct fire contact with German forces and then withdrew out of range. Next, they called for air support to devastate the defenders, and then they advanced in conjunction with the attached infantry under cover of artillery and tank destroyer fire.[63] This method proved successful in almost all of the cavalry's actions. The combined arms nature of these tactics had been standard cavalry practice for decades, although the cavalry proved highly dependent on outside formations for support due to its dismount-weak, lightly armored organization.

After two days of rest, on 9 August, the 17th CRS led the 15th MCG and Task Force A in the seizure of the town of Morlaix and its important rail and road bridges, thirty miles to the west of Guingamp. This success completed the task force's initial mission of seizing the important rail bridges from Brest to the base of the Cotentin Peninsula.[64] The following day, Middleton ordered Task Force A to protect the northern and northwestern flanks of the 6th AD as it invested the port of Brest. The two squadrons then moved out to conduct reconnaissance and clear the portions of the northwestern Brittany coast that the 6th AD had bypassed. The 15th CRS encountered strong resistance around the town of Plouguerneau, thirty miles to the west of Morlaix and thirteen miles north of Brest. A group of bypassed German defenders stubbornly held their ground, forcing the cavalry to dig them out of their positions. With assistance from the task force's tank destroyers and artillery support (most likely from the 6th AD), the squadron captured 227 Germans in the reduction of that pocket.[65]

While the VIII Corps fought its way to Brest in Brittany, the rest of the Third Army continued its attack to the east. Following the capture of Le Mans, on 9 August 1944, Patton directed Haislip's XV Corps to attack twenty-five miles north to seize the city of Alençon, as part of what would become the drive to close the Falaise Pocket. Alençon is twenty miles south of the key city of Argentan, one of the essential road junctions needed for a successful German withdrawal from the developing pocket. The 106th MCG's role in this action was to shield the eastern flank of the corps as it attacked north. The corps began its attack on 10 August, with the 106th MCG in their assigned role, as well as providing intelligence on the locations (or lack thereof) of German forces to the north in their former area of operations. This intelligence allowed the XV Corps to bypass a region that the 12th Army Group believed to be a German stronghold, but reconnaissance by the 106th MCG proved that area to be empty of enemy activity.[66] This information allowed the corps to not spend valuable time and effort clearing nonessential locations and to instead concentrate on its drive to the north.

Later in the evening of 10 August, well to the west of the rest of the Third Army's main drive toward Germany, Middleton directed Task Force A to secure a beachhead near the town of Saint Michel-en-Grève, thirteen miles to the northwest of Morlaix in Brittany. This would be used to offload supplies for the 6th AD, thereby shortening the logistics chain that now ran nearly two hundred miles from Brest to the Normandy landing sites. The 15th CRS, followed by the rest of the group, departed the Plouguerneau area at 0100 hours and arrived at their objective at 1200, having made the nearly fifty-mile journey in eleven hours, a fine time for a tactical road march under combat conditions, and an accomplishment that could not have been replicated by a slower and less mounted infantry regiment.[67]

Back in the east, the 3rd MCG (Brave Rifles) swung immediately into action on the afternoon of 10 August after joining the XX Corps earlier that week. The corps was in the process of swinging around the XV Corps. Major General Walton Walker, the corps commander, ordered the group to conduct reconnaissance to the east, between its widely scattered divisions that were in the process of shifting their attack from the south to the east. Then, once the group reunited its squadrons on the eastern flank of the corps, it was to continue reconnaissance in order to identify enemy positions and lead the corps' attack. The 3rd CRS conducted reconnaissance and liaison duties between the 80th ID near Evron and the 1st ID at Mayenne, a distance of approximately fourteen miles, while the 43rd CRS reconnoitered the region between the 80th ID and the 5th ID near Angers, a tremendous frontage of forty-seven miles. This movement took a little over a day, with the linkup between the squadrons occurring at 0700 on 12 August.[68]

The group then continued its movement east, ending on a line from Sées in the north to Blois in the south, a remarkable frontage of over eighty-five miles.[69]

Due to the continuing light resistance from the Germans in the region, the Brave Rifles continued their reconnaissance farther east, finally ending on the evening of 13 August along the line Orléans–Étampes, a forty-mile front for the cavalrymen. In three days, the group had covered approximately 120 miles, losing only one scout car in the process.[70] Moreover, the cavalry had discovered that the entire southern flank of the German Seventh Army was exposed and ripe for an encircling assault. The Germans had committed most of their combat power into the fighting around Mortain against the American First Army, leaving their southwestern flanks relatively open. This discovery would lead to a series of successful attacks by the XV Corps against the left rear of the German Seventh Army that would contribute to the gutting of this formation.[71]

On 15 August, the XX Corps shifted its direction of attack from the northeast to due east in order to not move in front of the XV Corps. The corps objective became the city of Chartres as well as the crossing points over the Seine River. Patton detached the 3rd CRS, sending them to assist the XII Corps in flank security at this time, leaving the 3rd MCG with only one squadron. The 43rd CRS led the corps in its movement to the Chartres region, since its patrols were already near the area as a result of its previous lunge across France. The cavalry moved slower on this assault, as German resistance began to stiffen along the approaches to the Seine. Although the cavalry could still bypass pockets of resistance, the small nature of most cavalry patrols combined with their light armor made patrolling inherently more dangerous as enemy opposition began to solidify. While a chance encounter with an anti-tank gun supported by a platoon of infantry could be a bad day for a tank or infantry company, it had the potential for disaster for a small cavalry patrol that typically consisted of an armored car and two jeeps. Thus, as the enemy began to appear in strength, the cavalry had to proceed in a more deliberate fashion in order to survive.[72]

On 15 August, as the XX Corps shifted its efforts east, Patton ordered the XV Corps to shift its attack from the northeast to the east toward the city of Dreux, sixty miles to the east of the corps' front line around Argentan, and only thirty-six miles west of Paris. Haislip tasked the 106th MCG to lead the way in this drive. The group began their mission early on 15 August, and despite heavy resistance they seized the town of Nogent-le-Roi along the Eure River, thirty-six miles west of Paris, an astonishing forty-eight miles from their starting positions.[73] This advance allowed the 79th ID to move rapidly to the Eure River to prepare for an assault crossing the following day.

Following the crossing of the Eure River, the 106th MCG led the corps to the northeast as it attacked to the Seine River northwest of Paris. The cavalry not only provided reconnaissance and security for the corps during this move, they also prevented German forces from escaping across the Seine. On 26 August, Haislip withdrew the group from the line for refit. The accomplishments of the group for the month of August earned them the following note in the corps after action report: "The part played by this unit throughout the campaign is particularly noteworthy. The group accomplished every mission assigned it in a superior manner."[74]

By the middle of August, as the XII, XV, and XX Corps attacked to the east, the VIII Corps' 2nd MCG moved in front of the 4th AD, conducting reconnaissance of German positions guarding the city of Nantes. This city lay at the southern corner of the Third Army's wheel into France. The group used its armor and firepower aggressively to discover the leading edge of the Wehrmacht's defenses, though heavy German fire from prepared positions prevented the lightly equipped cavalry from decisively closing with the enemy. In one particularly notable example, a troop of the 42nd CRS used assault guns to destroy a roadblock that was halting forward progress. However, despite initial success, the troop found itself unable to advance past the roadblock due to concentrated enemy fire, including massed small arms and artillery so intense that the small reconnaissance force withdrew.[75]

After the fall of Nantes, Middleton assigned responsibility for the entire region from Nantes to Angers to the 2nd MCG, a tremendous frontage of over forty-five miles oriented to the south along the Loire River. Moreover, the group was also responsible for the frontage to the west of Nantes, with the mission of preventing loose German formations in the Brittany Peninsula from interfering with friendly movements through the Rennes–Nantes corridor.[76] This sector had been the province of the entire 4th AD before its relief from the VIII Corps for missions to the east. Although the focus of battle had moved from this particular region of France as the VIII Corps invested Brest and the rest of the Third Army moved to the east, maintaining a presence in this vital hinge of the army prevented the disorganized German resistance in the area from coalescing into a threat that would draw combat power away from the spearheads. The remaining Wehrmacht along the French coast were strong enough to defeat small patrols of the 2nd MCG comprised of armored cars and jeeps; they most certainly would have caused grievous harm to the lightly defended supply columns keeping the XII Corps moving east.[77] Of course, given the extremely large area of responsibility, the cavalry patrols were rarely more than platoon strength, and often much smaller, so the threat should not be overestimated. However, the mission was essential to the success of the corps. Despite some small setbacks, the group succeeded in their mission of protecting the Third Army's hinge (see map 5).

On 17 August, the 3rd MCG swept around the German defenses at Chartres (forty-five miles southwest of Paris) in an effort to cut off the defense of that city. However, Wehrmacht defenses outside of the city of Étampes, approximately thirty miles east of Chartres, stopped the Brave Rifles in their tracks, defeating every effort to penetrate, infiltrate, or bypass.[78] Seizure of Étampes by the cavalry would have helped isolate Chartres by capturing one of the only major road junctions to that city outside of Paris still in German hands. The 7th AD had fought its way into the city on 15 August, but fierce counterattacks by the defenders had turned the battle into a multiple-day struggle that eventually involved the 5th ID as well as substantial corps artillery support.[79] Thus, the capture of Étampes would have greatly facilitated the success of the corps' attack and also prevented the escape of the Wehrmacht formations fleeing the fighting around Chartres. However, the 3rd MCG did not possess the combat power to fight their way through such heavy resistance. In the end, this failure meant little to the corps, as it succeeded in seizing Chartres, although victory at Étampes would have meant more Germans captured.

The following day, on 18 August, the XX Corps ordered the 3rd MCG to reconnoiter east to identify crossings over the Seine River. Additionally, elements of the 43rd CRS continued to patrol and con-

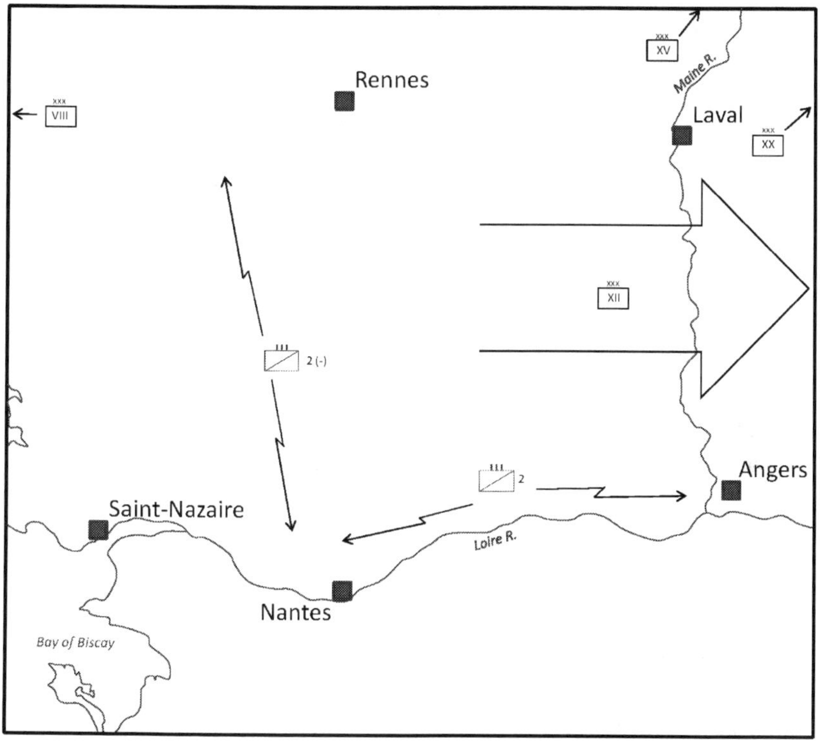

Map 5. 2nd MCG Sets the Outside Corner.

duct reconnaissance in the Chartres area. At one point during this operation the squadron was spread over forty-three miles, with Troop B engaged in combat near Rambouillet, nineteen miles northwest of Étampes, while Troops A and C fought their way into the vicinity of Fontainebleau on the Seine River, thirty-three miles south of Paris.[80] The 3rd MCG's movements were more successful now, as German resistance in the Paris region was collapsing, allowing greater freedom of maneuver to the lightly armored cavalry. However, the group (at this point, really only the 43rd CRS) still encountered heavy resistance that often had to be bypassed in order to achieve its reconnaissance objectives.

As August waned, the XX Corps began its drive to the Seine River with an eye farther east. On 20 August, Walker reinforced the 3rd MCG with engineers and tank destroyers and assigned it the mission of protecting the western flank of the 7th AD. The division needed the protection as it concentrated its combat power for an attack against a German strongpoint near the city of Melun, along the Seine River twenty miles south of Paris.[81] The extensive prior reconnaissance of the 3rd MCG allowed the corps to rapidly reach the river and then conduct assault crossings on the 23rd. The group's participation in the actual assault was limited to shielding the 7th AD's flank as it seized the city of Melun. However, its earlier efforts greatly increased the odds of success for the XX Corps as it breached German defenses along the Seine.

While the rest of the Third Army assaulted to the east, the 2nd MCG held their positions in the Nantes–Angers region for ten days, until 23 August, when the Third Army transferred the group from the VIII Corps to the XII Corps. The Dragoons then conducted offensive operations in central France, heading toward the province of Lorraine. The group moved a distance of nearly two hundred miles to join the corps that was operating seventy miles to the southeast of Paris.[82] The XII Corps assigned the 2nd MCG to relieve a squadron of the 3rd MCG (the 3rd Squadron) that was then protecting the corps' southern flank as it continued moving to the east. As the XII Corps was the southern element of the Third Army, the corps' right flank was also the southern flank of the entire army and army group, with all the German forces left in southern France beyond it.[83] On 26 August, the 42nd CRS attacked a regiment-size grouping of the German army and forced it to withdraw from the town of Carisey, less than thirty miles from the 4th AD's main effort assaulting the city of Troyes (eighty miles southeast of Paris).[84] This action prevented possible enemy interference in the decisive point of the corps' operations, and also stands as a good example of a defensive guard operation.

To the north of the XII Corps, the 3rd MCG crossed the Seine on 25 August 1944 at Tilly, a small town approximately four miles west of Melun and one of the 7th AD's bridgeheads. Once across the river, the cavalry continued their attack to the east, leading the 7th AD in its drive to the Marne River. Here the cavalry truly "earned their pay," discovering multiple roadblocks and ambushes in front of the division. Lacking the combat power to fight through these positions themselves, the cavalrymen passed on the locations and compositions of the enemy. Armed with this information, the 7th AD made short work of these

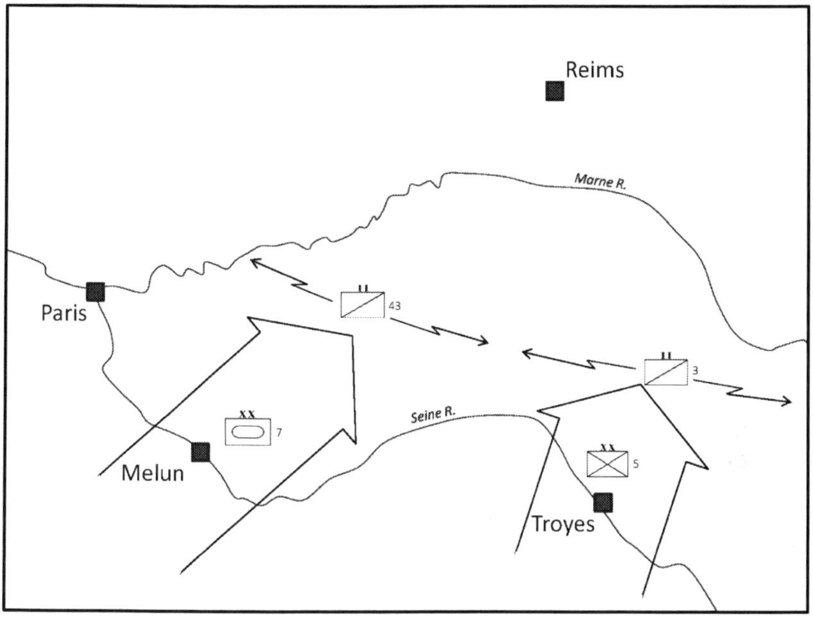

Map 6. XX Corps Assault to Reims.

attempts at delaying actions.[85] Interestingly, this battle is a textbook example of the kind of reconnaissance-only mission that was envisioned for the mechanized cavalry in 1942. Unfortunately, open battlefield operations like this turned out to be more of an anomaly than the norm for combat in western and central Europe.

The 3rd CRS returned to the 3rd MCG from the XII Corps on 26 August. The squadron linked up with the main body of the 3rd MCG at Nogent sur Seine, twenty-nine miles to the northwest of Troyes.[86] The 3rd CRS then moved out in a zone reconnaissance to the Marne River as it screened the 5th ID in its attack to the Marne. Thanks to the efforts of both squadrons, the XX Corps vaulted over the Marne River and seized the important city of Reims (see map 6).

By 28 August, the XX and XII Corps were either over or preparing to cross the Seine and attacking to the east and northeast. To the northwest of Paris, the XV Corps was in the process of wrapping up operations along the Seine and preparing to shift to the southern end of the Third Army. On this army's southern flank, the 2nd MCG's protective screen stretched a vast seventy miles, generally along the Loire

River.[87] The 2nd CRS manned this line, while the 42nd CRS conducted reconnaissance of additional crossing points along the Seine River. On 28 August, the XII Corps relieved the group of its screening mission, ordering it to prepare to conduct an offensive guard preceding the corps as it attacked to and past the Marne River.[88]

On 28 August, Patton attached Colonel Vennard Wilson's 106th MCG to the XII Corps as it conducted its assault across the Seine south of Paris, toward the Marne. Haislip's XV Corps was in the process of being pinched out between the First Army and the edge of the XX Corps, and thus did not need its cavalry during this period. The 106th MCG relieved elements of the 2nd MCG and the 35th ID that at the time were screening the southern flank of the corps. The group's screen would eventually reach a length of ninety miles, stretching in a diagonal line from Auxerre (eighty-five miles southeast of Paris) to Gondrecourt (140 miles east of Paris), although leavened in parts by elements of the 35th ID in the east.[89] This action would allow Eddy's XII Corps to mass its elements, including its own cavalry, on the decisive push to the east toward Metz.

While the bulk of the Third Army drove to and then over the Seine, the middle of August saw the 15th MCG serve as the main effort for Task Force A's drive to clear the northern Brittany coast of any remaining enemy forces. A German stronghold at Paimpol, twenty-two miles north-northwest of Saint Brieuc, was preventing the use of that town's port for logistical support of the fighting in Brittany. Although it was a small facility, the poor logistical situation of the Allied forces in general due to the limited flow through the Normandy beaches meant that any additional inflow would be welcomed. Therefore, Middleton ordered Task Force A to destroy the German forces at Paimpol.

The task force began operations on 15 August, with the cavalry in front. Over the next two days the cavalry and their sister units in the task force ground their way through the German defenses around Paimpol. By 17 August the town had fallen, along with over eleven hundred prisoners, and the last impediment to Allied use of the port of Saint Brieuc was gone.[90] The cavalry's actions in both the seizure of the bridgehead at Saint Michel-en-Grève and the capture of Paimpol contributed directly to the success of the logistical effort that would be needed to reduce the fortress of Brest.[91]

Following the fall of Paimpol, Task Force A, with its cavalry, moved to an assembly area approximately ten miles to the west and northwest of Brest. The rapid success of Operation COBRA had freed the 2nd, 8th, 29th IDs for use in Brittany.[92] Although the 6th AD and Task Force A had generally secured the peninsula, the region was still unsettled and not safe for moving large, unescorted truck columns. Therefore, the VIII Corps needed the task force to screen the divisional assembly areas approximately ten miles east of Brest. One squadron, the 17th, screened the corps assembly area to the east along a front of approximately fourteen miles; meanwhile, the 15th CRS screened the German-occupied Daoulas Peninsula to the west. This peninsula, located immediately to the southeast of Brest, was an essential piece of geography, as it provided positions to fire upon the city from the south. By 20 August the 15th CRS had managed to advance approximately halfway down to the peninsula, until it was stopped by strong German resistance centered on Plougastel, the primary city in the area. Over the next two days two infantry battalions relieved the 15th CRS, allowing the cavalry to simply maintain contact between the two formations rather than conducting offensive operations of their own. The squadron maintained this role until it was relieved on 28 August.[93]

While the 15th CRS fought in the Daoulas Peninsula, the 17th CRS, with attached tank destroyers, engineers, and armored artillery, moved to reconnoiter the Crozon Peninsula (the peninsula just south of the Daoulas Peninsula) on 26 August upon the completion of its mission protecting the arrival of the corps' main body. This peninsula dominated the naval approaches to Brest as well as the entire southern flank of the city. Its seizure would greatly complicate the German defense of the city. However, a German force, estimated to be a battalion, prevented the cavalry from entering the peninsula along the five-mile-long line from Saint Nic to Brigneun. A single squadron of cavalry, however reinforced, simply did not have the combat power to force this position. The 15th CRS rejoined the 17th CRS on 28 August, and the 15th MCG began preparations for an attack into the Crozon Peninsula.[94]

On 31 August, a patrol of the 15th CRS penetrated the German line, captured a company command post, and convinced the commander to surrender his entire company. This action dislocated the entire German position, forcing the defenders to withdraw in the early morning of 1 September, with another company surrendering en masse in the process. Apparently a 15th CRS trooper who had been captured spoke German, and he convinced the German company commander that continued resistance was pointless. By 2 September, the 15th MCG had advanced to the line Tal-ar-Groas in the south to Saint Efflez in the north. This approximately three-mile front, a little over halfway down the peninsula and eight miles from the original German defensive line, compressed the advancing cavalry and allowed the remaining Wehrmacht forces to hold their positions.[95]

While stymied in front of this line, the 15th MCG suffered grievous losses—not so much from the enemy, but from friendly airpower. On 3 September an air mission had a hung bomb that dropped on a 17th Squadron observation post.[96] Another flight witnessed the drop and, thinking that there were enemy troops present, bombed and strafed the command post of Troop A, 17th Squadron. Less than half an hour later, as a platoon from the same troop made its way through the town of Selgruc-sur-Mer, a squadron of B-17s dropped their entire load on the town, nearly wiping out the platoon. Then, to add insult to injury, the ambulances and medical personnel attending to the wounded were then strafed and bombed. The total cost to the 15th MCG from the "American Luftwaffe" came to thirty-three troopers killed or wounded.[97]

At the end of August the Third Army had two corps, the XII and XX, fighting east of the Seine; another, the XV Corps, was consolidating positions around Paris; and its last corps, the VIII, was conducting operations in the Brittany Peninsula. The XX Corps was in the process of capturing Reims, while the XII Corps was preparing to launch an offensive toward Metz.

On 5 September, while the 15th MCG still remained static in the Crozon Peninsula, the entire VIII Corps, including its cavalry, transferred to the command of the newly activated Ninth Army. The 15th MCG participated in a drive a few days later that cleared the German positions in the Crozon Peninsula. After this action, the group would clear fugitive enemy soldiers from Brittany and conduct area security operations in western France until the late fall.[98]

Meanwhile, far to the east, the main body of the Third Army continued its attack toward the German border. Eddy's XII Corp began its offensive on 30 August with two divisions abreast, the 80th ID to the north and the 4th AD to the south. The 2nd MCG led the assault, with a squadron in front of each leading division (the 2nd CRS preceding the 80th ID, and the 42nd CRS conducting reconnaissance for the 4th AD).[99] The Dragoons met little resistance as they drove to the Moselle River. By 2 September, elements of the 2nd CRS had reached the river at Toul, approximately eleven miles due west of the major city of Nancy, and conducted reconnaissance to find likely crossing points.[100]

The next two days saw the 2nd MCG conduct a series of patrols in order to ascertain enemy strength defending the river. To the north, the 2nd CRS required an extra day to close with the main path of the river due to its natural curve to the west, of which Toul was the apex. On 3 September, patrols of the squadron encountered a large number of German forces withdrawing across the Moselle River to the village of Mousson on the east bank. Additionally, the squadron identified a German headquarters with three anti-air guns in the vicinity of Marbache, seven miles to the south of Mousson. Finally, at least a company of Germans were identified in the town of Villey-Saint Etienne, approximately seven miles to the southwest of Marbache.[101] The villages of Mousson and Marbache were extremely significant, as these comprised two of three planned crossing sites for the 80th ID, the chosen main effort for the river crossing.[102] The division's attack occurred on the evening of 4 September, meeting fierce resistance from recently arrived and well-dug-in German reinforcements. The attack ultimately failed with heavy casualties.[103]

Although the army's official history of the Lorraine campaign states that "cavalry patrols operating west of the Moselle, indicated that the Germans were not in sufficient strength to make a stand on the east bank," the aforementioned reports seem to indicate otherwise.[104] An excerpt from the XII Corps after action report from 3 and 4 September reads:

> At 1028B, the 2d Cav Gp reported that bridges over the Moselle River had been blown by the enemy at . . . , and that the enemy were covering bridges at . . . by small arms and machine guns.

> . . . An enemy column estimated at 700 men, including artillery, was reported at 1515 at Xirocourt [nineteen miles south of Nancy]. It was believed to be heading north towards Nancy. . . . All bridges over the MADON River were covered by MG fire supported by artillery on the high ground to the east. Patrols of the 2d Cav Gp were unable at that time to penetrate to Nancy due to MG fire.[105]

The records of the 2nd CRS for this period are incomplete, but assessing even just the XII Corps records for these three days makes it difficult to argue as some have that there was an "intelligence vacuum" in front of the corps.[106] If there was such a vacuum, it was of the corps commander's own making. The 2nd CRS was only able to partially complete its doctrinal mission in the case of the 80th ID's attack on 4 September due to a lack of time to conduct reconnaissance across a broad, defended river. Additionally, it did not have the combat power to attempt a crossing to force the Germans' hands by making them reveal hidden defenses. The initial reconnaissance reports note the beginnings of a developing German security zone along the river and should have demanded a more in-depth reconnaissance prior to committing a third of the corps to an attack. However, perhaps the past month had bred overconfidence in the men and leadership of the XII Corps as well as the 2nd MCG. Regardless of the issue of fault, this episode stands as a strong reminder of the importance not only of identifying the enemy, but also of having a security force with enough strength to forcefully sound out the enemy if time does not permit a lengthy reconnaissance. Perhaps as penance for its perceived reconnaissance failures, the XII Corps withdrew the 2nd CRS from the line on 7 September and used it as a security force around the corps headquarters while the remainder of the corps closed on the Nancy battlefield.[107]

While the drama of the 2nd CRS and the 80th ID unfolded to the north, the 42nd CRS continued to probe to the east across the Madon River while maintaining a screen to the south, protecting the corps' flank against German forces arriving from southern France (see map 7).[108] Faced with both tasks, the squadron maintained a generally defensive posture, though it kept actively patrolling to its front and flank. To aid in this task, Eddy attached the 696th Armored Field

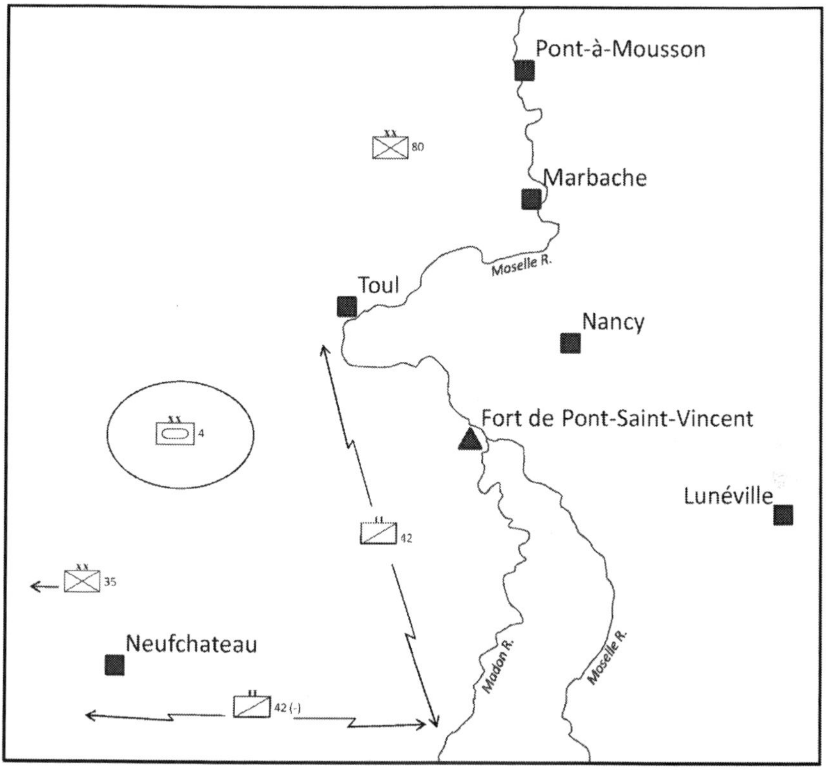

Map 7. XII Corps Preparing to Cross the Moselle.

Artillery Battalion to the rump 2nd MCG in order to provide immediate indirect fires. The first part of September would severely challenge the 42nd CRS, as large Wehrmacht formations made their way north into Lorraine. Despite the light nature of their equipment, the cavalry used the terrain to their advantage. Establishing observation points on several commanding heights, the cavalrymen called down extremely accurate fire on several German columns during this period, forcing their withdrawal.

Perhaps one of the most notable occasions came on 4 September, when Troop B, 42nd CRS, reinforced with some light tanks from Troop F, 42nd CRS, defeated a column of over one thousand German soldiers through a combination of artillery and direct fire, forcing their withdrawal and preventing their penetration of the corps' flank.[109] This achievement is extremely impressive considering that the cavalry were outnumbered at least five to one in this battle.[110] However, for perspective, it must be remembered that, once again, the Germans were retreating under continuous air attack and more interested in escaping to the north than in causing significant harm to the XII Corps.

To the north of the XII Corps, the XX Corps advanced east toward the Moselle as well. Following the capture of Reims around 28 August 1944, the 3rd MCG rested for a day, and on 30 August it led the corps' assault to the Meuse River. Walker ordered the cavalry to conduct a zone reconnaissance bounded on the north by Sedan and in the south by Saint Mihiel, a frontage of more than sixty miles. Enemy defenses along the Aisne River prevented the 43rd CRS from crossing, necessitating the commitment of Combat Command A, 7th AD, to clear the road. The 3rd CRS, with the luxury of not having to contend with attempting an opposed river crossing, penetrated German delaying positions along the main roads, reaching Verdun and seizing its bridges on the afternoon of 31 August.[111] Here the terrain played a significant role in success or failure. Where the terrain (and enemy situation) allowed the cavalry to use its mobility, they succeeded, but where they were faced with an obstacle (such as the Aisne) and had to fight their way ahead, the mechanized cavalry had to pass other units forward.

The beginning of September found the bulk of the XX Corps immobilized by a fuel shortage. However, the corps provided the lightly equipped 3rd MCG with enough to conduct probing reconnaissance missions to the Moselle River to set the conditions for future operations. On 2 September, a platoon of Troop B, 3rd CRS, penetrated all the way to Thionville, over seventy miles from their starting position. The platoon seized the Moselle River bridge in the town and held on for several hours before retiring due to the concentrated German response. The 43rd CRS also managed to infiltrate several patrols to the Moselle, establishing observation points along the river.[112]

On 4 September, Walker ordered the 3rd MCG to advance to the Moselle River and attempt to seize any remaining bridges. The group attacked in column of squadrons, with the 3rd leading and the 43rd trailing to exploit success. However, the group met intense resistance and was stopped short of the river. During this operation, on 5 September, group commander Colonel Frederick Drury and a small patrol became trapped by German forces. The colonel was captured along with some of his men.[113]

On 6 September, reacting to the failure of the 3rd MCG to reach the river, Walker committed the 7th AD to the assault, with the cavalry still in the lead. With the added weight of the 7th AD the group was able to gain the river, but no bridgeheads were seized and the cavalry were withdrawn from the front to allow the line divisions to conduct a deliberate assault over the river.[114] The failures of the cavalry from 4 to 6 September demonstrate the weaknesses of the mechanized cavalry in high-intensity combat, especially against an enemy in positions that cannot be bypassed. The lightly armed and armored cavalry simply did not have the firepower to bludgeon their way forward. The loss of the group commander during this critical operation did not help, either. Of course, it is also notable that the divisions that followed also struggled to achieve success. Walker gambled on the cavalry being able to seize a crossing before resistance hardened, but the Wehrmacht had had ample time to prepare their defenses due to the nearly weeklong delay caused by the Third Army's fuel shortages. Thus, what emerges from the XX Corps fight in early September is the story of a tough fight against a weakened but still dangerous and determined enemy.

From 7 to 14 September the 3rd MCG moved to the flanks of the corps, the 43rd CRS to the north to maintain contact with the V Corps of the First Army, and the 3rd CRS to the south to establish contact with the XII Corps. The 3rd CRS was further detached from the 3rd MCG and attached to the 5th ID. The 43rd CRS faced a difficult fight in closing the gap between the First and Third Armies, but by 14 September it had made contact with the 5th AD at Flaxweiler in Luxembourg.[115] The 3rd MCG was further aided in their efforts by the appointment of a new commander, Colonel James H. Polk, a personal selection by Patton. Polk, a long-serving cavalry officer, had family ties with Patton through his father, a West Point classmate of Patton. Notwithstanding the family ties, Polk had compiled a distinguished record on his own, including service as an instructor at West Point as well as stints as the executive officer of the 106th MCG in Normandy and the acting commander of the 6th MCG in France. In his work with the 6th Cavalry, Polk had worked directly for Patton's personal staff and had made an extremely good impression. In fact, Patton went out of his way to mention his reassignment of Polk in his letters.[116] Finally, Patton had previously commanded the 3rd Cavalry Regiment and had a vested interest in the success and reputation of his former command.

After establishing contact with the First Army, the 43rd CRS received orders from the XX Corps to patrol from Wormeldange, Luxembourg, to Garche, France, along the Moselle River, a frontage of over twenty-three miles. The squadron would hold this front from 14 to 19 September, during which time the 23rd Headquarters "Special Troops," 12th Army Group, established a fake armored division in the area through the use of various methods.[117] The cavalry participated in this deception by denying the Germans the ability to patrol into the region to confirm or deny the presence of that unit. Thus, during the first half of September, the 3rd MCG served not only as an economy of force for the XX Corps, but also aided in a diversion to draw German forces away from the main effort.

While the XII and XX Corps fought along the Moselle, Haislip's XV Corps, finished with its operations around Paris, moved to assembly areas to the east of Troyes, which was shielded by the 106th MCG, still in its screen southeast of the city. The Third Army's plan was to reinsert the corps along its southern flank to make contact with the advancing American Seventh Army. However, a large German salient was forming between the southern edge of the XII Corps and the leading edge of the Seventh Army coming from southern France. Therefore, the XV Corps would first have to destroy this bulge before it could fully come on line with the rest of the Third Army (see map 8).

On 10 September, the XV Corps regained control of Colonel Wilson's 106th MCG as it assumed responsibility for the southern flank of the Third Army, but it left them in their positions assigned by the XII Corps. However, Haislip cut the group's responsibility considerably, shortening their screen to only forty miles, leaving the cavalry with only the northern half of their original area.[118] The rest of the corps would fill in the southern portion of the group's original front.

The following day, the XV Corps attacked to the Moselle River between Charmes and Epinal. This move brought it alongside the XII Corps, then currently fighting along the Moselle. The 106th MCG led the corps in its attack, providing a security screen across the front of the 79th ID and the French 2nd Armored Division. The 106th

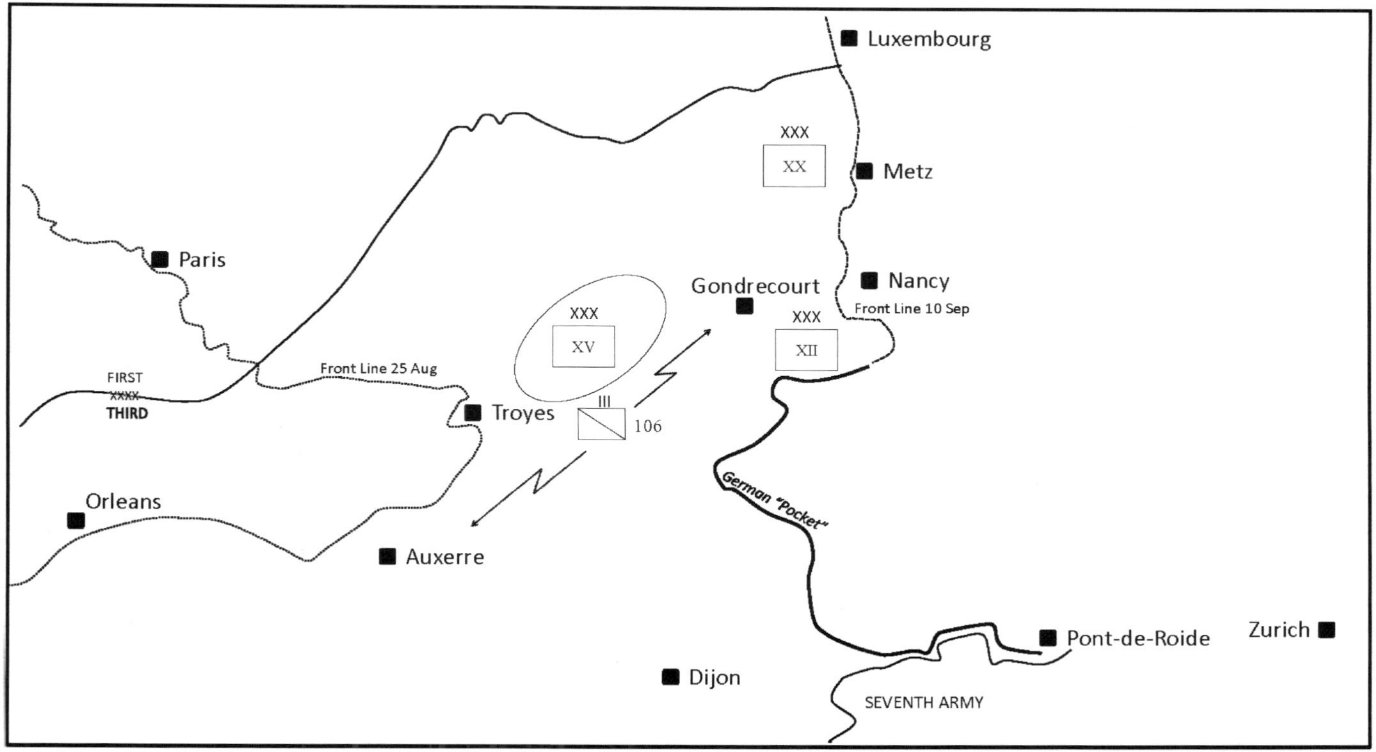

Map 8. 106th MCG Screens the Arrival of the XV Corps.

CRS reached the town of Charmes (twenty-one miles south of Nancy) on the evening of 11 September, another remarkable drive of thirty-seven miles—under combat conditions—from their starting positions around Gondrecourt. Despite the speed of the cavalry's advance, the group was unable to prevent the destruction of the bridges over the Moselle by the Germans. To the south, the 121st CRS encountered fierce resistance from the German 16th Infantry Division centered on the town of Mirecourt, ten miles west of the Moselle River. However, the rapid success of the 106th CRS to the north allowed XV Corps elements to engage the Germans from not only the west, but the north as well.[119] Additionally, the 121st CRS succeeded in identifying the main German defensive positions prior to being stopped, allowing for a rapid battle-handover with the follow-on regiments of the 79th ID and the French 2nd Armored Division. Finally, the cavalry, specifically the 121st CRS, maintained economy of force positions between the main combat elements of the corps, allowing them to concentrate combat power. The squadron's positions experienced German armor and infantry attacks on 13 September, but they defeated these assaults with relatively little loss.[120]

By 15 September the XV Corps had essentially destroyed the German 16th Infantry Division west of the Moselle River. The corps had estimated the division's original strength at seven thousand soldiers. The Americans had killed one thousand Germans, captured four thousand more, and destroyed the bulk of their equipment.[121] This action is a textbook example of cavalry in a corps battle. The 106th MCG identified the enemy's positions, as well as gaps in his defenses, and fought through his security zone. The battle was then handed off to the follow-on corps elements that used the information gathered by the cavalry to attack the enemy's most vulnerable points. Although this action was fought with complete air superiority against a somewhat disorganized foe, it is still a good example of the utility of corps cavalry on the modern battlefield.

From 15 to 18 September 1944, the 106th MCG participated in a war of patrolling and raids along the eastern bank of the Moselle River as the XV Corps awaited further orders. On 18 September, the Third Army ordered the corps to attack across the Moselle to the northeast, into the southern flank of the German forces that had assaulted into the flank of the XII Corps (this will be discussed in greater depth in the following chapter.) The 106th MCG again led the advance of the corps, although, due to the strength of the German forces in the region, the cavalry quickly gave way to the follow-on divisions. By 22 September the group was concentrated around the town of Lunéville, maintaining contact with the 2nd MCG to the north while protecting the XV Corps' northern flank.[122] Due to the intensity of the fighting that the corps had just endured as well as the expected difficulty of its next fight, the XV Corps would pause for approximately a week before beginning its next major battle to clear the Parroy Forest. It would start the battle under the auspices of the Third Army, but within a day transition to the Seventh Army.

The Army Information Service

In addition to using its corps cavalry in direct tactical and operational roles, the Third Army also used one cavalry group in a unique and demanding fashion. As a result of Patton's previous combat experiences in North Africa and Italy, he desired a direct form of intelligence from the battlefield straight to his headquarters, bypassing the traditional reporting channels, thereby enabling more rapid decision-making at the field army level. The 6th MCG had been chosen for this task, a mission that would be labeled the Army Information Service (AIS).[123] One squadron would fulfill the duties of the AIS, while the other in conjunction with the associated parts of the AIS squadron not needed for that role (the tank company and assault gun troop) would serve as a security force for the army headquarters and as a "hip pocket" reserve for the army commander.[124]

While the 6th MCG awaited the activation of the Third Army, it spent the month of July 1944 providing security for that headquarters and preparing for its role, a task involving the issue of several sets of nonstandard radio trucks to assist in extra long-range communications. Additionally, plans were finalized for the execution of the AIS. The two squadrons (the 6th and 28th) would rotate on a twenty-one-day cycle.[125] Generally, a reconnaissance troop was assigned to every corps headquarters (with a troop from the off-cycle squadron assisting as necessary), with platoons (detachments) to every division. At times of increased fluidity, sections (typically two jeeps and an M8 Greyhound with radio support) could be further assigned to the regimental level.[126] All these detachments then reported directly to the squadron operations center, co-located with the Third Army headquarters. This procedure dramatically sped up the flow of information to the army headquarters, as well as improved the accuracy, as raw data went straight to the army operations center without being filtered through so many layers as to be unrecognizable from the original report.

On 1 August 1944, the Third Army became operational and assumed command of the VIII, XII, XV, and XX Corps, then involved in conducting and exploiting the success of Operation COBRA.[127] The 28th CRS (supplemented by Troop B, 6th CRS) provided an initial set of fifteen detachments, spread across the four corps and eleven divisions of the Third Army. An additional detachment (for a total of sixteen) provided command and control for all AIS troopers in the Brittany Peninsula. The standard time for an AIS message to go from battlefield to army headquarters averaged two hours, twenty minutes, while the conventional channels took eight to nine hours.[128]

The AIS detachments moved across Brittany and central France with their assigned headquarters, providing such accurate and up-to-date intelligence that the official history of the northern France campaign states that "on occasion . . . the army staff was better informed on a particular situation than the corps directing the operation."[129] As the distances between the corps of the army grew, problems became apparent in the communications equipment that had not been fully tested before the operation due to the need for the army to maintain radio silence prior to COBRA.[130] The AIS detachments improvised by acquiring motorcycles, which were used for couriers. The cavalry's jeeps were also pressed into service as retransmission vehicles, enabling the widely scattered formations of the Third Army to communicate.[131]

During the early days of the Brittany campaign, the 6th AD experienced tremendous difficulties in communicating with the VIII Corps headquarters as the division rapidly advanced toward the city of Brest. The corps frequency was overloaded, requiring the division to fight for space and time to communicate with the corps. Moreover, as the 6th AD was the most distant formation, its radio calls were the most faint, and could be "stepped on" with greater frequency.[132] The AIS helped alleviate this division's communications problems by providing an additional channel of communications that was not jammed with corps-level traffic. Moreover, the cavalry were more heavily armed than the ad hoc couriers the division had been relying on, and thus could fight their way through minor resistance to deliver messages as well.[133] Although communications difficulties continued to plague the 6th AD and VIII Corps throughout their operations in Brittany, it is doubtful whether any form of meaningful communications could have occurred without the participation of the AIS.

As the month of August wore on, the 6th MCG continued in its dual role as AIS and security for the Third Army headquarters. On 27 August, the Third Army ordered the cavalry to send reconnaissance forces south to reconnoiter the Loire River from Orleans to Saumur, a stunning distance of one hundred miles. A single reinforced troop from the 28th CRS (Troop A) departed and spent two days covering that distance, ensuring the destruction of all bridges in the area and that no strong German forces were attempting to drive north into the army's wide-open flank.[134] The 4th AD had also screened this flank in its move to the east, but that had been more than a week prior, and the area had since only been covered by the XIX Tactical Air Command and the very thinly spread 83rd ID.[135] The cavalry met little opposition, but their presence provided the army headquarters with at least a measure of peace of mind until the 83rd ID could muster enough combat power in the region.

This screen mission attests to the mobility and flexibility of the cavalry. No other unit could have traversed this distance in such a short period of time. Moreover, although the cavalry were too lightly armed to have stopped a determined assault, their radio equipment and prior communications experience allowed them to remain in communication with higher headquarters much more easily than any other company-size formation in the army. Additionally, the combined arms nature of the cavalry allowed a tank-motorized team to be quickly assembled within a single day with almost no issues with interoperability of the units, as they all came from the same battalion-level headquarters.

By the beginning of September, the Third Army stretched no fewer than 475 miles from Brest to the Moselle River.[136] Throughout this huge zone, the 6th Cavalry's AIS squadron aided the army commander in maintaining a timely information flow in what would have otherwise been a communications disaster. As the members of the AIS all came from the same squadron, they were able to utilize their much less crowded battalion, company, and platoon radio nets to relay information from one detachment to another, much like a radio-based Pony Express. This ability to move information so quickly allowed Patton a degree of flexibility and battlefield awareness not often possible in combat, and nearly unheard of for such a large fight. Although the assault across France involved huge command and control difficulties, the mere fact that the army headquarters was able to manage such a large formation (at one point four corps) over a vast area speaks to the herculean efforts of the cavalry in support of the communications fight. Thus, the problems that existed would have been much worse without the presence of the 6th MCG operating in a behind-the-scenes role.

On 5 September, the commander of the 6th MCG, Colonel Polk, was relieved by the original commander, Colonel Fickett, who had missed the first month of combat due to injuries sustained in a traffic accident in June. Polk then assumed command of the 15th MCG, operating in Brittany, but General Patton immediately pulled him from that group after a mere three days with that unit so that he could replace the missing Colonel Drury, the captured commander of the 3rd MCG.[137]

On 18 September, the Third Army ordered a task force comprised of the assault gun troops (Troop E, 6th CRS, Troop E, 28th CRS) and the tank company of the 6th Squadron (Troop F, 6th CRS), with minor support elements, to support the 3rd MCG (Task Force Polk) in its operations along the Moselle River. This task force would perform yeoman work with Task Force Polk, providing fire support for numerous operations until 30 September, when the tankers and gunners returned to the control of the 6th MCG. This action also allowed these portions of the 6th MCG to gain valuable combat experience rather than wasting away guarding army headquarters.[138]

As the Third Army's operations began to solidify during the month of September, AIS operations became less crucial due to the ability of headquarters to establish more permanent (and efficient) communications methods. Moreover, when General Omar Bradley, commander of the 12th Army Group, relieved Patton of responsibility for Brittany and the VIII Corps, the distance from the farthest army element to the headquarters dramatically dropped. Additionally, at the end of the month the XV Corps departed the Third Army for the Seventh Army.[139] This now left the Third Army with two corps concentrated in the Metz–Nancy region, as opposed to four corps spread across the length of France.

Weather also began to hamper AIS operations, as the rain and mud of October 1944 seriously hindered the motorcycle couriers that had been so crucial earlier in the fighting. However, the static nature of the fighting in September and October allowed for the use of carrier pigeons, with the first birds being deployed at the corps level on 8 October. Although the loss rate for birds was rather small (3.6 percent for October), the unit records report that this method "proved to be not as rapid as radio communication."[140] However, the pigeons provided a useful alternative when radios failed.

The Third Army officially disbanded the AIS in November of 1944, as its services were no longer required. However, during its slightly more than three months of service the AIS had dramatically aided the Third Army's ability to command and control its forces as it spread over the largest contiguous geographic area that an American field army had ever occupied until the modern era. This achievement stands as one of the most important contributions of a regiment-size formation to operational success in the entirety of the American experience in the war. With only a single squadron of seven hundred troopers at a time, the 6th MCG enabled the most dramatic advance of an American army until the 1991 Gulf War. No other formation of this size can claim this level of operational importance.

By the middle of September the Third Army had completed one of the most remarkable assaults in the history of the U.S. Army. The successes of the Third Army were made possible in large part by the effective use of corps cavalry at the operational and senior tactical levels of war. These formations had fulfilled all the traditional roles of American cavalry as the army swept across northwest France. Much like the cavalry of the First Army, the Third Army's cavalry protected open flanks, screened ahead of advancing formations, and allowed corps to concentrate combat power against the enemy. The nature of the fighting in France also meant that cavalry proved even more important for the Third Army than for the First Army. The wide, sweeping nature of Patton's charge across France completely exposed his army's flanks. Cavalry protected those flanks, allowing combat power to be thrust forward. The army did use infantry divisions to help guard the flanks as well, but these units did not possess the mobility necessary to guard huge expanses effectively. Only the cavalry (and the armor divisions) had the ability to cover ground quickly and effectively. Finally, the corps cavalry protected the army through their screens by identifying German resistance and destroying it or finding bypasses. These actions allowed the army to continue to move at high speed, which also protected its flanks, as rapid advances dislocated and confused German reactions.

Seventh Army

While the 12th Army Group fought in Normandy and western France, forces that would eventually become the 6th Army Group landed in the south of France in Operation ANVIL. The American component of this force was the Seventh Army. Comprised of just a single corps, the VI Corps, this army joined with French forces to introduce a third army group to the Western Front as well as to confront the Germans in France, already reeling from the battles of the summer, with another direction of attack.

Major General Lucian Truscott's VI Corps was a very different corps than the rest of the American formations that fought in France. While the corps (if not all of the divisions) of the 12th Army Group were all new to combat prior to 6 June 1944, the VI Corps already had a detailed combat history, having fought extensively in Italy from Salerno forward. Just as the corps headquarters possessed a large amount of combat experience, its component formations were also battle-savvy, having survived some of the toughest fighting in the Italian campaign.

The corps cavalry of VI Corps were also experienced and combat hardened, although somewhat nonstandard compared to their brethren in other corps. Because the opening of the Mediterranean Theater had occurred before each corps received a mechanized cavalry group, the Seventh Army had assigned to the VI Corps the only cavalry available in the theater that was not organic to a division—the 117th CRS, originally of the New Jersey Army National Guard's 102nd Cavalry Regiment.[141] This squadron had deployed to North Africa to serve as security for the Allied headquarters. It had served in a variety of roles throughout 1942 and 1943, protecting key personalities, such as King George V, Prime Minister Winston S. Churchill, President Franklin D. Roosevelt, General George C. Marshall, General Dwight D. Eisenhower, and many others. The 117th CRS entered combat in Italy in the Rapido campaign in May 1944. The squadron would see combat with various corps of the Fifth Army throughout the summer until late July, when it left the front in order to prepare for Operation ANVIL. That month, thanks to the haggling genius of the squadron's logistics officer, the 117th traded its 75mm M8 Scott assault guns for 105mm M7 Priests in a deal that ostensibly included a couple of captured German Luger pistols.[142] This "arrangement" meant that the squadron would be entering combat with an assault gun troop that, in reality, was a true self-propelled artillery battery. Furthermore, although the 105mm still had the low muzzle velocity common with all howitzers, it would prove much more effective than the 75mm in the direct fire role. Sometimes size does matter, particularly in terms of explosives. A German tank that could shrug off a 75mm high-explosive round would be staggered by the much larger 105mm.

The VI Corps' plan for ANVIL involved landing all three of its divisions simultaneously to establish a broad beachhead.[143] Each division would receive one troop of the 117th CRS to assist in initial reconnaissance of the landing. Afterward, the 117th would reform and join other mobile elements to create a provisional mobile task force that would act as an expedient armored division, under the command of the corps deputy commander, Brigadier General Frederick Butler. The total task force consisted of the 117th CRS, two companies of tanks from the 753rd Tank Battalion, a battalion of infantry from the 36th ID, a company of M10 tank destroyers, a company of engineers, a battery of self-propelled artillery, and other assorted support formations. The purpose of this task force would be to isolate or at least harry German forces fleeing to the north.[144] This mission would prove particularly vital, as the three divisions of the corps would be heavily invested in securing the lodgment area and would not be prepared to move as quickly as necessary to block German escape.

Operation ANVIL began on 15 August 1944 with the cavalry landing alongside their infantry brethren. In fact, due to a mix-up in the landing craft assembly area, the support elements of Troop A (operating with the 36th ID) landed ahead of the infantry. Luckily, the cavalrymen were able to find cover until the main force arrived.[145] The rest of the squadron landed without incident and conducted reconnaissance for the three divisions of the corps as they attacked northward. By 17 August the separate troops had completed their initial missions and were consolidated along with the other elements of Task Force Butler around the town of Le Muy, approximately nine miles from the coast.

Here, the 117th CRS showed its true ingenuity in the face of daunting obstacles. The squadron had been ordered by the VI Corps to leave behind all nonessential support vehicles for the landing. These would follow in later waves. However, these vehicles included the squadron's mess trucks. As the cavalry expected to be forward of the corps' main body for quite some time, they considered this restriction somewhat onerous, as the troops would be forced to rely on canned rations for an undetermined amount of time. Thus, in true cavalry fashion, they improvised. The troopers loaded additional ammunition onto the mess trucks and repainted and modified the vehicles to look like ammunition haulers. Thus, on 17 August, two days after the landing, when Truscott arrived to check on the line, the cavalry were able to greet him with a hot cup of coffee straight from a mess truck—strictly against regulations, but welcomed nonetheless, and thus ignored. It also helped that the troopers of the 117th CRS were generous with their coffee and hot rations to soldiers of the 3rd ID, Truscott's old division.[146]

The cavalry led Task Force Butler forward on 18 August from Le Muy. After a slow start involving some serious fighting around the town of Draguignan, six miles north of the line of departure, the advance rapidly gained momentum. By nightfall the leading elements of the 117th CRS had advanced thirty-three miles in straight-line distance, but closer to fifty when the curving mountain roads are considered. The squadron encountered little resistance after the morning's fighting, as they took advantage of German confusion concerning how far the Americans had advanced. As a testament to that confusion, the cavalry overran the remaining staff of the German LXII Corps and its commander, General Ferdinand Neuling.[147] This corps commanded the easternmost portions of the German forces in southern France, and the capture of its commander and his staff certainly helped paralyze German coordination along that section of the front, although individual formations still continued to delay U.S. forces.[148] The advance of the cavalry placed Task Force Butler within ten miles of a major valley that could serve as a high-speed avenue north, paralleling the Rhône River valley.

The next day, the cavalry continued to lead the task force north. The squadron, augmented by some *Maquis* fighters, ran into a determined roadblock around Château-Arnoux-Saint-Auban, twenty miles north of their start positions. After a sharp fight the Germans surrendered, but only on the condition that they would be prisoners of the Americans, proving both the utility and the challenges of fighting alongside embittered and vicious allies.[149] While the cavalry consolidated around Château-Arnoux, Butler ordered additional elements, led by Troop B, east down a side valley to seize the town of Digne in order to prevent German forces stationed there from attacking into the flank of the task force. The cavalry identified the German resistance and aided the infantry and Maquis in taking several hundred prisoners. With the destruction of the threat to its flank, Task Force Butler continued, and the 117th CRS pulled into the town of Sisteron, sixty-five miles north of Marseille that night.[150]

On 20 August, the task force consolidated its positions while the 117th CRS conducted reconnaissance, scouting for more routes to the north. By the afternoon of 21 August, Truscott ordered Butler to seize the high ground to the north of Montélimar, sixty miles to the west of Sisteron, along the Rhône River. Major German forces were retreating along the river valley, and a blocking position at Montélimar could effectively destroy much of the enemy in southern France. The 117th CRS received the task of leading the task force there due to their mobility. The cavalry received their orders at 1400 and seized their objectives by 1900, owing to the speed of their vehicles and a general lack of German resistance along the route. Immediately upon their arrival, the squadron destroyed a forty-vehicle convoy headed north along the Rhône. The cavalry would seize positions along a nine-mile front, running along a ridge north of Montélimar. From these positions they could interdict German traffic moving north along the highways on either side of the Rhône River.[151]

The next day, 22 August, desperate fighting erupted for the 117th CRS as elements of the 11th Panzer Division attempted to fight their way through the cavalry's blocking positions. The squadron, reinforced with medium tanks and tank destroyers, defeated a determined assault from the town of Montélimar itself, but later in the day German forces surrounded a cavalry platoon protecting the task force's flank in a town nine miles to the east of Montélimar. The fortuitous arrival of the squadron's Troop A (which had been conducting a blocking mission in the Alps) as well as reinforcing elements of the 36th ID helped seal the penetration.[152]

Over the next several days, the VI Corps committed the entirety of the 36th ID as well as elements of the 45th ID to the battle to block the Rhône Valley. Additionally, the 3rd ID attacked north from Avignon, pressing the Germans from a second direction.[153] The 117th CRS participated in the swirl of battles around Montélimar, protecting the flanks of infantry regiments, providing fire support, and defending portions of the line. In one memorable instance the assault gun troop, equipped with their nonstandard (for the cavalry) 105mm howitzers, destroyed over fifty German vehicles attempting to escape along the river road.[154] When the battle of Montélimar ended on 29 August, the German forces had taken severe losses, though they had not been completely trapped and destroyed. Without the mobility of the 117th CRS, American forces could not have arrived as early as 21 August, meaning more German forces could have escaped unscathed.

While Montélimar may be described as a defeat due to the failure of VI Corps to trap the 11th Panzer Division and other German formations in the Rhône Valley, it is hard to imagine a different result. The Seventh Army in August did not have an armored division, so it had to improvise with lighter and less capable forces. The fact that Task Force Butler even presented the opportunity for trapping German forces in the Rhône Valley stands as a testament to the success of that improvisation. The 36th ID could have perhaps moved faster. However, the assets that would have speeded the division were instead used to motorize large portions of Task Force Butler. Without the task force, the infantry would have had to fight their way through the ground that Butler cleared. Truscott made a choice. Ultimately, it was not as successful as he wished, but it still inflicted damage upon the enemy.

While the fighting around Montélimar consumed Task Force Butler and the 36th ID, the 45th ID continued to advance to the north, seizing the town of Meximieux, ninety-two miles north of Montélimar. By 1 September, Truscott had withdrawn the 117th CRS from their positions along the Rhône and moved it north to support the 45th ID's continued drive.[155] German defenses, built around the 11th Panzer Division, had stiffened in front of the city of Bourg-en-Bresse, thirty-three miles northeast of Lyons. The 117th CRS conducted reconnaissance for the 45th ID and, acting on orders from the corps commander, managed to seize the town of Montrevel-en-Bresse, nine miles northeast of Bourg, and immediately astride the supply lines of the 11th Panzer Division holding that city. The Germans reacted violently, attacking the cavalry troop inside the town with overwhelming force. After fighting all day on 3 September, the Germans forced Troop B of the 117th CRS to surrender, and a platoon of Troop A lost all of its vehicles. The official history of the campaign faults Truscott for tasking the 117th CRS far beyond its capabilities, a solid assessment.[156] The records of the New Jersey cavalry are much more emphatic about their feelings on this particular battle. Their attitude was not helped when, in his memoirs, Truscott asserted that the cavalry had been caught sleeping at Montrevel. Considering the evidence of the all-day battle and the town's enduring loyalty to the 117th Cavalry (the NJARNG and Montrevel maintain a relationship to this day, with exchanges and reenactments), Truscott was wrong and may have been trying to pass off blame for such an embarrassing defeat. Perhaps, like his comrade Manton Eddy in the XII Corps, Truscott was feeling a pinch of "victory disease" and did not take the German threat as seriously as he should have.

After the battle at Montrevel, the squadron reformed and reorganized to reconstitute its Troop B. Then, on 4 September, Truscott committed the squadron to protecting the left flank of the 3rd ID as it attacked north toward Besançon. The entire 6th Army Group was advancing north, with the VI Corps (which was the entirety of the Seventh Army at this time) in the center, the French I Corps on the right along the Swiss border, and the French II Corps on the left advancing on the west bank of the Saone River.[157] At this point, the 3rd ID was the rightmost formation of the VI Corps, keeping a loose connection with the French I Corps to the east. The 36th ID advanced to the west, and the 45th ID followed the 3rd ID. As the 3rd ID moved around

Besançon, the cavalry screened the division from German forces operating in the city, and then protected its flank as it attacked the city.[158]

On 6 September, the 117th CRS moved to protect the VI Corps' left flank as it continued its attack north.[159] This protection proved particularly important, as the Allied advance bypassed numerous German formations. Moreover, the sheer size of the 6th Army Group's axis of advance meant that huge gaps existed between the component armies. Essentially, German and Allied formations were all streaming north simultaneously, often along the same routes. Complicating the matter further, German forces (particularly the 11th Panzer Division) in front of the Allied forces were fighting a delaying action. Thus, even though the VI Corps advanced in the center of the army group formation, it may as well have been operating alone in terms of mutual support. A prime example of this situation occurred on 8 September. While the 36th ID attacked north around the west side of Besançon, the 117th CRS attacked to the southwest against German forces moving north around the town of Saint Vit, seven miles southwest of Besançon, and well behind the main elements of VI Corps.[160]

To mitigate the confusion of the advance, the VI Corps ordered the 117th CRS to make physical contact with the French II Corps to the west. The cavalry accomplished this task on 10 September.[161] At this point, the squadron was conducting one of the hardest missions available. They were protecting a force moving at a relatively high speed while moving themselves, and maintaining contact with not only another moving formation, but also one from a different nation using a different language. They were doing this at slightly better than half strength after the losses incurred at Montrevel, while moving through enemy territory. Meanwhile, the VI Corps continued its attack north of Besançon. By 11 September, the 117th CRS, working in conjunction with the 36th ID, covered a forty-mile stretch of front with loose patrols, although this front would shrink to twenty-eight miles the next day as the French II Corps closed on the left.[162]

By the middle of September, the 6th Army Group had closed on the southern flank of the 12th Army Group (the Third Army's XV Corps). In order to better arrange his forces, Major General Jacob L. Devers shifted the French II Corps to the right of the VI Corps, making the Seventh Army (again, just the VI Corps) the leftmost element of the army group. This shift would keep American forces concentrated, particularly at the army group boundary, where the American forces would join with their countrymen, minimizing the problems inherent in any boundary. At the least, the soldiers on both sides of the line would speak the same language.[163]

Truscott's VI Corps was to attack to the northeast toward Strasbourg while maintaining contact with the Third Army to the north. The 117th CRS would continue to protect the left flank of the corps until 19 September. On that date the cavalry reached the town of Epinal, thirty miles south of Nancy along the Moselle River.[164] The 45th ID, which had been on the corps' right, had finally been relieved by French forces and now moved to the left flank, behind the cavalry. The 117th CRS screened the arrival of the 45th ID. Upon completion of this mission, the 117th moved to the right flank (south) of the corps, where it would protect that flank and maintain contact with the French II Corps.[165] The squadron would maintain this mission as the VI Corps slowly fought its way over the Moselle.

Despite their small size, the Seventh Army's corps cavalry managed to have an impact much larger than any other battalion in the army in the opening days of the France campaign. The 117th CRS not only conducted reconnaissance and screening operations, speeding the advance of Task Force Butler; it also served as a highly mobile blocking force, albeit with uneven results. At Montélimar the cavalry's actions helped the VI Corps savage the retreating German forces. At Montrevel it would be the Germans who would rip apart the cavalry. Despite major setbacks, like the loss of nearly 50 percent of the squadron in a single battle, the 117th CRS still managed to aid the VI Corps' rapid advance to the Moselle. Although the inability of the Seventh Army to catch and destroy all German forces in southern France is often painted as a failure, it did inflict serious damage upon them. The corps cavalry of that army helped make that happen. In fact, without the presence of the 117th CRS, the VI Corps would not have moved as quickly or been able to commit the same amount of combat power against the retreating Germans.

The attack of the 12th Army Group across northwest France still stands as a monumental touchstone in U.S. military history. The First Army held the focus of the bulk of German forces in the region, while the Third Army blitzed through central France in under a month. To the south, the attack of the 6th Army Group also demonstrated the speed of the Allied armies. The effective use of corps cavalry contributed greatly to the success of the larger force in all of these cases. These formations, often conducting unheralded screening and reconnaissance operations, were key ingredients in making the 12th and 6th Army Groups' offensives so successful.

The speed, firepower, and mobility of the cavalry allowed them to accomplish missions that would have consumed much larger formations. While infantry regiments possessed vastly more combat power, they did not have the ability to cover ground quickly without mounting highly vulnerable trucks. Moreover, in the army of the ninety-division gamble, infantry regiments were a precious commodity on the front line. It made little sense to strand a division or even a regiment well behind the lines in the highly mobile fighting of the France campaign when that unit would be needed elsewhere. Although the Allied commanders would on occasion do exactly that, it was something to be avoided. The cavalry, on the other hand, could fight on the move, making them less vulnerable to ambush, a particularly useful trait in the confused, fluid environment of France in the late summer of 1944. Additionally, their small size meant that they could be sent to the flanks without a major loss of combat power to the front. Finally, their mobility meant that they could rapidly catch up to the front without additional augmentation, something no other unit outside of an armored division could claim.

All of these traits, combined with the nature of the fighting in France, made cavalry a highly useful and prized asset for corps and army commanders. The commanders of all three armies leaned heavily on these groups to fill the niche cavalry had long held in American military thought. The France campaign in particular screamed for just such an organization, and for the most part, the mechanized cavalry groups delivered.

5

The Bitter Fall

During the fall of 1944, the Allied armies slowed and then stopped on a line from southeastern France to the Netherlands. German resistance had finally stiffened to the point that they were able to achieve limited successes. The terrain in this part of Europe also aided the German efforts. In the south, General Alexander Patch's Seventh Army faced the daunting Vosges Mountains, considered a major military obstacle since Roman times.[1] Farther north, General George S. Patton's Third Army first had to fight through the German defenses near Metz along the Moselle River, a venerable fortress. Moreover, Metz merely marked the beginning of a massive fortified zone stretching from the Moselle through the repurposed positions of the Maginot Line, past the Saar River, and into the Siegfried Line. Complementing the manmade obstacles in this region, the terrain becomes steadily rougher the farther east one travels. General Courtney Hodges's First Army also faced daunting physical barriers in the form of the Ardennes and the Hürtgen Forests. Additionally, the First Army had the dubious honor of being the first American forces to test the strength of the Siegfried Line. The newly formed Ninth Army, under General William Simpson, faced a different set of problems as it attacked across the lowlands and rolling hills of the Maastricht corridor. While perhaps less rugged than the terrain to the south, this route was also one of the natural invasion corridors into Germany and thus was heavily defended. Backstopping all of these impressive obstacles was the Rhine, one of the great rivers of the world, guarding the final approach into Germany. Finally, to complicate the Allied situation even more, massive supply issues surfaced at the beginning of September 1944. These shortages, brought about by the lack of functioning ports close to the Allied front line, hindered the American advance. The supply issues would not fully be resolved until late in the fall, with lingering problems persisting until early 1945.

All of these factors combined to give the Rhineland campaign a distinctly different feel from the more mobile fighting across France. The Germans would present few, if any, open flanks for the cavalry to exploit, requiring a more direct approach in most cases. While the cavalry would be hampered by these conditions, so was the rest of the U.S. Army in northern Europe. The army still needed cavalry missions (security, reconnaissance, economy of force). Thus, while the character of the fighting changed, the cavalry's importance did not.

First and Ninth Armies

The middle of September saw the First Army continue its drive toward Germany. Contrary to the popular myth that the dash across France had faced no resistance, Hodges's First Army had been in constant contact with German forces from Normandy to Belgium. The army's initial objective for the next part of the campaign would be the ancient city of Aachen, guarding the southwestern approaches to the massive industrial complex of the Ruhr. The dense Hürtgen Forest dominated the terrain south of the city, presenting a major obstacle in any attempt to maneuver around the major urban area.

The main effort for the First Army in this region would be conducted by Major General Joseph Collins's VII Corps, while the V Corps would make a supporting attack into the Bitburg area to the south, ostensibly to protect the VII Corps' flank. In reality, the two corps, separated by dozens of miles and extremely rugged terrain, would be hard pressed to conduct any sort of mutual support or coordination. Hodges had decided to halt the XIX Corps (north of the VII Corps) in western Belgium to compensate for the growing fuel shortages and to allow his two most advanced corps (V and VII) to continue their attack, as mentioned in the last chapter.[2]

After its success around Mons, the VII Corps continued its drive to Aachen, past the city of Liege. Colonel Tully's 4th MCG, relieved by the V Corps of their mission protecting the right (eastern) flank of the VII Corps, reassembled in the rear. On 4 September Collins ordered the cavalry to again protect the corps' right (southern) flank as it advanced to Liege. This support was essential, as the corps sector was over thirty-five miles long. Collins believed that this front was too wide, considering the terrain and nature of the German defenses. Therefore he grouped his three divisions in one-third of the corps zone, leaving the 4th MCG responsible for nearly two-thirds of the corps area.[3] This concentration of force would prove critical for the VII Corps as it engaged in the vicious, close-in fighting that typified the battle of Aachen and the Hürtgen Forest. These battles proved close enough for the American forces. They would have been impossible if the divisions committed to these actions also had been required to cover the remaining one-half to two-thirds of the corps sector.

Multiple small actions against German delaying forces marked the 4th MCG's attack to the east. In one notable action near Waillet, Belgium (twenty-five miles southwest of Liege), the cavalry engaged in a running fight, destroying four half-tracks and several trucks while driving the rest of the German force farther to the east.[4] By 11 September, the 4th MCG attacked into the town of Malmedy, having advanced over fifty miles from their start positions near Dinant. The fight for Malmedy would be short but violent, as the cavalry used overwhelming firepower to defeat the scattered German resistance in the town.[5] The 4th MCG would continue its advance to the German border. When it came to rest there by 18 September 1944, the group's area of responsibility accounted for approximately a third of the entire VII Corps sector, from just north of Losheim to just south of Monschau.[6] The group's percentage of the corps line had shrunk as Collins attempted to maneuver his divisions around the city of Aachen and the Hürtgen Forest.

To the north of the VII Corps, the XIX Corps had finally closed on the Albert Canal by 11 September. Unfortunately, all the bridges across the canal and the Meuse were strongly held by the enemy or had been destroyed. Therefore the XIX Corps expected a vicious fight to cross the canal and maintain its momentum to the German border. However, just eight miles south of the cavalry's positions around Eben Emael, the VII Corps had already constructed a bridge at Liege for its own use. The XIX Corps commander, Major General Charles Corlett, arranged for a small task force from his formation to cross the corps boundary, move north back into the XIX Corps sector, and seize a bridge in the vicinity of Maastricht. A full division would have overloaded the temporary American-built bridge, disrupting the flow of VII Corps units and supplies. Additionally, the attacking force had to have the ability to move quickly, not only to take advantage of the penetration of the German flank, but also to get out of the way of the VII Corps.[7] Thus, a reinforced cavalry group made perfect sense. Not everyone in the corps agreed with this course of action, with the commander of the 30th ID arguing vociferously against the plan. Corlett shut dissent down by placing a bet with him on the success of the mission.

Colonel Biddle's 113th MCG, reinforced with two motorized infantry companies from the 30th ID, a company of tank destroyers, and a company of engineers, set off on the morning of 1 September.[8] The cavalry task force met determined German resistance in their attack to the north on the east bank of the Meuse, only managing to advance a couple miles to the north of their crossing point. Due to the fierce resistance encountered by the 113th MCG, Corlett adjusted his plan and directed the 30th ID to build a bridge just north of Liege to a point on the east bank already seized by the cavalry. Corlett also attached the 113th MCG to the 30th ID, first to guard the bridgehead, then to protect the division's right (southern) flank as it attacked north to seize Maastricht and beyond. As the attack progressed, the 125th CRS would remain attached to the 30th ID, protecting that division's flank, while the rest of the group moved into corps reserve on 15 September.[9] With the cavalry's attack only being a partial success, the issue of the wager between the 30th ID's commander and the corps commander apparently was dropped.

On 20 September, as the XIX Corps continued its attack toward the German border, the Redhorse (minus the 125th CRS, still attached to the 30th ID) moved to the northern end of the corps zone, relieving elements of the 2nd AD along a ten-mile front to protect the corps' left flank.[10] The corps was preparing its offensive to break into the Siegfried Line north of Aachen. Corlett's plan involved the 30th ID penetrating the German defenses, allowing the 2nd AD to exploit. As such, the armor division needed its forces that had been protecting the corps' left flank concentrated and ready for action.[11] However, as the weather worsened, the corps postponed the attack, waiting for the veteran 29th ID to join the corps, fresh from its actions at Brest.[12]

While the VII and XIX Corps attacked through northern Belgium, to the south the V Corps continued its advance to the east over ground that would become famous as the site of the Battle of the Bulge in a couple months. The three divisions of the corps had spread out, with the 4th ID in the north pushing past Saint Vith and into the rugged terrain of the Schnee Eifel. The 28th ID, immediately to the south of the 4th ID, attempted to penetrate the Siegfried Line near the town of Roscheid, eleven miles south of Saint Vith. The 5th AD concentrated its efforts near Wallendorf, eighteen miles south of Roscheid. The armor was far away from the infantry due to the need of the corps commander to maintain contact with the Third Army to the south and the VII Corps to the north. The terrain also pushed the two infantry divisions into approaches well north of the 5th AD's axis of advance. The V Corps commander alleviated some of his problems by attaching the 102nd CRS to the 28th ID. The division then assigned the squadron the job of maintaining contact between the 28th ID and the 5th AD over a front of more than eleven miles. The rest of the 102nd MCG joined the 4th ID, protecting eight miles of its left flank and keeping contact with the 4th MCG and the VII Corps to the north.[13] The cavalry would maintain their positions for the balance of September as the V Corps tried, unsuccessfully, to penetrate the Siegfried Line.

To the north, in the VII Corps sector, the 4th MCG spent the latter half of September in a fight characterized by reconnaissance patrols and short, sharp clashes against German probes. Meanwhile, the VII Corps gathered for its assault on Aachen and the Hürtgen Forest. On one particularly notable day, 13 September, the 4th CRS engaged a combined arms German force around the town of Elsenborn, nine miles east of Malmedy. The cavalry captured two Panzer IV tanks, an anti-tank gun, and seventeen prisoners. They also destroyed an additional Panzer IV tank. A measure of the cavalry's effectiveness in their flank guard can be seen by a POW report wherein a German prisoner reported they believed that the 4th MCG was in actuality a "reinforced Panzer Division."[14] Although this report may have been somewhat hyperbolic, there is no denying the fact that the Germans did indeed see the 4th MCG as something of a threat, as evidenced by the number of low-level attacks aimed at driving the cavalry back. On at least two occasions, on 17 and 18 September, the 4th MCG repulsed company-size German attacks heavily supported by artillery.[15] Once again, though minor affairs in the larger scope of the fighting around Aachen, the cavalry's actions prevented additional German interference with the main battle while allowing the main American formations to concentrate on their objectives. It was the quintessential economy of force mission.

While the 4th MCG experienced limited successes in its guard along the southern portion of the VII Corps line, the corps itself soon sputtered to a halt against the Aachen and Hürtgen Forest defenses. The divisions of the corps attempted to grind their way forward against heavy German defenses manned by several German formations, including newly arrived units like the 12th Volksgrenadier Division, just in from the Eastern Front. This infusion of new troops, combined with sturdy defenses and proximity to arms depots, helped stiffen German resistance enough to slow and then stop Collins's attack.[16]

As the VII Corps continued to be consumed by the fighting around Aachen, Bradley conducted a major reorganization of his front line. The Ninth Army, then in command of only the VIII Corps, had finished the reduction of Brest and was now ready to assume a place in the line against Germany. Bradley placed this army in V Corps' sector, allowing the First Army to concentrate its forces against the Siegfried Line. Hodges then shifted the V Corps north on 1 October to the fifteen-mile zone that had been previously held by just the 4th MCG.[17] This would now mark the second time in two months that a corps had taken over a sector held mostly by a single cavalry group.

Obviously, the movement of an entire corps into a new sector is an operation fraught with potential danger. Infantry divisions that would be formidable opponents when deployed for battle are now highly vulnerable mounted in columns of trucks moving toward assembly areas. The entire 102nd MCG, reinforced by the 5th AD's reconnaissance squadron, was therefore pressed into service to protect the arrival of the corps into its new sector. As elements of the VIII Corps began arriving in the V Corps sector in late September, the 102nd MCG was released from its flank guard positions and sent to relieve the 4th MCG, then holding the future positions of the corps. The New Jersey cavalry completed the initial battle handover with the 4th MCG by 1 October. The reinforced group then screened the arrival of the corps elements, holding a line eleven miles long.[18] After the arrival of the corps' divisions, the 102nd MCG maintained an outpost line forward of those divisions' assembly areas until the infantry were ready to move into the line. By 10 October the two infantry divisions had moved forward in the southern portion of the corps zone, relieving the 102nd MCG of that portion of the corps line. For the rest of the month of October the 102nd MCG would hold the northern half of the corps sector (eight miles), maintaining contact with the 4th MCG and the VII Corps to the north, while the 4th and 28th IDs conducted limited attacks and probes of the Siegfried Line to their south.[19]

After being relieved by the V Corps, the 4th MCG shifted north, assuming five miles of front from the southernmost division of the VII Corps, the 9th ID.[20] This shift allowed the 9th ID to focus its efforts on the Hürtgen Forest, which was proving to be a desperately difficult fight. Prior to the 4th MCG's move, the 9th ID's front had been nearly twenty miles. Now that front had been reduced to nine.[21] This reduction in front allowed the 9th ID to attack with two full regiments along a three-mile front toward the town of Schmidt. This assault would bog down in a bloody morass after advancing three thousand yards at the cost of forty-five hundred casualties.[22] While the assault remains controversial, it is a fact that the 9th ID could not have mustered the requisite combat power for the attempt without the presence of the cavalry. The 4th MCG would retain these positions for the entire month of October as the 9th ID slogged its way forward.

To the north, in the XIX Corps' sector, the beginning of October would find Colonel Biddle's 113th MCG whole again, with the arrival of the 125th CRS from its attachment to the 30th ID. The XIX Corps also gave the group a new mission, attaching it to the newly arrived 29th ID. The 29th ID's task was to attack north in support of the 30th ID's assault farther south along the corps line. Corlett hoped that this assault would break through German positions north of Aachen, helping the corps flank the city and drive to the Roer River. Over the objections of the Biddle, the 29th ID ordered the 113th MCG to make a frontal assault across two miles of open ground to seize the town of Havert, Germany, north of the group's line. The Redhorse opened its attack on 2 October, supported by medium tanks from the 747th Tank Battalion. The cavalrymen met fierce resistance that included anti-tank guns, minefields, massed artillery fire, and well-entrenched infantry. After an extremely tough fight that included at least one battalion-strength German counterattack, the cavalry ceased their attack on 4 October, having made no gains.[23] Although the cavalry had failed in their attack, so had the rest of the 29th ID. The terrain, coupled with the German defenses, simply did not allow for a successful frontal assault. The group would spend the rest of October along its ten-mile front on the extreme north of the American line, allowing the 29th ID to focus its efforts farther to the east.[24]

In the middle of October, the 12th Army Group rearranged its lines once more. The Ninth Army headquarters took command of the northern wing of the army group, assuming control of the XIX Corps and Major General Alvan C. Gillem Jr.'s newly arrived XIII Corps. This move would allow the First Army to focus on Aachen and the Hürtgen Forest by giving the Ninth Army the job of clearing the region north of Aachen. Middleton's VIII Corps would be left in place in the Ardennes, where it would serve as a rehabilitation headquarters for units wrecked in the Hürtgen Forest or for breaking in formations new to the front. These moves were in preparation for a general offensive across the front that would consume much of November and December, coming to a halt only when the Germans began Operation WACHT AM RHEIN, otherwise known as the Battle of the Bulge.

As the Ninth Army assumed control of the northern end of the 12th Army Group line, the boundary between the American and Commonwealth army groups shifted such that the 113th MCG's sector now actually belonged to the British XXX Corps. However, the British did not have any units capable of holding the cavalry's front, so the 113th MCG worked closely with the British, holding this sector for their Commonwealth comrades while still maintaining active command relationships with the XIX Corps.[25] The beginning of November also saw the group reinforced by the 17th CRS. The 17th normally belonged to the 15th MCG, but that group with its other squadron was conducting rear area security in western France. The 17th CRS had recently been released from duty guarding the Ninth Army headquarters.[26] On 7 November, the XIII Corps took command of the extreme left of the American line, which included the 113th MCG. On 11 November, Gillem gave operational control of the 113th MCG to the British XXX Corps as the British assumed more of the corps sector in preparation for a general Ninth Army-wide assault to the east. On 13 November, the British Guards Armored Division assumed control of the 113th MCG's sector, allowing the cavalry to return to American control.[27]

Farther to the south, at the beginning of November, the First Army temporarily transferred the Schmidt sector, along with the 4th MCG, to the V Corps in order to allow the VII Corps to concentrate on its attack past Aachen. What this meant in real terms for the cavalry was that their artillery support and any other attachments would now come from the V Corps, as the VII Corps required all of these assets for its upcoming assault. The 4th MCG would retain its positions, but north of the cavalry the V Corps' 28th ID would replace the worn-out 9th ID of the VII Corps. Furthermore, the cavalry could expect little help, as Major General Leonard Gerow's V Corps now took the mission of attempting to take the key town of Schmidt.[28]

Gerow's own cavalry, the 102nd MCG, would play a major role by maintaining a large part of the corps line, allowing half of the V Corps' infantry strength to be drawn northward to attack Schmidt. This attack would also end in bloody failure, costing 6,184 casualties.[29] As with the case of the 9th ID's attack, the advisability of such an effort was questionable. However, the failure of both operations cannot be attributed to the American forces being too spread out or being disrupted on their divisional flanks. In other words, although both the 9th and 28th IDs failed at Schmidt, the 4th and 102nd MCGs had done everything within their power to offer support.

On 10 November, the 102nd MCG relieved the 4th MCG of the Lammersdorf–Monschau sector as the 4th MCG reverted back to VII Corps control. Collins was in the process of planning for a major offensive aimed at the city of Cologne on the Rhine River and needed his cavalry to assist in the fighting. The 1st and 4th IDs would attack together, supported by the 8th ID of the V Corps. The 8th ID had replaced the wrecked 28th ID after its failed assault on Schmidt in late October.[30] This assault would take the corps straight through the Hürtgen Forest in a headlong drive to smash through German resistance. The offensive began on 16 November, with the 24th CRS being committed with the 4th ID that day. The cavalry squadron protected regimental supply lines and patrolled between various regiments of the 4th ID over the next three weeks, allowing every possible infantryman and engineer to be pushed forward into the assault through the tangled woods. The 4th CRS would be attached to the 1st ID and be committed on 23 November.[31] The troopers screened the boundary between the 1st ID and the 4th ID to the south.[32] This connection was especially vital in the broken terrain of the Hürtgen in order to prevent enemy infiltration along unit boundaries.

While the 4th MCG participated in the VII Corps' direct assault through the Hürtgen Forest, to the south the 102nd MCG held its positions stretching eight miles from Monschau to north of Lammersdorf. This sector now comprised the center of the V Corps' somewhat schizophrenic line, with the 8th ID participating in the Hürtgen Battle to the north, while the 99th ID held its positions to the south in an extended line that connected with the VIII Corps just north of the Losheim Gap.

On 7 December, the VII Corps passed the 9th and 83rd IDs through the 1st and 4th IDs to continue the assault. The 4th MCG's squadrons simply joined the new divisions without relief.[33] In a particularly odd twist, unique to the Second World War army, the 4th MCG headquarters, which had continued along behind the lines while its squadrons fought underneath divisions and not under group control, was attached to the newly committed 5th AD. The armor division then attached its own armored reconnaissance squadron to the 4th MCG, meaning that that unit would reenter the fight without any of its organic combat formations, but instead with units belonging to a completely different formation. The 4th MCG (in its rather odd configuration) then joined that division as it attacked along the corps' southern flank in a sector stretching from Kufferath (three miles south of Düren) to the border with V Corps' 8th ID, approximately three miles east of the town of Hürtgen.[34] The group at that time consisted of just the 759th Light Tank Battalion (a long-time attachment) and the 85th CRS (organic to the 5th AD). The division tasked the cavalry with protecting its southern flank and maintaining contact with the 8th ID through the rugged, heavily forested terrain. As the corps offensive slowed, and then passed through the Hürtgen Forest by mid-December, the two squadrons of the group, first the 4th CRS and then the 24 CRS, returned to group control.[35] The actions of the 4th MCG during this offensive highlighted the advantages of having a small, highly mobile formation capable of maintaining contact between main body elements, a task long associated with American cavalry.

While the First Army's offensive to clear the Hürtgen proceeded through the second half of November, the Ninth Army launched a supporting offensive to the north aimed at the Roer River. The Ninth Army relieved the 17th CRS from the XIII Corps and sent it to protect the right flank of the XIX Corps, holding a nine-mile front from Jülich to Düren along the Roer, thirteen miles east of Aachen. The cavalry squadron would aid the 30th ID and, later, the 29th ID as those divisions cleared the final yards to the Roer River and then settled into defensive positions.[36]

On the other side of the corps, Biddle's 113th MCG protected the XIII Corps' left flank, maintaining contact with the British, as the group remained static waiting for events to become more fluid. On 27 November, the XIII Corps attached the 113th MCG to the 84th ID as it fought its way north to seize the towns of Beeck and Lindern, four miles east and northeast of Geilenkirchen, nearly on the Roer River. The cavalry relieved two regiments of the 84th ID that were screening the town of Beeck, allowing those regiments to attack north to the Roer River. The cavalry then worked closely with the remaining regiment of the 84th ID in seizing Beeck. This proved to be a vicious fight, as the German defenders comprised elements of the *Panzergrenadier* regiments of the 10th Panzer Division. The fighting lasted until 2 December, with the cavalry and infantry finally proving victorious.[37] Over the course of November, particularly the last week, the Redhorse earned twenty-nine Silver Stars and eighty-three Bronze Stars.[38] The action of the 113th MCG during this time was that of an offensive economy of force effort. Although the unit had conducted some reconnaissance, it had participated in the fighting, the same as any infantry regiment. While certainly not the most efficient use of the cavalry, in this particular case the 84th ID had required more combat power than it possessed to accomplish its objectives. Therefore, the cavalry proved to be a useful force multiplier in helping to seize a secondary but still important objective.

The 113th MCG settled into new defensive positions in mid-December just south of the Roer River, once again holding the extreme left of the XIII Corps line (and thus the extreme north of all American forces).[39] The corps line stretched in an arc facing northeast from the Dutch-German border to the Roer River just north of Jülich. Gillem arrayed his forces with the 113th MCG on the left (north), the 84th ID in the center (with control of the 113th MCG), and the 102nd ID on the right (south).[40] The group would participate in a force rotation plan with the rest of the 84th ID in preparation for continued offensive operations later in December.

On 12 December, the 11th MCG, also under the XIII Corps, arrived at the front. The corps assigned the new cavalrymen to the 102nd ID on the corps' right so that the 11th MCG's squadrons could relieve infantry battalions, allowing them to pull off the line and recover from the brutal fighting of late November. The division did not intend to use the cavalry to attack along this front, merely to hold the positions in an economy of force role so that the infantry regiments of the 102nd ID could reconstitute. This rotation would prove very welcome to the infantry, who had endured weeks of living in the cold and damp on the front lines.

Farther to the south, in the First Army sector, the V Corps received two additional divisions in mid-December to seize the Roer River dams—the newly arrived 78th ID and the veteran 2nd ID, fresh from a stint in the Ardennes under the VIII Corps. These dams were vital, as their destruction would cause flooding along the Roer that could cripple any crossing. Gerow's V Corps, the center corps of the First Army (VII Corps to the north, VIII Corps to the south), was perfectly placed directly to the east of these dams to attempt to take them. The 2nd ID in the south would attack northeast from the vicinity of Rocherath in the 99th ID's sector. The 78th ID in the north would attack east through the 102nd MCG's sector aimed directly at the Paulushof and Urft dams. The 102nd MCG and 99th ID held the corps line, allowing these two divisions to mass for their assault. The 2nd ID would require partial assistance from the 99th to make any sort of forward progress due to the ferocity of the German defense. The 78th ID would succeed well enough to completely screen the 102nd CRS, although not enough to seize their objectives yet. The attack of the V Corps would continue up to and through the first hours of the Battle of the Bulge.

The Siegfried Line campaign had placed significant demands on the First and Ninth Armies, and their corps cavalry groups had proven essential to overcoming those obstacles. While the Northern France campaign had seen rapid advances, this new phase of the war witnessed a return to positional warfare. In this fight, the First and Ninth Armies' corps cavalry demonstrated their versatility by fighting in a variety of roles. The most important of these roles in this campaign was acting as an economy of force, holding huge stretches of the front for the infantry. Positional warfare consumes infantry at a horrendous rate. Unfortunately, the U.S. Army did not have enough infantry divisions to fully cover its front, much less absorb the kind of casualties seen in places like the Hürtgen Forest, the plains north of Aachen, or the Eifel region south of Aachen. The cavalry of these two armies allowed their corps to concentrate their precious infantry regiments where they would do the most good. Therefore, the American methodology of victory through massive application of resources in support of tactical maneuver only worked because the corps cavalry were doing their jobs. In other words, the broad front only looked that way because of the presence of corps cavalry.

Corps cavalry also aided the First and Ninth Armies through security operations, either on the flank or to the front, with the dash of the 113th MCG across Belgium being particularly memorable. These operations prevented German interference with the movement of the American corps and armies across the battlefield. The 4th MCG screened the arrival of a corps twice in this campaign.

While the actions of the First and Ninth Armies during this period have been generally tainted with the controversy of the Hürtgen Forest, both still contributed greatly to the success of the overall campaign. Despite often bloody fighting, these two armies ground their way to the Roer River, inflicting serious losses on the Germans. Without their corps cavalry this fight would have proven to be impossible.

Third Army

While the First Army engaged in the brutal positional fighting around Aachen and the Hürtgen Forest, the Third Army experienced its own slugfest in the French province of Lorraine throughout the second half of September and into the winter. The army's initial attempts to vault the Moselle River to the north and south of Metz had failed, with both the XII and XX Corps taking heavy casualties. Additionally, the Third Army lost two of its corps to other armies at this time. The VIII Corps, still mired in Brittany, came under the command of the Ninth Army. The XV Corps, holding the southern end of the Third Army line, transferred to the newly arrived Seventh Army, which had just completed its assault from southern France after Operation ANVIL.

The Third Army would continue its assault under Eisenhower's broad front strategy, although it would not be the 12th Army Group's main effort. The First Army would retain that privilege as it attacked toward the German industrial heartland in the Ruhr. The Third Army's objective was Germany's secondary industrial region, located in the Saar Region. However, to reach its objective the Third Army would first have to penetrate the German line along the Moselle and isolate or reduce the fortress system around Metz.

Major General Manton Eddy's XII Corps, south of Metz, would be the initial Third Army main effort to isolate the city. As such, it would first have to cross the Moselle south of Nancy and then drive to the northeast. However, before the corps could accomplish these tasks it had to generate the necessary combat power, as it still had a full division, the 35th ID, strung out to the west as a consequence of the rapid movement across France. In order to concentrate the 35th ID, Eddy called on Colonel Charles Reed's 2nd MCG, already conducting screening operations along the corps' flank.

On 7 September, the XII Corps attached a tank destroyer battalion, equipped with M18 Hellcats, to the 2nd MCG as it assumed a greater role in the protection of the corps' flank.[41] This allowed the 35th ID, which had been covering the corps' extreme western flank, to concentrate in preparation for an assault across the Moselle south of Nancy.[42] The next day, the 42nd CRS conducted an assault on Fort de Pont Saint Vincent, a fortification overlooking the confluence of the Madon and Moselle Rivers, which also dominated much of the ground that the 35th ID would have to cover in preparation for its assault across the Moselle.[43] The attack was fraught with difficulty, owing to the general lack of foot soldiers in the cavalry troops, but skillful use of the squadron's assault guns, light tanks, and attached artillery allowed the Dragoons to succeed in their attack, as well as defeat a concerted dismounted counterattack the next day. On both occasions, the cavalry's heavy firepower proved decisive, although on the second day they were also aided by recently captured defensive positions that helped compensate for their lack of numbers and survivability. Once the 42nd CRS had secured the objective, it then handed it over to the 35th ID in preparation for their planned offensive. The possession of this fortification would prove important to both the 35th ID and the German army, as evidenced by continued fighting for the position for the next several days until additional American advances past the river made further German attempts to regain the position fruitless.[44]

The actions of the 2nd MCG, specifically those of the 42nd CRS, greatly facilitated the eventual assault crossing of the Moselle by the 35th ID over the next couple days. The group's reconnaissance and constant skirmishing between the Madon and Moselle Rivers had identified the majority of enemy strongpoints, allowing the infantry to bypass them and quickly strike the weak points in the German defenses.[45] Additionally, the group protected the southern flank of the division as it assaulted forward, allowing more force to be projected into the main effort. Finally, by direct actions, such as holding bridges over the Madon River and the seizure of Fort de Pont Saint Vincent, the group allowed the 35th ID to penetrate the German security zone with relative ease and attack into the main enemy defensive positions.

On 11 September, the reinforced reconnaissance battalion of the 4th AD assumed the mission of guarding the flank of the XII Corps. Additionally, Haislip's XV Corps was advancing along the XII's southern flank, lessening the responsibilities of the flank guard. This shift allowed the 2nd MCG (minus the 2nd CRS, which was still conducting security around the corps headquarters) to cross the Moselle and protect the southern and eastern flanks of Combat Command B (CCB) of the 4th AD as it fought to envelop the city of Nancy.[46] The Dragoons continued in this mission, often engaged in heavy contact, as they moved across the front of a buildup of German counterattack forces, including elements of the 15th Panzergrenadier Division, the 111th and 113th Panzer Brigades, and the 21st Panzer Division.[47] Due to the difficulties encountered by the cavalry, the XII Corps released the 2nd CRS back to the group on 15 September 1944 in order to allow them to continue to protect the rear of CCB, 4th AD.[48] This infusion of combat power allowed the 2nd MCG to commit to a squadron-size assault on Lunéville on 16 September. This town was a major road junction controlling access to Nancy. Possession of it would greatly assist in isolating Nancy as well as preventing German interference with the 4th AD's envelopment of the city. The mixed bag of various Wehrmacht formations left in the region after the advance of the 4th AD fought hard for Lunéville, but they did not have the combat power to counter the combined strength of two cavalry squadrons working in concert.[49]

In the early morning of 18 September, elements of the 111th Panzer Brigade attacked the 42nd CRS, then occupying Lunéville. The cavalry estimated this initial attack as "six [Panther] tanks and two companies of infantry."[50] The group attempted to ambush this force with the 42nd CRS's assault gun troop, but their 75mm low-velocity guns were insufficient to penetrate the armor of the German tanks, and the cavalry's defense crumbled in the face of tanks that they could not stop. The Germans destroyed three guns (half of the assault gun troop) in the initial encounter. The squadron conducted a delaying action, having more success against the German infantry than their armor. The difficulties of their infantry kept the Germans at bay until approximately 1100 that morning. This time allowed the remainder of the group to withdraw to better positions and for reinforcements from the 4th AD to arrive.[51] These reinforcements forced the Germans to break off their attack. Although the attack had not inflicted much damage on the American main body elements, the 2nd MCG—and the 42nd CRS in particular—had taken serious losses, including its commanding officer, Colonel Reed, who was badly wounded in the engagement.[52] Moreover, the losses to the assault gun troop of the 42nd CRS, the heaviest anti-tank firepower organic to the cavalrymen, would take at least three months to recover.[53]

The action at Lunéville stands as a perfect example of a defensive security operation. The 2nd MCG absorbed the blow that otherwise would have fallen on the main body of the 4th AD while its attention was focused to the north and west. Moreover, the cavalry held long enough to allow the corps commander to react and develop the situation under his own terms. The resulting battle, though hard fought, could have been much bloodier for the Americans had the cavalry not been in position. Unfortunately for the cavalry, their equipment was not well suited for such a role. The assault guns assigned to the squadrons were the only vehicles the cavalry organically owned that were capable of defeating even some German armor. Although the U.S. Army struggled with German tanks as a whole during the Second World War, the cavalry were particularly challenged. Each group possessed a mere twelve weakly armored vehicles with any chance against heavy armor. However, the cavalry were constantly placed in situations wherein they encountered enemy tanks. This scenario forced the cavalrymen to take often inordinate risks. In the case of Lunéville, the 2nd MCG accomplished its mission, but at an excessively high cost. Still, the cavalry had done its job. They had slowed and bled the German attack until sufficient combat power could be brought upon the enemy, acting as the "crumple zone" for the corps.[54]

The remainder of September saw the 2nd MCG maintaining a screen along the southern flank of the XII Corps and contact with the XV corps to the south. A continuation of the German counterattack begun against the 2nd MCG flared to the north and east of the group's positions, involving large elements of the 4th AD. This fighting also pulled away the armored reserve left with the group after the Lunéville fighting, leaving the cavalry on their own once more.[55] However, except for some artillery barrages and light probing, the Germans did not test the 2nd MCG for the rest of September, as their attention was on the large tank battles occurring around Arracourt.[56]

While the XII Corps managed to cross the Moselle in the south and begin the isolation of Metz, the XX Corps continued to struggle in front of the city itself, as it failed to make appreciable headway against such fortifications as Fort Driant. The 90th and 5th IDs both battered themselves senseless in repeated assaults, trying to crack this line.[57] The actions of the XX Corps during this time would serve as brutal reminders of the dangers of attacking well-entrenched enemies directly.

Colonel James Polk's 3rd MCG held the northern end of the corps line, allowing the infantry divisions to concentrate on the fighting around Metz. On 19 September, the XX Corps established Task Force Polk, attaching the 135th Combat Engineer Battalion, the 6th Cavalry Task Force (comprising two assault gun troops and a light tank company of the 6th MCG), and the 1st Battalion of the 1st Regiment, Paris Division. These forces were added to provide the understrength group (the 3rd CRS, though reattached, was still south patrolling a gap between the 90th and 5th IDs) with enough combat power to hold an additional eight miles of front while becoming more aggressive in patrolling. The task force conducted reconnaissance across the river, identifying portions of three Wehrmacht formations (36th Panzergrenadiers, 19th ID, and 559th ID) in its area of responsibility.[58]

On 24 September, the 3rd MCG relived the two regiments of the 90th ID in order to allow that division to mass for its attacks against the northern side of the Metz fortified region, giving the cavalry a front of nearly twenty miles along the Moselle River, centered roughly on Thionville.[59] The task force continued to hold its positions along the flank, allowing the infantry and armored divisions of the corps to mass their efforts against the Metz forts.

As October began, Walker attached the 135th Combat Engineer Battalion, the rest of the 1st Regiment, Paris Division, the 2nd Regiment, Paris Division (the French forces were all organized under Group Lorraine), the 1st Battalion of the 330th Infantry Regiment, and the 807th Tank Destroyer (TD) Battalion to Polk's task force. Additionally, the 3rd CRS had now rejoined the group, providing Colonel Polk with a tremendous amount of combat power, though some of it perhaps dubiously equipped.[60] On 13 October 1944, the XX Corps removed the poorly equipped Free French Group Lorraine from Task Force Polk, seriously curtailing the infantry strength of the cavalry, although removing a fairly large administrative and logistical headache.[61] The remainder of the month saw a war of outposts, with both sides sending patrols across the Moselle River in an attempt to gain insights into the other's intentions (see map 9). Although there was a fair amount of give and take, the 3rd MCG generally gave better than they received.

As the 3rd MCG fought its security battle at the north end of the Third Army line, the 2nd MCG spent the majority of October conducting minor reconnaissance patrols and probes as it held the extreme south of the XII Corps line in an economy of force role. Toward the end of the month, the XII Corps planned a limited attack involving the newly arrived 26th ID in order to "blood" the unit as well as establish better positions for future offensive operations.[62] This attack would

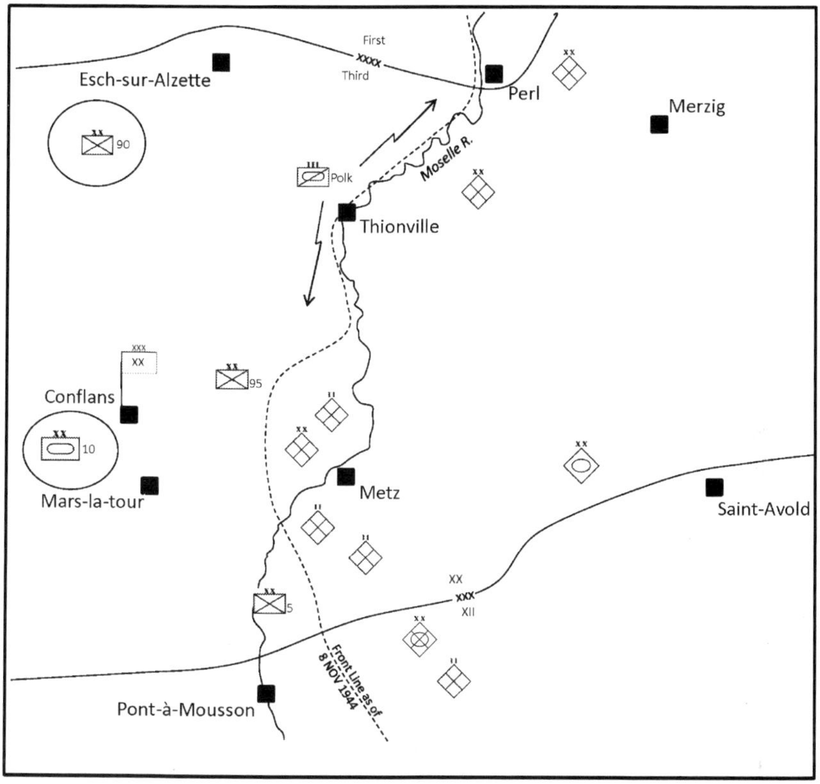

Map 9. XX Corps Positions at the Beginning of November 1944.

seize the Moncourt Ridge. However, the southern end of the ridge in the 2nd Group's sector dominated the approaches to the 26th ID's planned point of attack. Thus, the XII Corps ordered the cavalry to seize this portion of the ridge in order to facilitate the success of the 26th ID. The 42nd CRS dismounted and attacked on 20 October in column of troops on an extremely narrow (less than two miles) front. Despite some fierce resistance from the German defenders, the squadron achieved its limited objectives, thereby aiding in the success of the 26th ID's assault five days later.[63]

As November began, the Third Army prepared for a major offensive with the aim of isolating Metz and driving to the Saar River. Walker's XX Corps would fight its way across the Moselle and then use this bridgehead to pass the bulk of its divisions across, most notably the

10th AD, for an advance east and south, enveloping Metz as well as driving to the German border. Eddy's XII Corps would assault from the south, meeting the 10th AD to the east of Metz. The XX Corps' plan involved the 90th ID making an assault crossing of the Moselle near the town of Koenigsmacker, in the 3rd MCG's sector. The Brave Rifles' role in the battle would be to occupy the 90th ID's zone, allowing the entire division to be withdrawn from the line of battle in order to allow it to train and prepare. Additionally, the cavalry were to screen the river line in their sector to prevent the Germans on the far side from learning of the impending attack. These shifts left Task Force Polk covering the entire northern third of the corps line.[64]

However, before the planned assault could begin in the Koenigsmacker area, a small, battalion-size German outpost on the west bank of the Moselle in Berg inside the cavalry's zone had to be reduced. The Germans in this position could identify forces moving up to conduct an assault crossing as well bring accurate fires on the planned staging areas.[65]

The attack on Berg started early on the morning of 4 November when a platoon of Troop A, 43rd CRS, attacked dismounted to seize the dominating high ground to the north of the town. Despite initial success, a German company-size counterattack drove the troopers off the hill, wounding five and capturing five. The next morning, the squadron attacked the town itself with Troop B reinforced with a platoon of engineers, supported by F Company (the light tank company). The fighting for the town took a brutal four hours and required the light tanks to spearhead the penetration into the town in order to protect the pinned-down dismounted cavalrymen. Additionally, the 705th TD Battalion suppressed German forces in the town of Malling, immediately across the Moselle, preventing their interference in the operation. Once the 43rd CRS had secured the town, Troop A attacked the high ground from which they had been repulsed the day before. The 689th Field Artillery Battalion preceded the attack with a massive barrage of eighty 155mm rounds in under three minutes.[66] After such a crippling blow, the Germans on the hill put up little resistance as Troop A recaptured the hill. The squadron captured a total of forty-five German soldiers and inflicted an estimated sixty additional casualties.[67] Over half of the casualties inflicted on the Germans seem to have occurred in the final stages, when the assault guns opened fire on boats carrying soldiers attempting to escape to the east bank.[68] The cost to the cavalry was fairly substantial, with four dead and thirty-six wounded.[69]

The attack on Berg is a great example of a deliberate security zone battle. The cavalry were not only preventing German infiltration of American lines, but in this battle the group also destroyed a German outpost that would have given early warning about the impending attack of the 90th ID. The destruction of an enemy security zone is a vital component of a successful operation, particularly a high-risk one, such as a contested river crossing in bad weather like the planned XX Corps assault.

The 3rd MCG had provided a major service to the 90th ID's assault by removing the threat to the potential bridgehead that Berg had posed. Additionally, the cavalry's screen along the Moselle prevented the Wehrmacht from identifying the buildup of the 90th ID in the Cattenom area. This was no small feat, as the infantry had massed two full regiments for the assault. According to later prisoner reports and captured documents, Task Force Polk had been so successful in their efforts that the attack at Koenigsmacker came as a complete surprise.[70] It also did not hurt that the Americans attacked in extremely poor weather. This role of providing a security zone to allow friendly forces to mass for an assault is one of the oldest missions in the mounted lexicon, and is still practiced to this day. Additionally, the cavalry's reconnaissance of the crossing point smoothed the 90th ID's initial efforts crossing the river.[71] Therefore, the 3rd MCG had truly won the reconnaissance fight, imposing a "fog of war" for the enemy while creating as clear a picture as possible for their own forces. The 3rd MCG executed this mission nearly perfectly in early November 1944.

The 90th ID's assault across the Moselle began on 9 November, supported by Task Force Polk's artillery and assault guns. Due to the requirements of the assault, Walker stripped the task force of its engineer and tank destroyer battalions. As some consolation, the cavalrymen were given a portion of another tank destroyer battalion. Additionally, on this day, Corps attached the task force to the 83rd ID, which was back under XX Corps control for the purposes of the offensive across the Moselle. The cavalrymen quickly moved to their new positions to the north along the river, relieving elements of the 83rd ID so that the infantrymen could participate in the fighting to the south. The 3rd MCG's new front along the Moselle ran twenty miles north from their old northern boundary. The group held these positions until 11 November, when the 83rd ID was returned to the First Army, whereupon the cavalry returned to XX Corps control.[72] This series of events had been instigated by a political struggle over resources between the First and Third Armies. The Third Army had wanted the 83rd ID to help in its November attack, while the First Army wanted the division to hold its line. The result was a compromise that pleased no one. The Third Army received the division for a very short period, and in return had to deploy the XX Corps cavalry to hold the 83rd ID's positions. Thus, Patton had one of his three cavalry groups tied down not supporting the attack and a division that he could barely use.

In conjunction with the XX Corps assault on the north end of the army line, Eddy's XII Corps initiated another offensive on 8 November to close the jaws of the Third Army around Metz. The 2nd MCG, still working with the 26th ID on the southern flank of the corps, performed two key roles in this attack. At the onset of the fighting, the Dragoons moved about a kilometer forward of the 26th ID's positions in order to protect the infantry as they moved from their defensive positions into the attack. After passing the 26th ID's soldiers forward of their position, the cavalry maintained a screen protecting the southern flank of the 26th ID and XII Corps as they advanced to the northeast.[73] This screen was doubly important due to the fact that the southern flank of the XII Corps was not only the southern boundary of the Third Army but also of the 12th Army Group. Additionally, Haislip's XV Corps to the south was conducting its own assault, complicating the coordination between the two corps. Therefore, the cavalry performed a vital mission in ensuring that the flanks of the 26th ID, XII Corps, Third Army, and 12th Army Group were secure, allowing combat power to mass forward without worrying about a German strike behind their spearheads.

Another example of the cavalry's impact on the larger battle can be seen on 16 November, when elements of the 2nd MCG relieved an entire infantry regiment (the 101st) of the 26th ID that had been holding the shoulder of the division's penetration. Two days later, that regiment would participate in a renewed divisional-level assault.[74] Unbeknownst to the group, they were aided in their efforts to guard the corps' flank by the general lack of large German mechanized formations in the region, as the Wehrmacht were massing their formations to the north in preparation for their December counteroffensive.

In the middle of November, Task Force Polk (3rd MCG) moved across the Moselle River through the Koenigsmacker bridgehead that it had helped establish. Then the cavalry relieved elements of the 90th ID from the responsibility of holding the northern shoulder of the bridgehead, allowing the infantry to mass forces in their drive to the south to envelop the city of Metz. As the XX and XII Corps joined around Metz, they masked the city with minor combat power and then turned east to attack toward the Saar River. Simultaneously with their relief of the 90th ID, the 3rd MCG moved east, mopping up German forces bypassed by the 10th AD as it had stormed through the region on a deeper envelopment of the city. The XX Corps also ordered the cavalry to attack north to the vicinity of Saarburg, a major crossing over the Saar River, nineteen miles to the northeast of Koenigsmacker. This move would accomplish two goals. The first would be to seize a crossing over the Saar River. The second would be to protect the northern flank of the 10th AD and 90th ID as they encircled the city of Metz.

The 3rd MCG began their move on 14 November, with their drive to the north kicking off in earnest on 17 November. The next day saw both squadrons engaged in heavy urban combat as they fought from town to town north into the Saar–Moselle Triangle. On 18 November the cavalrymen advanced a little over a mile on a five-mile frontage. The addition of the M18 Hellcats of the 705th TD Battalion proved decisive in much of the fighting, as their 76mm high-velocity cannons were able to destroy most German positions with a few well-placed rounds, which was vastly superior to any organic firepower carried by the cavalry. The fighting around and in the town of Büschdorf, Germany, was typical of the day's action. A company-size formation of Germans (approximately one hundred men) entrenched behind roadblocks attempted to resist the efforts of Troop C (reinforced by a platoon of M18s and a squad of engineers) and Company F, 43rd CRS, as they assaulted into the town. The cavalry used its tanks and tank destroyers to suppress the enemy, its engineers to clear the roadblocks, and then dismounted cavalrymen moving under the suppressive fire to clear the enemy from their positions.[75]

The next day, 19 November, Task Force Polk advanced to portions of the Siegfried Line. While the 43rd CRS on the eastern flank made limited progress (one mile), seizing its objectives for the day, the 3rd CRS on the western flank met such determined resistance from heavily entrenched German forces in bunkers and pillboxes that they were obliged to withdraw to their start lines. These actions are indicative of cavalry in an offensive security mission. The 3rd MCG fought its way forward, through the initial enemy defensive positions, until it came against the main line of resistance. After it gained contact with that line, it attempted to develop the situation further and identify weak points as well as trying to penetrate by itself. This information helped Walker make informed decisions about how to commit his combat power in a fluid environment.[76]

After the 3rd MCG encountered such heavy resistance in the Saar–Moselle Triangle, Walker ordered the group to be relieved by the 10th AD in an attempt to use greater combat power to force a way through. The cavalrymen, once relieved, were to go into reserve, the first rest the group had received since 10 August.[77] The 10th AD tried for five days to break through the defenses that had stymied Task Force Polk, but ultimately failed. Thus, on 27 November, the Brave Rifles found themselves back along the same line, as the XX Corps pulled the bulk of the 10th AD off the front to rest it in order to prepare for exploitation to the east once the rest of the corps (the 5th, 90th, and 95th IDs) crossed the Saar River.[78] Walker assigned the task force the responsibility for screening the entire base of the Saar–Moselle Triangle, a frontage of seven wooded and hilly miles, studded with enemy defensive positions. During the first week of December, the XX Corps ordered Task Force Polk to take over the remainder of the 10th AD's position, adding another two miles to their front and allowing the division to be completely pulled back into reserve, a move that would have great benefits for the Third Army within the month.[79] Additionally, the cavalry's mission allowed the corps to continue its attack to push the rest of its formations to the Saar River without worrying about the threat of a counterattack from the north. The German forces in the Saar–Moselle Triangle had been extremely active and aggressive, so there existed a very real threat that a spoiling attack from this region could have dislocated the corps' main effort attack to the east.

On the southern end of the army line, Eddy split the 2nd MCG on 22 November, sending the 42nd CRS and group headquarters to the north to work with the 80th ID and to maintain contact with the XX Corps. The 2nd CRS remained in the south to maintain a liaison between the XII Corps and the XV Corps of the Seventh Army.[80] Although no record seems to remain for the reason behind this shift, it is reasonable to assume that the recent offensives undertaken by the entire Third Army had shaken loose the connections between the various corps, and great care had to be taken in order to ensure that gaps which the Germans could exploit in a counterattack did not develop. The lightly armed but highly mobile cavalry were perfect for such a mission.

As December started, and more divisions began arriving at the front, the XII Corps could plug these units into its line. This allowed the corps to pull first the 2nd CRS (by now returned to the group), and then the 42nd CRS from the line for rest and recuperation. From 8 to 14 December the troopers recovered from the previous campaign and prepared for the next.[81] At the end of this period the group moved to the town of Sarreguemines, seven miles to the south-southeast of Saarbrücken. There, they joined the 35th ID as it prepared to continue its offensive to the northeast. The group relieved the 137th Infantry Regiment from its position holding the western edge of the division line, allowing the 35th ID to mass combat power along its desired axis of attack. They maintained that position for a week, allowing the 35th ID to continue its assault against the leading edges of the Siegfried Line.[82]

As the cumulative effects of months of fighting through rugged terrain and stiff defenses wore down elements of the Third Army, Patton decided that the needs of the front outweighed his need to keep Colonel Edward Fickett's 6th MCG in reserve. Therefore, at the beginning of November 1944, the Third Army had reorganized the group, attaching the 5th Ranger Battalion, Company C of the 602nd TD Battalion, and Company B of the 293rd Combat Engineer Battalion to what became known as Task Force Fickett.[83] The task force then spent the remainder of the month of November training as a unit in preparation for general combat operations.

On 1 December, the Third Army committed Task Force Fickett to the XX Corps as that formation attacked to the Saar River. A German salient on the west bank of the Saar River, with elements of the German 36th ID, had developed between the XX Corps to the north and the XII Corps to the south.[84] However, as the main efforts of either corps were well to the north or south of the region, committing major elements of line divisions would have diluted their efforts—thus Task Force Fickett's presence on the battlefield. They relieved elements of the 42nd CRS, 2nd MCG, at Saint Avold, fifteen miles to the southwest of Saarbrücken and the Saar River, on 1 December and prepared to begin their attack the next day. The task force organized for combat with each of the three recon troops (the 28th CRS was detached) reinforced by a company of rangers, a platoon of assault guns, and a squad of engineers.[85]

Task Force Fickett attacked on 2 December on a two-mile front against the towns of Carling and L'Hôpital, along the Saar. The Germans put up fierce resistance, and even with the addition of a full battalion of rangers the cavalry were unable to clear the two objectives until three days later, on 5 December, when they received massive artillery support. The cavalrymen continued their attack for the next two days against weakening resistance to the Saar River, where they were stopped due to the inability of the XII Corps to reduce the fortified town of Forbach to the south, which would have threatened any further penetration.[86] This attack destroyed a salient that had threatened the XX Corps' Saar bridgehead at Saarlautern, and it did so without the commitment of main corps forces.[87] Though this action was not a major effort, it was a regiment-size battle that otherwise would have drawn precious resources needed for the main effort—a textbook example of an economy of force attack.

The difficulties encountered by Task Force Fickett in clearing the small objective of L'Hôpital highlight the limitations of the cavalry. The 6th MCG, especially when it only had one squadron present, did not have enough combat power to seize two firmly held objectives without massive reinforcement. The addition of a ranger battalion, by itself, nearly doubled the amount of soldiers in the task force, and increased the number of soldiers available for infantry operations by an order of magnitude. The cavalry did possess the firepower in this particular case to punch their way through enemy defenses, thanks to a lack of German armor, but without the rangers their attack would have failed.

On 8 December, Task Force Fickett relieved a reinforced regiment of the 5th ID. This left the cavalry manning a front of approximately seven miles centered roughly on Saarlautern. The presence of Task Force Fickett allowed Walker to completely withdraw the 5th ID from the front. This division then took advantage of their time off the line to train for attacks against fortified positions and bunkers, clearly in preparation for an assault across the Saar River and into the teeth of the Siegfried Line.[88] Thus, the cavalry were able to assume a division frontage in an economy of force mission. As the XX Corps had just completed a grueling offensive through the Lorraine region, any chance to rest a division was a golden opportunity.

The Third Army continued low-level operations until the middle of December as it prepared for the next phase of the assault into Germany. Walker's XX Corps held positions stretching in a line from the Moselle River southeast along the Saar. Eddy's XII Corps then maintained the rest of the Saar front, linking up with the Seventh Army southeast of Saarbrücken. Corps cavalry anchored both flanks, with the 3rd MCG on the left tying into the First Army and the 2nd MCG on the right connected to the Seventh Army. The 6th MCG held the army center, tying both corps together. Patton planned to rest his army briefly, then plunge across the Saar and into Germany. However, events negated that planning and sent it moving in an entirely new direction. Still, the events of the fall demonstrated that the army could do more than simply attack through open terrain. Patton's soldiers had ground through part of the most densely fortified region in the world, fighting through the Metz fortifications, parts of the Maginot Line, and slamming into the Siegfried Line.

Without the presence of the cavalry, the Third Army could not have accomplished everything that it attempted. From the 2nd MCG's screening of the XII Corps attack around Nancy to the 3rd MCG's defensive guard on the Moselle, the army's corps cavalry made substantive contributions to the success of the overall army. Patton needed formations for security, reconnaissance, and to fill in as economy of force where needed. The cavalry groups met this need and allowed the army to fight its way past the Moselle to the Saar.

Seventh Army

By late September the Seventh Army had expanded to include the XV Corps, formerly of the Third Army. This corps stretched from Lunéville thirteen miles to the southeast. The corps cavalry group, the 106th MCG, occupied the northern end of this line, facing the Forest of Parroy, a heavily defended German strongpoint. The two divisions of the corps, the 79th ID and the French 2nd AD, held sectors south of the cavalry, splitting the corps zone evenly between them. To the south, the VI Corps continued its offensive toward Strasbourg, but it met serious German resistance in the foothills of the Vosges Mountains. The 45th ID held the northern end of the corps zone and the 36th ID occupied the center, while the 3rd ID slogged through the southern portion of the Vosges, just to the north of Belfort. The VI Corps cavalry, the 117th CRS, began the period attached to the 3rd ID, protecting its right flank and maintaining contact with the French to the south.

On 29 September, Major General Lucian Truscott moved the 117th CRS from the southern flank of the VI Corps to its northern flank. There, the cavalry was responsible for protecting the flank as well as maintaining contact with the French 2nd AD of the XV Corps. Due to supply difficulties as well as overall exhaustion hitting its main infantry divisions, the VI Corps would shift to a defensive posture while making limited attacks toward Saint Dié-des-Vosges. The 117th CRS joined a regiment of the 45th ID in securing the northern end of the corps zone, while the remaining regiments of the division fought their way east through the Mortagne Forest.[89]

The cavalry assumed positions on the corps' left flank, near the town of Anglemont, on 1 October 1944. There they established a roadblock and sent patrols to the north and east. The squadron spent the rest of the month holding their positions, although they actively patrolled and raided German positions around Baccarat to the north.[90] From this position they could protect the juncture of the two corps of the Seventh Army as well as conduct reconnaissance in support of not only the VI Corps, but the XV Corps as well. As the cavalry held their ground, the VI Corps prepared for the offensive that would carry it through the Vosges to Strasbourg and the Rhine River.

Before the VI Corps could initiate a general attack, Haislip's XV Corps to the north had to clear the significant German defenses in the northern portion of its zone. As long as German forces still held their positions, the XV Corps could not advance, and thus any advance by the VI Corps would have a hole in its northern flank that would simply invite a German counterstroke. Therefore, the VI Corps' attack was also delayed as the XV Corps cleared the obstacles to its front.

The cornerstone of German defenses in the XV Corps sector was the Parroy Forest, four miles to the northeast of Lunéville. Laced with old fortifications and trenches from the First World War as well as more modern improvements, the forest was garrisoned by elements of the 11th Panzer Division reinforced with an assortment of other German formations, including portions of the 15th Panzergrenadier Division.[91] The Marne-Rhine Canal flowed east to west past the forest, guarding its northern flank. The forest also stood as the most significant obstacle between the XV Corps and the Saverne Gap—a high-speed avenue through the north end of the Vosges Mountains, thirty-eight miles east of Lunéville.

The XV Corps' attack to clear the forest began on 28 September 1944, preceded by a massive bombing and artillery preparation. The 79th ID had the responsibility of clearing the forest, while Colonel Vennard Wilson's 106th MCG attacked to their north along the Marne-Rhine Canal to protect the flank and maintain contact with the XII Corps. The cavalry, with an attached battalion of tank destroyers, made steady progress, seizing a pair of small towns on either bank of the canal.[92] The following day, the 106th MCG fought off a determined German counterattack that threatened to penetrate between the seam of the two American corps. In the ensuing battle, a combination of cavalry, tank destroyers, and close air support destroyed thirteen Panzer IV tanks, two Panzer V (Panther) tanks, four self-propelled guns, and two half-tracks. The cavalry also inflicted nearly one hundred casualties on the Germans.[93] Although the attached tank destroyer battalion certainly played a huge role in this victory, they were not the only factor, considering the inherent weaknesses of tank destroyers without support, particularly against dismounted infantry. Additionally, the group history records that day that "the P47s were in their glory."[94] Therefore, the best description of the fight is that the cavalry slowed and channeled the German armor into kill zones for the tank destroyers and fighter-bombers, while suppressing German infantry. Thus, the cavalry used combined arms to defeat a significant threat to the northern flank of the XV Corps (or perhaps to the southern flank of the XII Corps).

On 2 October, the 106th CRS moved south into the forest, staking a firmer hold on the leftmost infantry regiment of the 79th ID. Two days later, the 106th CRS staged an attack on German forces holding a major road junction one mile from the western boundary of the woods. After the initial assault forces became pinned down by intense fire, another troop enveloped the German line, forcing them out of their positions. The attack resulted in the road junction falling into American hands, along with fifty-one prisoners from the 113th Panzer Brigade.[95] This success aided an attack by the 79th ID to the south, as the cavalry took control of the northern half of the forest, allowing the infantry to concentrate their strength.

On 9 October, the 106th MCG joined the 79th ID in a major push against the German defenders of the wood. The cavalry and infantry met with success, although it came at a grinding pace, slowed by minefields, wooded terrain, and fierce resistance. Finally, by 13 October, the 79th ID and 106th MCG could claim that the Parroy Forest was secured.[96] In this action, the cavalry had fought in a fierce security fight, guarding the flank of the 79th ID as it slugged through the forest.

After the seizure of the Parroy Forest, the 106th MCG held its positions on the northeastern side of the woods, running patrols to gauge German strength to their front and maintaining contact with the XII Corps (primarily the 42nd CRS). The 79th ID would attack on October 21, seizing the town of Réchicourt-le-Château, seven miles east of the Parroy Forest. After this attack, the 44th ID relieved the 79th ID so that that division could reorganize in preparation for a general offensive in November.[97] Of note, the 106th MCG did not pull into reserve, although it also had suffered in the heavy fighting. However, the nature of the cavalry's mission and their mobility allowed the group commander to rotate cavalry units off of the immediate front more easily than with an infantry formation.

On the southern end of the XV Corps line, the French 2nd AD seized the town of Baccarat to the north of the VI Corps' 117th CRS on 1 November. The next day the cavalry, reinforced by a battalion of engineers, relieved the French of the town, as well as their positions to the east. This relief would take two days as the squadron replaced French forces over a four-mile front. The cavalry would then spend the next two weeks in their positions at the extreme northern end of the VI Corps, waiting for the 45th ID to close on the city of Raon-l'Étape to the south. The squadron would assist the infantry's attacks by slowly flanking the city from the north, putting pressure on the defenders from a second direction.

On 9 November, the 45th ID would be replaced by the newly arrived 100th ID (the 103rd ID would relieve the 3rd ID to the south).[98] This division would complete the seizure of Raon-l'Étape by 11 November 1944.[99] This action is a clear demonstration of cavalry acting not only in a flank security role, but also as an economy of force that prevented the enemy from focusing his efforts against the main American attacks.

On 13 November, the XV Corps began its part of the general army offensive. The corps' plan was to seize the town of Sarrebourg, attack through the Saverne Gap, and advance past the Vosges Mountains at least as far as the Rhine.[100] The 44th ID to the southeast of the 106th MCG would be the main effort, while the cavalry would launch supporting attacks to their immediate front, just east of the Parroy Forest.[101]

The 106th MCG's initial attacks failed to make much headway, although that hardly mattered, as the 44th and 79th ID's attacks achieved their objectives, dislocating the German defenses in front of the cavalry. On 17 November, the group advanced east to the town of Moussey, five miles outside the Parroy Forest. The cavalry's primary function remained maintaining a connection with the XII Corps to the north (elements of the 2nd MCG), a task complicated by the XV Corps' attack that was outstripping its northern neighbor.[102] By 19 November, the advance of the XII Corps had relieved the 106th MCG of the need to patrol the vicinity of the Parroy Forest. The freed cavalry quickly moved to keep a closer watch on the left flank of the XV Corps as it attacked to the east and northeast.[103] This security allowed Haislip's forces to move even faster because they no longer had to look over their shoulder at an open flank. This speed would translate into the French 2nd AD blasting through the Saverne Gap and toward Strasbourg before the Germans could reorder their defenses. In fact, the XV Corps briefly trapped the 553rd Volksgrenadier Division on the western side of the gap, although the Germans were able to escape.[104]

To the south of the XV Corps, the 117th CRS continued their attack on 19 November, continuing to protect the VI Corps' flank as it fought across the Meurthe River as part of the Seventh Army offensive. The next day, the entire corps attacked to the east. The cavalry spent the next five days clearing the northern side of the Vosges along the Neufmaisons–Badonviller road (the modern D8), six miles east of Baccarat.[105] This ground occupied an awkward spot for the VI Corps, as it could shelter German resistance but was off the main line of attack for even its northern division, the 100th ID. Additionally, the XV Corps to the north had other responsibilities to the north and east, leaving the 117th CRS, reinforced with a battalion of infantry, to clear this zone in an obvious demonstration of an economy of force mission. This region needed to be dealt with, but if the corps had committed a division or even a regiment to the effort, that would have slowed its entire attack. But sending the lone infantry battalion by itself would not have been enough, as it did not have the requisite mobility or firepower to accomplish the task. Only the cavalry, paired with a small infantry force, could do the job.

By 23 November, the XV Corps had fully penetrated the Vosges Mountains at the Saverne Gap, with several divisions (the 79th and 45th IDs, the French 2nd AD, and the 14th AD) on the eastern side of the mountains. The French 2nd AD would seize Strasbourg that night. The 106th MCG continued to screen on the western side of the range, north of the gap and south of the town of Sarre-Union.[106] Two regiments of the 44th ID supported the cavalry, as the Saverne Gap was simply too important to hold lightly.[107] Thus, the XV Corps had a perfect defense in depth established—the cavalry in front to identify, slow, and bleed the enemy, and infantry in battle positions to block or counterattack.

In a desperate attempt to stem the American advance, the Panzer Lehr Division attacked from the vicinity of Sarre-Union south, directly into the 106th MCG, on 23 November (see map 10). The attack consisted of two columns, totaling approximately twelve Panzer IV tanks and twenty-five Panzer V tanks, with accompanying infantry. The German attack pushed the cavalrymen back several miles, but not before the Americans inflicted damage on their attackers. The troopers eliminated a small number of tanks and a large amount of infantry through the use of artillery, small arms, and their own vehicles.[108]

The infantry regiments of the 44th ID engaged the German forces,

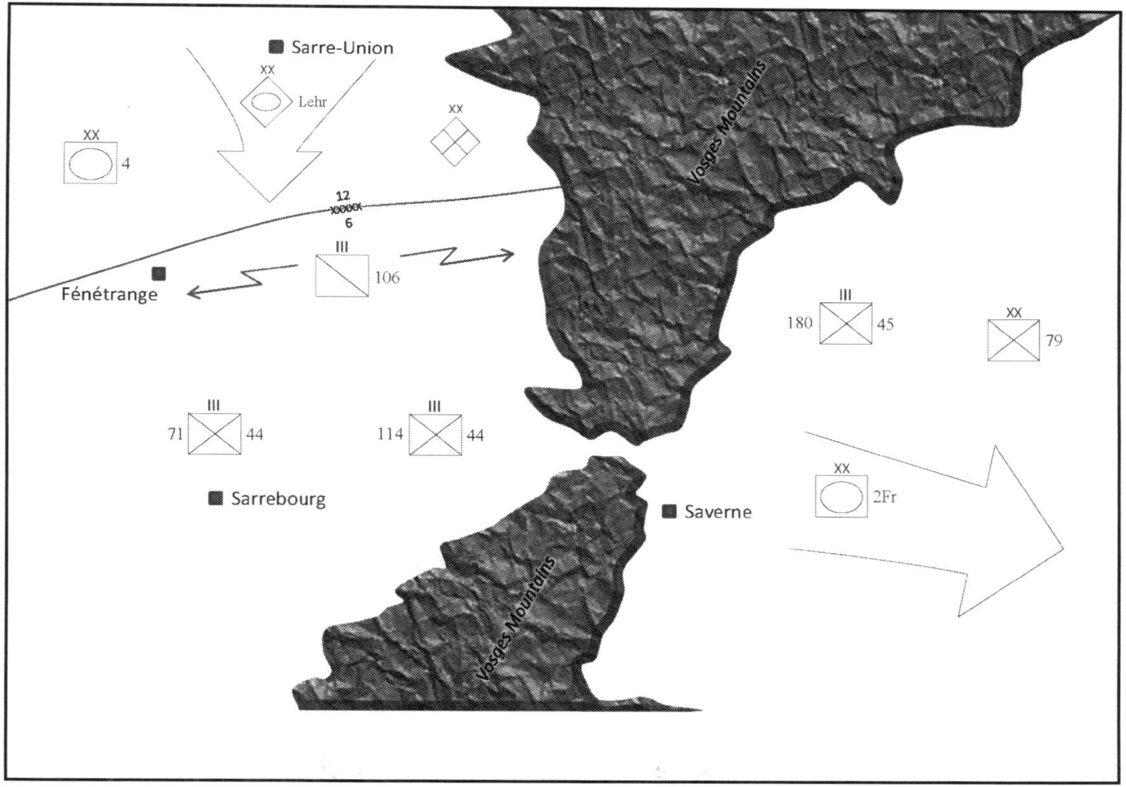

Map 10. 106th MCG Guards the XV Corps' Flank.

further damaging the attack. The German counterattack would be doomed by the commitment of the 4th AD's CCB from the west, over the army group boundary. Although fighting persisted until 25 November, the Germans never seriously threatened or slowed the advance of the XV Corps east of the Vosges.[109]

Although the 106th MCG failed to block the German attack, they still succeeded in their mission. Just like the 2nd MCG at Lunéville, the cavalry acted as a "crumple zone" for the rest of the corps. They met the first waves of the attack, identified the axes of advance, inflicted casualties, and withdrew after buying some time for the infantry to prepare. If the cavalry had been more robustly equipped, the story might have been different, but they were not. As such, they fought within the limits of their equipment and, at the end of the fight, achieved their mission. Most importantly, no German force entered the Saverne Gap.

While the XV Corps fought off the German counterattack, on 24 November the VI Corps' 117th CRS continued their attack, seizing the town of Raon-sur-Plaine, thirteen miles northeast of Raon-l'Étape. This town lay on one of only two major east-west highways in the northern portion of the Vosges Mountains. The country's success allowed CCA of the 14th AD to seize the critical town of Schirmeck, which controlled the confluence of two major routes through the mountains and was one of the last easily defended locations before the Vosges gave way to the Rhine plain.[110] Due to the success of the corps' attack through the Vosges, the 117th CRS found itself behind the American lines after the capture of Schirmeck. The French 2nd AD had captured Strasbourg in a lightning attack from the northwest on 23 November, so the VI Corps debouched from the mountains toward (relatively) friendly territory.

After the arrival of the XV Corps along the Rhine River in late November, Eisenhower ordered the Seventh Army to turn north. The new army group boundary would run north from the Rhine-Marne Canal, west of Bitche to Ramstein. The divisions of the XV Corps were already arrayed in an east-west line oriented into the new zone. The divisions of the VI Corps were still exiting the Vosges Mountains, clearing Strasbourg, and fighting to clear the Colmar Pocket to the south along the Rhine River.[111]

On 26 November, Truscott relieved the 117th CRS from the 100th

ID, which was moving to the XV Corps, and attached it to the 3rd ID, then operating to the north of Strasbourg. By 28 November, the squadron found itself manning an outpost line along the Rhine River, from just outside the city to seven miles north. The squadron would hold their positions, maintaining contact with the 79th ID to the left for a short while, as the VI Corps turned its attention south toward Colmar and the reduction of German forces in the Vosges Mountains.[112]

While the VI Corps passed responsibility for the northern portion of the Colmar Pocket to the French First Army, the XV Corps attacked north. With the corps split by the northern Vosges Mountains, the 106th MCG was employed to patrol the mountains between the two halves, centering its sector on the town of Wingen-sur-Moder, twelve miles north of Saverne. The corps made limited progress fighting through the rough terrain. However, without the connective tissue provided by the cavalry, the advance might have been even slower as the divisions of the corps struggled to communicate laterally.[113]

By 5 December 1944, the VI Corps had reoriented to the north, assuming command of all divisions east of the Vosges, while the XV Corps controlled the western flank of the mountains. The VI Corps was now arrayed with the 45th ID to the left, maintaining contact with the XV Corps, the 78th ID in the center, and 117th CRS maintaining contact between the rest of the corps and the Rhine.[114]

As the VI Corps prepared to attack north on the eastern portion of the mountains, the XV Corps continued its attack on the western side. The 106th MCG held their positions in the northern Vosges Mountains, maintaining contact between the two corps, providing lateral communications. The group also conducted aggressive patrols through the rugged terrain forward of their line, toward the city of Bitche, nine miles to the north. The 106th MCG's activity prevented German forces from slipping behind the advancing American infantry as well as alleviating the lateral coordination problems inflicted by the Vosges Mountains. The cavalry's task was made harder by the fact that the VI Corps remained relatively static as the XV Corps advanced.

The VI Corps resumed its offensive on 9 December, attacking north toward the German Rhineland. The 117th CRS advanced alongside the infantry divisions, keeping contact with the Rhine on the right. By 15 December, the cavalry entered the town of Lauterbourg, on the French-German border, while the rest of the corps advanced to their west, making contact with the southern portions of the Siegfried Line southwest of Mannheim.[115] The next day, the VI Corps relieved the cavalry of their offensive mission and ordered them to assume a fifteen-mile-long defensive screen along the Rhine.[116]

The 106th MCG would continue to advance with the XV Corps, their task greatly eased by the advance of the VI Corps to their right. By 15 December, the group was operating to the east of the city of Bitche, protecting the flank of the 100th ID as it fought through and to the north of the city.[117] The group patrolled the Vosges until 20 December, supporting the XV Corps' continued efforts to breach the Siegfried Line south of Pirmasens.[118] The Seventh Army would end the month holding its positions, slowly grinding its way forward until the Battle of the Bulge put a halt to its activities.

The fall of 1944 had seen the Seventh Army successfully break through German defenses along the Rhine, through the Vosges Mountains, and seize the key city of Strasbourg. In so doing, Patch's army would be the first of any Allied army to reach the Rhine in substantial strength. The army's cavalry had played a key role in this success. Fighting in offensive and defensive security missions, the 106th MCG and 117th CRS had protected their parent formations, enabling successes elsewhere along the line. In the most dramatic example of this, the 106th MCG fought in a corps battle that prevented the entire army from being cut off at the Saverne Gap. The army's cavalry also performed well in the economy of force role, allowing the infantry of the VI and XV Corps to batter their way through stubborn German defenses in the Vosges Mountains. Without question, the presence of the cavalry in the Seventh Army allowed that army to succeed and drive to the Rhine as well as it did.

As the Allied advance slowed and then stopped in the fall of 1944, corps cavalry continued to play a major, albeit somewhat different role. Security operations became less frequent, whereas economy of force defensive missions grew in importance and regularity. In fact, this particular role would be the cavalry's major contribution during the period. The American solution to German fortifications generally involved the massive application of combat power against a small point. However, the sheer size of the front required the U.S. Army to be spread from north of Aachen to Strasbourg, a massive frontage of over two hundred miles. Thus, in order for the Americans to fight in their preferred style they would have to have smaller units cover large portions of the front. The cavalry fit this role perfectly.

Moreover, a front involving ten corps spread across four field armies divided among three army groups meant that the American front in the fall of 1944 was nothing but a pieced-together patchwork of vulnerable boundaries. With the infantry focused on attempting to smash through the German defenses, it fell to the cavalry to ensure that these crucial patches of ground were covered and that lateral communications remained open. While certainly not glamorous, the cavalry's success in these missions ensured that the line infantry and armor divisions of the corps could concentrate on their objectives without worrying about spoiling attacks around their flanks.

Therefore, the corps cavalry of the army played a substantial role in the fighting throughout the fall of 1944. Although the character of the fighting had changed, the importance of the cavalry had not. The corps and armies still required security, reconnaissance, liaison, and economy of force missions. The cavalry were just the units to accomplish them, particularly as casualties mounted in the infantry and armor divisions. Soon, however, the cavalry would face their greatest test as the Germans unleashed two counteroffensives that would eventually involve nearly every American unit in the theater and lead to one of the greatest defeats as well as one of the most significant victories of American arms.

6

A Desperate Winter

The German offensives of December 1944 and January 1945 placed the U.S. Army in a position that it has not often held—that of the operational defense. Known as Operation WACHT AM RHEIN (the Bulge) and Operation NORDWIND (the offensive into the Seventh Army), both operations occurred in heavily broken terrain and bad weather. The corps cavalry played important roles in the fighting over these two months, figuring prominently in some of the most famous and infamous actions of this extremely difficult time for the army.

The Wehrmacht caught the Allied armies at the conclusion of their November offensives that had been geared to establish conditions for an assault to the Rhine. In the north, the Ninth Army had just completed its assault to the Roer River and was consolidating its positions. Lieutenant General Courtney Hodges's First Army had finally broken through the worst of the Hürtgen Forest and was in the process of destroying the last shreds of German resistance west of the Roer in its area. Additionally, the First Army's V Corps was still in the process of fighting toward the Roer River dams, just north of where the main German blow would land on the VIII Corps. Lieutenant General George S. Patton's Third Army, fresh from a successful crossing of the Moselle, had spent the latter part of November and early December slowly battering its way forward against portions of the Siegfried Line along the Saar River. Finally, Lieutenant General Alexander Patch's Seventh Army had closed to the Rhine River, seizing Strasbourg after a bitter and exhausting fight in the Vosges Mountains. Patch's forces had now turned their attention north and were slowly probing the Siegfried

Line, defending the southern shoulder of the Saar–Palatinate region of Germany. Thus, by mid-December all four of the American armies were exhausted, bloodied, and in need of refitting after the brutal Siegfried Line campaign. What they received instead was the Germans' last major offensive punch of the war. The corps cavalry of these armies would, in most cases, help the American field armies catch their breath or concentrate their dwindling combat power on the most vital points.

First Army

Before an analysis of the First Army's actions or the contributions of its cavalry in the Battle of the Bulge can be conducted, a thorough understanding of how exactly the American forces had come to be there and why they were arranged as they were is critically important. These choices would shape one of the biggest disasters that the U.S. Army ever faced in the European Theater of Operations. Therefore, a full accounting of the unit dispositions of the VIII Corps is in order.

The story of the First Army in the Battle of the Bulge actually starts with the introduction of Major General Troy Middleton's VIII Corps under the Ninth Army into the Ardennes in early October. Prior to this time, Major General Leonard Gerow's V Corps had occupied this sector and made some limited gains into the Siegfried Line. Middleton's 2nd ID took responsibility for the northern portion of the sector, maintaining tenuous contact with the southern elements of the new V Corps line to the north, while the 8th ID moved to the south of the 2nd, ostensibly maintaining contact with the Third Army, although the distances involved were rather dramatic. On 11 October, the Third Army relinquished the 83rd ID, including its frontage, to the VIII Corps (then still under Ninth Army), increasing that corps' frontage to eighty-eight miles.[1] Colonel Mark A. Devine Jr.'s 14th MCG and the 9th AD arrived on 20 October fresh on the continent and bringing the corps to full strength. The 9th AD would commit its Combat Command B (CCB) to support the 2nd ID in the north, its division artillery to the 83rd ID in the south, and the balance of the division to the reserve. The 14th MCG also split, with the 18th CRS moving to the 2nd ID and the 32nd CRS joining the 83rd ID.[2]

The 18th CRS took over the Losheim Gap region, stretching from just north of the town of Losheim south to the town of Kobscheid, a straight distance of nearly five miles but much more than that with bends in the line included. This sector is relatively open, and flatter than the areas to the north and south. Even today, it stands as an obvious movement corridor from the northeast to the southwest.[3] The 32nd CRS would move around quite a bit, first covering a sector for the 83rd ID, then the 8th ID, and finally ending in group reserve by 7 December.[4]

The VIII Corps organization would continue to fluctuate as it traded fresh divisions to Major General Joseph Collins's VII Corps in exchange for battle-worn ones. The 8th ID exchanged positions with the exhausted 28th ID, and the 83rd ID changed out with the damaged 4th ID. These exchanges further weakened the corps position, as its eighty-eight miles of front were difficult enough to hold with three full infantry divisions, much less with only one full-strength one and two that had just sustained massive casualties.[5] Finally, on 11 December, the newly arrived 106th ID took over the 2nd ID's positions as that division prepared to move north to participate in the V Corps' offensive south of the Hürtgen Forest. The VIII Corps attached the full 14th MCG to the 106th ID to support this new division as it settled in. In real terms, this simply meant that the 32nd CRS returned to group control, while the 18th CRS continued to hold the same positions it had been in since mid-October. A single company of towed tank destroyers and a battalion of self-propelled artillery rounded out the cavalry's complement for its defense.[6]

As the corps defensive line stood in disarray, so too did its cavalry dispositions. The 14th MCG's position in the Losheim Gap consisted of eight strongpoints spread over a five-mile front.[7] None of the positions were mutually supporting, and there was a two-mile gap between the cavalry and the southern elements of the V Corps (the 99th ID) and a 1.5-mile gap between the 14th MCG and the 106th ID to the south. Moreover, the official history claims that although there were American minefields in the area, neither the 14th MCG nor the 2nd ID knew their locations.[8] This failure seems particularly unforgivable, as the 18th CRS had been in these positions for nearly two months by the time of the German offensive.

Compounding the cavalry's problems was the fact that one of the three reconnaissance troops of the 18th CRS had been pulled by the 106th ID to support one of its infantry regiments, leaving the squadron with only two reconnaissance troops, a tank company, a towed tank destroyer company, and an assault gun troop to patrol its large sector.[9] While Devine discussed using the 32nd CRS as a mobile reserve in his plans, apparently no thought had been given to using the 32nd to buttress the extremely weak original line. The cavalry did not expect a major attack in their sector, and thus they believed that the 18th CRS would be enough to delay and weaken a minor German attack, while the 32nd CRS could then use its mobility to move to, block, and destroy any penetration.[10]

Another curious problem in the deployment of the VIII Corps was the choice of defensive positions. The 106th ID held positions in the Schnee Eifel, a rugged piece of terrain that had served as part of the Siegfried Line and would be a hard position to take in a frontal assault. The Losheim Gap area, by contrast, should be considered a high-speed avenue of approach. So why was the lightest formation in the division defense across the most likely route into the division's or corps' rear? When the V Corps attacked this position in September, it had made some limited gains, with cavalry watching its flank near the Losheim area. Thus, when the 2nd ID took over from the V Corps, it had simply replaced infantry units with infantry units, and cavalry units with cavalry units, regardless of whether that made sense when viewed from a defensive perspective. When the 106th ID arrived, it simply followed suit. Additionally, cavalry covering the flank and connecting units made sense and had been a standard practice, so the dispositions remained.[11]

As is evident from the above description of the central Ardennes region, the American army had relegated it to a backwater status and did not pay too much attention to ensuring that a proper defensive line had been established. The constant rotation of units, the expectation that under-strength divisions could hold lines that would stretch full-strength formations, and the general lack of defensive planning all point to a sector that the entire army considered to be a very low priority. Some of this attitude reflected the general consensus of the American leadership from General Dwight D. Eisenhower to Middleton that, even in the unlikely event of a German offensive in this region, there simply was nothing worth defending until well past the Meuse River.[12]

When the German offensive began in the Ardennes on 16 December 1944, the 14th MCG found itself under attack by portions of the 6th Panzer Army in the north (3rd Fallschirmjäger Division) and the 5th Panzer Army in the south (major elements of the 18th Volksgrenadier Division).[13] Due to the scattered nature of the 18th CRS's defenses, the Germans penetrated the group zone from the start, surrounding large elements of the squadron and bypassing others. Some portions of the cavalry gave a good accounting of themselves, with a reinforced platoon in the town of Krewinkel, two miles south of Losheim, holding off perhaps the better part of a German battalion for a couple of hours.[14] However, numbers can matter, and the disjointed and heavily outmanned cavalry simply could not hold.

Colonel Devine committed the 32nd CRS in the morning of the 16th but quickly realized that he had no hope of rescuing any of his forward units. Therefore, at 1100 he ordered the 32nd CRS to establish a defensive line two miles behind the group's original front in order to cover the withdrawal of the 18th CRS. The displacement of this squadron proved particularly hazardous, with Troop A of the 18th CRS being completely surrounded. The troop destroyed or abandoned its heavy equipment and dispersed as small groups, attempting to escape and return to friendly lines. By the evening of 16 December, around 21 percent of the troop had rejoined the 14th MCG.[15] The group continued to fall back, ending the first day of the Battle of the Bulge along a three-mile line about two miles behind their secondary line.[16] However, this line proved not only temporary but also irrelevant, as the Germans had already blasted a hole between the cavalry and its adjacent units on either side. Thus, the 14th MCG had already failed in its mission to protect the boundary between the V and VIII Corps.

As the Germans continued the attack through the night and into 17 December, the 14th MCG continued to retreat, establishing a new line approximately 4.5 miles to the west of its positions the previous night and three miles northeast of Saint Vith. The withdrawal had been costly. Troop A of the 32nd CRS had been surrounded at Honsfeld and forced to disperse in an attempt to escape after destroying or abandoning its heavy equipment. One officer and forty-three enlisted men reported back to the group headquarters.[17] Troop B of the 32nd CRS, after being pushed back initially by strong German forces, managed to fight an isolated delaying action that held on for two hours prior to being ordered back.[18] However, once the 14th MCG ensconced itself in its new positions, it was generally out of contact with German forces and in a position to help protect the key town of Saint Vith.

By 1530 of 17 December, Colonel Devine ordered the remnants of the 14th MCG back to a line five miles northwest of Saint Vith. Traffic and confusion led to the group not arriving at its destination until late that night. Additionally, at 1830, the group commander's element engaged part of a German armored column two miles northeast of the assembly area in a fight that destroyed both American jeeps, although all personnel survived and escaped. Unfortunately, the strain of seeing his formation shredded and the trauma of this near-death experience proved too much for Devine. At 2300 he turned over command to the commander of the 18th CRS and collapsed. Devine was evacuated as a non-battle casualty the next day.[19]

As the remnants of the 14th MCG attempted to regain order and the new commander tried to assert control over the disordered mass, Middleton ordered the cavalry back to its positions northeast of Saint Vith. At 0220 on 18 December, the group executive officer, Lieutenant Colonel Augustine D. Dugan, finally made it back to the command near Poteau after escaping from the same ambush that had shaken Colonel Devine. He divided the remains of the group into two task forces and took the larger of the two in an attempt to follow Middleton's orders. This task force encountered a significant German force and was driven back seven miles northwest of Saint Vith. By the afternoon on 18 December, the commander of the VIII Corps relieved Dugan from command and ordered the 14th MCG attached to the 7th AD, then defending the Saint Vith salient. The remnants of the 14th MCG were organized into a provisional squadron that was then parceled out to various points of the Saint Vith defense. On 30 December, the group regained control of its disparate elements near Oneux, Belgium (eleven miles south of Liege), and began to rebuild. Over the course of fourteen days in combat the group lost 20 percent of its officers, 33 percent of its enlisted strength, and 53 percent of its vehicles.[20]

The 14th MCG had failed in its mission of protecting the flank of the 106th ID. After the collapse of the 14th MCG, two regiments of the 18th Volksgrenadier Division penetrated the cavalry's zone and then turned southwest behind the 106th ID's defensive positions. Another regiment of the 18th penetrated the weakly held boundary between the 106th ID's southern and middle regiments. The result was a double envelopment of the northern two regiments of this green American division. This action would lead to the largest mass surrender of U.S. troops since the Civil War. Half of that envelopment, and the stronger half at that, had come through the 14th MCG's sector. Additionally, the army official history of the campaign notes that the only portion of the 106th ID front that saw a massive force imbalance was in the cavalry's sector.[21] The cavalry's preparation against a massive attack left much to be desired, but then that had not been the thought behind the disposition of the entire corps. If it had, the corps would have been deployed in much greater depth, with stronger forces supporting the cavalry, perhaps allowing the 14th MCG to repeat the feats of the 2nd and 106th MCGs, who had succeeded in similar circumstances. Therefore, perhaps the 14th MCG could not have succeeded regardless of it actions.

Perhaps the most questionable action of the cavalry was its withdrawal on 17 December from the Born position to Poteau, when it was out of contact and actually in fairly decent positions. Most likely the shock of seeing the 18th CRS essentially destroyed and the 32nd CRS heavily buffeted had unnerved Colonel Devine to the point where his confidence had been thoroughly shaken. His actions later that night would certainly support this hypothesis.

While the German offensive shredded the 14th MCG and the rest of the VIII Corps, the New Jersey cavalrymen of the 102nd MCG and the V Corps fought their own desperate battles over what would become the northern shoulder of the Bulge. As noted earlier, the V Corps was engaged in an offensive toward the Roer River dams with the 2nd, 99th, and 78th IDs in the middle of December. The 8th ID held the extreme north of the line, tying in with the VII Corps still fighting to the east of Aachen. The 102nd MCG held the center of the corps line from Lammersdorf to Monschau, with the 99th ID holding the south, tying in with the VIII Corps and the 14th MCG. The 78th ID attacked in the north of the 102nd MCG's sector, screening the 102nd CRS from any further contact. The 2nd and 99th IDs advanced in the south, with the 2nd attacking through the center of the 99th ID's sector, with one 99th ID regiment (395th Infantry) to the north (and tied into the 102nd MCG) and the other two regiments to the south.[22]

The German plan of attack for the V Corps sector involved a penetration of the southern end of the 99th ID's sector and the 14th MCG's zone along the natural avenue of advance through the Losheim Gap with elements of the 277th and 12th Volksgrenadier Divisions, as well as the 3rd Fallschirmjäger Division, all belonging to the 1st SS Panzer Corps. The intent of this corps was to advance to and cross the Meuse, with the ultimate objective of Antwerp. The German LXVII Corps to the north would support the attack of the 1st SS by attacking through Monschau and seizing the Eupen–Malmedy road. This attack would protect the northern flank of the 1st SS Panzer Corps, block any movement of American reinforcements south toward the German penetration, and isolate the 2nd and 99th ID's (see map 11).[23]

The 38th CRS occupied a curving front of nearly six miles from just east of Konzen (two miles north of Monschau) south along the Mützenich Ridge (northwest of Monschau), through the town, and linking up with 3rd Battalion of the 395th Infantry (3/395th) (part of the 99th ID) that held the town of Höfen. Of note, the cavalry's sector was nearly twelve times longer than that held by the larger but significantly less mobile infantry battalion.[24] The cavalry were also supported by a platoon of tank destroyers, a reinforced company of engineers, and a group of three artillery battalions (one 105mm and two 155mm).[25]

On 16 December the initial German attacks on the Monschau–Höfen area came from four battalions of the 326th Volksgrenadier Division, heavily supported by artillery.[26] This division, while certainly not counted among the elite German formations, could be considered to be of average quality for the period. Thus, the cavalry and their brethren in the infantry were fighting solid troops and not simply the "old men and boys" that permeates American thinking about Volksgrenadier divisions. In point of fact, the Volksgrenadier divisions were mostly rebuilt formations with veterans at their core, while the Volksturm were primarily filled with "old men and boys." The similarity in terms has often led to their conflation in popular history.

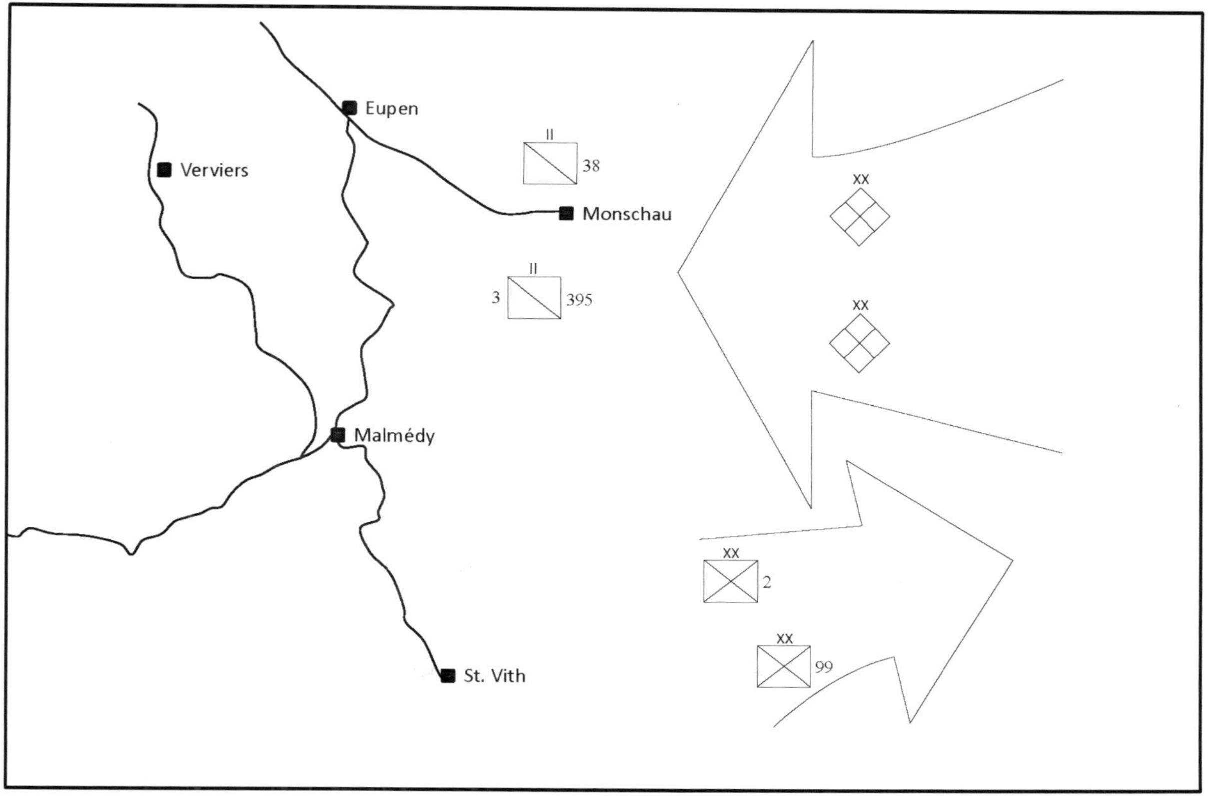

Map 11. Cavalry and Infantry Hold the Shoulder, 16 December.

Both the 38th CRS and the 3/395th held firm in their positions, inflicting casualties equal to approximately 20 percent of the committed German formations.[27] The Germans continued their attacks on 17 December, launching eight different assaults, from platoon to company strength, against the 38th CRS. The fighting often grew desperate, with the Germans effecting a company-size penetration of the cavalry's line at one point during the day. The cavalry (reinforced by their attached engineers) and dramatic artillery support blocked and then destroyed the penetration. By the end of the day, the 38th CRS counted eighty-eight German bodies inside their lines, with another eighteen men captured.[28] A final attack on 18 December against the 3/395th Infantry failed after a brutal fight. After this last repulse, the Germans would not conduct another major attempt to seize this region for the rest of the offensive.[29]

The successful defense by the cavalry and infantry in this sector from 16 to 18 December ensured that the 326th Volksgrenadier Division would fail to cut or even threaten the communication lines of the 99th and 2nd IDs. The importance of the cavalry and 3/395th's stand cannot be overstated. The 99th and 2nd IDs would slow and eventually halt the German Sixth Panzer Army in a series of desperate and bloody battles around Rocherath, Krinkelt, and Bülingen. These divisions were then reinforced by the 1st and 30th IDs, who aided in solidifying the northern shoulder of the Bulge. These divisions could not have arrived in time if the Monschau–Höfen position had fallen, allowing the Germans to block the vital routes south.[30] Moreover, if the 326th Volksgrenadier Division had been successful, the 99th and 2nd IDs could have been isolated and either forced into headlong retreat or surrender. Therefore, although the 38th CRS saw little fighting in the Bulge after 18 December, it is not an exaggeration to argue that its actions directly contributed to the success of the V Corps' vital defense of the northern shoulder. The cavalry also allowed the corps to concentrate combat power where it was most needed without having to commit valuable infantry formations to hold its flanks.[31]

Fighting to protect the corps' flank during a defense is a textbook example of a security mission. The example of the 38th CRS is also yet another demonstration of how security missions can look just like regular combat missions. The difference, as always, lies in the intent behind the mission.

While the 14th and 102nd MCGs participated in the desperate fighting at the beginning of the Battle of the Bulge, to the north the 4th MCG, now commanded by Colonel John McDonald, continued its contributions to the VII Corps' assault to the Roer River. The group had spent the middle of December protecting the flank of the 5th AD as it attacked to the east past Aachen. After the bulk of the division, and the VII Corps in general, had reached the Roer River, a small pocket of German resistance west of the river remained in a roughly one-square-mile area centered on a trio of towns three miles northeast of Hürtgen. American intelligence reported it as approximately a battalion from the German 6th Fallschirmjäger Regiment. This pocket would have to be destroyed in order to prevent it from interfering with the 5th AD's or VII Corps' preparations for operations across the Roer. The division tasked its CCB, reinforced with the 4th MCG, to destroy this pocket. The Americans would be attacking from the north and west against this position. The 4th MCG would seize the two easternmost towns, while the 2nd Battalion of the 334th Infantry Regiment attacked the westernmost one.[32]

The 4th CRS attacked on 20 December. After some initial success penetrating the German defenses, the attack bogged down into a vicious fight as the cavalrymen fought to destroy the last German strongpoints in the first objective town. The squadron would emerge victorious, but not before four troop commanders and three troop executive officers became casualties.[33] Additionally, the squadron lost about 25 percent of the enlisted strength of its three reconnaissance troops in the fighting.[34] The 24th CRS continued the attack on 21 December, seizing a key ridge that dominated the sector with assistance from the neighboring 121st Infantry Regiment. The cavalry pressed their attack, with Troop C seizing a trench line just north of the final town in the pocket in a bayonet charge. The 4th MCG consolidated its positions that night in preparation for a final assault the next morning.[35]

This short battle demonstrated the cavalry's ability to fight as an economy of force, destroying a German stronghold without requiring a large commitment from the corps' infantry divisions. These divisions could then take that time to prepare for future combat operations, upping the chances for their success. This fight is also an example of a flank security mission, as the cavalry removed a threat to the corps' main body that could have caused problems for future operations.

Before the 4th MCG could finish their mission along the Roer, Collins pulled the group out of the line in preparation for a move south to help contain the growing crisis in Belgium. The VII Corps had already donated a couple of divisions to the hard-pressed V Corps, and now General Omar Bradley of the First Army had ordered the VII Corps headquarters with its corps troops to the south to assist in the battle. Major General Charles Corlett's XIX Corps assumed responsibility for the VII Corps sector, as well as some of its divisions.[36] Collins took charge of a forty-mile sector west of the XVIII Airborne Corps, which was itself holding a line west of the battered V Corps. The British XXX Corps would be to the right (west) of the VII Corps.[37]

Collins ordered his cavalry south to join the 2nd AD, already en route to the growing northern shoulder of the Bulge. He needed to gain information as to what was going on in the new corps sector as well as determine the best places to defend and potentially strike back. The cavalry along with the armored division possessed the requisite speed to quickly arrive and accomplish these missions.

The 4th MCG assembled its forces behind friendly lines by midday on 22 December and moved over eighty miles, arriving around Haversin, Belgium (twenty miles southeast of Namur), at 0330 on 23 December. The 4th CRS almost immediately made contact with a combined arms German column of eight tanks and a company of infantry, attacking from the southwest. The Germans defeated the initial cavalry screen consisting of attached tank destroyers, and it took a concerted squadron effort to finally defeat this force by early afternoon on 23 December.[38] This fight, desperate as it was, allowed the cavalry to achieve at least part of their mission. They had found the enemy (or the enemy had found them) and had established a baseline from which the corps could operate.

The next two days would be a whirlwind of orders, rescinded orders, and changes of mission as the VII Corps attempted to grasp the chaotic situation on the northern flank of the Bulge. Finally, the VII Corps attached the 4th MCG to the 2nd AD, as that division was attacking south through the same zone as the cavalry. The division ordered McDonald's 4th MCG to seize and hold the town of Humain (four miles southeast of Haversin). This attack would cut the main supply route for the 2nd Panzer Division then attacking through the area to the west.[39] The group assigned the mission to Troop A of the 4th CRS, reinforced with a platoon of tank destroyers. The troop seized the town early on Christmas morning, but was driven out by a company of infantry supported by three Panther tanks at 0700.[40]

McDonald reinforced the 4th CRS with elements from the 24th CRS as well as portions of the 759th Light Tank Battalion. The reinforced task force again assaulted Humain at midday, and although it managed to gain a small foothold in the town, it was forced to withdraw under heavy fire shortly thereafter. The 2nd AD then sent further reinforcements in the form of a reinforced composite company of tanks from the 66th and 67th Armor Regiments and a platoon of 90mm tank destroyers from the 702nd TD Battalion. This attack, launched at 1600, was also halted and forced to withdraw. That night, as the cavalry were preparing for yet another attempt, the commander of the 2nd AD ordered a halt to the operation.[41] The 24th CRS then settled into a screening mission of Humain that would last until 27 December. The cavalry maintained observation over the town, conducted harassment fires, and laid minefields to prevent a German attack out of the town. On 27 December, the CCB of the 2nd AD moved to take the town, assisted by the 24th CRS, but the VII Corps ordered the division to hand off responsibility for the town to the 84th ID.[42]

The fighting at Humain highlighted the problems of an economy of force operation. The 2nd AD had committed what it considered to be just enough force to isolate the 2nd Panzer Division. Unfortunately for the 4th MCG, the Germans proved remarkably sensitive to an attack at Humain and committed more force than the Americans to the fight there. Thus, what should have been a merely supporting attack for the 2nd AD quickly developed into a much larger operation. This kind of thing happens often in confused meeting engagements, much like what was occurring in central Belgium during late December. Just as in the story of the 14th MCG, economy of force only works when the enemy does not decide to make that sector its primary effort.

While the cavalry did not have the combat power to reduce the town by itself, neither did the substantial reinforcements from the

CCB. Thus, while the 4th MCG's efforts to clear Humain can be considered a failure, it should be seen in the light of a tough action against an enemy force that proved difficult for much larger forces to overcome. From a positive light, the attack at Humain certainly diverted some German resources north from their attack to the west, thereby achieving at least a portion of the VII Corps' intent. In fact, while the cavalry fought to cut the German's lines of communication, the bulk of the 2nd AD met the 2nd Panzer Division in open battle to the west, dealing that formation a major blow.[43] Though the cavalry did not play a direct role in this victory, it certainly helped by splitting German attention.

While the 24th CRS fought desperately at Humain, the 4th CRS conducted reconnaissance to the corps' right flank, gaining contact with the British XXX Corps and helping to stitch together the ad hoc line that was in the process of forming. After the 24th CRS was relieved of its duties around Humain, it joined the 4th CRS in a screen that stretched from the Meuse River to the east for eighteen miles, in front of the 2nd AD, allowing the division to regroup and prepare for future operations. As the line stabilized, the 2nd AD withdrew into assembly areas, along with the 4th MCG, which reverted to corps control.[44]

As the New Year began, the First Army opened its offensive to close the Bulge. The army's main effort would be conducted by the VII Corps, attacking with the 2nd and 3rd ADs in front, followed by the 83rd and 84th IDs.[45] The British XXX Corps attacked alongside the corps to its west, while the XVIII Airborne Corps attacked to the east. Collins's VII Corps would be separated from the XXX Corps by the Ourthe River. The corps attached the 4th MCG to Task Force Church, a part of the 84th ID. This task force was to closely follow the 2nd AD, destroy any pockets of resistance the armor bypassed, and ease the passage of the rest of the 84th ID. The cavalry's mission would be to protect the corps' right flank along the Ourthe River.[46]

The cavalry began moving on 3 January, following the 2nd AD as it attacked to the south. It screened the line of the Ourthe River, established roadblocks, and conducted route reconnaissance for the advancing elements of the 84th ID. The flank screening mission was particularly vital, as the XXX Corps was not necessarily advancing at the same rate as the VII Corps. Therefore, the cavalry were needed in order to prevent German elements to the west from infiltrating between the 2nd AD and 84th ID. The 84th ID dissolved Task Force Church on 7 January, leaving the flank protection mission solely to the 4th MCG. However, the division reinforced the cavalry with a battalion of infantry. The 4th MCG continued its role of flank protection, assuming the role of command and control of the entire flank of the 84th ID.[47]

On 10 January, the 2nd and 3rd ADs halted their advance in order to allow the 84th and 83rd IDs to pass through and continue the attack. The presence of the 4th MCG connecting the forward positions of the 84th ID and 2nd AD helped ease this transition in the west.[48] By this point, the front line had advanced to within about fourteen miles north of Bastogne. The 84th ID took the 4th MCG's attached infantry battalion away on 11 January 1945 and ordered the cavalry to conduct a supporting attack along the Ourthe River (the division's western flank) as the infantry regiments attacked to the south. The 4th MCG attacked on 12 January, seizing two towns along the Ourthe. The 24th CRS also attacked and took another town that would dominate the flank of the 84th ID's attack. This fight, against an estimated battalion of German infantry, proved difficult, but the cavalry eventually succeeded, inflicting forty dead and taking thirty-three prisoners.[49]

Unfortunately for the 4th MCG, the 84th ID had altered its scheme of maneuver, and the attack that the cavalry were supposed to have been supporting never happened. Thus, the Germans were able to shift combat power against the 24th CRS, driving them north out of the town. On 13 January the infantry division initiated its attack, originally slated for the previous day. The cavalry continued their advance, meeting only light resistance as they continued to keep contact between the division and the Ourthe River. On 14 January, Troop A of the 24th CRS made contact with leading elements of the 17th Airborne Division, marking the juncture of the First and Third Armies. By 15 January, the closure of Third Army's VIII Corps and the British XXX Corps from the west made the cavalry's mission redundant, and the VII Corps returned the 4th MCG to corps control and pulled the group off the line.[50]

The 4th MCG would be recommitted to the VII Corps line on 17 January in the sector of the 3rd AD. The group screened a portion of the division's front, preventing German movement in their area. The cavalry continued this mission until their sector was closed out of the line by the advance of friendly formations on 22 January, whereupon it was withdrawn from the line yet again. The group then spent the rest of the month refitting from its exertions around the town of Andenne, Belgium, nine miles east of Namur.[51]

The actions of the 4th MCG during the advance of the VII Corps in January were highly typical of American cavalry. The group protected the flank of the corps, both in a screening role (along the Ourthe River) and in direct action against German forces that threatened the main body's advance. These missions were necessary, but the commitment of the forces required to accomplish them from the main line divisions of the corps would have dramatically weakened the efforts of the VII Corps as it fought south through the dense Ardennes region.

The corps cavalry of the First Army proved to have a dramatic impact, both positive and negative, on the First Army during the Battle of the Bulge. While the 14th MCG participated in one of the largest disasters the U.S. Army would experience in the Second World War, the 102nd MCG's actions—more specifically, those of the 38th CRS—prevented a bad situation from getting worse. Both of these actions highlight the importance of security operations. The disaster that consumed the 14th MCG and the 106th ID is a great example of how a failed screen can lead to catastrophic consequences. On the other hand, the success of the 102nd MCG proved that a successful security operation can set the stage for even more successes later in a battle.

The First Army's cavalry also demonstrated their worth in the rapid response to the German offensive. The 4th MCG had the mobility to quickly pull out of one battle, move across Belgium, and enter the fight in time to help stem the German tide. The confusion that invariably accompanies an enemy penetration needs to be sorted prior to an army implementing effective countermoves. The reconnaissance provided by the 4th MCG aided in this effort. No other unit in the American army had the ability to get to the battlefield so quickly and also possessed the training and equipment to gather the information that commanders needed to bring order out of chaos.

Third Army

While the First Army absorbed the German offensive into the Ardennes, the Third Army would emerge as the principle striking arm for the initial Allied response on the southern shoulder of the Bulge. The actions of the Third Army in mid-December would highlight the flexibility and mobility of the U.S. Army in 1944. In fact, if his advance had not already made him a household name, Patton's attack north to relieve Bastogne would have done so, considering the breathtaking speed with which he adjusted his army's direction of attack and how quickly it moved in the new direction. This advance has long enthralled historians and military practitioners alike.[52] The army's corps cavalry groups played an integral part in Patton's ability to adjust so quickly and decisively.

In the middle of December, the Third Army possessed three corps: the XX, XII, and III. Major General Walton Walker's XX Corps held the northern portion of the army line. Its left flank rested on the Moselle River, eleven miles east of Luxembourg City. The corps' front then ran southeast to a point south of Saarlautern (modern-day Saarlouis). Colonel Polk's 3rd MCG anchored the corps' left flank, holding approximately thirteen miles of front. This allowed the three infantry divisions of the corps—the 90th, 5th, and 95th—to concentrate on the Siegfried Line across the Moselle. The corps also possessed a small bridgehead across the Saar around Saarlautern. Major General Manton Eddy's XII Corps retained responsibility for the southern half of the army zone. The corps line stretched in a concave arc from its boundary with the XX Corps to a point along the Saar River east of Sarreguemines. Colonel Reed's 2nd MCG anchored the corps' right flank, while Colonel Fickett's 6th MCG held a divisional frontage on the left. In between, the 6th AD, 35th ID, and 87th ID made slow progress against the Siegfried Line. Major General John Millikin's III Corps, newly arrived in the Third Army's area, supervised the reduction of Metz.

On 16 December, the 28th CRS returned to the 6th MCG in the center of the army line. This same day, the Third Army began a massive restructuring of its front line. The III Corps, which had just finished operations around Metz, received a place in the army line between the XX and XII Corps. This meant that Task Force (TF) Fickett would move from the XX Corps to the III Corps.[53] However, on 19 December, the III Corps was alerted for a move north to participate in the developing counteroffensive as part of the Battle of the Bulge. As the Third Army's initial plans left the 6th MCG in place on the Saar River, the cavalry moved under the command of the XII Corps on that day. However, the next day the XII Corps was also pulled to the north as part of the army counteroffensive, leaving TF Fickett with the XX Corps.[54] In a period of five days the cavalry had changed higher headquarters three times without moving an inch, a true demonstration of the modularity inherent in the army during the Second World War.

On 22 December, on the far right of the army line, elements of the 44th ID relieved the 2nd MCG and the group moved to join the XII Corps as it participated in the counterattack into the southern flank of the Germans then besieging Bastogne.[55] The XII Corps assigned the 2nd MCG the important missions of maintaining the eastern flank of the corps along the Moselle River as it assaulted north and of maintaining contact with the XX Corps. However, because Eddy realized that the cavalry did not have enough organic combat power to fully hold the flank against a determined assault, the group was heavily reinforced. Task Force (TF) Reed, as the 2nd MCG came to be called during this time, consisted of the 2nd and 42nd Squadrons, a tank destroyer battalion, two general support engineer regiments, and a battalion of 105mm artillery.[56] Furthermore, two additional battalions of artillery were in direct support of TF Reed.[57]

On 23 December 1944, the 2nd MCG and its attachments relieved a regiment-size formation of the 4th ID and assumed its positions along the Moselle, a frontage that would eventually stretch over twenty-five miles north from its anchor at Thionville as the Dragoons extended their front as the corps advanced. This area of responsibility was over four times the size of any of the infantry divisions (4th, 5th, 80th) of the XII Corps attacking north (see map 12).[58]

The cavalry's ability to cover so much ground allowed the XII Corps to mass its combat power in the drive against the southern shoulder of the Bulge. The highly mobile nature of the cavalry, especially in comparison to the generally dismounted infantry, allowed the group to cover this ground more effectively than could a similarly sized infantry formation. Without the presence of such a unit as the 2nd MCG, the

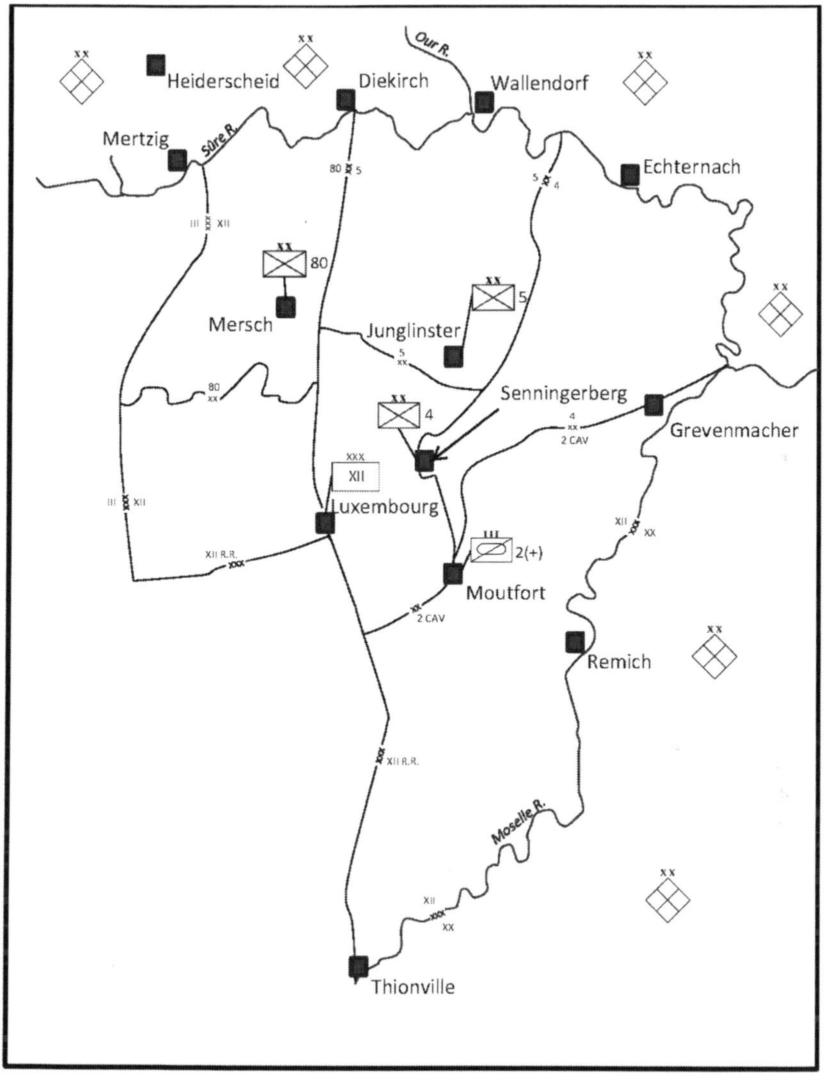

Map 12. 2nd MCG Holding the XII Corps' Flank.

corps commander would have been forced to detail more troops to protect the flank in order to achieve the same degree of protection offered by TF Reed. Moreover, that infantry was put to much better use in the heavy fighting to the north for which the lightly protected and numerically inferior cavalrymen were unsuited.

On Christmas Eve 1944, the 106th MCG of the XV Corps, Seventh Army, assumed responsibility for TF Fickett's zone as part of a general readjustment of boundaries in the Saar in order to better allow the XX Corps to maintain its front. The Seventh Army was shifting west to cover more of the Third Army's line as that army reoriented two of its three corps north against the threat of the Bulge. Patton decided that the XX Corps did not need two cavalry groups (the other being the 3rd MCG) and that the need for cavalry was greater along the southern shoulder of the Bulge, although the 5th Ranger Battalion was to stay with the XX Corps and not follow the 6th MCG north. Thus, the cavalrymen were once again attached to the III Corps, which was in the process of beginning its attack into the German southern flank.

The assault by the III Corps would give the Third Army two corps holding the southern flank of the Bulge. Eddy's XII Corps on the right would hold the shoulder, with its right flank anchored along the Moselle and protected by TF Reed. Millikin's III Corps would constitute the army striking arm, aimed for Bastogne and the beleaguered 101st Airborne Division. The battered VIII Corps would soon fall under the purview of the Third Army and hold the army left and the tip of the German penetration, but the newly arrived formations that would constitute this corps were still moving into position and would not be ready for action for several days.

The 6th MCG pulled into an assembly area in the vicinity of Arlon late in the day on 24 December. Colonel Fickett was given two separate missions in support of the 4th AD. The III Corps attached the 6th CRS (reinforced) directly to the 4th AD with the mission of maintaining contact with the 26th ID to the division's east (right). The rest of the task force was ordered to screen the western flank (left) of the 4th AD in the Neufchâteau region, which was essentially in the air, as there were only fragments of the wrecked 28th ID in the area, facing elements of the German 130th Panzer Lehr Division (see map 13).[59]

On Christmas Day the 6th MCG moved into the attack. The presence of the 6th CRS on the 4th AD's right allowed the 26th ID to focus their efforts on a concentrated attack rather than attempting to keep pace with the rapidly moving armor. This relief of the 26th ID proved especially important, as that division had a long, hard fight as it attempted to force its way across the Sûre River.[60] Additionally,

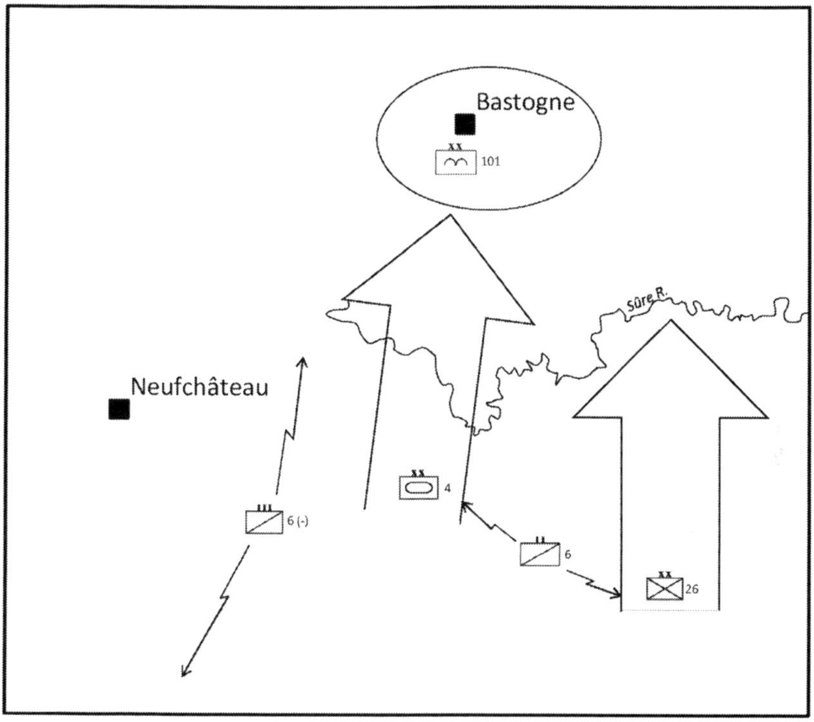

Map 13. Protecting the 4th AD's Drive to Bastogne.

Combat Command Reserve (CCR), 4th AD, was relieved of that area as well, allowing it to lend weight on the division's left near Neufchâteau, where the III Corps' after action report stated "the situation of the 101st Airborne was reported as critical." Moreover, the protection offered by the remainder of the 6th MCG allowed the 4th AD to mass its efforts in an all-out drive to relieve Bastogne, which it reached on 26 December.[61]

On 28 December, the 6th CRS returned to group control as it continued to protect the western flank of the 4th AD and III Corps, as well as reconnoitering the German dispositions in the area and attacking enemy outposts if possible. The cavalrymen were relieved of their front on 30 December by the 87th ID and the 11th AD of the VIII Corps as they attacked into the German positions. Some of these attacks made good initial headway, thanks in part to the cavalry's aggressive actions having stripped the Germans of much of their security zone.[62] Following the attack of the VIII Corps, the 6th MCG moved behind the corps line and into reserve.

The 6th MCG's actions during the III Corps' relief of Bastogne are highly typical of traditional American cavalry operations, although they did not match the newer doctrine established after 1942 for mechanized cavalry. Protecting open flanks and maintaining communications between scattered units were long part of horse cavalry doctrine and practiced often. By their actions, the troopers of the 6th MCG contributed immeasurably to the success of the 4th AD in relieving the 101st Airborne Division. Furthermore, they also conducted a true reconnaissance mission along the flank of the corps, and their efforts aided a subsequent attack by two full divisions.

South of the fighting to relieve Bastogne, TF Reed spent the latter half of December and the beginning of January still in position along the Moselle River guarding the flank of the XII Corps. The period was characterized by active patrolling and small attacks to gain key ground. One such attack involved the use of Troop C of the 2nd CRS to seize the small town of Machtum, held by German forces amounting to an under-strength platoon. The attack proved highly successful; only three cavalrymen were wounded in the entire affair, while they killed nine Germans and captured fourteen.[63] However, the town was very small, mostly consisting of a single street that was a third of a mile long.[64] Additionally, the troopers were heavily supported by artillery and attacked with better than a 3:1 ratio of troops. While taking nothing away from the bravery and skill of the cavalrymen of C troop, the attack on Machtum serves to highlight the limitations of the mechanized cavalry in direct combat.

After the relief of Bastogne on 26 December, the Third Army continued its efforts to destroy the German forces in the Bulge. Eddy's XII Corps held the southern shoulder and faced a dramatic obstacle to its front in the form of the Sauer River. Millikin's III Corps remained the main striking arm of the Third Army as it attacked in the center, to the east of Bastogne. The VIII Corps attacked on the army left, pushing on the Bulge from the front and driving German forces east.[65]

By the beginning of January, the III Corps had experienced success to the northeast of Bastogne, but German forces around the town of Harlange, southeast of Bastogne, still stymied any American advance.

This resistance created a salient bulging to the east of Bastogne, splitting the formations of the III Corps. On 2 January, the corps attached the 28th CRS of the 6th MCG to the 35th ID to aid in holding a sector facing the developing Harlange Pocket, allowing that division to concentrate a precious infantry battalion at the main effort to the north. The 6th CRS remained in reserve, patrolling between the 26th and 35th IDs, providing rear area security for both divisions, and allowing maximum combat power to be provided forward. On 9 January, the 6th MCG (with the 28th CRS back under its control) took a portion of the front on the southwest corner of the Harlange Pocket between the 35th ID and 26th IDs as both divisions continued their attack north. Although not in their orders, the group attacked "when it became apparent . . . that the Germans had so organized the ground that it was impossible for the infantry on both flanks to advance."[66] The cavalry used their combined arms to neutralize numerous enemy positions, often substituting firepower for manpower.

The next day, the 6th MCG continued a deliberate assault against the German defenders of the pocket, seizing the towns of Harlange and Watrange, and then continuing the assault north to Sonlez, where they made contact with the 90th ID, closing the Harlange Pocket.[67] The assault to Sonlez was entirely at the discretion of the group commander, but this action effectively destroyed the German defenses around Harlange. The enemy in this region, though somewhat battered from a month of heavy fighting, had held against the 26th, 35th, and 90th IDs for over eleven days. Moreover, the cavalry seized eight 88mm guns, five Nebelwerfer rocket launchers, and three hundred German prisoners.[68] These numbers meant that the 6th MCG attacked an undersized regimental formation that was well entrenched and supported.[69] Thus, the cavalrymen almost certainly did not have the generally accepted ratio of 3:1 superiority in numbers prior to their attack, though their firepower helped somewhat. Additionally, the attack was conducted on a limited front, only a couple of miles wide. However, this frontage was standard for much larger infantry units and armor combat commands. For their actions in this battle the 6th MCG was awarded a Presidential Unit Citation, the highest honor that can be given to any American unit.[70] The fighting in the Harlange Pocket demonstrates the ability of the cavalry to succeed in direct combat under the right conditions.

Note that the 6th MCG was only reinforced with an additional company of engineers and a company of tank destroyers for this action, and thus did not have the luxury of the significant numbers of dismounted soldiers that an infantry unit possessed.

The destruction of the Harlange Pocket allowed the III Corps to shorten its line and consolidate in preparation for further offensive operations. The 90th and 35th IDs relieved the 6th MCG and then moved through and past the cavalry. From 13 to 18 January, the cavalry task force moved to corps reserve and refitted after their labors during the offensive. On 19 January the group received a battery of armored artillery and another company of tank destroyers from the III Corps in preparation for reentering the line. On 20 January, the 28th CRS (reinforced) relieved two regiments (the 101st and 104th) of the 26th ID, allowing them to be committed to the corps drive to the north and northeast. Once again, the cavalry were operating on a division frontage of approximately four miles. The following day saw the cavalry seize a bridgehead over the Wiltz River, seize the small town of Winseler, and then capture the larger town of Wiltz, two miles to the east, which was promptly taken over by the 80th ID of the XII Corps as it advanced from the south.[71]

On the eastern end of the Third Army line, Eddy attached four newly arrived battalions of combat engineers to the 2nd MCG to replace the two general support engineer regiments that were then working with the cavalry at the end of January.[72] This seemed to follow the new custom in the XII Corps of placing engineer units with the cavalry for training as infantry while aiding in protecting the corps' flank. This practice worked well for the 2nd MCG also, as it provided the group with large numbers of dismounted soldiers, a feature missing in its own table of organization and equipment. Finally, Eddy attached the headquarters of the 9th TD group (with no organic units of its own) to TF Reed in order to assist in command and control of the various elements of the task force.[73] This headquarters would serve as a third combat command headquarters for the cavalry (which had been limited to two battalion-level maneuver command posts), thereby increasing the flexibility of the organization.

To the south of the main battle area of the Bulge, the 3rd MCG held its positions, though the XX Corps reorganized after the loss of the 10th AD to the VIII Corps. The 90th ID was ordered out of its Saar River bridgehead, and TF Polk was attached to it. The contraction of the 90th ID's frontage allowed it to take some of the cavalry's responsibilities, shortening the group's line to a mere four miles of front.[74] For the rest of December the cavalry held their positions while conducting active patrolling to maintain current information on enemy positions and strengths in their front, as well as maintaining contact with their brethren in the 2nd MCG across the Moselle River. This action, while uneventful, proved incredibly helpful for the Third Army, as the cavalry covered enough ground to allow the XX Corps to stretch its already limited resources.

In the first part of January 1945, the XX Corps relieved TF Polk from the 90th ID and attached it to the 94th ID, in conjunction with those two divisions exchanging battle-space. As this change took place, the 94th ID moved the cavalry to a four-mile front on the eastern flank of the division, along the Saar River, as the division prepared for combat operations against the Saar–Moselle Triangle. As the infantry continued their attacks north, the 3rd MCG extended its front to ten miles, relieving 94th ID infantry regiments of the necessity of guarding the Saar River as they attacked to the north. The entire period was characterized by active patrolling and artillery exchanges, but little movement. At the end of the month the cavalry were returned to XX Corps control.[75]

Corps cavalry proved to be indispensable for the Third Army during the Battle of the Bulge. Patton used his groups in every conceivable manner. The 3rd MCG conducted economy of force defensive operations along the Saar, helping a reduced XX Corps hold most of the original army front. The 2nd MCG operated a huge security screen along the entire flank of the XII Corps, allowing that corps to focus its divisions on extremely narrow frontages without significant fear of a German attack into their flank. The 6th MCG provided reconnaissance and security to the III Corps, and then participated in a direct assault against the Harlange Pocket. These actions allowed for the rapid relief of Bastogne, as well as directly contributing to the defeat of the German forces on the southern shoulder of the Bulge.

Every single corps operation conducted by the Third Army relied extensively on cavalry support. Therefore, the cavalry ensured the success of this army in one of its most crucial battles. In fact, the legend of the Third Army's 90 degree pivot and attack into the Bulge would not have happened without the presence of corps cavalry. Therefore, in this particular case, Patton's cavalry not only impacted his army's success, but also played a significant role in the overall army group and theater victory in this campaign.

Ninth Army

The Battle of the Bulge struck just as the Ninth Army was concluding its offensive to the Roer River. The army's two corps, the XIX Corps on the right, just north of Aachen, and the XIII Corps on the left, and to the north, were in the process of recovering from the brutal fighting of late November and early December. Cavalry anchored the XIII Corps line on both flanks, with Colonel Biddle's 113th MCG Redhorse holding the extreme left, while Colonel A. A. Frierson's 11th MCG Blackhorse reinforced the right. The 17th CRS of the 15th MCG reinforced the right flank of the XIX Corps, helping the 30th ID maintain contact with the VII Corps of the First Army to the south.

When the German offensive began on 16 December, the Ninth Army's offensive operations ceased almost entirely, with the army becoming a force provider to the First Army as that formation struggled to contain the growing threat. From 17 to 20 December, the Ninth Army relinquished control of the 7th and 2nd ADs, as well as the 30th, 84th, and 75th IDs. On 26 December, the army lost three more divisions, the 5th AD, the 83rd ID, and the British 51st Highland Division, to the fight around the Bulge. Additionally, the army assumed control of the First Army's VII Corps sector, stretching its line to an astounding forty miles. Complicating matters, the army now had a grand total of only five divisions to hold this front—the 78th, 8th, and 104th IDs in the XIX Corps, and the 102nd and 29th IDs in the XIII Corps.[76] Put another way, each division had to maintain eight miles of front, compared to the typical three to five miles to which they were accustomed. Due to these massive personnel losses, the Ninth Army assumed the defensive until the German offensive could be subdued. Aiding the army were its two cavalry groups plus the 17th CRS. Another help was the flooded Roer River that flowed across the majority of the Ninth Army front, protecting both sides from sudden thrusts.[77]

The cavalry of the Ninth Army initially held their positions, although this changed as demands on the army grew. The 11th MCG soon found itself holding the entire old frontage of the 102nd ID, as that division's line doubled in length.[78] Just before Christmas 1944, the XIX Corps' 113th CRS (part of the 113th MCG) assumed a regimental sector of the 8th ID along the Roer while the Ninth Army ordered the 125th CRS (the other squadron of the group) under army control for special missions. This disposition allowed the 8th ID commander to concentrate his infantry in the rugged terrain south of this relatively open stretch, where more troops were required to maintain a consistent front.[79] The cavalry, with their mobility and firepower, could cover the open ground more effectively. Of course, this risk was the same as that taken at Losheim by the 106th ID and 14th MCG, but those formations did not have a fairly imposing river guarding their front.

For the balance of December and early January, the Ninth Army, including its cavalry, conducted a series of patrols along the front in order to gain intelligence, prepare for future combat operations, and keep the Germans off balance. The 11th MCG participated in an elaborate deception operation meant to convince the Germans that the American forces in the area were substantially stronger than in actuality.[80] Although the group history records this operation in great detail, the actual utility of it is fairly questionable. The German military had committed all its strength to its twin offensives in the Ardennes and Vosges. Thus, though the threat of a major German offensive may have played at the minds of the Ninth Army, the reality was that there was no strength left to conduct such a strike. While the deception operation may have convinced the local German forces, it is doubtful that they rearranged their already stretched force structure to deal with this perceived threat.

On 13 January, Major General Alvan C. Gillem Jr. of the XIII Corps attached the lone 17th CRS to the 11th MCG, giving the group a strength of three cavalry squadrons. On 26 January, the 102nd ID conducted a limited attack to bring the Americans to the Roer. This operation supported a British attack to the north that was slowly clearing German forces west of the Roer.[81] The 11th MCG aided in this attack by seizing two objectives and protecting the flank of the main infantry attack to the south. The Blackhorse succeeded in their mission, assisting in the overall success of this minor assault.[82] The 11th MCG would continue to hold their lines until pulled into the XIII Corps reserve on 2 February.[83]

The 113th MCG spent January bifurcated, with one of its squadrons, the 125th CRS, detached for duty with the Ninth Army. Simpson was concerned about German parachute infiltration of the army rear area and had detailed the 125th CRS to use its mobility to conduct roving patrols behind the lines to hunt down and destroy these suspected saboteurs. Although the cavalry seemed to view these operations as little more than "make-work," the intent behind them was serious. The discovery of German infiltrators, speaking English and wearing U.S. uniforms, in the early stages of the Battle of the Bulge had badly spooked the American high command. The cavalry were perfectly equipped to handle the task, and such a mission fit with long-established patterns of use for cavalry.[84]

Although the Ninth Army did not make any major advances from mid-December to the end of January, it played an important role during this time. It provided the strength needed to contain and then defeat the German penetration. Moreover, it also maintained and actually improved upon the American positions in the Aachen region. The 11th and 113th MCGs played a key role in the army's efforts by helping to cover the thinly stretched front in economy of force operations. They also conducted security operations, protecting the limited attacks that were conducted by the army, and contributed to the rear echelon's piece of mind by patrolling against the threat of German infiltrators.

Seventh Army

As the crisis in the Ardennes continued to grow, the Third Army required more strength along the southern shoulder of the Bulge. With two of its three corps committed north, the Third Army had to hold most of its original frontage with one corps—Walker's XX Corps. Eisenhower ordered General Alexander Patch's Seventh Army to move its boundary with the Third Army twenty-seven miles west to shorten Walker's line. In order to accomplish this task, Patch called a halt to both of his corps' attacks. The two corps remained split by the Vosges Mountains, with Haislip's XV Corps to the west and Truscott's VI

Corps to the east. However, the VI Corps gave the 103rd ID to the XV Corps, as Patch viewed the ground between the Saar River and the Vosges (XV Corps' sector) as the most dangerous. That division, plus Colonel Wilson's 106th MCG and elements of the 12th AD, held the new ground gained from the Third Army.[85] However, Eisenhower soon called on the Seventh Army for two divisions for a theater reserve. This stripped the army of the 36th ID and 12th AD, leaving it holding a 126-mile front with just five infantry divisions, one armored division, and one and a half cavalry groups. Elements of three newly arrived infantry divisions were en route, and their formations already present in the line were transformed into three ad hoc task forces that would hold large portions of the Seventh Army line, particularly along the Rhine. The 106th MCG anchored the XV Corps' left, while a fourth task force, comprised of the 117th CRS, the 94th CRS (of the 14th AD), the 62nd Armored Infantry Battalion (also from the 14th AD), and a tank destroyer company occupied the center of the army line in the Vosges Mountains, under the aegis of Task Force Hudelson.[86] Thus, the cavalry performed a similar mission to their brethren in the Ninth Army by helping a manpower-strapped army hold a suddenly much larger front.

TF Hudelson took over the old positions of the 106th MCG on 23 December 1944. The 117th CRS settled on the left, linking with the 100th ID around Bitche; the 94th CRS (under the command of the 117th CRS) held the center; and the 62nd Armored Infantry Battalion maintained the right portion of the zone, tying in with the 45th ID at the town of Dambach. Overall, the task force front was about ten miles of extremely broken, forested terrain.[87] The next week would be spent reinforcing and improving positions.

At 0100 on the morning of 1 January, elements of four German Volksgrenadier divisions struck TF Hudelson, aiming for the Saverne Gap as part of Operation NORDWIND. This assault had the intention of seizing the gap and linking up with another German assault that struck the center of the XV Corps line farther west in an attempt to encircle part of the XV Corps as well as threaten the rear of the rest of the Seventh Army (see map 14).[88]

The forward positions of both the 117th and 94th CRS soon found themselves engaged with heavy German forces. In fact, the Ger-

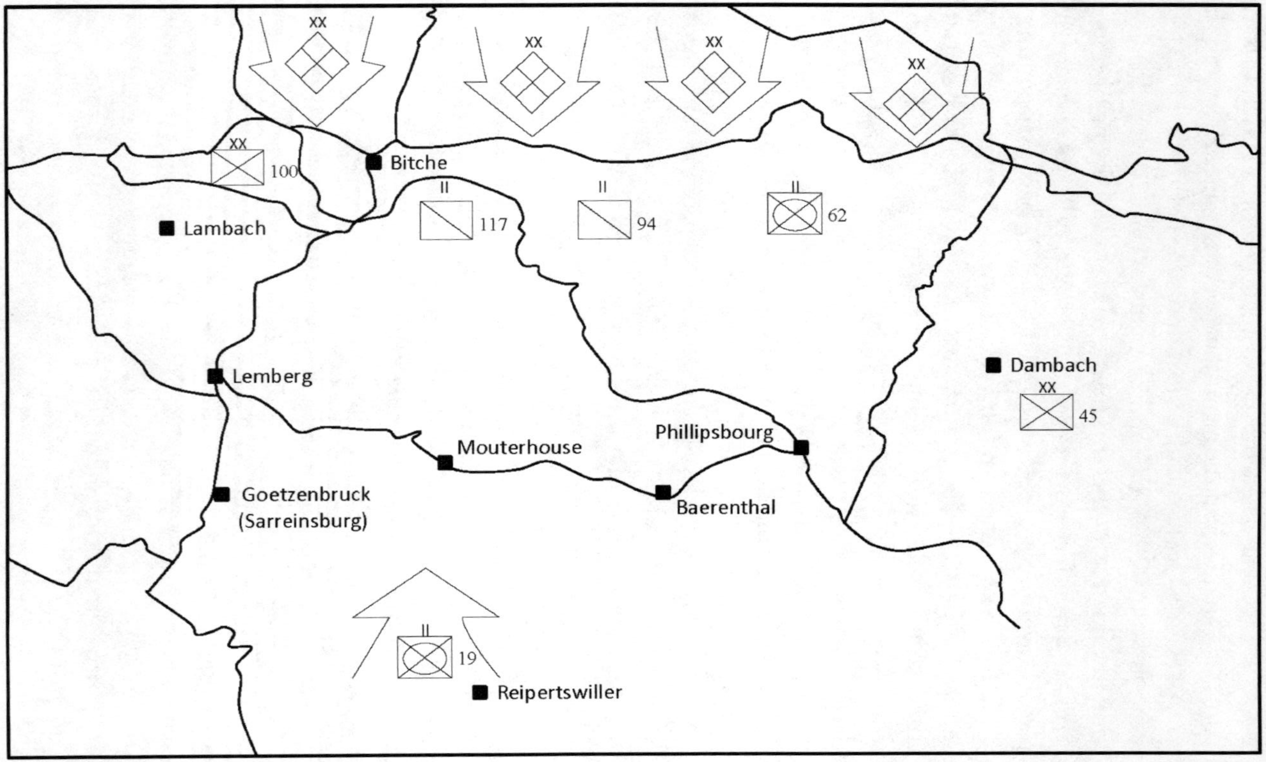

Map 14. Task Force Hudelson in NORDWIND.

mans had committed approximately ten thousand infantry against the approximately twenty-three hundred infantry of TF Hudelson and the rightmost regiment of the 100th ID, a ratio of about four to one.[89] Despite a desperate defense supported by artillery, by 0330 the cavalry found themselves outmatched and the 117th CRS's commander, Lieutenant Colonel Charles Hodge, ordered a withdrawal. Unfortunately, due to slippery conditions, battle damage, and enemy capture of roads, the forward cavalrymen were forced to abandon a large amount of equipment.

The 117th CRS established a new defensive line approximately two miles to the south. Reinforced by the 19th Armored Infantry Battalion, the cavalry held this line all morning against successive waves of German attacks. As the day progressed, German infiltration seized the towns of Mouterhouse and Baerenthal to the east of the squadron. The loss of these towns unhinged the cavalry position (and forced the 117th CRS headquarters to flee). Subsequently, the cavalry and 19th Armored Infantry Battalion retreated another three miles to hold a five-mile line from Goetzenbruck to Reipertswiller.[90] The 117th CRS was relieved on 2 January by the 179th Infantry Regiment of the 45th ID and sent to the corps' rear to recover. The squadron had taken only thirty-nine casualties, but their vehicles losses were extreme, with twelve armored cars, thirty-eight jeeps, six light tanks, and two half-tracks reported as lost.[91]

Due to the cavalry's retreat, a gap opened between the 100th ID's rightmost formation holding the town of Lemberg and the 117th CRS. Several historians have commented on this "dangerous" gap in the American lines in the literature on this battle, starting with the after action report of the XV Corps.[92] However, a critical examination is required before passing harsh judgment. The 399th Infantry, the rightmost regiment of the 100th ID, occupied defensive positions just to the southwest of Bitche with two battalions. The third battalion was arrayed in depth approximately a mile south, around the town of Lambach. The precipitous withdrawal of the cavalry did force the 399th Infantry to bend back and orient more to the east, so that by the end of the day their eastern elements occupied positions around the town of Lemberg, two miles south of their initial positions.[93] The left flank of the 117th CRS's line at the end of 1 January rested at the town of

Goetzenbruck, less than two miles south. Furthermore, the German forces in this area that could immediately use this hole consisted of a single Volksgrenadier division, or perhaps two, both already severely used in the first day. Behind these initial forces, the exploitation force for this entire portion of the German offensive was a single mountain division—the 6th SS. While this division was very capable, it did not have the mobility to rapidly exploit such a hole and make a difference.

Thus, the cavalry's retreat certainly posed a problem for the XV Corps, particularly for the 399th Infantry Battalion. However, the danger was not as great as some of the literature and even the XV Corps report has implied. Moreover, the cavalry had accomplished their mission of delaying long enough for its parent corps to bring additional assets to bear. Considering that the odds were significantly against TF Hudelson (significant elements of four division against three battalions), the U.S. forces performed admirably. While these Volksgrenadier divisions were not considered the elite of the German Army, neither were they horribly inferior. Additionally, although the German forces might not have been of the highest caliber, at a certain point numbers begin to have their own effect.

Although the German attack through the mountains would continue to make small gains over the next couple of days, it would culminate at the town of Wingen-sur-Moder, just three miles south of where the 117th CRS stopped on 1 January. Thus, although this battle is certainly not a textbook example of how to conduct a fighting withdrawal, the cavalry did well enough, and certainly outperformed their counterparts in the 14th MCG (who faced much heavier odds in worse conditions).

To the west of the VI Corps and the 117th CRS, the 106th MCG extended their front and relieved the XX Corps' 6th MCG and 5th Ranger Battalion on 24 December. The 106th MCG thus occupied a front that was approximately seven miles long, stretching from just south of Saarlautern to a point six miles west of Saarbrücken. The 95th ID of the XX Corps was to the group's left, while the 103rd ID of the XV Corps held the right. The cavalry's mission was to maintain the connection between the two corps and protect the left flank of the XV Corps.[94]

While the 117th CRS fought its desperate action on 1 January,

German forces launched another major attack against the XV Corps that same day to the west of the mountains, with the intent to link up with the eastern assault element of NORDWIND near the Saverne Gap. The main effort in the XV Corps sector would be against the eastern portion of the corps zone, the area of the 44th and 100th IDs. The 106th MCG, holding the corps' extreme left flank, would be struck by a force of approximately regimental strength that was a supporting effort designed to threaten the corps' flank and fix Allied strength in that region.[95]

The initial German drive pushed the 106th MCG back approximately a mile before they were able to halt the attacks. The cavalry spent the next three days, 2–4 January, attempting to retake the ground lost, but the group was stymied by heavy German artillery fire and stiff resistance. By 5 January, the cavalry had made some limited gains but had not fully succeeded in driving the Germans back to their start lines.[96] However, holding or retaking ground was not the primary point of the 106th MCG's mission. The cavalry were in a security role, thus making their success dependent on the impact to their secured formation. The links between the XV and XX Corps were never seriously threatened, and despite limited German gains on 1 January, the left flank of the XV Corps was never in jeopardy. Granted, the 106th MCG fought against a supporting effort. However, their fight did not draw off substantial combat power from the American main effort. Thus, in the end the action on the far left of the XV Corps line proved to be a minor diversion that cost the Germans more in terms of combat power than it did the United States—the essence of an economy of force as well as a security mission.

After the trauma of their battle on New Year's Day, the 117th CRS spent the bulk of January in the VI Corps reserve, patrolling supply routes while receiving new vehicles. As the cavalry recovered, the corps conducted a controlled withdrawal south from the German border in order to concentrate strength to defeat the continued German attacks from Operation NORDWIND that were threatening to tear the VI Corps apart. As part of these withdrawals, the corps pulled off the Rhine River just north of Strasbourg, creating a German salient around the town of Gambsheim. The 117th CRS, now under the command of Lieutenant Colonel Harold Samsel, entered the line on 19 January to help contain this salient. The New Jersey cavalrymen were emplaced on the southern end of the corps zone and oriented to the east, holding a five-mile stretch from Hoerdt (six miles north of Strasbourg) in the south to Weyersheim in the north. The cavalry were attached to the 36th ID, and their positioning allowed the division to concentrate its forces to meet the continued German attacks raining in from the north and east. The rest of the month passed quietly, as the cavalry's positions were not tested, although the 36th ID did see plenty of action to its north.[97] While the 117th CRS saw little action in this phase of the fighting, their ability to conduct an economy of force operation helped the 36th ID and VI Corps to finally shut down the last gasps of the German offensive.

The 106th MCG would continue to hold its line along the Saar for the rest of January, conducting patrols and improving its positions. On 9 February, the newly arrived 101st MCG, under the command of Colonel Charles McClelland, would relieve the 106th MCG, allowing the latter to move into corps reserve. The 106th MCG remained in corps reserve through February and most of March as they prepared for the resumption of the Seventh Army's assault into Germany.[98]

The corps cavalry of the Seventh Army demonstrated the true value of security operations and economy of force in January of 1945. The 106th MCG's security screen made the German attack against the extreme left of the army line a nonevent. This battle could have had repercussions across the XV Corps line precisely when the corps was already absorbing two additional blows in its center and right. The 117th CRS's fight in the Vosges is a great example of a cavalry unit in an economy of force role adapting to challenging circumstances. Their sector, originally a low priority due to the terrain, soon became a high priority through enemy action. Despite this shift from anticipated low threat to an actual high threat scenario, the cavalry's delaying action worked exactly as it should have, allowing reinforcements to reach the line. Thus, in both instances the cavalry fulfilled their role in the army battle. Without these formations, Patch's army would have struggled to handle Operation NORDWIND as well as it did.

From the Ninth Army in the north to the Seventh Army in the south, corps cavalry played a huge role in the U.S. Army's response to the German winter counteroffensives. Like free safeties in football, the cavalry moved across the width and breadth of the battlefield, filling in wherever they were needed. Although the Americans found themselves on the defensive for a large portion of this campaign, the cavalry groups demonstrated their versatility and utility in this form of warfare as well.

The cavalry were not perfect. The failure of the 14th MCG looms large in this chapter of American military history. The defense of the 117th CRS in the Vosges Mountains, while successful, is still controversial. Other successes of the cavalry could be attributed to the weak nature of their opponents. The 102nd MCG's victory at Monschau and the 106th MCG's stand along the Saar were both against second-line German formations committed to subsidiary efforts. However, in each of these cases the threat was real and could not be ignored, regardless of whether it was an SS Panzer Division or a depleted Volksgrenadier formation. Some American unit would have to engage with and defeat the German threat or allow it to succeed. Otherwise the Wehrmacht could have inflicted major casualties. In fact, the 106th ID fell not to a Panzer or Fallschirmjäger division, but to a Volksgrenadier division. Therefore, regardless of the quality of some of their enemies, the cavalry still performed valuable service during this period.

Thanks to the successes and action of the cavalry from the Netherlands to Alsace, the Allied forces drove the Germans back from their deepest penetrations. The First and Third Armies would continue their counterattack, attempting to drive the enemy past their original positions. Thus, there really was no true end to the Battle of the Bulge, but merely a change in the location of the fighting that would persist into the spring. These battles would set the stage for the Allies' dramatic offensives of March and April that would take them to and over the Rhine.

7

To the Rhine

The two months after the close of the Battle of the Bulge would witness the destruction of most of the organized resistance the Germans could muster on the Western Front. However, despite the impending demise of the Nazi state, the remaining forces of the SS and Wehrmacht continued to put up fierce, often fanatical resistance.

The Allied armies on the continent, refitted after the grueling fighting of December and January, stood poised to make the final drive to the Rhine River, the last natural obstacle defending Germany's western frontier. The Commonwealth 21st Army Group in the north had liberated all of the southern Netherlands and was poised along the lower Rhine and Roer Rivers. The Ninth Army, now attached to the 21st Army Group, occupied the region just north of Aachen and was preparing to make an assault crossing of the Roer. The First Army had regained control of its old sector from the Ninth in late January, stretched from Aachen to the Eifel region, and was preparing to assault to the Rhine. The Third Army continued offensive operations through the Eifel and as well as throughout the Saar-Palatinate. To the south, the Seventh Army, half of the 6th Army Group, having already reached the Rhine in part, had just finished defeating the NORDWIND offensive and was preparing to assault into southern Germany.

Third Army

At the end of January, the Third Army was arrayed on a very wide front. The northern portion of the army line was held by Major General Troy

Middleton's VIII Corps, stretching twenty miles, from Losheim to just inside the Luxembourg border. This corps would continue its attack, begun as part of the reduction of the Bulge, driving on the city of Prüm, a major highway junction north of Bitburg. Major General John Millikin's III Corps, to the south of the VIII Corps, also continued its assault east, oriented across the Our River and on the highway linking Prüm to Bitburg. Farther south, Major General Manton Eddy's XII Corps, finally unleashed after nearly two months of inactivity, would attack north over the Sauer River toward Bitburg. Major General Walton Walker's XX Corps would continue to anchor the army right and await its opportunity to return to the fight.

Colonel Edward Fickett's 6th MCG continued to advance along the III Corps' right (southern) flank in late January and early February, keeping pace with the 26th ID and then the newly arrived 17th Airborne Division, as well as maintaining contact with the XII Corps to the south as the entire army attacked to the Our River. This contact became steadily more important as the Third Army wheeled to the east after the reduction of the Ardennes Bulge. Attempting to keep entire corps on line during such a maneuver is extremely difficult, so the cavalrymen earned their pay by preventing bypassed German formations from inflicting damage on the corps' rear echelons.[1]

On 4 February, the Third Army reorganized its front lines as it completed its turn to the east. The III Corps' zone was dramatically expanded from seven to eighteen miles. The corps ordered the 6th MCG to assume the sector of the XII Corps' 5th ID as that division moved south to be used in the XII Corps' upcoming offensive. Task Force Fickett (the 6th MCG) thus expanded south, assuming a frontage of nearly five miles (more than a normal division's) along the Our River.[2] The Germans on the east side of the river were heavily entrenched in the Siegfried Line. The cavalry were especially important to the III Corps because the ongoing reorganizations of the Third Army in late January had left it with only the 6th AD and 17th Airborne Division.[3] Thus, with only two full "striking arms," the corps had to use its cavalry to cover everything else in order to allow those two divisions to concentrate their forces for the best chances of success. The cavalry were given a battalion of combat engineers to aid in improving their positions. Task Force Fickett continued to hold its positions on the southern end of the corps line, while the 6th AD and 17th Airborne attacked across the Our River into the teeth of the Siegfried Line, establishing small bridgeheads on 7 February thanks to their ability to concentrate their combat power.[4] This fight proved to be so vicious that General George S. Patton labeled the assault crossings as "Homeric."[5] Five days later, the 12th Army Group assigned the III Corps headquarters to the First Army, leaving all of the corps' remaining divisions and the 6th MCG with the Third Army. Middleton's VIII Corps assumed command of the sector and these formations.[6] This reorganization kept the group on the extreme southern end of what was now the VIII Corps line.

At the beginning of February, Eddy's XII Corps began planning its next offensive across the Moselle and Sauer Rivers. As the attack would be fighting through portions of the Siegfried Line, the attacking divisions would need to mass their efforts in order to penetrate the heavily fortified and rugged terrain. Thus, Eddy ordered Colonel Charles Reed's 2nd MCG to assume over seven additional miles of front that had belonged to the 76th ID. (Eddy did relieve the 2nd of a small sector to the southwest that was now safely behind friendly lines. However, the revised line still stretched over nineteen miles.)[7] This extension of frontage for the cavalry allowed the infantry divisions to attack along fronts that were less than four miles wide.[8] Additionally, two of the task force's four combat engineer battalions (the 284th and 1252nd) were relieved from cavalry control and attached to Combat Command A (CCA) of the 6th AD in preparation for that division's mission to exploit success in the upcoming offensive.[9]

The XII Corps offensive began on 7 February 1945. A fierce three-day battle to gain bridgeheads across the Sauer River ensued, with victory coming slowly and with great difficulty. In fact, more than a week into the attack the corps had barely moved more than a couple of miles beyond the river.[10] Without question, if the three infantry divisions of the corps (76th, 5th, 80th) had had to cover more frontage, they would not have had the combat power to force their way across the river without accepting substantial risk all along their lines.

On 19 February, Eddy ordered TF Reed (the 2nd MCG) to conduct an assault across the Moselle to seize the town of Wincheringen in order to support the attack of the 10th AD of the XX Corps to the southeast. This assault was part of the clearing of the Saar–Moselle

Triangle that had bedeviled the Third Army (including the 3rd MCG) since November.[11] Wincheringen was believed to be held by garrison troops or members of a Volksgrenadier division.[12] The 2nd CRS, reinforced by engineers, led the dismounted attack. The assault proved a great success, with the Dragoons seizing their objectives prior to the arrival of the elements of the 10th AD that were supposed to assist in the attack. The squadron lost five killed and twenty-two wounded while capturing thirty-four Germans and killing an unknown number.[13] The casualty ratio is indicative of not only the superior firepower of the cavalry but also the growing combat skills of the group. Even though they were facing rear echelon troops, a night assault across a defended water obstacle is difficult even in the best of circumstances.

With the success of the attack on Wincheringen, the 2nd MCG was now able to focus more of its attention to the northeast, as the XX Corps was now coming alongside its eastern flank. This shift allowed the cavalry to concentrate more combat power along the remaining length of its screen in preparation for combat operations across the Sauer River.[14] This fight is a good example of a flank security mission in a complex offensive against an entrenched enemy.

While the XII Corps fought around Bitburg, to the north and the far left of the Third Army line, the VIII Corps continued its attack on Prüm and the region between that city and Bitburg. On 12 February, TF Fickett (the 6th MCG) ordered its attached engineer battalion to clear Vianden west of the Our River. This fight turned into a grueling seven-hour slugfest despite the support of the cavalry's assault guns, tanks, and artillery.[15] Needless to say, a battle like this was no place for an engineer battalion to serve as the main effort, even a combat engineer battalion. Unfortunately, the task needed to be accomplished and the only element in the task force with the dismounted strength to properly fight an intense urban battle was the engineers. If the cavalry had attempted the fight without them, the reconnaissance troops would surely have been decimated with little gain.

With the capture of Vianden, the stage was set for the cavalry to begin their own attack across the Our River. On 14 February, the VIII Corps removed TF Fickett's attached engineer battalion, as it was needed to support corps operations elsewhere.[16] The group planned to begin the attack on 19 February as part of the larger VIII Corps assault to breach the Siegfried Line. The corps' main effort was to be in the north, with the 90th ID and 11th AD, with a subsequent supporting effort just to their south with the 6th AD.[17] The cavalry's task was to fix the German defenders to their front, preventing them from withdrawing and interfering with the attacks to the north. Furthermore, the added pressure of attacks all along their line would help dilute German artillery support and hopefully confuse them as to the location of the American main effort.

The initial attacks by both squadrons proved successful in getting across the river, with the 6th CRS getting its entire strength across at Keppeshausen and the 28th CRS establishing a bridgehead at Vianden. However, German resistance was fierce, with the defenders fighting for every yard. At Vianden, Troop B of the 28th lost twenty-seven men just in the fighting around the town.[18] This was an appalling 20 percent casualty rate for that troop, assuming that it was at full strength at the beginning of the attack (which is doubtful). The heavy casualties stand as a testament to the fierce fighting still being encountered in late February. However, despite the vicious fighting, both squadrons got across the Our River, beating back German counterattacks.

The next several days saw slow, bitter progress for the cavalry as it fought its way forward, still protecting the corps' flank. On 22 February the group managed to gain a little over a mile with assistance from the 80th ID to its south.[19] German resistance finally cracked on 24 February, and the group attacked to the northeast to Waxweiler, eleven miles from the cavalry's bridgeheads and ten miles northwest of Bitburg. The task force then took over a short line along the Prüm River from Waxweiler to the town of Mauel, two miles to the south. The group also retained the responsibility of protecting the corps' southern flank for the next couple of days as the 80th ID of the XII Corps came up from the south and on line with the VIII Corps.[20]

The month of February started much the same as the rest of the winter had for TF Polk (the 3rd MCG), as they continued their mission of holding the center of the XX Corps line between the twin efforts of the Saar bridgehead and the fighting in the Saar–Moselle Triangle. On 21 February the XX Corps attached the 5th Ranger Battalion to assist the cavalrymen in maintaining their link with the 94th ID as it attacked to the north.[21] TF Polk used the rangers to clear some enemy pillboxes along their northern flank. Despite the benefits offered to the cavalry by the rangers, the XX Corps withdrew them from the task force on 24 February. The group continued to maintain their positions until 27 February, when the corps readjusted its boundaries and organization in preparation for follow-on operations after the clearance of the Saar–Moselle Triangle by the 10th AD and 94th ID.

General Walker, the commander of the XX Corps, began concentrating his forces to give the corps' main effort the best chance at success. Therefore, he assigned the 26th ID to assume most of TF Polk's and the 94th ID's frontage along the Saar River. This move allowed the 94th ID to concentrate on its bridgehead at Saarburg, from which they would launch their attack. Walker then attached TF Polk to the 94th ID in order to allow the latter to further concentrate its infantry regiments at the main point of attack to the northeast, toward Trier. Thus, the cavalrymen assumed a seven-mile squadron screen along the Saar.[22] Walker's reorganization allowed him to mass the 94th ID against the German fortifications defending the western approaches to Trier.[23]

By the end of February the Third Army had captured Prüm (VIII Corps) and Bitburg (XII Corps), but it had not reduced a bulge of German forces between those cities. Walker's XX Corps had also cleared the Saar–Moselle Triangle, a position that had frustrated the corps since December. This success placed the corps within striking distance of Trier.

March would prove to be an interesting month for the Third Army, as it would participate in two major offensives aimed in divergent directions.[24] To the north, the First Army was about to launch Operation LUMBERJACK, the offensive that would take that army to the Rhine. The Third Army would play a key role in that operation by acting as the southern half of a double envelopment of German forces west of the Rhine and north of the Moselle. The Seventh Army, south of the Third, also had plans for March. That army was to attack north through the portion of the Siegfried Line that protected the southern flank of the Rhineland. The Third Army would also play a role in that offensive, striking south and east from the Moselle, behind the forces facing the Seventh Army, and driving to the Rhine.

On 28 February, Middleton's VIII Corps resumed its attack on the northern end of the army line to set the conditions for the First

Army's Operation LUMBERJACK. The corps' first priority was to clear the Bulge of German forces still resisting between Prüm and Bitburg. It would then continue the assault over the Kyll River east to the Rhine near Koblenz. As part of the corps' offensive, the 6th MCG crossed the Prüm River and engaged in a nasty fight for the control of the high ground east of Waxweiler, as well as the town itself. It took both squadrons the better part of two days to clear the objective. The group continued their attack to the east, fighting against steady German resistance. In the fight to clear the roads east of Waxweiler, every single NCO in one platoon of the 6th CRS became a casualty in one day's fighting.[25] The cavalry continued their offensive, fighting their way forward across the Nims River at Lasel in a bloody two-day fight against German Volksgrenadiers.[26] On 4 March, TF Fickett (the 6th MCG) advanced four miles against weakening resistance, seizing a number of towns, culminating with the village of Neuheilenbach, less than two miles west of the Kyll River and ten miles north of Bitburg.[27] During this entire attack, the cavalry not only had to make steady progress and keep pace with their flanking divisions; they also had to maintain contact with the XII Corps to the south in order to prevent breaks in the army line.

On 5 March, the VIII Corps ordered TF Fickett to move north to assist the 87th ID in maintaining contact with First Army and protecting the corps' northern flank. The group maintained this mission until 8 March, when their presence was no longer required thanks to advances by the 106th ID of the First Army.[28] On 8 March, the group again moved out to protect the northern flank of the corps, following the 11th AD as it attacked to the Rhine River. As the 11th AD was more interested in gaining ground, it fell to the cavalry to destroy any remaining enemy resistance as well as to maintain contact with the First Army to the north. The actions of the cavalry in the advance aided the rapid movement of the VIII Corps to the Rhine, as it did not have to commit portions of its armored divisions to security tasks. On 12 March, the 6th MCG relieved both the 6th and 11th ADs from their positions along the Rhine River in the Andernach–Koblenz region.[29] The cavalry were generally unchallenged in this area, but their presence allowed two full armored divisions to be withdrawn from the line and prepared for further exploitation after the crossing of the Rhine.

A week later, the 28th ID relieved the 6th MCG, which was sent to a rest area in the rear.[30]

To the south of the VIII Corps, the XII Corps offensive to the east of Bitburg continued through the end of February and into March 1945. By 2 March, the 2nd MCG's screen along the Moselle River was no longer necessary, and the XII Corps removed all of the task force's attachments. The corps then attached the group with its two remaining squadrons to the 76th ID.[31] The 76th ID had already crossed the Sauer River and was now looping in front of the 2nd MCG's front, headed to the southeast. The division assigned the cavalry the mission of clearing the pocket of Germans between the 2nd MCG (on the Sauer River) and the southern flank of the 76th ID. The troopers accomplished this mission with enthusiasm after nearly two months of limited activity along the Moselle River. The two squadrons quickly cleared the pocket of disorganized German forces that had been dislocated and cut off by the thrust of the XII Corps to Bitburg as well as the more localized *manoeuvre sur les dérrieres* of the 76th ID. By 3 March, the group established a screen along the Moselle and Kyll Rivers in order to protect the 76th as it cleared the remaining German forces in the zone.[32]

Eddy's entire corps was closing on the Moselle and preparing to assault farther south and east to the Rhine. The 76th ID gave the 2nd MCG the mission of covering the southern flank of the division (and thus the corps) as the attack progressed. The group also had to maintain the connection with the XX Corps to the south. Essentially, the 2nd MCG was the hinge between the XII Corps swinging down from the north across the Moselle and the XX Corps attacking due east.

The corps' offensive began to gather momentum as it struck deep into German territory headed toward the Rhine, and soon the cavalry were making dramatic advances alongside the rest of the corps. The German defenses crumbled, although some units still fought hard, as was the case at the town of Zemmer (approximately two miles to the east of the Kyll River) on 7 March. The Germans defended the town with an under-strength battalion backed by rocket and tube artillery. The 42nd CRS attacked with dismounted elements of Troop A supported by a platoon of light tanks (from Company F), a platoon of attached tank destroyers, and a platoon of assault guns. The heavy firepower of the supporting elements as well as the rapid assault of the cavalrymen broke the German defenders. The squadron killed ten Germans and captured sixty-one for little loss in the assault.[33] This action is yet another example of the cavalry conducting security missions, fighting to protect the flank of advancing formations. If the cavalry had not been able to clear the enemy from their front, the advance of the XII Corps would have had to slow in order to prevent a gap from opening in its flank.

By 12 March, the 2nd MCG's zone, along with the 76th ID's, had been pinched out by the closing of the XX Corps to the south and the movement of the 89th ID to the north. Eddy relieved the group of attachment to the 76th ID and moved it to the north of the corps sector. There, the 2nd MCG conducted a screen along the Rhine River, protecting the northern flank of the XII Corps as it attacked east toward the Mainz–Wiesbaden region.[34] The cavalrymen allowed the corps to mass combat power forward by preventing enemy forces on the right (or northeastern) bank of the Rhine from conducting spoiling attacks into the lightly defended rear. The Dragoons used artillery and massed fires from its assault guns and light tanks to break up concentrations of German forces on the right bank as well as to harass any visible enemy movement. This protection allowed the lead divisions of the XII Corps to increase their speed without having to worry about providing for their own flank or rear security.

While the XII and VIII Corps assaulted through the Eifel to the north in early March, the XX Corps continued a deliberate advance south of Trier and the Moselle River. On 2 March, the 94th ID ordered TF Polk (the 3rd MCG) across the Saar to assume defensive positions to the east and southeast of Trier as part of the effort to expand the overall Saar bridgehead. The group occupied an approximately seven-mile defensive line along the Ruwer River, relieving CCR, 10th AD.[35] This move allowed the corps to "lighten the load" of the 10th AD, which was simultaneously sustaining a drive to the northeast along the northern bank of the Moselle toward Koblenz while maintaining forces in readiness to exploit bridgeheads over the Kyll or Ruwer Rivers.[36] Additionally, the presence of the 3rd MCG holding the northern flank of the division allowed the 94th ID to concentrate its infantry regiments for a series of battles over the extremely brutal terrain south of Trier. This type of fighting required large amounts of infantry and was not conducive to rapid vehicular movement. Therefore the cavalry held their ground, allowing the infantry to "earn their pay" to the south.

The period of 3 to 16 March 1945 witnessed a war of raids and small battles for hilltops, much like what would be seen in Korea six years later (though without the extensive trench and bunker systems). As the terrain did not allow for much heavy vehicular maneuver, the assault guns, tank destroyers, and light tanks (by now the heavier and better-armed 75mm M24 Chaffee) assumed static firing positions or were held in reserve to counterattack enemy penetrations. Though the cavalry were perhaps undermanned for such a fight, their heavy allocation of machine guns allowed them to maintain their positions in the face of most attacks. Furthermore, as the German forces in the area did not possess large mechanized formations (which the restrictive terrain prohibited regardless), the task force was relatively secure in their, by now, accustomed role on the front line in a defensive posture.

On 8 March, the XX Corps relieved TF Polk from the 94th ID, placing the cavalry under corps control. The following day, Colonel George Busbey's newly arrived 16th Mechanized Cavalry Group was placed under the command of TF Polk, creating the 316th "Provisional" Cavalry Brigade, comprised of TF Polk with all prior tank destroyer, engineer, and artillery supports, the 3rd MCG, and the 16th MCG. The corps' plan involved the cavalry making a diversionary attack on the northern flank of the corps' line to draw German forces out of position prior to a general offensive set to begin on 13 March (see map 15).[37]

The 16th MCG assumed positions alongside the 3rd MCG, relieving elements of the 43rd CRS in order to allow that squadron to mass combat power to conduct a shaping attack on high ground to the north of Waldrach, a key town in the German defenses, four miles southeast of Trier. On 12 March, the 43rd CRS began the brigade attack as planned. Although the Germans stoutly held their positions with 88mm fire as well as intense artillery support, the cavalry managed to seize their limited objectives. The defenders' artillery support was unusually high, noted by both the group and the corps, and was explained by the fact that the cavalry were the only force in the corps attacking at that time, thus attracting the attention of every German battery within range. The attacks had been conducted dismounted

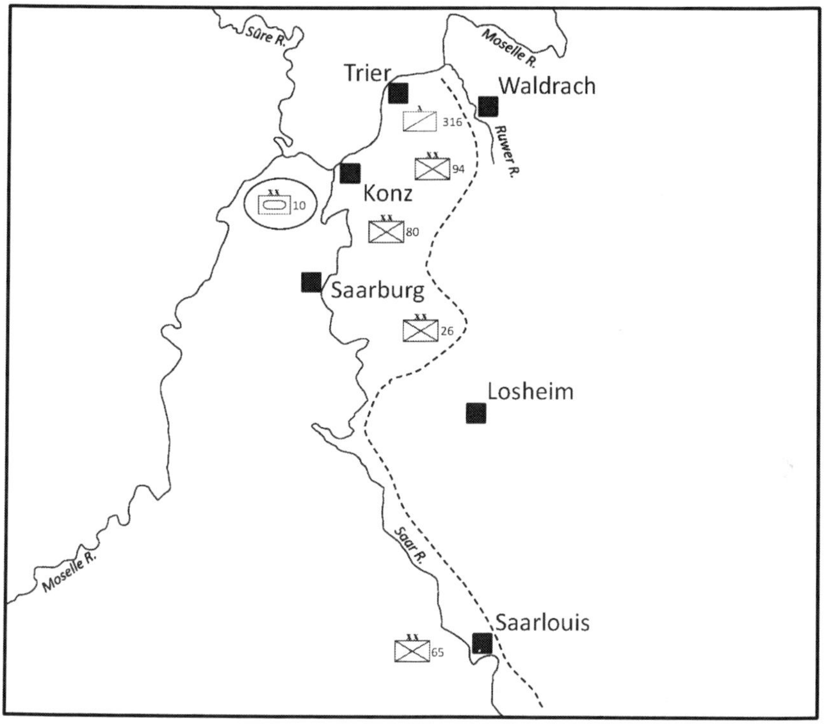

Map 15. XX Corps March 1945.

but were supported by the light tanks of the squadron's tank company as well as attached tank destroyers. Casualties for the squadron (all three reconnaissance troops, the tank company, and the attached tank destroyer company) amounted to four dead, twenty-three wounded, and four missing. German 88mm anti-tank fire destroyed four tank destroyers as they attempted to suppress those weapons.[38]

Upon the success of the 43rd CRS's attack on 12 March, the 16th CRS relieved the 43rd CRS of their newly conquered ground and supported the attack of the 19th CRS on the ridgeline dominated by the towns of Sommerau and Morscheid immediately to the south of Waldrach.[39] Seizure of this position would drive the Germans back approximately two miles, deprive them of the best defensive positions in the area, and unhinge the defense of Waldrach.

The 19th CRS's attack went well, consuming the day of 13 March. This attack then set the conditions for the 16th CRS to conduct an attack on the primary objective of Waldrach on 14 March. By now the group possessed the high ground to the north and south of the town. Despite these disadvantages, the Germans defending the town stubbornly clung to their positions with heavy artillery support. The 16th CRS attempted to seize Waldrach from the west, but the Germans stopped it outside the town with heavy fire. The attack resumed the next day, with the 16th CRS attacking from the north and the 19th CRS from the south. Although a blown bridge prevented the 19th CRS from entering Waldrach, the 16th CRS succeeded in clearing the town in bitter house-to-house fighting.[40]

As the 16th MCG fought in Waldrach on 13 March, the 3rd CRS in holding positions to the south repulsed a small German counterattack of fifty soldiers supported by three tanks and artillery support. Despite being forced from their initial positions, the cavalrymen defeated the attackers, destroying one tank and inflicting a number of casualties on the German infantry at the cost of three dead and thirteen wounded. The Germans also managed to destroy one armored car and damage two light tanks.[41]

The 316th Brigade's attacks to the east and southeast continued, with all four squadrons participating. The advance was slow due to heavy German resistance, but steady. The terrain in this region was particularly difficult, consisting of the foothills of the Hunnsbrück Mountains. A series of wooded ridges ran from the south to the Moselle River, directly across the corps' line of attack. The 3rd MCG discovered that they could use their mobility to quickly move their troops to the fight, but that most of their actual combat was conducted on foot, much like any other formation.[42] On 16 March, Troop B of the 43rd CRS and a platoon of Company F (the tank company) were ambushed as they attempted to seize the highway intersection three miles to the east of Fell. German forces opened fire at close range with 88mm cannons, destroying the entire platoon of tanks and forcing the patrol back, with twenty men wounded or captured.[43] Subsequent attempts to reconnoiter the enemy revealed no further information, but cost four additional troopers missing in action. The German defense eventually was outflanked by elements of the XII Corps, and assessment of the enemy positions revealed that it had been held by at least a battalion with four 88mm guns and four 105mm guns.[44]

This fight demonstrates the inherent dangers of reconnaissance. The cavalry probably were feeling somewhat cocky by this point in the war and were not as careful as they should have been. Cavalry can only do its job of finding and fixing the enemy if it survives to report. A line of last positions reported does very little to aid the higher commander. Much like the example of Colonel John B. Reybold of the 15th MCG in August 1944, overly hasty reconnaissance results in casualties, wrecked vehicles, and not much else.

On the afternoon of 16 March 1945, the XX Corps halted the 316th Brigade's attack. The rest of the corps' attacks had met success (though still facing determined if disjointed defenses) and the efforts of the cavalry brigade were no longer necessary on that front. Consequently, Walker removed the 16th MCG and all remaining tank destroyer and engineer attachments from the control of the 3rd MCG and ordered the 3rd MCG to the rear to become a part of the Supreme Headquarters Allied Expeditionary Force (SHAEF) Reserve.[45]

Though the direct impact of the cavalry's actions in this offensive may be hard to assess, a force of two cavalry groups, the size of one infantry Regimental Combat Team (the cavalry group was long on firepower but short on personnel), had attacked on a divisional frontage. This assault had allowed the corps to mass its efforts where it willed, while also steadily pressuring the enemy in its zone, preventing the Germans from conducting an economy of force mission there as well. In its short existence, the 316th Provisional Cavalry Brigade advanced approximately fifteen miles. The contributions of this ad hoc brigade did not end with just the XX Corps. As the cavalry's actions enabled the corps' success, the corps' breakthrough into the rear of the German forces facing the Seventh Army helped unhinge the entire German defense in the Saar–Palatinate salient. Finally, this incident stands as the only time in the entire history of the U.S. Army in the Second World War where a full mechanized cavalry brigade fought as envisioned in prewar horse cavalry doctrine.

By 18 March, the XX Corps offensive had succeeded in penetrating German lines and all units were making good progress. The corps ordered the 16th MCG to continue its advance to the east along the southern bank of the Moselle, protecting the corps' left flank while maintaining contact with the XII Corps to the north. The XX Corps was advancing due east now, cutting behind the German forces resisting the Seventh Army to the south. By 21 March 1945 the group had advanced to the vicinity of the mining town of Idar Oberstein, thirty miles to the east of their start positions. German resistance west of the Rhine had begun to collapse, and the cavalrymen met little opposition in their drive.[46] On 23 March, the group seized the town of Essweiler, eleven miles to the northwest of the city of Kaiserslautern.[47]

While the 16th MCG continued their attack, the 3rd MCG's travails continued. No sooner had the last elements of the 3rd MCG closed on the group's assembly area in Trier on 19 March than Walker ordered the group back into the fight, this time to support the 65th ID. This division had held the line of the Saar River on the southern edge of the corps, right at the point of the Saar–Palatinate German salient. While the northern portion of the XX Corps had continued the attack to the east-southeast, the XXI Corps of the Seventh Army had attacked to the northeast. The result was a pocket of German forces stuck in a wedge on the eastern bank of the Saar River near Saarbrücken, with the 65th ID to their front, other XX Corps elements (the 26th ID and 10th AD) to their rear, and the 70th ID of the XXI Corps closing from the south. The XX Corps had ordered the 65th ID to clear this pocket before assuming duty as the corps reserve. On 20 March, the 65th ID sent the 43rd CRS to the south, where it protected the division's southern flank along a frontage of ten miles and maintained contact with the XXI Corps to the south. The 3rd CRS moved in front of the division's main body, protecting it against enemy delaying efforts. A single company of the 245th Combat Engineer Battalion was attached to the cavalry in support of their efforts. German defenses in the area had crumbled after the 65th ID had forced a crossing of the Saar River, and the 3rd MCG's advance was swift and virtually unopposed. The mission took approximately two days to accomplish, at the end of which the Brave Rifles were again moved to rest areas in the corps' rear. During this period the troopers assisted in guarding temporary prisoner-of-war camps in Kaiserslautern.[48]

From the early spring and the fight to exploit the German retreat from the Bulge to late March and the wild ride to the Rhine through the Saar–Palatinate, Patton's corps cavalry showed their skill in traditional cavalry roles. Beginning this phase of the war in mainly defensive security roles along the Saar and Moselle, the Third Army's cavalry groups rapidly transitioned to offensive security operations and economy of force supporting attacks, as well as providing liaison and coordination between adjoining corps and field armies while those formations attacked at high speed through the Rhineland. Thus, the cavalry contributed to a huge victory and helped the Third Army destroy twelve German divisions in its drive to the Rhine.[49]

Although the Germans were facing critical shortages in manpower and equipment by this point in the war, they were still dangerous. The hard fighting encountered by the Third Army in the Eifel as well as the Hunnsbrück Mountains reflect the desperation and intensity of the Wehrmacht as they fought to hold the Americans from the Rhine. Therefore, actions such as the 316th Cavalry Brigade's fixing attack in mid-March still proved necessary. The line divisions and corps of the army still needed reconnaissance and security missions completed. Thus, the corps cavalry still had an important role to play.

Ninth Army

After spending the entire period of the Bulge in essentially a holding pattern, the Ninth Army stood poised in early February to play a leading role in the Allied assault to the Rhine River. The army, since 21 December under the control of the British 21st Army Group, would launch half of that army group's planned offensive to crush German forces west of the Rhine. The Canadian First Army would launch Operation VERITABLE to the north, complemented a few days later by the Ninth Army's Operation GRENADE to the south. The British Second Army would be prepared to attack to support either offensive.[50]

The Ninth Army would attack with three corps—the XVI Corps on the extreme left, the XIII Corps in the center, and the XIX Corps on the right, opposite Cologne. All three corps would be oriented northeast in the general direction of Düsseldorf, across the Cologne Plain.[51] The attack would begin with the XIX Corps, supported by the VII Corps, crossing the Roer, clearing the Hambach Forest, and securing the flank of the army. Then the XIII and XVI Corps would cross the Roer in an attempt to link up with Canadian forces advancing from the northwest.[52]

The XIX Corps' 113th MCG, the Redhorse, began the month of February being relieved by the 8th ID of the VII Corps and moving north from their positions near Düren to join the 29th ID west of Jülich. The group relieved that division's 115th Infantry Regiment along a front from Lammersdorf to Fron-Hoven. The cavalry helped screen the arrival of the 30th ID into the sector, then joined that division when the 29th ID shifted slightly north as the XIX Corps massed combat power for its assault.[53] When Operation GRENADE began on 23 February, the cavalry held their positions.

On 26 February, the 113th MCG was finally committed by Major General Raymond McLain's XIX Corps in support of its southern flank. The group, reinforced with a light tank battalion and a tank destroyer battalion, was to secure the southern edge of the corps and link with the 4th MCG, then holding the northern edge of the VII Corps' bridgehead. The Redhorse held these positions for a day, and then on the night of 27 February conducted an attack on a key town in support of CCB of the 2nd AD. This town lay directly on the corps' southern boundary, and enemy forces there could disrupt corps operations northward. The group advanced with both squadrons and, finding the town unoccupied, soon had the entire vicinity under firm control.[54] The group continued its advance on 28 February, clearing the town of Bedburg. That night McLain withdrew the cavalry from the line and placed them in reserve due to the constricting of the corps' front. The 113th MCG would remain in the corps reserve throughout the first week of March, until the 9th, when it was ordered to relieve the 4th MCG from its sector along the Rhine River north of Cologne, allowing that group to be committed farther south to support the Remagen bridgehead.[55]

To the northwest of the XIX Corps, the XIII Corps began its own attack to the northeast on 23 February, with the 84th ID on the left (west) and the 102nd ID on the right (east).[56] Major General Alvan C. Gillem Jr., the corps commander, kept the 5th AD ready to exploit any penetrations. The 11th MCG, the Blackhorse, was also kept in corps reserve ready to assist where needed. Gillem did not commit his cavalry until 28 February, when the leading elements of the 84th ID had penetrated nearly twenty miles north of the Roer and were seven miles southeast of Venlo. That division had advanced faster than the easternmost elements of the XVI Corps to the right, and it now had an extremely long open flank. Gillem attached the 11th MCG to the 84th ID with the task to protect this flank.[57] Although German forces were certainly in disarray, the possibility of a limited counterattack against the rear of the 84th ID could delay the corps' advance and allow more German forces the chance to consolidate or withdraw.

Thus, on 28 February the Blackhorse crossed the Roer River and established its screen to protect the left flank of the 84th ID. Each squadron took responsibility for a ten-mile stretch of front, allowing the group to cover a full twenty miles, or over four times the normal frontage of a division. Both squadrons encountered moderate German resistance in the form of roadblocks backed by anti-tank guns. Despite suffering casualties, the cavalry were able to accomplish their primary mission of ensuring that these German forces did not interfere with the advance of the 84th ID.[58]

As the XVI Corps advanced along the left flank of the XIII Corps, the 11th MCG rolled up its screen to the north. The 44th CRS, relieved of its mission by the advance of the 8th AD on 1 March, moved to seize bridges across a minor river in order to facilitate the movement of the 84th ID north. Later that same day, the 36th CRS, also relieved by the advance of the 8th AD, moved to screen almost four miles of the 84th ID's flank. The cavalry also sent patrols three miles northeast into the division's objective for the night of 1–2 March.[59] This reconnaissance would smooth the infantry's attack the next day.

The XIII Corps' advance continued throughout 2 March, with the divisions wheeling to the east to meet the Rhine River. The 44th CRS moved to screen a four-mile section of the flank, while the 36th CRS helped consolidate the gains the group had already achieved. Additionally, the corps attached a towed tank destroyer battalion to the group, adding to its firepower.[60] The group continued its mission on 3 March, leapfrogging its squadrons along the flank of the 84th ID as it advanced to the Rhine River seventeen miles north of Düsseldorf. The 44th CRS defeated a German counterattack supported by rockets and artillery, preventing the enemy from interfering with the 84th ID's advance. By 5 March the group had reached the Rhine, and the XIII Corps pulled the cavalry off the line as the 5th AD and 84th ID closed around it.[61]

The XIII Corps so valued the contributions of the 11th MCG to its success that a special notation of the group was included in the corps' after action report of Operation GRENADE. The report noted that the rapidity of the corps' movement required exposed flanks until adjacent units could close. It stated that "this was overcome by using corps reserve units on the right flank and by the employment of cavalry on the left flank."[62] As the left flank was the longer and more exposed of the two, the employment of the corps cavalry group along that flank simply made sense. Without the employment of the 11th MCG, the 84th ID and the XIII Corps in total would not have been able to move so fast, at least not without accepting significantly more risk to its support echelons and potentially more casualties to those important units.

Upon the completion of the cavalry's immediate combat role, Gillem put the group to work from 8 to 12 March 1945 canvassing the civilian populace for fugitive enemy soldiers attempting to evade back to German lines, as well as identifying any potential items of military use. In the course of these duties, the Blackhorse would capture nearly one thousand suspected German soldiers as well as twelve train engines and 143 rail cars that were then pressed into the service of the Ninth Army. On 12 March the cavalry assumed responsibility for an approximately six-mile front along the Rhine just north of Düsseldorf, where it would spend the next two weeks conducting patrols across the river.[63]

The final corps in Operation GRENADE, the XVI Corps, would see its true baptism of fire in this campaign, as it had just been activated over the winter and sent to the extreme left of the Ninth Army line. The corps cavalry group, Lieutenant Colonel Robert Quinn's 15th MCG, had arrived in mid-February after conducting operations against German pockets in France, although one of its squadrons had arrived in December and participated in limited combat over the winter. The corps began its attacks on 23 February, much like its sisters to the east. The 35th ID attacked on the right, while elements of the 79th ID attacked in the center, with the 8th AD holding the far left, tying in with the British Second Army. At first the XVI Corps maintained the cavalry in reserve, as the frontal assaults against the German forces still south of the Roer, and then the assault crossings of that river, did not require their services.[64]

After the success of the initial attacks of the assault elements, particularly those of the 35th ID, on 27 February the XVI Corps ordered the 15th MCG to relieve the 8th AD from its section of the front on the corps' left, so that it could be committed behind the 35th ID to exploit its success. This freeing of the 8th AD would lead to some spectacular gains for the XVI Corps over the next week. On 28 February the group conducted a reconnaissance of the town of Roermond along the Maas. This town had served as the anchor of the German defenses in the region. After finding it deserted, the cavalry were able to be withdrawn from their defensive positions in order to be committed to the corps' attack toward Venlo in support of the Commonwealth forces closing from the west.[65]

On 1 March the 15th MCG, reinforced by a battalion of self-propelled artillery and a company of engineers, crossed the Roer River and commenced a reconnaissance in zone toward the city of Venlo. The roads proved heavily mined, so the cavalry used their light vehicles to find routes through the forest, allowing them to reach their objective by the afternoon of 2 March. This city was the boundary between the British Second Army and the XVI Corps, and from Venlo the corps shifted its efforts northeast toward the Rhine. The corps commander tasked the 15th MCG to protect the left (northern) flank of the 35th ID and the corps as it attacked east. The cavalry also had to gain and then maintain contact with British forces advancing north of the corps.[66]

The second mission for the 15th MCG proved easier than the first. The British Second Army was advancing toward the cavalry, so after only a day of pushing north the group made contact with their allies around the towns of Walbeck and Geldern, approximately eleven miles northeast of Venlo on 3 March. German forces held Walbeck strongly, and after probing the defenses the cavalry allowed a battalion task force of the 35th ID to destroy the enemy.[67]

The next eight days (4–11 March) would see the 15th MCG continue to screen the left flank of the 35th ID on an approximately five-mile front. The cavalry also destroyed scattered pockets of German resistance in their zone, preventing them from disrupting the attack of the 35th ID or 8th AD.[68] By 11 March the group had been pinched out of the line and moved briefly into the reserve as the XVI Corps shifted to defensive positions along the Rhine River. The corps history labeled the contributions of the cavalry to this operation as "invaluable," particularly favoring the liaison mission the group performed between the British Second Army and the American Ninth Army.[69] Although seemingly insignificant, communications between adjacent units, particularly those belonging to different higher headquarters, are always critical. Moreover, in rapidly changing situations like that north of the Roer in early March 1944, commanders cannot wait to use the chain of command to disseminate and gather information, but instead must depend on lateral communications.

The corps cavalry of the Ninth Army truly earned their pay in Operation GRENADE. These formations acted primarily in a security role during this period as the army smashed its way across the Roer. Security proved to be a major concern for the corps of the Ninth Army, as they needed to maximize combat power forward to expand bridgeheads, but they also had to guard against counterattacks from German formations still alongside the river. These enemy formations proved to be fairly strong, as they had been expected to hold the front line. Thus, the cavalry often found themselves facing tougher resistance than some of the lead elements of the infantry and armor divisions that had broken through.

The coordination and liaison mission of the cavalry also proved essential to the Ninth Army. The physical location of this army lay between the main efforts of two army groups from different nations, both of which required the support of Simpson's forces. If the Ninth Army had failed, the 12th and 21st Army Groups' advances could have been physically separated, leading to the potential for German spoiling attacks against one or the other. Although this situation may not have been catastrophic to the Allied armies, neither would it have been ideal. Additional casualties and a slowed advance would have prolonged the war, increasing suffering and national resource expenditure. Therefore, the ability to quickly move along the flanks and make contact with adjacent units proved particularly vital for not only the forces of the army, but also for keeping the entire theater line coherent and organized.

First Army

The First Army would open its post-Bulge operations with a quick assault into the Eifel region opposite Monschau with the V and XVIII Corps. The V Corps attacked from its positions along the old northern shoulder of the Bulge, directly into the region south of the Roer dams. The XVIII Corps attacked to the south, along the boundary of the Third Army as it advanced toward the city of Prüm. This offensive had the aim of maintaining pressure on the German forces retreating out of the Bulge. Additionally, there may have been some hope in the 12th Army Group headquarters that a major success in the Eifel might shift the main effort of the Allied Expeditionary Force south from the 21st Army Group sector to the Americans.

The V Corps assault in late January and early February would consist of the 99th ID in the south, the 9th ID in the center, and the 78th ID in the north. The 78th ID, beginning in late January under the XIX Corps, attacked north of Monschau with the objective of the southern end of the Roer reservoirs. On 2 February, the 78th ID rejoined the V Corps after over a month's separation during the Battle of the Bulge.[70] Colonel Cyrus Dolph's 102nd MCG supported this attack by relieving infantry formations along the northern flank of the 9th ID as it attacked toward the town of Schleiden, ten miles east of Monschau, on 31 January 1945. The cavalry also maintained contact between the 78th and 9th IDs as they attacked eastward until the two divisions pinched the cavalry out of the line.[71] The cavalry's actions, though limited in this offensive, proved valuable. The ability of the cavalry to quickly move to and hold terrain made them quite useful in situations such as this.

Despite this promising early success in late January and early February, Eisenhower ordered the offensive halted in order to shift the main effort of the 12th Army Group north to the Cologne Plain, and south into the Saar. The First Army would protect the flank of the Ninth Army, then preparing for Operation GRENADE, the planned offensive that would take that army to the Rhine.[72] However, before GRENADE could take place, the Roer River dams, particularly the Urft and Schwammenauel dams, sixteen miles southeast of Aachen and on the east side of the Hürtgen Forest, would have to be seized. With hostile control of the dams, any attack across the Roer was vulnerable to deluge if the Germans decided to open the floodgates.[73]

The 9th ID seized the Urft Dam on the south side of the reservoir on 4 February, while the 78th ID, reinforced by elements of the 82nd Airborne Division, attacked toward the Schwammenauel Dam on the north side, just to the east of Schmidt, the focus of much hard fighting for many months. On 4 February, the 311th Infantry Regiment of the 78th ID seized the town of Rurberg on the west side of the Roer reservoir. The 102nd MCG relieved the infantry so that the regiment and the rest of the division could continue the assault north toward Schmidt, which finally fell on 7 February.[74] The cavalry again used their firepower to suppress German forces in the vicinity and hold their positions, enabling the infantry to mass forces against the division and corps main objective.

The damage to the Schwammenauel Dam during the fighting in early February along with the attendant flooding of the Roer River would create a lost month for the First and Ninth Armies. Neither saw much fighting, although both were making massive preparations for the planned offensives that would take these two armies to the Rhine. The VII Corps would participate in Operation GRENADE, supporting the Ninth Army in its drive to the Rhine. The rest of the First Army, including the VII Corps, once released from GRENADE, would take part in Operation LUMBERJACK, the destruction of German forces west of the Rhine. The First Army had also reorganized, with the V Corps now holding the southern end of the army line, from the Kyll River to just south of Schmidt, the III Corps in the center, from Schmidt to south of Düren, and the VII Corps from Düren to Jülich, and the boundary with the Ninth Army.

Colonel John McDonald's 4th MCG moved with the rest of the VII Corps in early February back to the Roer. The corps placed the cavalry, reinforced by a light tank battalion, a company of engineers, and tank destroyer battalion, in reserve, with the expectation that they would guard the left flank of the corps bridgehead, tying in with the XIX Corps to the north. The corps would attack over the Roer River to the Erft River, approximately eleven miles to the east, in order to protect the XIX Corps' flank. The corps' plan for the initial phase of LUMBERJACK involved attacking with the 8th ID south of Düren, and the 104th ID to the north. The 3rd AD would follow to exploit any penetrations, and the 99th ID would remain in reserve.[75]

The VII Corps attack began on 23 February. After two days of fierce fighting, the 8th and 104th IDs secured the bridgehead, and the rest of the corps, including the 4th MCG, began to cross. The corps tasked the cavalry to relieve elements of the 104th ID holding the towns of Oberzier and Ellen, four miles north of Düren. These towns anchored the northern end of the corps bridgehead and dominated any approach to the crossing points. The cavalry accomplished this mission and then aided the 104th ID in an attack to clear a portion of the Hambach woods just to the north of these towns. Additionally, the group made contact with elements of the XIX Corps, thereby tying together the two corps bridgeheads.[76]

The 4th MCG would continue to expand its sector of the bridgehead while maintaining contact with the 113th MCG of the XIX Corps. On 27 February the group protected the flank of the 3rd AD as it seized the large town of Elsdorf, immediately to the east. The cavalry faced a stiff fight, clearing trenches and wood lots, but it pushed through the crumbling German defenses, seizing 270 prisoners.[77] Elsdorf was the last major town before the Erft River, and the 3rd AD would have two bridgeheads over the river before the end of the day. Although the German defenses were crumbling under the weight of the combined Allied assault in GRENADE, the 4th MCG certainly made the advance of the 3rd AD easier and more fluid. The 3rd AD and 104th ID encountered fierce resistance from the German 9th Panzer Division in Elsdorf. If the attacking formations also had been responsible for clearing and securing their own flanks, the fighting might have bogged down short of the river.[78] In addition to conducting offensive security tasks along the 3rd AD's flank, the cavalry also was maintaining contact with the XIX Corps, which by 27 February required a line over eight miles long, stretching from the Roer to past Tollhausen.[79]

On 28 February, the VII Corps attached the 4th MCG to the 3rd AD. The cavalry had been closed out of the front as the 3rd AD met the XIX Corps along the Erft.[80] The cavalry spent two days protecting the division's crossing point along the river as well as conducting refit from their operations before being attached to the 99th ID. The First Army had assigned to the VII Corps the mission of seizing the city of Cologne on the Rhine River, and generally east of the corps' current location. The 8th and 104th IDs would be the main effort, while the 3rd AD secured the northern end of the city. The 99th ID would be the northern edge of the corps and would continue the mission of maintaining contact with—and protecting—the southern flank of the XIX

Corps. As the northern element of the 99th ID, this task would fall to the 4th MCG.[81]

The 4th MCG began their attack on 2 March 1945, moving to the Erft River. The group continued the advance the next day, seizing the two towns that dominated the road network on the corps' flank. During the night of 3 March, the VII Corps relieved the 4th MCG from the infantry and attached them to the 3rd AD. That division had created a gap between itself and the 99th ID as it attacked directly to the Rhine River from Worringen (nine miles northeast of Cologne) to just north of Cologne. Although the German forces were highly disorganized and damaged by now, the 3rd AD's trains and supply lines were still vulnerable, as it had moved faster than the 99th ID, which had yet to reach the Rhine. Therefore, the cavalry moved in one night from the northern flank of the 99th to its southern flank in preparation for an attack the next day. Other than an armored division combat command, no other formation in the corps had the mobility to shift position so rapidly and the firepower to accomplish the mission.[82]

On 4 March, the 4th MCG began its attack, making rapid advances and quickly closing the gap that had threatened the rear of the 3rd AD. By 5 March, the group had reached the town of Dormagen, twelve miles north of Cologne and along the Rhine River. There, the German defenders put up a tremendous defense in an all-day, building-to-building fight through dense industrial facilities as well as urban terrain. The cavalry used dismounted troops and firepower to clear the German defenses in a deliberate attack. By midday on 6 March the 4th MCG had cleared the Germans from over five miles along the west bank of the Rhine, encompassing a large bend of the river.[83] While the cavalry fought north of the city, the bulk of the corps seized Cologne—one of the largest German cities and a major industrial center.[84]

As the VII Corps closed to the Rhine, on 8 March the First Army also assigned the corps the mission of seizing the city of Bonn, fifteen miles south of Cologne. This task had originally belonged to the III Corps, but that corps' focus had shifted with the seizure of the Remagen bridgehead. Although the VII Corps received the 1st ID to assist in this task, the corps had also just received an extra fifteen miles of front and the task of reducing a major city. The corps was also in the process of planning an assault across the Rhine. Every unit possible would be needed for this new focus. Thus, the corps ordered the 4th MCG to relieve the 99th ID, allowing that division to be withdrawn from the line and moved south. This shift meant that the cavalry were now manning a sector along the Rhine from Worringen to Neuss (across the Rhine from Düsseldorf), eleven miles of straight-line distance, but much more considering the bends in the river. The cavalry were now manning nearly two divisions worth of front between the 3rd AD in the south and the 113th MCG to the north.[85]

To the south of the VII Corps, the III Corps launched its attack as part of LUMBERJACK. When the III Corps moved north from the Third Army to the center of the First Army line in mid-February, it also assumed command of Colonel Lawrence Smith's 14th MCG. The group had spent the past month and a half rebuilding, with a brief stint of action by the 32nd CRS supporting the 82nd Airborne in its operations in early February around Schmidt. On 25 February, elements of the III Corps' 1st ID crossed assault bridges built by the VII Corps around Düren and attacked south into the corps' area of operations on the east bank of the Roer. By 27 February, the 1st and 9th IDs had secured a bridgehead, with the 1st holding the northern end, linked to the VII Corps, and the 9th driving south along the riverbank to the boundary with the V Corps. That same day the 14th MCG crossed the Roer and began its assigned mission of protecting the corps' southern flank.[86]

The next day, the 14th MCG, reinforced with a company of tank destroyers and another of combat engineers, began its attack south to the V Corps boundary. This move took them across the front of the 9th ID, then occupied in clearing the eastern bank of the Roer around the town of Nideggen as well as building more bridges across the Roer. The cavalry only advanced a little more than a mile before encountering a German counterattack involving tanks as well as infantry. The group defeated the German assault, but in the process was stopped for the day themselves.[87]

The situation at the end of the day on 28 February presented the commander of the III Corps with a choice of what to do with his cavalry. The 1st ID had made solid gains in the past two days and was now seven miles east of the Roer. The 9th AD had also made good progress and had advanced six miles southeast of the bridgehead at Düren. The task of the 1st ID was to seize the city of Bonn, while the 9th AD, supported by the 9th ID, was to advance as fast as possible and attempt to seize a Rhine crossing as well as protect the northern flank of the V Corps. Neither of these two missions involved a protracted fight well to the southwest of and behind the corps spearheads, which was what was currently consuming the 14th MCG and 9th ID. What the corps needed was mobile security to the east in support of both divisions. While the 9th AD had the ability to provide for its own security through organic assets, the 1st ID possessed merely a single reconnaissance troop. It also had an attached medium tank battalion, but if that unit was involved in security operations it could not support the division's main effort. The corps cavalry possessed the necessary mobility and firepower to accomplish the task. This is one of the reasons why cavalry exists. Therefore, on the night of 28 February, the corps commander detached the 32nd CRS from the group and attached it to the 1st ID. The rest of the group followed on 2 March, reinforced with a tank destroyer battalion.[88]

The 14th MCG spent a day in assembly areas behind the 1st ID, then moved on 4 March to defend crossing points along the Erft Canal in the vicinity of Nörvenich, seven miles east of Düren. This move relieved the 26th Infantry Regiment of the 1st ID from this duty, allowing that regiment to continue the attack toward the Rhine. Additionally, the group relieved the 18th Infantry Regiment in the northern portion of the division zone, allowing the 1st ID to concentrate on a more southeasterly direction toward Bonn.[89]

The following day, 5 March, the 14th MCG attacked in its zone to clear German resistance between the Erft Canal and the Rhine. The two squadrons conducted an envelopment of German forces while fixing their attention with a frontal assault. The 32nd CRS attacked directly into weakening German resistance, advancing seven miles east of the Erft Canal. The 18th CRS moved north into the 8th ID's sector and attacked to the southeast, destroying German resistance in a series of four towns. This attack defeated the German forces between the III and VII Corps and protected the flank of the 1st ID as it attacked toward Bonn.[90]

After their attack on 5 March, the 14th MCG spent the next two days clearing the remaining German forces in their sector and relieving elements of the 1st ID to their south so that division could focus more combat power on Bonn. On 7 March, the 9th AD seized the Ludendorff Bridge over the Rhine at Remagen, completely refocusing the efforts of the III Corps.[91] The First Army ordered the corps to drop all other considerations and get combat power across the Rhine. As part of these adjustments, the 1st ID, along with the 14th MCG, joined the VII Corps. The cavalry attacked east to the Rhine River and protected the northern flank of the division as it attacked into Bonn. The cavalry eventually settled on a front approximately five miles along the river. Additionally, the group continued its mission of maintaining contact with the division to the north of the 1st ID, by now the 104th ID.[92] This security allowed the 1st ID to rapidly clear Bonn and prepare for operations on the east bank of the Rhine.

The V Corps' 102nd MCG spent the month of February holding the town of Rurberg near the Roer dams with one squadron while the other remained in reserve. Additionally, the cavalry received the new M24 Chaffee. The M24 and its 75mm gun proved vastly superior to the 37mm-armed M5 Stuart that it replaced.[93] The cavalry now held the northern edge of the V Corps zone, connecting it with the III Corps to the north.

On 27 February, the V Corps began its part in Operation LUMBERJACK with limited attacks by the 69th ID in the south of the corps zone. On 2 March, the 102nd MCG with the 2nd Ranger Battalion attached crossed the Roer at Rurberg and cleared the peninsula created by the Roer Reservoir. This movement was in conjunction with the attack of the 2nd ID to the south of the cavalry. The group spent the next two days clearing minor German resistance from the peninsula while waiting for developments in the rest of the corps sector. On 5 March 1945, German resistance began to break, and the V Corps ordered the 102nd MCG to advance as rapidly as possible, protecting the northern flank of the corps as well as maintaining contact with the 78th ID of the III Corps to the north. This task would be complicated by the fact that the 2nd ID would not simply be advancing along a straight line, but wheeling southeast as it moved, lengthening their northern flank with every hour on the attack.[94]

The 102nd MCG advanced rapidly, moving over thirteen miles to the east on 5 March. The next two days produced spectacular advances as the cavalry rapidly closed to the Ahr River at the town of Ahrweiler, a further twelve miles to the southeast. While the German forces put up scattered resistance that was occasionally fierce, the cavalry were able to use their mobility and firepower to good effect.[95] After the group had closed upon the Ahr River on 7 March (also famous as the day of the Remagen Bridge seizure by the III Corps), the V Corps ordered it to continue south, protecting the left flank of the 2nd ID as it closed the trap on German forces to the west. The cavalry continued to move quickly, seizing large numbers of prisoners, including the commander of the German 5th Fallschirmjäger Division, who had stayed overlong attending to last-minute details before retreating over the Rhine with his division.[96]

On 9 March, elements of the 2nd ID met the leading edges of the Third Army's 6th MCG advancing from the south, closing the pocket on German forces west of the Rhine. The 102nd MCG had played an important role in this operation. The V Corps had required an extremely mobile force with enough firepower to overcome resistance to protect the outer edge of its wheel while keeping contact with the III Corps as it attacked along a more direct route to the Rhine. The cavalry met this need perfectly, particularly when reinforced by a battalion of rangers. The 102nd MCG allowed the 2nd ID to focus on trapping German forces without looking over its shoulder, and it also allowed the III Corps to drive to the Rhine without worrying about its southern flank. On 10 March, SHAEF ordered the 102nd MCG headquarters along with the 38th CRS south to join the Seventh Army's VI Corps. The 102nd CRS would remain in assembly areas in the V Corps zone as the corps closed to the Rhine River, south of Remagen.

The actions of the cavalry groups of the First Army greatly aided the overall success of this formation in Operation LUMBERJACK. While rarely leading the army assault, the cavalry provided highly valuable service on the flanks in security and coordination roles. The flank security role proved particularly valuable as the army wheeled south after penetrating the German lines. This wheel meant that both flanks of the army were exposed, requiring a security screen. Although the Germans did not have the ability to take advantage of this situation, they could have interdicted the corps' supply lines and inflicted additional casualties on the army's rear echelons. Such actions would have only slowed the First Army, but they still would have hurt. Moreover, force protection is important, and accepting unnecessary risk would have been negligent for the American commanders.

Finally, the security provided by the corps cavalry allowed the First Army to be more aggressive. While the seizure of the Ludendorff Bridge at Remagen did not directly involve a cavalry group, they did have an indirect presence. The 102nd MCG's liaison and security mission linking the V and III Corps together gave the III Corps the peace of mind to throw its divisions headlong toward the Rhine without having to worry about the rear becoming compromised. Thus, Hodges's cavalrymen earned their pay in the drive to the Rhine. Although the army would have succeeded without them, particularly at this point in the war, it would have struggled more as infantry and armor units peeled off to perform cavalry tasks. While certainly not the most glamorous or exciting missions, these jobs needed to be done.

Seventh Army

The Seventh Army spent the bulk of January repelling a series of German assaults that had begun on New Year's Day and continued throughout the month. Late in the month, the newly arrived XXI Corps would join the French First Army in the destruction of the Colmar Pocket. That corps' cavalry group, Colonel Charles McClelland's 101st MCG, would not participate in that action, as they relieved Colonel Vennard Wilson's 106th MCG just south of the Saar River on the extreme left flank of the Seventh Army.

While the XXI and XV Corps consolidated their positions to the west of the Vosges in February, the VI Corps fought to regain some of the ground it had lost. The 36th ID in particular faced a fierce fight to eliminate the Gambsheim salient, a thumb-shaped protrusion of German forces extending five miles south of the Moder River with its back to the Rhine. Lieutenant Colonel Harold Samsel's 117th CRS would aid the 36th ID in its fight by anchoring the division's right flank, allowing the infantry regiments to fight their way into and through Gambsheim. The cavalry would aid the infantry through reconnaissance and fire support throughout the first week of February. On 7 February, the 36th ID pulled the 117th CRS off the line and moved them to hold a five-mile front along the south bank of the Moder River. The New Jersey cavalrymen relieved the 141st Infantry Regiment, allowing that unit to be placed in reserve, and thus, by extension, allowing the entire division to rotate regiments off of portions of the line still undergoing intense action.[97] This capability proved to be a tremendous aid to the 36th ID as it fought its way forward. The squadron remained along the Moder River for the rest of February as the VI Corps built strength to resume the offensive.

By early March, the Seventh Army had defeated the German counteroffensive, participated in the destruction of the Colmar Pocket to the south, and reoriented itself to resume offensive operations to the north. This offensive would be coordinated with the Third Army to destroy German forces operating in the Saar–Palatinate salient, essentially that part of Germany to the west of the Rhine River and south of the Moselle. The Third Army, having already fought a bitter fight through the Siegfried Line, would attack from the line of the Moselle to the south and east. The Seventh Army still faced its portion of the Siegfried Line and would have to attack north through the German fortifications, then wheel to the east so as to remain on line with the Third Army.[98]

To accomplish its task, Patch arrayed his army three corps abreast, oriented to the north. On the left flank, the XXI Corps, with two divisions, maintained contact with the Third Army at the apex of the German salient around Saarlautern. The army center was maintained by the XV Corps, with six divisions, from east of Saarbrücken to the Vosges. Finally, the VI Corps anchored the right with five divisions (one of them French) stretched from the Vosges to the Rhine. The army plan was fairly straightforward. All three corps would attack north in zone, through the Siegfried Line. Major General Frank Milburn's XXI Corps would seize Saarbrücken, while the XV Corps would attack along an axis Zweibrücken–Kaiserslautern. The VI Corps would simply plug north on the east side of the Vosges (see map 16).[99]

Before the XXI Corps could begin its offensive, it first had to clear German forces from the southern bank of the Saar River as well as the ground to the front of the Siegfried Line. The Germans had gained this ground during Operation NORDWIND, and now the Americans needed to recapture it prior to beginning operations to the north. The 63rd ID

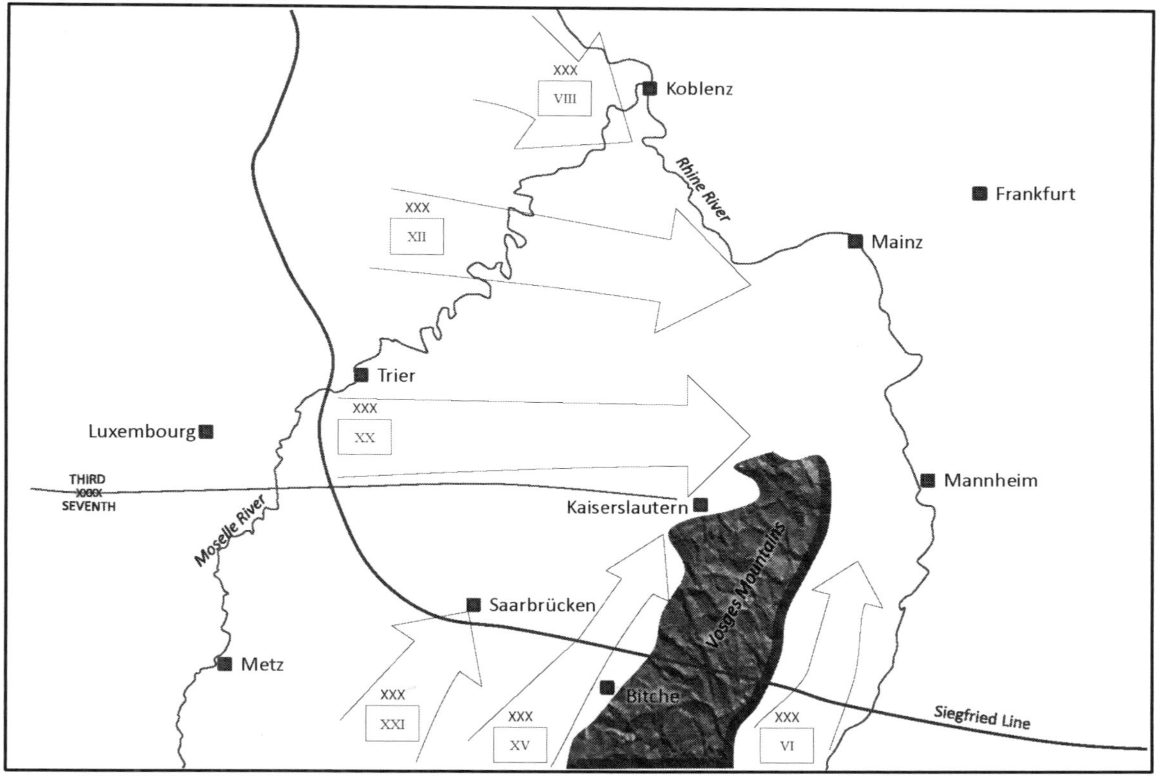

Map 16. The Destruction of the Saar–Palatinate Salient.

attacked on the corps' right, while the 70th ID advanced to the left. On the corps' left flank, the 101st MCG patrolled vigorously along its seven-mile front from Emmersweiler on the right to Wadgassen (along the Saar) on the left. As part of the general corps operations to close to the Saar, the cavalry prepared to attack north in mid-March 1945. On 13 March, the group's patrols discovered evidence that the Germans were withdrawing from the southern bank of the river. Therefore, the next day, the cavalry attacked along the breadth of its zone, closing the mile and a half to the Saar by nightfall, clearing the weak German resistance remaining on the western bank.[100] This reconnaissance sped up the corps' timetable and saved resources, as it no longer had to plan to seize this area.[101]

On 15 March, the XXI Corps began its portion of the army offensive. The 70th ID on the corps' left made slow headway against stiff German resistance in Saarbrücken. However, the 63rd ID began to make good progress on the right. This uneven advance opened a gap between the two infantry divisions. Therefore, on 17 March, the corps moved the 101st MCG from its positions on the corps' left to protect the left flank of the 63rd ID, maintaining contact with the 70th ID. The cavalry relieved an entire infantry regiment of the 63rd ID along a three-mile line facing Saarbrücken to the west. This relief allowed that regiment to be used in the fighting in the Siegfried Line to the north.[102]

By 20 March, German resistance was starting to fade. To take advantage of this, the 63rd ID ordered a reinforced troop of the 101st MCG to infiltrate through the German lines and take the key town of Sankt Ingbert, six miles to the northeast of Saarbrücken. Control of this town would almost completely isolate the defenders of Saarbrücken, who were still frustrating the 70th ID. The troop seized the town by that afternoon, with the rest of the group clearing German resistance to the south. Upon relief by the infantry of the 63rd ID, the cavalry screened the division's flank along a five-mile front from the Saar River to Sankt Ingbert, facing Saarbrücken.[103] The cavalry's actions helped the 63rd ID achieve its objective, the city of Neunkirchen, by 21 March.[104] The capture of this city would break the Americans nearly free of the rugged terrain around the Saar River, allowing for more rapid movement.

While the XXI Corps battled its way through the Siegfried Line around Saarbrücken on the Seventh Army's left, the supersized XV Corps (six divisions) launched the army's main effort in the center. This corps attacked on 15 March with three divisions. The 45th and 3rd IDs attacked directly north toward the city of Zweibrücken. The 100th ID, to the right of those divisions, would first clear the Bitche fortresses that had stymied the Seventh Army in December. The other two infantry divisions of the corps maintained defensive positions to support the attacks, while the 6th AD was kept in reserve.[105] The corps inserted the 106th MCG between the 3rd ID and the 100th ID.[106] This position allowed the cavalry to maintain contact between the two divisions as they attacked in slightly different directions. Moreover, as the corps expected Bitche to be a more difficult fight than what was facing the 3rd ID, it presumed that the 3rd ID would advance faster than the 100th ID and might open its right flank to a counterattack.

On the opening day of the offensive, the 106th MCG advanced approximately two and a half miles, seizing the town of Lengelsheim, three miles north of Bitche and along a lateral route that fed into the main road leading into Bitche from the north. The capture of this town allowed the cavalry to communicate better with the 100th ID as well as block German movement into or out of the area. During the next several days the cavalry steadily advanced, protecting the flank of the 3rd ID as it attacked into Germany. The group's advance was aided by the 100th ID's rapid seizure of Bitche on 16 March, allowing the cavalry to move north, perhaps more rapidly than expected.[107]

By 19 March, the 106th MCG had crossed the German border and was conducting operations along a three-mile front, almost exactly in between Pirmasens and Zweibrücken. The same day, the rapid advance of the 100th ID would remove the need for the cavalry to protect the 3rd ID's flank, as the two divisions were now relatively on line and connected. By this point, the XV Corps was experiencing success across its entire front, and on 20 March it committed the 6th AD to exploit the penetrated German defenses and attack toward Kaiserslautern.[108] Additionally, the 3rd and 100th IDs began to move very rapidly. Haislip placed the 106th MCG to the right of the 3rd ID and ordered the cavalry to protect the infantry's flank as they moved as quickly as possible to the north and then to the east. This protection allowed the division to accelerate, as units stopped having to concentrate on security and thus were able to focus on their front. On 22 March, the cavalry moved into the lead of the 3rd ID, escorting a motorized regiment through the northern Vosges Mountains, from Kaiserslautern to Bad Dürkheim.[109] Although the territory covered by the cavalry and infantry during this time had already been covered by the armored divisions of the Third and Seventh Armies, the armor had not taken the time to consolidate the ground. Therefore, large numbers of disorganized German units and individuals still littered the battle-space and posed a threat to truck-mounted infantry. The attack would end on 23 March with the XV Corps on the Rhine. The 106th MCG would move to positions along the Rhine north of Worms to reconnoiter possible crossing sites and to prevent German intrusion upon American plans.[110] The cavalry's reconnaissance and security during this period greatly aided the quick and cheap success of the corps.

As the German salient in the Saar–Palatinate collapsed with the Third Army assaulting from the north and the Seventh Army from the south, the American line began to constrict. The XXI Corps' front was blocked by the advance of the Third Army's XX Corps to the north and the Seventh Army's XV Corps to the east. Therefore, on 22 March, the Seventh Army moved the XXI Corps headquarters with its corps units to a new sector of the front, taking over the XV Corps' 100th and 71st IDs. These divisions were moving rapidly east of Pirmasens, heading toward the Rhine River.

The 101st MCG moved behind the front-line divisions of the XXI Corps, destroying pockets of German resistance, sweeping up fugitive German soldiers, and generally securing the rear areas of the corps. By 24 March, the cavalry had landed on a twelve-mile line east of Pirmasens and Kaiserslautern in the extreme northeastern side of the Vosges Mountains. There the group halted and conducted area security operations in the corps' rear as the XXI Corps prepared to cross the Rhine and continue the assault deeper into Germany.[111] While these operations seem negligible, they were critical during this period. With at least two German field armies smashed in the Saar–Palatinate, the potential for large numbers of fleeing enemy soldiers to cause mischief in the corps' rear areas was high. While these individuals could not stop the American advance, they could certainly disrupt and slow it down by attacking supply lines and command nodes.

While the 101st and 106th MCGs supported the XXI and XV Corps to the west, the 117th CRS joined the VI Corps in its offensive directly north. At the beginning of March, the corps moved the squadron from the 36th ID into reserve. The squadron would spend nearly two weeks waiting to be called forward. On 13 March, the corps committed the 117th CRS to the left flank of the 42nd ID. The cavalry's new positions were fairly familiar, as the positions along the 42nd ID's flank in the Vosges east of Bitche were the same ones that they had held in January. The 42nd ID's mission in the upcoming offensive would be to assault directly through the northern Vosges Mountains. The cavalry's task would be to protect the left flank of the division, conduct reconnaissance in zone, and maintain contact with the 71st ID of the XV Corps to the west.[112]

The attack of the 42nd ID began on 15 March with the rest of the Seventh Army. The 117th CRS, after allowing a battalion of infantry to pass through its lines, moved out on its mission of securing the division's flank. Within three days of the initial attack the cavalry's patrols had advanced approximately twelve miles, placing the squadron to the east and northeast of Bitche. By 23 March the squadron had attacked to just east of Pirmasens. At this point the armored divisions of both the Seventh and Third Armies had reached the Rhine, and the infantry divisions of the XXI and XV Corps were closing on the river as well. Thus, the Germans facing the VI Corps were cut off and placed in a hopeless situation, though that did not stop several units from futile displays of resistance.[113]

After the general collapse of German resistance in the region, the VI Corps detached the 117th CRS from the 42nd ID and used the cavalry to conduct roving patrols and checkpoints throughout the northern Vosges. The intent was to capture fugitive German soldiers in order to prevent them from harming the American advance. The squadron was reunited with its New Jersey brothers in the 102nd MCG, which had been detached from the First Army. The reinforced cavalry continued this mission until 29 March, when the 102nd MCG was ordered back to the First Army and the 117th CRS was directed by the VI Corps to assemble in preparation for a move across the Rhine.[114]

The Seventh Army's cavalry, much like their brethren in the other armies, made their greatest contributions in the spring of 1945 in the guise of flank security and coordination. These actions proved doubly important for Patch's formation, as it had to not only fight its way north, but then also pivot on its axis to the east, linking up with the Third Army on the fly and in the middle of the turn. This move, difficult enough by itself, was further complicated as these two armies reported to different army group headquarters, requiring even more deft coordination than normal.

The terrain and nature of the Seventh Army's zone also complicated Patch's task. The Vosges Mountains separated the VI Corps from the other two army formations, meaning that a solid front advance was simply out of the question. Additionally, all three corps had to fight through the Siegfried Line, a more difficult task for some than others. Moreover, the XXI and XV Corps would then have to turn through these mountains in order to reach the Rhine. Adding in the different distances required of each corps in the attack meant that, rather than a solid line advancing, the Seventh Army attack would resolve into a series of individual corps and divisions scrambling their way forward in only the barest approximation of a front. Therefore, the security as well as flank coordination provided by the cavalry proved particularly valuable to the Seventh Army as it worked to maximize its combat power while minimizing friendly losses.

The fighting in the spring of 1945 witnessed corps cavalry proving their utility again, not only in the open field running that characterized late March, but also in the bitter positional fighting that began the period. The fact that the groups proved useful in both kinds of warfare and their ability to rapidly transition from one to the other speaks to their overall versatility.

While cavalry conducted economy of force operations, their greatest contributions in March came in the realm of coordination and flank security (as opposed to an offensive or defensive guard). This period saw three army groups comprised of seven armies move forward within the span of a month. The U.S. Army alone had twelve corps moving nearly simultaneously over a 250-mile front. So many moving pieces over so vast an area meant that the chances of gaps in the lines, confused boundaries, or oversights increased into the realm of certainty.

The corps cavalry were among the best tools available to Eisenhower and his generals to help mitigate the chaos.

Although by the spring of 1945 German defeat appeared inevitable, the war continued. Without the cavalry, the American army would have struggled to coordinate and protect its far-flung formations as they moved to crush the last remaining organized enemy units. This challenge would continue with the last assault into the heart of Germany. The campaign would see the need for firepower and mobility, two hallmarks of the cavalry.

8

Sabers through the Reich

By the middle of March, the Allied armies stood poised along the Rhine River, ready to launch the offensive that would end the war in the west. The Ninth Army, still attached to Field Marshal Bernard Montgomery's 21st Army Group, stretched from a point between Düsseldorf and Cologne in the south to the town of Wesel in the north. Lieutenant General Courtney Hodge's First Army, with a foothold already across the Rhine at Remagen, would use the middle of the month to steadily transfer most of its combat power into that bridgehead, while still maintaining contact with Lieutenant General William Simpson's Ninth Army and Lieutenant General George S. Patton's Third Army on its flanks. The Third Army, fresh from its victories in the Saar–Palatinate, linked up with the First Army at Koblenz and stood ready to leap the Rhine and drive toward Frankfurt. Lieutenant General Alexander Patch's Seventh Army, having joined the Third Army north of Worms, also prepared its own crossing in support of the 12th Army Group's efforts.

General Dwight D. Eisenhower and his Supreme Headquarters Allied Expeditionary Force (SHAEF) planned a series of assaults that would overload the German defenses and bring Allied armies into the heart of Germany. Simpson and Hodges planned a massive envelopment of the Ruhr industrial region, while Patton and Patch plotted drives deep into central and southern Germany. SHAEF also planned for the British 21st Army Group to vault across the Rhine (using the American Ninth Army to protect its southern flank) and drive through northern Germany along the North European Plain to the Elbe River.

By this point in the war the German military struggled to bring any coherent combat forces to bear. In the north their forces facing the British and American armies were perhaps the best rested, considering the long planning cycle of the 21st Army Group. However, these units had also been stripped of significant forces to help reinforce the German center. In this sector, the U.S. First Army, already across the Rhine thanks to its *coup de main* at Remagen, faced an assortment of desperate German defenders that may have lacked organization but benefitted from almost all the reserves that Berlin could spare for the Western Front. Farther south, the American Third and Seventh Armies faced a collection of battered units that had escaped from the fighting in the Saar–Palatinate as well as hastily collected reserves.

Although the terrain along portions of the front still proved challenging, the overall weakened state of the Wehrmacht by late March 1945 meant that once the Allies could get sufficient combat power across the Rhine, the Germans would be unable to form an effective defensive line to delay or stop them. However, this did not mean that many German formations gave up easily and without a fight. The fighting after the Rhine would be characterized by engagements that were as brutal and vicious as they were fleeting.

First Army

After the seizure of the Ludendorff Bridge over the Rhine at Remagen on 7 March, the First Army rapidly made the bridgehead on the east bank its primary mission. However, alliance politics as well as traffic congestion at the crossing point delayed the army's buildup, as the 12th Army Group limited the amount of combat power allowed on the eastern bank.[1] Essentially, Montgomery insisted that his formations still receive priority in their assault to the Rhine and that even though the First Army was already across the Rhine, it should subordinate its efforts to the 21st Army Group.[2] Despite this official restraint, Hodges would push as hard as possible to get as much combat power across the Rhine as he could.

Major General John Millikin's III Corps, the first corps across the Rhine, soon encountered a number of problems in expanding the bridgehead. First and foremost was the problem of communicating with the elements of the corps across the river. Ordinarily, wire was the standard means of communicating at the division or corps level. However, due to the intensity of German artillery, as well as the inherent problems of stringing wire across a river as wide as the Rhine, this method proved unreliable. Radio was the other means of communication. However, the corps and division nets were jammed with traffic, as the III Corps literally threw almost every asset it could toward the bridges. Additionally, the corps still had to control divisions on the west bank of the Rhine as well as the fight on the east bank. The initial forces across the river, elements of the 9th AD and 9th ID, soon found themselves hard pressed to talk to the corps and coordinate among themselves.

The corps' solution ripped a page from the Third Army's playbook of the previous fall by calling for the cavalry. On 8 March, the III Corps directed Colonel Lawrence Smith's 14th MCG to provide radio teams to the headquarters of the two divisions across the Rhine, the crossing point, and the corps headquarters. This secondary radio net helped ease the command and control burden on the corps and allowed them to more efficiently move troops across the river and manage the fight on the east bank.[3] The cavalry accomplished this task as it was finishing its duties north of Bonn supporting the 1st ID.

Millikin also faced the problem of protecting the Ludendorff Bridge and the subsequent engineer bridges built around it. Traffic control at the crossing points was also a problem. Units from the 9th ID were taking care of these tasks, but they were needed by their division in the fight to the east. On 10 March the 14th MCG was released from the 1st ID and VII Corps and rejoined the III Corps. The corps immediately put the cavalry to work protecting the bridges and controlling traffic, relieving the 9th ID units. The handover was completed by 12 March, and the group remained at these tasks until 23 March, when it was relieved by the 8th Tank Destroyer (TD) Group.[4]

As the III Corps fought to expand its bridgehead, the First Army began funneling Major General Joseph Collins's VII Corps to the east bank of the Rhine. On 10 March 1945, the army boundary shifted south so that the Ninth Army's 113th MCG could relieve the VII Corps' 4th MCG from its positions along the Rhine, north of Cologne. The 4th spent five days in reserve refitting their equipment before being committed back on 16 March along an eight-mile front on the west bank of the Rhine River north of Cologne.[5] The commitment of the cavalry, along with the continued presence of the 8th and 104th IDs, allowed the VII Corps to completely pull its armored division, the 3rd AD, off the line and rest it for future operations.

The period from the recommitment of the 4th MCG to the line until 20 March saw the group hold their positions along the Rhine with half of the VII Corps, while on the east bank the 78th and 1st IDs attacked north to expand the bridgehead and assist the III Corps to the east. By 20 March, the corps had advanced to the Sieg River, a small tributary that flowed into the Rhine River opposite Bonn. To aid the two divisions fighting on the east bank, the VII Corps attached the 4th CRS and a combat command of the 3rd AD to the 78th ID. The cavalry secured a five-mile front along the Sieg River from the Rhine River. This allowed the 78th ID to concentrate infantry combat power on clearing a three-mile segment of the Sieg River line to the east of the cavalry. This river line would serve to anchor the American defense of the northern shoulder of the bridgehead.[6]

The V Corps would cross the Rhine on 21 March. Hodges assigned the corps to the southern portion of the Remagen bridgehead and ordered it to seize Limburg. This city was a major crossing point along the Lahn River, a Rhine tributary that flowed along the southern flank of the American bridgehead. Possession of Limburg would allow the First Army to move across the Lahn at will and prevent easy German movement against the American right. The corps attacked without its cavalry, the 102nd MCG, as the group headquarters with the 38th CRS had been detached to the Seventh Army's VI Corps. The 102nd CRS remained with the corps, but it spent the first days of the corps' attack on the west bank of the Rhine combing the corps area for straggling Germans. The group headquarters and the 38th CRS would arrive in the VI Corps area on 24 March, and without seeing action would be ordered to return to the V Corps on 28 March.[7] Thus, half of the corps cavalry group would be involved in essentially a wild goose chase for half the month.

On 24 March, the First Army began its offensive to break out of the Remagen bridgehead and encircle the Ruhr. Initially all three corps of the army attacked east to the Giessen–Marburg line, Collins's

VII Corps in the north, Major General James Van Fleet's III Corps in the center, and Major General Clarence Huebner's V Corps in the south.[8] Then the army shifted north in a great wheel. Collins's axis of attack would be from Marburg to Paderborn with the additional task of linking up with the Ninth Army, which was attacking from the west toward Paderborn. His corps would also be responsible for maintaining contact with the Rhine River, essentially creating the southern shoulder of the soon-to-be Ruhr Pocket. Van Fleet commanded the middle formation, attacking generally northeast from the Marburg region to the Eder River, twenty-five miles to the north, where it would be pinched out by the VII and V Corps. Huebner's corps took the outside track, attacking north from Giessen, around the III Corps to the north of Kassel (see map 17).[9]

The VII Corps began its attack to the east on 25 March, with the 3rd AD passing east through the 1st ID in the north and the 104th ID in the south. The two infantry divisions then followed and supported the armor. The 78th ID maintained contact with the Rhine and anchored the left flank of the corps as it attacked to the east and north.[10] That same day, the VII Corps returned the 4th CRS to the 4th MCG as it prepared to aid the corps in the offensive.[11] As the 3rd AD, fully rested from its time out of the line, broke through the German lines and began its exploitation to the north, the corps required a mobile element that could rapidly relieve elements of the 1st ID in protecting the left flank of the corps, keeping pace with the 3rd AD. This protection was vital, as this flank was the inner wall of the developing Ruhr Pocket, and any German attempt to escape from the pocket would strike through this portion of the corps.

Thus, on 28 March the VII Corps committed the 4th MCG between the 78th and 1st IDs. That day, the cavalry relieved two regiments of the 1st ID, covering over ten miles of front along the Sieg River, so that they could continue the attack north.[12] On 30 March, the 78th ID relieved the 4th MCG of its security mission. Collins then ordered the group to seize the two critical road junctions of Brilon and Büren (twenty-three and fourteen miles south of Paderborn, respectively) in order to prevent German forces from escaping through the gaps between the 3rd AD and the following infantry. These two towns controlled most of the east-west roads in the northeast portion of the

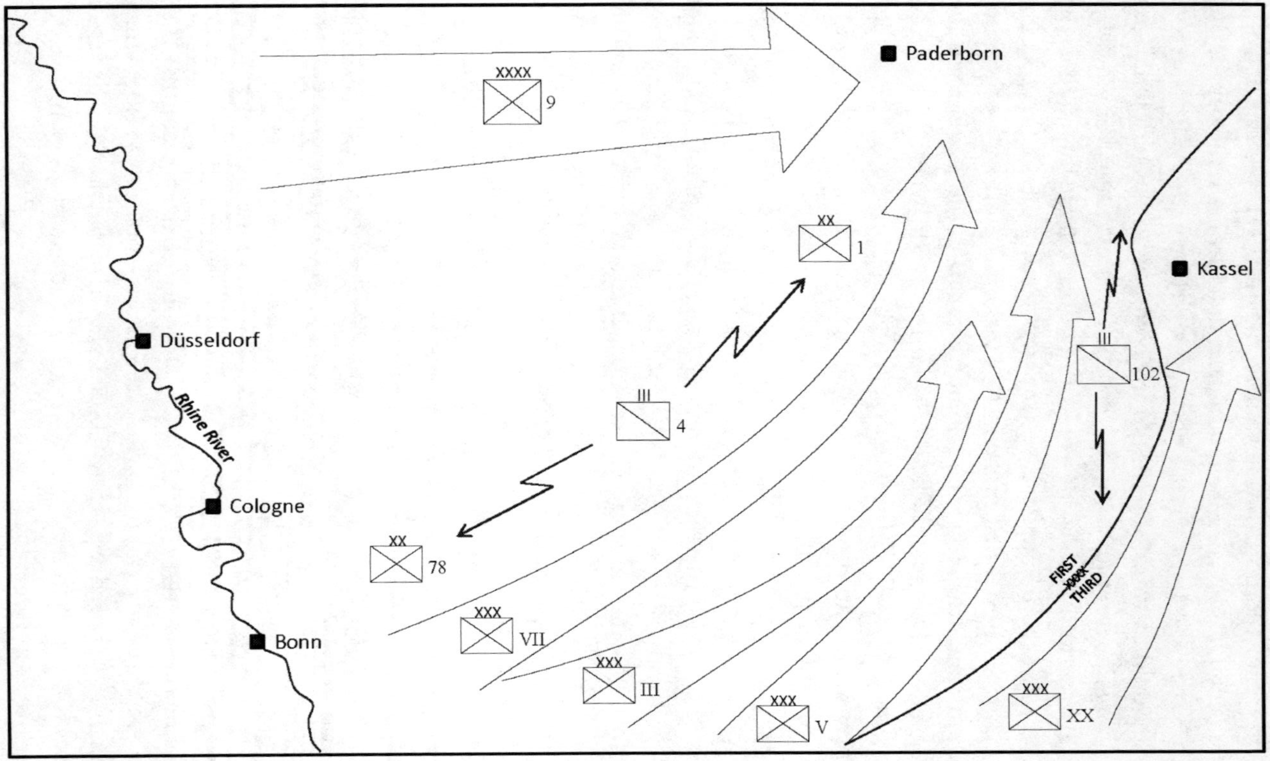

Map 17. The Encirclement of the Ruhr.

developing Ruhr Pocket. The cavalry could move quicker than the 1st ID and reach these towns first, plugging the hole through which Germans were escaping. The corps also reinforced the cavalry with a battalion of the 1st ID to give them additional dismounted ability to aid in blocking German fugitives.[13] This operation could be considered a continuation of the cavalry's security mission, just in a new location, and in an offensive posture.

The first two days of the 4th MCG's attack saw the group making good progress, advancing thirty-five miles, well over halfway to its objective of Brilon. Throughout the attack, small company-size elements of Germans supported by tanks and assault guns attempted to block the group's advance. Although this resistance slowed the attack, the Germans could not stop the cavalry due to the latter's ability to bring down superior firepower and maneuver around them.[14]

On 1 April, the 9th ID took over the mission of securing the town of Büren, and the 4th MCG concentrated on seizing Brilon, which the group occupied later that day. The capture of these towns helped complete the inner seal around the now fully developed Ruhr Pocket. The next day, the 4th MCG, now attached to the 104th ID, attacked to the west, cutting the roads leading out of the Ruhr Pocket. During the next week the 4th MCG participated in a series of actions to the west and north of Brilon as they fought to prevent German forces from escaping from the pocket's northeast corner. The group repulsed several German counterattacks attempting to break out of the perimeter, experiencing particularly heavy fighting around the town of Olsberg, four miles southwest of Brilon. The Germans had concentrated a fairly significant force in this town, as it served as a natural staging point for an attack on the American positions in Brilon, due to the road net and shape of the terrain. The 4th MCG fought a number of actions along the periphery of Olsberg, even managing to push a couple of combat patrols into the center of the town before having to withdraw them due to heavy resistance.[15]

As the 4th MCG and 104th ID fought around Brilon in the northeast corner of the Ruhr Pocket, the rest of the VII Corps turned its attentions to the east, into central Germany, on 4 April. In the fighting around Brilon, the 4th MCG demonstrated that it not only could conduct an offensive security mission, but also that it could hold a defensive screen against a fairly determined—and desperate—enemy. Moreover, the cavalry aided the 104th ID in holding its small corner of the Ruhr Pocket while the primary attention of the corps had been elsewhere.

The 14th MCG spent the first part of the III Corps' drive north in assembly areas in the corps' rear, preparing for commitment. On March 28 the corps attached the 18th CRS to the 99th ID and the 32nd CRS to the 9th ID. These squadrons assisted these two divisions in providing flank and rear security as they raced to the north. On 31 March the squadrons returned to group control.[16] The corps had achieved its objectives and had been pinched out of the advance north. At that time, the First Army assigned the III Corps to participate in the destruction of the Ruhr Pocket to the west, while the V and VII Corps attacked to the east. This move required a substantial adjustment of the corps, as it required reorienting from the north to the west. The 14th MCG aided the III Corps in this adjustment by assuming responsibility for the sectors held by the 9th and 99th IDs, clearing them of hostile remnants and protecting key infrastructure, such as dams and power stations.[17]

While the VII and III Corps attacked east and north, the V Corps began its attack to set the outside edge of the Ruhr Encirclement and maintain contact with the Third Army to the south (and eventually, east). On 26 March, Huebner committed the 102nd CRS to the east bank of the Rhine. The squadron relieved elements of the 9th AD two miles north of Koblenz and across the Rhine. The cavalry, reinforced with the 2nd Ranger Battalion and the 62nd Armored Field Artillery, were to protect the southern flank of the 9th AD as it attacked toward Limburg. This relief freed the 9th AD of enough combat power to concentrate its forces upon the city, seizing it just before midnight on 26 March. Additionally, the squadron was responsible for maintaining contact with the Third Army, to the south at Koblenz.[18]

By 28 March the 9th AD had passed through Limburg to the south and east. The 102nd CRS moved from the Rhine to relieve elements of that division two miles southwest of Limburg in Diez. There the squadron again protected the southern flank of the 9th AD and the corps as they attacked to the east and north. The cavalry would be relieved by elements of the Third Army's VIII Corps later that night, allowing the 102nd CRS to continue to move north in their mission of protecting the V Corps' flank.[19] Additionally, Huebner ordered the cavalry to conduct traffic control, preventing non-V Corps units from entering the corps zone due to its narrowness.[20] At this time, the V Corps was passing to the right of the III Corps, which had stopped at the Edersee (a large reservoir eighteen miles southwest of Kassel), pinching out the corps. However, the army zone had not expanded, and the V Corps had only about a nine-mile width between the III Corps to the west and the XX Corps to the east. By 1 April, the squadron was arrayed along a twelve-mile front facing east toward Kassel. There the cavalry released elements of the 9th AD to continue the attack north to Warburg (twenty miles northwest of Kassel), the northern limit of advance for the V Corps. The 102nd MCG with the 38th CRS, now back under the control of its parent corps, relieved the 102nd CRS from their line on 2 April, and that squadron then moved to protect the corps headquarters, thirteen miles west of Kassel.[21] The 38th CRS continued the 102nd's mission of sweeping up remnants of German formations left in their zone and patrolling to the east to maintain contact with the XX Corps. In just over a week the 102nd MCG had transitioned from a defensive security mission to an offensive security mission while also providing economy of force measures and conducting area security for the corps. This flexibility is what made the cavalry so useful to the army.

The reduction of the Ruhr Pocket began on 4 April with the XVI and XIX Corps of the Ninth Army attacking from the north. The First Army began its attack the next day, with the III Corps on the right (north) and the XVIII Corps on the left (south). The newly formed 15th Army held the west bank of the Rhine opposite the pocket and did not engage in active combat. This vicious battle would rage until the middle of April and would constitute one of the most crushing defeats ever inflicted on the Germans by the Allies.[22]

The attack of the III Corps consisted of the 9th ID to the north, the 7th AD in the center, and the 99th ID to the south. The 14th MCG performed two functions. The group headquarters and the 18th CRS conducted rear area security behind the advancing divisions, clearing out fugitive German soldiers and protecting key infrastructure whose damage might delay the advance of the corps. Van Fleet attached the

32nd CRS to the 9th ID with the task of protecting that division's northern flank in the vicinity of Brilon, on the northeast corner of the pocket, so that it could concentrate combat power forward.[23]

On 8 April, the 5th ID moved forward to replace the 9th ID, which became the corps reserve. The 32nd CRS continued its mission of protecting the flank of the attacking division in the north, but now it was attached to the 5th ID. By 10 April, the XVI Corps had closed on the 5th ID's northern flank. At the same time, the division's southern flank had opened due to rapid advances. Therefore, the 32nd CRS moved to the southern flank of the 5th ID and continued its mission, allowing maximum combat power to be pushed forward. By 12 April, the 5th ID relieved the 32nd CRS of its duties and sent it back to the 14th MCG. The 9th ID was leaving the III Corps for the VII Corps, and their departure left a gap in the corps zone. The cavalry, which had been conducting an area security mission in the corps' rear, now gained the 9th ID's sector.[24] The group continued in this mission until 16 April 1945, when the pocket had been destroyed. The III Corps ordered the cavalry to assist the First Army prisoner collection point at Brilon that was overrun with surrendered Germans, liberated Allied prisoners, and displaced persons. In one day (17 April), the corps would process over nine thousand prisoners. The total count of prisoners would reach over 317,000.[25] While not necessarily a specific cavalry mission, the 14th MCG was the best-placed unit in the corps to assist in processing this mass of humanity while the line divisions of the corps rested from the fighting to reduce the pocket. Moreover, the cavalry's vehicles proved handy, for this mission requiring moving people around a huge area to handle administrative tasks.

With the closure of the Ruhr Pocket in early April, Hodges wheeled two corps, the V and VII, to the east, keeping on line with the Ninth Army to the north and the Third Army to the south. The III and XVIII Corps were left to reduce the Ruhr in conjunction with elements of the Ninth Army. The attack to the east would be marked by extremely rapid advances, delayed occasionally by fanatical German resistance.

Huebner's V Corps began its advance to the east on 5 April along the axis of Kassel to Leipzig. Initially, the 102nd MCG with the 38th CRS maintained their positions east of Kassel. The 102nd CRS would continue as corps headquarters security for the rest of the month. By

9 April, as the corps passed to the south of the Harz Mountains, the 102nd MCG (minus the 102nd CRS) would be ordered to protect the corps' left (northern) flank. The corps was advancing at such a rate that open flanks were becoming a serious problem, particularly to the north as the VII Corps became engrossed in the Harz Mountains.[26]

As the V Corps approached the city of Leipzig in mid-April, the 102nd MCG (still only with the 38th CRS) would take the northern portion of the 2nd ID zone, allowing that division to focus its infantry regiments against the desperate German defenders of the city. Despite a general breakdown in German order, the fight devolved into an intense urban fight, requiring large amounts of infantry—troops that were free to act because the cavalry were protecting their flank.[27]

Once the city of Leipzig was firmly invested, Huebner relieved the 102nd MCG and the 38th CRS from flank security duty, and the cavalry spent the last half of April sweeping the corps' rear area for German stragglers and would-be guerrilla forces. This is a textbook example of area security, a task at which cavalry excels due its high mobility. On 27 April, Troop B of the 38th CRS escorted Huebner to the official linkup with the Soviet Army on the Elbe River, although the actual meeting had occurred two days prior with elements of the 69th ID.[28] Meanwhile, the 102nd CRS, in addition to their headquarters security duty, guarded over ten thousand German prisoners for the V Corps.[29]

In early May, the V Corps moved south into Czechoslovakia toward the city of Pilsen, now under the command of the Third Army.[30] The corps seized the city on 6 May. The 102nd MCG moved into Czechoslovakia, but it was not committed to the fight before the end of hostilities on 9 May.[31]

With the destruction of the Ruhr Pocket, the III Corps was now well behind friendly lines and out of contact with the enemy. On 17 April, the 12th Army Group ordered the corps to join the Third Army, now attacking across central Germany. The 14th MCG moved with the corps nearly 250 miles to Iphofen, fourteen miles southeast of Würzburg. The III Corps and the 14th MCG would finish the war with the Third Army.[32]

On 8 April, the advance of elements of the 9th ID and 17th Airborne Division closed out the 4th MCG's area of responsibility on the northeast corner of the Ruhr Pocket. Collins's VII Corps reassumed control of the group from the 104th ID, and he ordered it to assemble near Bad Driburg, eleven miles east of Paderborn. The corps had a problem in the form of heavy German resistance in the Harz Mountains, a range that lay directly in the center of the VII Corps' axis of advance to the Elbe River.[33] Collins wished to bypass the region initially but required a mobile screening force to hold the western entrances of the mountains. The 4th MCG fit the bill. Thus, on 9 April, he ordered the group to prepare to move in advance of the 1st ID to seize the key towns of Osterode and Clausthal-Zellerfeld in the western Harz (see map 18). Control of these two towns would allow the Americans to dominate the western portion of the mountains. The corps attached a battalion of infantry, a company of tank destroyers, a company of engineers, and the 759th Light Tank Battalion to assist in the attack.

To accomplish this mission, the 4th MCG organized into three task forces. The two squadrons each received a company of infantry, a platoon of tank destroyers, a section of two medium tanks, and a platoon of engineers. The two squadrons would attack abreast on over a division frontage of approximately eight miles, forcing their way forward.[34] The final group task force, serving as the reserve, would be built around the 759th Light Tank Battalion reinforced with a company of infantry and a platoon of engineers.[35]

The 4th MCG crossed the line of departure on the Weser River on 10 April. It advanced over twenty-five miles east, fighting its way through scattered but occasionally fierce resistance. By the next day the group had reached the Harz Mountains, accomplishing their mission of advance guard for the 1st ID as it attacked east. In doing so, the cavalry either destroyed or located and identified most German resistance in the division's zone of advance, thereby speeding its movement.

The 4th CRS, attacking toward Clausthal-Zellerfeld in the western Harz, soon found that it could not force its way through the tight terrain. The 26th Infantry Regiment of the 1st ID passed through that squadron on 12 April and continued the attack toward the city, with the squadron in support. The 4th CRS would remain in this region for the next three days, assisting the 26th Infantry in clearing the area around Clausthal-Zellerfeld of German forces.[36]

While the 4th CRS fought its way through the western Harz, the

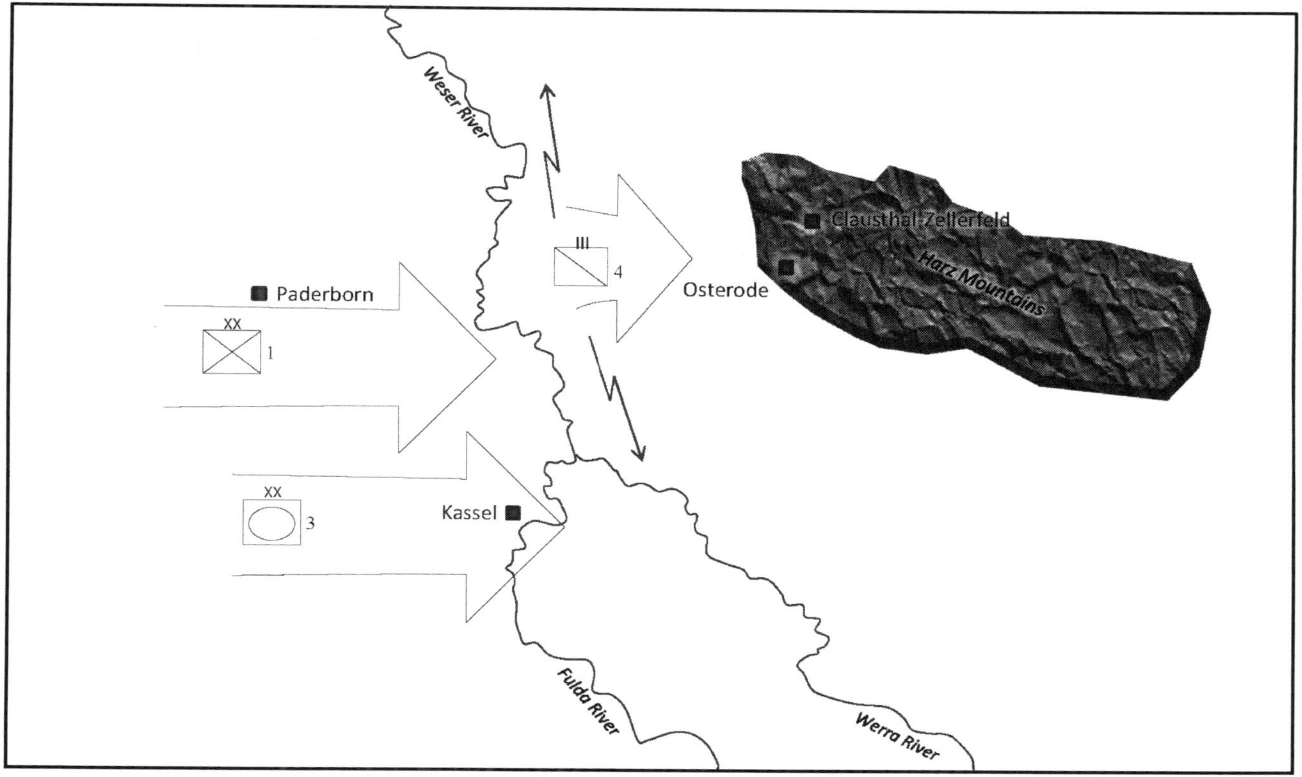

Map 18. 4th MCG Leads VII Corps to the Harz Mountains.

rest of the group moved to the southern edge of the mountains. There, the group formed part of Task Force MacDonald, a compilation of a battalion of infantry, the 24th CRS, a self-propelled artillery battalion, and a light tank battalion. The 1st ID ordered the task force to seize the towns of Hohegeiss and Benneckenstein, five miles north of Ellrich. The seizure of these towns would help protect the right flank of the 16th Infantry Regiment as it attacked toward the town of Braunlage, directly in the center of the Harz Mountains and the intersection of all the major east-west and north-south roads in the region.[37]

TF MacDonald began its attack on 14 April 1945. German resistance proved fierce, supported by tanks and self-propelled guns. However, despite the inherent advantages of defending and the rugged terrain, the Germans could not muster enough strength to keep the cavalry task force back. American infantry led the assault, with the cavalry using their firepower to provide direct support. By the end of the day Hohegeiss had fallen, and Benneckenstein was seized on 15 April.[38]

The 4th CRS returned to the 4th MCG on 15 April as well, and it relieved a regiment of the 104th ID of its responsibility for a series of blocking positions along a thirteen-mile front on the southwestern edge of the Harz Mountains.[39] This relief allowed the 104th ID to continue the corps' advance east toward Halle and the Elbe River.[40] The next day, the group swept the south-central portion of the region for any remaining resistance as well as any fugitive German soldiers attempting to evade capture.[41] Thanks in part to the actions of the 4th MCG, the 1st ID seized the critical town of Braunlage and proceeded in the complete destruction of the Harz Pocket.[42]

On 18 April, when elements of his VII Corps had already reached the Elbe River, Collins ordered the 4th MCG east to Mansfeld to join the 83rd ID. That division had the task of clearing German resistance between the Harz Mountains and the corps' northern boundary. Much the same as before, the group organized into combined arms task forces to maximize the use of the cavalry's firepower and the attached infantry's manpower. The group attacked on 18 April, moving from east to west, clearing German resistance as they went. Although some enemy forces were determined to fight, most were quickly subdued, and by 20 April the cavalry had secured all of their objectives. Clearing a zone of broken and straggling enemies is a long-standing traditional use of cavalry, and the 4th MCG demonstrated that some things had not changed over the centuries.[43]

As Eisenhower had ordered all Allied forces to halt at the Elbe, an objective that had been reached by 24 April, the 4th MCG would spend the rest of the war conducting area security missions around the Aschersleben region, just to the northeast of the Harz Mountains.[44] This mission, although far from glamorous, also harked back to traditional American cavalry roles, this time from their frontier days. Soon, most of the First Army's cavalry would be filling similar roles in their new guises as constabulary regiments, helping to administer a defeated and broken Germany.

The First Army's positions along the Elbe lay over six hundred miles in a straight line from the Normandy beaches. The most battle-hardened of any American field army in the ETO, the First had witnessed an immense array of combat, having been in continuous contact with major German formations since 6 June 1944, an amazing 338 days of battle. The last full month of combat had proven no less intense than any other portion of the war. Despite the Wehrmacht's utter inability to offer sustained coherent resistance, large portions of it continued to bitterly resist in many areas as fanatical commanders—and the SS in particular—sought their own personal Götterdämmerung.

The First Army's corps cavalry played a major role in the destruction of German forces in the Ruhr and central Germany. No other organization had the mobility and firepower to contain the vast numbers of German soldiers attempting to escape the Ruhr Pocket. While two infantry divisions anchored the perimeter for the army, a cavalry group provided the flexible connection between them that could expand as necessary. Cavalry also conducted a flank guard on the outside of the Ruhr perimeter, preventing any interference with the sweep of the army northward.

The security provided by the cavalry allowed the divisions and corps of the First Army to move rapidly, preventing any organized German resistance from coalescing. Additionally, the securing of vital infrastructure helped pave the way for a more rapid resumption of a semblance of normality for the civilian populations in the occupied territories. Finally, the administrative and local security performed by the groups allowed for a more stable rear area for the First Army. This stability allowed for more and larger supply columns to reach the front lines, allowing the combat formations of the army to focus on the task at hand. Without its cavalry, the First Army would have been forced to commit an even larger share of its combat power to basic security in a conquered area, thereby perhaps prolonging the fight or allowing the Americans to suffer more casualties.

Third Army

The Third Army had drawn up three corps abreast on the Rhine by late March. Major General Troy Middleton's VIII Corps held the left just south of Koblenz, maintaining contact with the First Army's Remagen bridgehead just to the north. Major General Walton Walker's XX Corps occupied the army center, holding positions across the Rhine from Wiesbaden. Major General Manton Eddy's XII Corps held the south, maintaining contact with the Seventh Army north of Worms.

Eddy's XII Corps would be the first to cross on the night of 22 March 1945, near the town of Oppenheim, west of Darsmstadt. It would be followed by the VIII Corps on 25 March and the XX Corps on 28 March. Once across the Rhine, the Third Army would pivot to the northeast for the drive into Germany as well as linking up with the First Army near its Remagen bridgehead. The Seventh Army would advance along its right flank and clear most of southern Germany.[45]

On 23 March, the VIII Corps' 6th MCG was sent forward to relieve the 87th ID so that it could concentrate for its assault crossing of the Rhine two days later. The 6th MCG held a nine-mile front (nearly a corps-level length of line), aided by a single battalion of the 87th ID who were left in place so that the division would have its own forces at the actual point of attack (see map 19).[46] Despite the 87th ID's leaving that one battalion in place, the presence of the 6th Cavalry contributed directly to the success of the VIII Corps' first crossing of the Rhine by allowing the assault division to pull nearly completely off the line, reorganize, and mass at the decisive point.

As the 87th and 89th IDs widened the VIII Corps' Rhine bridgehead, TF Fickett (6th MCG) received new orders on 26 March to pass through the two divisions and attack across the breadth of the corps zone as an advance guard. To accomplish this mission, the VIII Corps

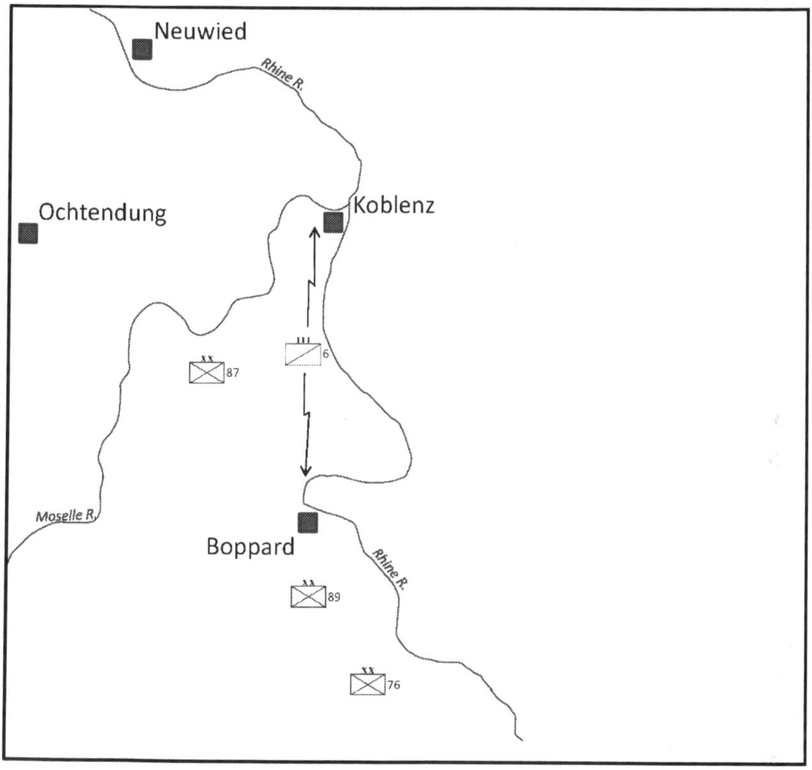

Map 19. VIII Corps Preparing to Cross the Rhine River.

configured Task Force Fickett with its two squadrons, a battalion of artillery, two tank destroyer companies, two infantry companies (from the 76th ID), and a company of engineers.[47] The cavalry further organized into five subgroups, generally centered on the reconnaissance troops. The following day, 27 March, the newly reformed TF Fickett crossed the Rhine River and began its assault. The first day, all elements made substantial progress in attacking to the east, averaging fifteen miles from the river.[48] The attack resumed on the following day. The group advanced nineteen miles, with leading elements a mere fifteen miles north of Wiesbaden and the XII Corps' bridgehead. By 29 March, the cavalry had advanced fifty miles, participating in the joining of the VIII and XII Corps' bridgeheads and driving deep into enemy territory.[49]

German resistance proved sporadic, but still deadly in places. On 28 March, the 28th CRS ran into serious resistance from the 6th SS Mountain Division at the town of Schmitten, twelve miles northwest of Frankfurt. There, the Germans ambushed a platoon from Troop C, severely mauling it, as well as a platoon sent in to rescue the beleaguered cavalrymen. By the end of the day the cavalry had sustained thirty-six casualties and lost one light tank, one tank destroyer, and every jeep that entered the town. The resistance proved so great that the squadron was forced to bypass the town, leaving it to the following infantry to reduce.[50]

This action showed the hazards of pushing light cavalry forward into an uncertain battlefield. However, despite suffering heavy casualties, the cavalry were still able to achieve their objectives as well as protect the main force of the infantry from such an ambush. A heavier cavalry force might have achieved the same results with fewer casualties, but the result for the corps would have been the same.

Farther to the south, Patton detached the 16th MCG from the XX Corps on 25 March and attached them to the XII Corps. Eddy's XII Corps needed a cavalry formation to relieve Charles Reed's 2nd MCG, which had been protecting its northern flank along the Rhine River, so that the 2nd MCG could participate in the exploitation of the Rhine bridgehead. The 16th MCG made the forty-mile move in a single day, taking responsibility for fifteen miles of Rhine riverbank along the XII Corps' flank near Mainz.[51] Although this sector had become relatively quiet due to the success of the XII Corps' assault crossing of the Rhine, a screen still needed to be maintained to provide security for the corps' vulnerable logistics elements scrambling to keep pace with the rapidly advancing armored columns.

After being relieved by the 16th MCG, the Dragoons hastened to catch up to the leading elements of their parent corps. By this time, the XII Corps had succeeded in crossing the Rhine south of Mainz and was attacking north toward the city of Frankfurt to link up with the XX Corps, which was preparing to cross the river. The corps ordered the 2nd MCG to reprise their screening mission, this time conducting a mobile guard of the corps' southern flank as it moved ever deeper into Germany. Additionally, the group was to maintain communications with elements of the XV Corps of the Seventh Army (for most of this time, this meant the 106th MCG) to the south as it attacked alongside the XII Corps.[52] The connection would prove important, as both armies were moving at high speed and needed to reduce as many potential problems and frictions as possible.[53]

Two days after their arrival in the XII Corps, the 16th MCG received a more active mission. Eddy attached the group to the 80th ID as it continued the attack across the Rhine River. This move would provide the XII Corps with cavalry protection on both flanks, allowing it to concentrate all available combat power forward. On 29 March, the group crossed the Rhine and assaulted to the west to protect the flank of the 80th ID as it attacked to the north and east. By nightfall, the group had reached the town of Wiesbaden, six miles north of Mainz. Over the next two days the group continued to keep pace with the 80th ID, protecting the northern flank of that division and the XII Corps. German resistance was generally light or nonexistent. However on 31 March, Troop B of the 19th CRS engaged a group of SS twelve miles north of Frankfurt. The cavalrymen could not dislodge the German defenders and were forced to pass the reduction of the town to an element of the 5th ID.[54] Although the cavalrymen would have liked to have had the combat power to finish the Germans, the handover was entirely within the bounds of an offensive security fight. The troop identified the enemy, developed the situation, and then passed the fight to follow-on forces. A heavier cavalry force might have been able to fight through more resistance without calling on the main body, but the concept remains the same. On 1 April, Bradley relieved the 16th MCG from the XII Corps, assigning it to the newly forming Fifteenth Army. This army had responsibility for administering conquered German territory and needed a unit with the mobility and flexibility of the cavalry. The troopers of the group would spend the last month of the war conducting rear area security and dealing with displaced persons.

In the center of the Third Army line, Walker's XX Corps ordered Colonel James Polk's 3rd MCG forward to protect bridges over the Main and Rhine Rivers in the Mainz region on 26 March following the assault crossing of that river a few days earlier.[55] Three days later, on 29 March, Walker called the group to the front of the corps to lead the exploitation from the Rhine bridgehead. With the 6th AD to the north and the 4th AD to the south, and the 65th ID trailing, the Brave

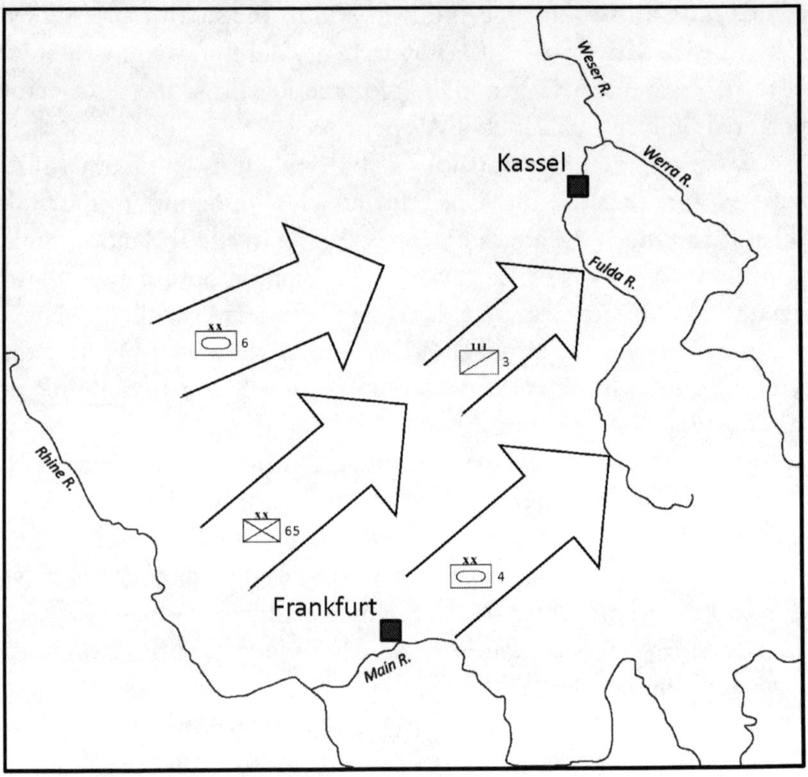

Map 20. XX Corps' Assault to the Fulda River.

Rifles moved out at top speed against light resistance (see map 20). By the end of the day the group had covered twenty-five miles and was in the northern suburbs of Frankfurt.

During the next several days the 3rd MCG led the XX Corps deeper into Germany toward the Fulda River, with the 3rd CRS to the north and the 43rd CRS to the south.[56] However, on 31 March the cavalrymen met stiff German resistance to the west of the Fulda River, south of Kassel. The Wehrmacht had assembled a large force comprised of elements of the 5th Fallschirmjäger Division, the 6th SS Mountain Division, and other hastily assembled formations, backed by tanks and anti-tank guns and protected by minefields and field fortifications.[57] These defenses had stopped the 4th and 6th ADs to the north and south of the cavalry as well. Moreover, the First Army's V Corps to the west of Kassel was also encountering its own problems with the German forces in this region. It appeared that a deliberate assault would be required to clear this block of resistance. Thus, the cavalry moved to a defensive posture to protect the 65th ID as it moved up to prepare to assault through this new defensive belt. This advance demonstrates the true potential of cavalry in a fluid situation. The cavalry had advanced over ninety miles in three days, a substantial achievement even with the near collapse of German resistance, and allowed the 65th ID to move from the Rhine to the Fulda River in trucks without having to dismount and fight.[58]

On the southern flank of the Third Army, Eddy's XII Corps continued to advance to the east during the first part of April 1945, keeping its station between the XX Corps and Seventh Army's XV Corps. The 2nd MCG continued to protect the corps' right (southern) flank while maintaining contact with the Seventh Army. On 2 April, in conjunction with the XV Corps' 106th MCG, the 2nd MCG liberated 3,328 U.S. prisoners and 3,205 Allied prisoners, including a Russian major general, near Bad Orb.[59] The cavalry continued their advance to the southeast against lessening resistance. Due to the lack of threat along the corps' flank, the XII Corps ordered the 2nd CRS to be detached from the group (splitting it nearly in half) and to provide route security along the corps' main supply route.[60] This mission was extremely vital to maintain the momentum of the attack. Large numbers of German units had been bypassed in the rapid advance, and although these isolated and often broken formations posed little danger to the main combat units of the corps, they were deadly to the lightly guarded supply columns keeping the forward units going. Though not as glamorous as duty on the front or flank, rear area security is just as important.

To the south of the XII Corps, the 3rd MCG spent the first couple of days in April 1945 conducting a reconnaissance of the German positions around Kassel in preparation for the 65th ID's attack. On 2 April, the XX Corps launched a coordinated attack with the 65th ID, the 4th AD, and the 6th AD, completely rupturing the German positions along the Fulda River.

On the northern end of the Third Army line, the VIII Corps had been pinched out by the closure of the First Army from the north and the movement of the XII Corps to the south. As such, the corps would shift south, taking over the XX Corps' positions. In preparation for the move, the VIII Corps withdrew most of the supporting elements of TF Fickett, leaving the 6th MCG with its two squadrons, an artillery battalion, and a company of combat engineers.[61] On 3 April, the 6th MCG relieved the 3rd MCG along the Fulda River from Rothenburg to Bad Hersfeld in preparation for the transfer of the Kassel region from the XX Corps to the VIII Corps. The VIII Corps would continue the attack east while the XX Corps cleared the Kassel Pocket.

While waiting for the larger corps reorganization to shake out, the XX Corps ordered the 3rd MCG to clear the forests and roads leading into Kassel as the 80th ID cleared the city. The majority of this mission posed no difficulty for the cavalrymen except for a determined defense of two towns three miles to the north of Kassel by a company of German infantry supported by twelve 88mm guns.[62] The group did not close with and engage this garrison, but instead chose to stand off and blast them with concentrated artillery fire. Thus, the cavalry destroyed what could have been a nasty surprise for a column of infantry through proper reconnaissance and then application of firepower.

After its assumption of the XX Corps sector, the VIII Corps attacked in column over fifty miles east toward the town of Gotha, with its armor to the front, followed by the infantry and then the cavalry.[63] The 6th MCG's task was to round up German stragglers left behind by the main corps advance. Although not a particularly desirable task, the corps needed a highly mobile formation that could maintain order in its rear areas as it moved with all possible speed to the east. The cavalry were well suited to the role, even if they were not particularly fond of it. Additionally, as the corps moved deeper into eastern Germany, small groups of German Army forces aggressively sought out rear echelon forces. Thus, the cavalry were tasked to maintain a screen to the north of the corps between the widely separated echelons of divisions.[64]

As the VIII Corps advanced, the XX Corps' 3rd MCG, now reinforced with engineers and tank destroyers, moved into assembly areas on 6 April to await further orders. The next three days saw the cavalry move from one position to the other along the Kassel Pocket as the XX Corps slowly reduced the German forces inside. On 9 April, the group prepared for further operations as the 80th ID cleared the Erfurt–

Weimar area. On 10 April, the 80th and 76th IDs penetrated the German defensive positions, and the 4th and 6th ADs passed through them to exploit the breakthrough. The 3rd MCG's orders were to protect both flanks of the corps while also maintaining continuous contact between the fast-moving armored divisions leading the corps and the slower infantry divisions behind them. By 13 April, the XX Corps was approaching the Czechoslovakian border, with the 3rd MCG scattered throughout the corps zone, weaving elements together with communications, as well as maintaining contact with the V and VIII Corps on the flanks.[65]

On 11 April the VIII Corps resumed its advance, this time heading to Czechoslovakia. Colonel Fickett split his 6th MCG into two elements for this mission. The 28th CRS committed a troop to operate as a liaison with the XX Corps to the north.[66] This activity meant that the two corps could advance on a broad, widely separated front without the flank units of either corps being confused about the whereabouts of their counterparts. This information prevented gaps from appearing in the army line as well as reducing the potential for fratricide or simple traffic jams as units moved through the same region. The 6th CRS operated in a security role between the leading and trailing edges of the VIII Corps, preventing any Wehrmacht stragglers from impeding corps logistics or communications.

On 15 April, the VIII Corps ordered the 6th MCG to cross the Saale River and attack to the corps' limit of advance near the Czechoslovakian border in order to identify any remaining German formations in the axis of advance. The group moved out rapidly, making good progress and fighting their way through scattered German resistance. By this point in the war the cavalrymen generally did not have to bypass any strongpoints, but simply had to apply enough firepower until the Germans surrendered. However, on at least one occasion, in the forest of Greiz, where remnants of the 11th Panzer Division were found, the cavalry were unable to force a surrender and had to leave a serious pocket of resistance behind for the rest of the corps.[67] The group also seized key bridges, allowing the follow-on infantry to advance at a rapid pace.[68] On 20 April the group entered the 1938 borders of Czechoslovakia.

While the XX and VIII Corps fought around Kassel and the Fulda

River, the XII Corps on the southern end of the army line continued its attack southeast into southern Germany with the 2nd MCG still protecting the right (southern) flank. On 10 April, German forces, discovered to be about three hundred SS supported by three tanks, made a small stand against the 42nd CRS around the town of Gleicherweisen, just to the north of the Bavarian border.[69] The squadron made a concerted attack with all three line troops supported by the assault guns and light tanks of Troop E and Company F. Although the 2nd MCG failed to clear the enemy fully from their positions, the cavalrymen seized enough key terrain in order for them to mask the remaining Germans and bypass the position. Three days later, the 42nd CRS was maneuvering against the city of Bayreuth, fifty miles to the southeast and deep in the heart of Bavaria. By this point, German resistance had nearly ceased, with the cavalrymen capturing 312 enemy soldiers in a single day.[70] After the fighting around Bayreuth subsided on 16 April, the XII Corps ordered the group to move to the rear and conduct maintenance and resupply operations for two days. During this time the 2nd CRS rejoined the group after completing its rear area security mission.

The 2nd MCG moved back into action on 18 April, this time protecting the northern flank of the XII Corps as it attacked toward Czechoslovakia. The Wehrmacht's resistance stiffened as the group moved east. On 20 April, a battalion-size element of Germans attempted to prevent the Dragoons from seizing the town of Aš, just inside the Czechoslovakian border, thirty miles to the northeast of Bayreuth. After heavy fighting, the group, reinforced by the 358th Infantry Regiment, drove the Germans from the town, taking 250 prisoners.[71]

As the Third Army plunged deeper into Germany, American planners became worried about the potential for German forces to coalesce in the Bavarian Alps in a so called "National Redoubt." In order to prevent this from happening, the Third Army was reoriented from its eastern assault to a southern direction.[72] To aid in this new offensive, the First Army's III Corps, out of a job since its participation in the destruction of the Ruhr Pocket, joined the Third Army. This corps was inserted just to the north of the Seventh Army, actually assuming large portions of that army's sector. The XX Corps shifted from its position in the north of the Third Army to the center, moving around the VIII and XII Corps to enter the line between the III Corps and the XII Corps.

Van Fleet's III Corps ordered the 14th MCG, reinforced by the 400th Armored Artillery Battalion, to protect the northern flank of the corps as it attacked south. The group was also to seize bridges over the Donau near the town of Kelheim.[73] The 14th MCG attacked south of Fürth on 22 April, and by the next day it had advanced nearly twenty-six miles to the southeast. With the addition of an engineer company, the group continued its attack south, still along the northern flank of the III Corps. By 24 April, the group laagered just north of the Donau River crossing at Kelheim. The cavalry attacked the next day and, after an all-day battle generally conducted at long range, forced the Germans defending the town to surrender. Unfortunately the bridge had already been destroyed.[74]

By 29 April, a bridge had been constructed over the Donau and the 14th MCG joined the rest of the III Corps in the attack south to the Isar River. The group began its attack at 1400 on 29 April, and by 0900 the next morning it had reached its objectives east of Landshut along the Isar, an advance of nearly thirty-six miles in nineteen hours.[75] The cavalry continued the attack, crossing the Isar on 1 May and attacking to the Inn River the next day, an advance of over twenty-five miles, matching the pace of the rest of the III Corps. On 3 May, the Third Army ordered the III Corps to halt and consolidate positions. The corps, along with the 14th MCG, would remain along the Inn until 8 May. On that day, the 14th MCG moved to Erlangen, just north of Nuremberg, to conduct military government activities.[76] During a ten-day period, the group had advanced over 120 miles while protecting the lead elements of the III Corps in a great example of an offensive guard.

While the III Corps joined the Third Army, Walker's XX Corps conducted a dramatic move, reorienting to the south while moving behind the VIII Corps. On 17 April, the 3rd MCG and the 80th ID began a 120-mile move to the south, to assembly areas around Bamberg.[77] Upon arrival at the staging areas, the group's new task organization included the 5th Ranger Battalion, two companies of the 811th Tank Destroyer (TD) Battalion, and a company of engineers from the 245th Combat Engineer Battalion.[78] On 22 April the 3rd MCG moved to the front of the XX Corps to begin the attack, with the 3rd CRS leading the 71st ID and the 43rd CRS leading the 65th ID. Based on past experience, Polk task organized his formation especially for this mission: "Using the six reconnaissance troops of the Group as the basic unit, each of the reconnaissance troop[s] had a light tank platoon [M24] attached, a TD Platoon [M18], a company of Rangers and a squad of Engineers."[79] These small battlegroups possessed enough combat power to deal with most of the remaining German resistance in Bavaria, and they proved highly successful in protecting the infantry divisions of the corps as they attacked toward Regensburg and the Danube River. Once the infantry divisions reached the Danube, the 3rd MCG moved to protect the corps' northern flank. On 28 April, the group crossed the Danube River in a continuation of the attack to the south. The following day the cavalry captured a depot containing "95,000 large gas bombs with the capacity to kill every person in Bavaria." By the end of the month the Brave Rifles had led the XX Corps nearly to the Austrian border along the Isar River. Additionally, as the threat against the group diminished, the XX Corps removed most of the cavalry's attachments, leaving it with only a company of the 260th Combat Engineer Battalion.[80]

On 4 May 1945 the 3rd MCG crossed the Inn River and continued east, protecting the corps' move to the east as it attempted to link up with the advancing Soviet forces. Two days later the 3rd CRS liberated the concentration camp at Ebensee in Austria. The next day, the group received orders to cease all offensive operations in preparation for VE day on 8 May. At this point the cavalry were over fifty miles deep into Austria. The 3rd MCG's actions during this period demonstrate the utility and power of the cavalry in security operations, as it prevented German interference with the advance of the XX Corps. Granted, the enemy had little left by this point, but the above incidents show that they still had the capacity to inflict casualties and fight.

As the Third Army moved south, Bradley ordered the VIII Corps to remain behind on the Czechoslovakian border under the control of the First Army. The 6th MCG spent the rest of April along defensive positions on the Weisse Elster River from Gornitz to Rossbach. The cavalrymen conducted their last attack on 6 May, when the group assaulted across the river as part of a limited corps offensive. However, they were stopped on 7 May due to the impending cease-fire.[81]

The 2nd MCG participated in one of the most remarkable episodes in the cavalry's history at the end of April. Troop A of the 42nd CRS attacked and seized the town of Hostouň in Czechoslovakia in an effort to rescue Allied prisoners. This town contained not only approximately three hundred friendly prisoners of war, but also a remount station containing approximately 670 horses, including a significant number of the Lipizzaner Stallion breeding herd.[82] Once this was reported to General George S. Patton, he ordered these horses removed from Czechoslovakia, which was to fall under the Soviet occupation zone. Thus, shortly after the cessation of hostilities, on 12 May, Operation COWBOY occurred in which the cavalrymen returned to their equestrian roots and rode or herded this irreplaceable stock of horses into the U.S. occupation zone.[83]

The 2nd MCG would continue reconnaissance and screening operations inside Czechoslovakia until the official cessation of hostilities on 8 May. Shortly after the success of Operation COWBOY, the group along with all remaining American forces withdrew from Czechoslovakia and took up positions along the German side of the new border. The rest of the Third Army would also draw up on this border and begin to conduct area security operations in central and southern Germany as part of the beginning of occupation duty.

The cavalry of the Third Army played a substantial role in this final campaign. The security provided by their offensive guards allowed several infantry divisions to be motorized, speeding the overall movement of the corps. In fact, some of the speed for which the Third Army would be famed came as a result of the corps cavalry's protection. Still more of the speed would come from the cavalry destroying German opposition or finding bypasses for the main force before the enemy had the chance to delay Patton's columns.

The Third Army's cavalry also helped ensure success by providing links between far-flung and rapidly moving units, not only within the army, but with the adjacent formations as well. This coordination proved vital when Eisenhower and SHAEF directed the army to make a massive, nearly ninety-degree turn south to interdict the alleged German national redoubt. With so many moving pieces in this action, the only way to ensure even a semblance of order was for there to be significant lateral communications between units. The cavalry helped make that happen. Thus, although Patton's cavalry did not win the campaign by themselves, they certainly made the victory easier.

Seventh Army

The Seventh Army paused for only a short period after its destruction of German forces in the Saar–Palatinate region. The Third Army had already established a Rhine bridgehead on 22 March, just north of the army group boundary. The Seventh Army's XV Corps would follow four days later, on 26 March, with a two-division assault around Worms—the 45th ID to the north, and the 3rd ID to the south. Major General Edward Brooks's VI Corps drew up its combat power south of Major General Wade Haislip's XV Corps and prepared to cross the Rhine through the bridgehead and then advance to the southeast. Major General Frank Milburn's XXI Corps, initially consumed with clearing German stragglers from the army rear, would follow the XV Corps and be inserted between it and the VI Corps. Once across the Rhine, the Seventh Army was to advance into southern Germany, seizing the important cities and preventing resistance from coalescing in the mountainous extreme south and Austria.[84]

The XV Corps' 106th MCG crossed the Rhine on 27 March at Worms. The next day, the group led the 3rd and 45 IDs in the corps' advance to the northeast toward Aschaffenburg and the Main River as well as the Third Army's Rhine bridgehead. A cavalry squadron led each division, and the 106th CRS on the left also had the mission of maintaining contact with the XII Corps' 2nd MCG to the right. The 121st CRS on the right met several German delaying actions and roadblocks, slowing their arrival on the Main. Although these obstacles were not pleasant for the cavalry, the troopers protected the infantry in the main body, preserving them for later fighting.[85]

German resistance stiffened against the XV Corps in Aschaffenburg, so while the infantry divisions cleared the city of enemy, the 106th MCG moved from the corps' front to the left flank, relieving elements of the 2nd MCG who had secured a bridgehead over the Main River north of the city.[86] After the corps destroyed German resistance in Aschaffenburg by 1 April, it turned to the northeast, aiming for the area south of Fulda. The 106th MCG continued to screen the corps' left flank, essentially on a line from Hanau to Fulda, during the five days it took for the corps to move to the area.[87]

As the XV Corps expanded the army bridgehead and began its movement north, the XXI Corps began to cross the Rhine on 30 March, led by Colonel Charles McClelland's 101st MCG. The corps would take the center of the Seventh Army bridgehead, relieving the XV Corps from that sector so that it could focus on its attack to the northeast. The 101st MCG, arranged in a series of combined arms task forces, moved forward over thirty miles east of the river, taking up a ten-mile front and relieving elements of Haislip's XV Corps that had held that portion of the line. The group then screened the arrival of the rest of the XXI Corps, particularly the 4th ID, into their positions on the line. The 4th ID had been motorized in trucks to give it greater speed, but with mobility came vulnerability, and thus the importance of the cavalry's screen to protect it as it came into position.[88]

The VI Corps' 117th CRS crossed the Rhine on 30 March at Mannheim. The corps was in the process of moving its combat power across the river and preparing for offensive operations to the east as the southern element of the Seventh Army. The VI Corps gave the squadron the responsibility of patrolling Mannheim as well as protecting the pontoon bridges across the river. The situation in the city was fragile, with displaced persons, newly liberated slave laborers, and defiant Hitler Youth and other violent elements all mixing together. The corps could not take the time to fully pacify the city with its infantry, which were needed to flesh out the bridgehead. Thus, while the corps waited to conduct mobile operations, the cavalry proved useful in helping to maintain order.[89]

In the center of the Seventh Army line, as part of the XXI Corps' and Seventh Army's general offensive, the 101st MCG moved in front of the 4th ID on 31 March, conducting an offensive screen. They would protect the movement of the division as it attacked to the east. By 2 April, the cavalry encountered heavy German resistance north of the town of Bad Mergentheim, twenty-one miles south of Würzburg. After spending 2 and 3 April fighting in an attempt to break through the German lines, the cavalry passed two regiments of the 4th ID through on 4 April to complete the destruction of the enemy. While the infantry continued the fight, the cavalry moved to the flanks and continued reconnaissance of the German lines around Bad Mergentheim. By 7 April, the 4th ID had defeated the desperate defenders and was prepared to resume its advance to the east.[90] This action stands as a perfect example of an offensive guard. The cavalry moved in front of the infantry, defeated the enemy security zone, engaged the German main line of resistance, developed the situation, and then passed the fight to the main body. Instructors at the cavalry and armor school at Fort Benning today would find no fault in how this operation occurred.[91]

While the XXI Corps attacked due east from Worms, to the south the VI Corps began its attack on 1 April 1945. The 10th AD, followed by the 63rd ID, advanced toward the Neckar River around Heilbronn. On 3 April, the VI Corps reached the river and encountered the southern portion of the same German line that had stopped the XXI Corps to the north. While the 63rd ID fought to penetrate the German defenses, the VI Corps called the 117th CRS forward to conduct liaison duties between it and the XXI Corps to the north. The cavalry performed this mission for over a week, as well as conducting screening operations protecting the left (northern) flank of the 63rd ID. The cavalry's liaison mission would prove particularly useful when the two corps conducted several cross-boundary operations in support of one another.[92]

On the northern end of the army line, the XV Corps began a wide wheel to the southeast, aimed generally on an axis Coburg–Bamberg–Nuremberg after it reached the Fulda region. This movement brought the corps across the front of the XXI and VI Corps (see map 21). Beginning on 5 April, the 106th MCG would spend three days on the corps' left flank, protecting the 45th ID as it attacked south. As the advance picked up steam, the corps ordered the 106th MCG to move in front of the 45th ID and screen its advance on Bamberg, while still protecting the left flank of the corps.[93] On 14 April the 45th ID seized the city of Bamberg. The cavalry was protecting their flank.[94]

As the XV Corps, on the left wing of the Seventh Army, completed its pivot to the south, the XXI Corps continued its drive southeast toward Nuremberg. On 8 April, the 101st MCG left the 4th ID to join the 12th AD. This division was still fighting around the city of Schweinfurt, twenty miles north of Würzburg, but already had plans to shift south. The 12th AD gave the cavalry a tank company and a self-

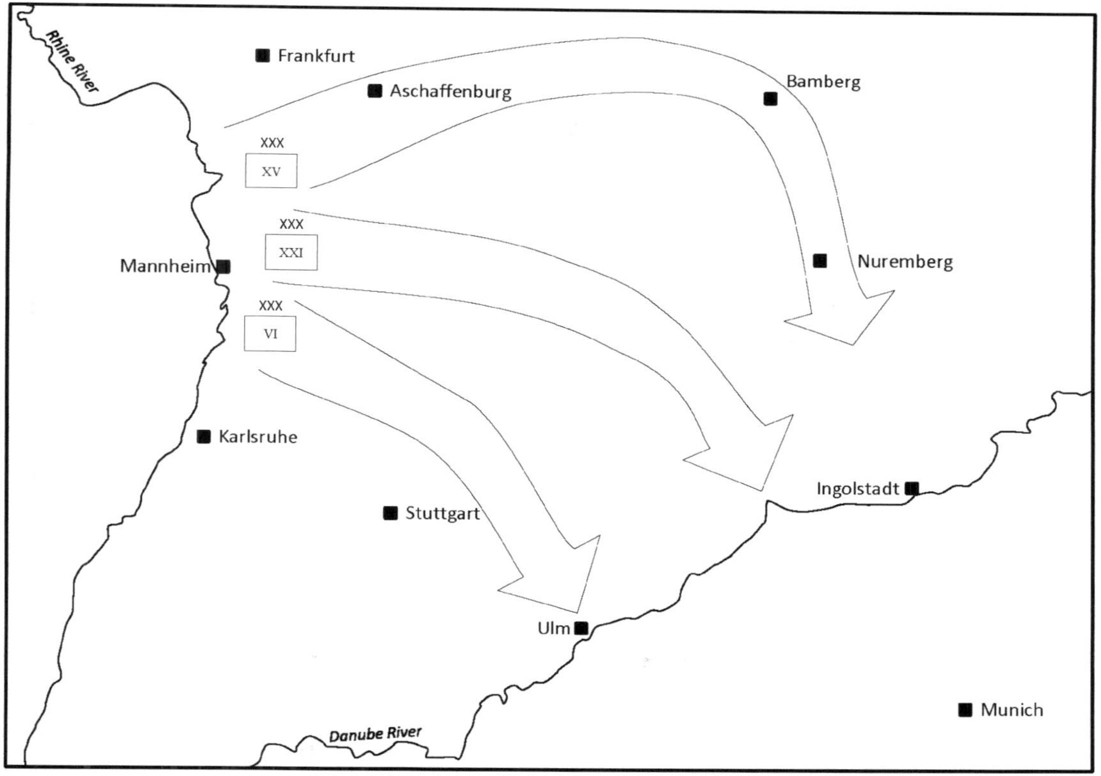

Map 21. Seventh Army's Assault from the Rhine.

propelled artillery battalion and assigned it a fifteen-mile-wide sector. The group was to conduct a reconnaissance in force of the zone, from a region southeast of Würzburg to just north of Rothenburg, a depth of approximately sixteen miles. The 12th AD's own cavalry squadron, the 92nd CRS, would do the same to the 101st MCG's north. The combined cavalry would lead the 12th AD southeast toward its objective of Ansbach, an important crossroads twenty miles southeast of Nuremberg.[95]

The 101st MCG marched on 9 April, but it soon ran into heavy defenses along the Tauber and Gollach Rivers, approximately eighteen miles south of Würzburg. The next day, after German resistance continued to stymie the cavalry, the 12th AD committed its CCR into the battle. The 101st MCG then transitioned to protecting that combat command's flanks. The armor made better progress, but soon desperate German actions forced it to stop. The fighting continued over the next three days, with the CCR spearheading the fight while the cavalry advanced along its flanks.[96]

On 14 April 1945, the 101st CRS was detached from the group to provide cavalry cover to the 4th ID. To compensate the group for its loss, the 12th AD attached its own 92nd CRS to the 101st MCG. The division ordered the cavalry to advance up the center of its zone, with CCR to the left and CCB on the right. The entire division was oriented on Ansbach in order to attack Nuremberg from the southwest. German resistance was finally beginning to fade, and the cavalry and armor made good progress, bypassing pockets of resistance and continuing their drive south.

While the XXI Corps continued its assault south to envelop Nuremberg, the VI Corps rested and reorganized for a couple of days before resuming its offensive to the south on 16 April. The 117th CRS maintained its position on the left flank of the corps, protecting the 63rd ID while that division fought slowly south against still tough resistance. The cavalry also maintained contact with elements of the XXI Corps as it advanced on the VI Corps' flank.

By 18 April, the XXI Corps had made substantial progress, with the 12th AD seizing Ansbach and the 101st MCG establishing a screen to the southeast of the city. That day, the Seventh Army shifted corps boundaries, making the XV Corps responsible for Nuremberg, while the XXI Corps would pass to the west of the city. The next day, the 101st CRS would rejoin the 101st MCG. That same day, a troop of the 116th CRS was attacked after dark by a reinforced company of SS. A brutal battle ensued, often degenerating into hand-to-hand fighting. However, the security measures of the cavalry and their firepower eventually won out, inflicting crippling losses on the attackers. Thus, even when the war seemed nearly over, the German military possessed the capability to strike back.[97]

The attack of the VI Corps to the south continued as the corps passed to the east of Stuttgart. The corps moved the 117th CRS to its right flank to support the 100th ID on 19 April. This division had met stiffening resistance in the vicinity of Stuttgart, and the addition of the cavalry protecting its flank would allow the infantry to concentrate their efforts.[98] The squadron would support the 100th ID for the next two days as it attacked toward Stuttgart, and by 22 April it would be committed to clear the division's rear areas of bypassed pockets of resistance as the infantry continued their forward progress.[99]

On the northern/eastern flank of the Seventh Army, the 106th MCG continued to screen the left of the XV Corps as it attacked toward Nuremberg after the fall of Bamberg. By this stage, every corps in both the Seventh and Third Armies was moving so rapidly that the idea of a solid front was more fiction than reality. Although German forces were badly wrecked by mid-April, they could and did turn and engage in serious fighting. Thus, the importance of flank protection would continue until the end of the war. The 3rd and 45th IDs would attack Nuremberg from the north, while the 106th MCG and elements of the 14th AD enveloped the city to the east, preventing any defenders from escaping or last-ditch reinforcements from entering.[100]

The XXI Corps' 12th AD began moving again on 20 April 1945, with the reinforced 101st MCG leading the way south to the Danube River. The cavalry destroyed German roadblocks and small pockets of resistance, only having to pass off German forces to the following armor once. The next day, the 12th AD broke into separate columns, with the combat commands racing alongside the cavalry. By 22 April, the 101st MCG reached the Danube twenty-two miles northeast of Ulm.[101]

While the XV Corps' infantry cleared Nuremberg on 21 April

1945, the 106th MCG continued its reconnaissance, encountering a firmly held line eighteen miles south of the city. The cavalry, unable to penetrate this line, passed it off to the 45th ID, who quickly forced the enemy to retreat on 23 April. Upon the defeat of this delaying force, the group led the 45th ID on a high-speed advance south toward the Danube River while still maintaining contact with Third Army's III Corps on the left. The infantry and cavalry worked in close tandem, with a battalion of infantry riding on the cavalry's vehicles for additional mobility. The group reached the Danube on 25 April. Finding the bridges blown, they went into reserve until the infantry could establish a bridgehead.[102]

To the west, while the XXI Corps' 101st MCG had failed to seize a crossing over the Danube, the 12th AD succeeded on 22 April. On 24 April, the group crossed the river on the armored division's bridge and led the division south. Despite German resistance and counterattacks, the cavalry maintained their momentum, seizing a bridge over the Wertach River on 26 April. The group made such good progress that by 28 April they were operating due east of Munich on the Lech River. That day the cavalry advanced over the river, screening the crossing of the remainder of the 12th AD the next day. On 30 April, the 101st MCG would advance to within fifteen miles of Munich (from the southwest) before being halted and shifted to the 4th ID, as the Seventh Army transferred responsibility for that city to the XV Corps.[103]

At the extreme right of the Seventh Army line, on 23 April the VI Corps transferred the 117th CRS to the 103rd ID, now holding the corps' right flank. The cavalry protected the flank of the division and also made contact with elements of the French First Army, who were advancing from the west. The 10th AD had already reached the Danube, so the 103rd ID would advance behind the armor and, in the process, arrive on the corps' left flank. On 25 April, the 103rd ID attacked to reach the Danube to the east of Ulm. However, the VI Corps withdrew the 117th CRS from the division so that it could support the 44th ID, now on the right of the corps (west). The squadron would support the 44th ID for the balance of April, protecting its flanks, securing its rear areas, and maintaining contact with the French to the west while the infantry fought to clear Ulm and then advance south. The 103rd ID would receive the newly arrived 115th MCG as compensation for the loss of the 117th CRS. This group had spent the majority of 1945 in positions around Saint Nazaire, containing German forces there. The 115th would protect the flank of the 103rd ID as it advanced on the corps' left (east).[104]

As the VI Corps advanced south into the German Alps in early May, it used the 117th CRS and 115th MCG to secure its supply lines, conduct roadblocks to find fugitive German soldiers, and otherwise conduct general area security. The cavalry would be attached to a number of the corps' divisions over the first two weeks of May, but the mission was always the same. The end of the war would find the cavalry of VI Corps conducting these operations throughout Austria.[105]

The XXI Corps' 101st MCG at the beginning of May was leading the 12th AD through the Inn River valley. On 5 May the corps would attach the group to the 101st Airborne Division so that it could lead the way into the region around Berchtesgaden. Along the way, the cavalry would capture Field Marshal Albert Kesselring and his staff, as well as the Japanese ambassador to Germany. The 101st MCG would end the war conducting area security operations and patrols in the German Alps and the Austrian Tyrol.[106]

The XV Corps' 106th MCG crossed the Danube on 27 April, and then led the 45th ID south to Munich while still covering the left flank of the corps. While the XV Corps cleared Munich on 29 and 30 April, the cavalry advanced to the southeast of the city. On 2 May the 121st CRS accepted the surrender of the Hungarian 9th Infantry Division.[107] By 4 May, the cavalry were in Salzburg. The group would continue to patrol northern Austria, collecting German stragglers and conducting area security. On 7 May, Troop B of the 121st CRS would rescue King Leopold of Belgium, the last real mission undertaken by the group before the end of hostilities.[108] The cavalry received this mission because of their ability to move extremely rapidly with a large amount of firepower. Although the king's guards were not expected to put up a fight, a weaker detachment might have encouraged foolish behavior, while a slower one might not have arrived quickly enough to satisfy political requirements.[109]

The Seventh Army ended the war occupying southwest Germany and Austria. Its cavalry quickly transitioned to either constabulary roles or began preparing for shipment to the Pacific. These formations had proven to be critical operational players for Patch's army in this campaign. They had led the divisions of the army out of the bridgehead, providing frontal security, identifying German strongpoints, and finding bypasses where appropriate. These actions allowed the Seventh Army to quickly and effectively defeat the last desperate German defensive positions on the east side of the Rhine. Although victory would probably have come anyway, the actions of the corps cavalry streamlined the process and prevented as many unnecessary losses as possible.

The cavalry had also allowed the Seventh Army to conduct a fairly complex series of operational maneuvers, with entire corps shifting axes of attack, accounting for the change in direction of the Third Army as well as that of the French First Army. The coordination along the flanks of the corps of Patch's formation allowed these shifts to happen with a minimum of chaos. While crossed units may not have lost the war, particularly in April of 1945, they would have induced confusion and perhaps led to more friendly fire incidents than were occurring through the normal friction of war. Thus, the corps cavalry proved critical in this last stage of the war in Europe.

Ninth Army

The Ninth Army crossed the Rhine as part of the 21st Army Group's Operation PLUNDER. After controversy in the planning stages over the role of the American forces, Montgomery committed the Ninth Army to a supporting role in protecting the right flank of the army group by seizing a limited bridgehead from Wesel and the Lippe River in the north and Duisberg and the Rhine-Herne Canal in the south (approximately fifteen miles of front).[110] The commitment of the rest of the Ninth Army seemed almost an afterthought for the commander of the 21st Army Group, as he focused most of his attention on his main effort, the British Second Army.[111]

By late March 1945 the Ninth Army had three corps abreast along the Rhine River. In the north, along the boundary with the British Second Army, lay Major General John Anderson's XVI Corps with four infantry divisions and one armored division. The corps stretched approximately eight miles south from the British forces. The 30th ID held the northern half of the corps zone, while the 79th ID held the southern. The remaining divisions of the corps were behind the line in preparation for the assault. To the south of the XVI Corps, Major General Alvan C. Gillem Jr.'s XIII Corps occupied a front of over sixteen miles anchored in the south across from Düsseldorf. The 84th ID held the northern portion of the corps zone and the 102nd ID held the center, while Colonel A. A. Frierson's 11th MCG, the Blackhorse, held the southern portion. Finally, Major General Raymond McLain's XIX Corps, with three infantry divisions and an armored division, held over twelve miles of front from Neuss to Worringen. Most of this sector had originally belonged to the First Army, but the Ninth Army had assumed control of it in order to allow the former to concentrate its combat power in the Remagen bridgehead. The XIX Corps split its line evenly between the 95th ID and Colonel William Biddle's 113th MCG, the Redhorse.[112]

In the north, the XVI Corps attack began on 24 March, with the 30th and 79th IDs attacking abreast across the river. The 75th ID, reinforced with Colonel Robert Quinn's 15th MCG, held the river line in order to allow the two assault divisions to maximize their strength forward. The cavalry served as the mobile reserve for the 75th ID, guarding bridges and protecting key supply routes forward. On 25 March, the 15th CRS moved across the Rhine to relieve elements of the 30th ID's 119th Infantry Regiment on a small island just south of Wesel at the mouth of the Lippe River.[113] The town of Wesel was the junction point between the Ninth Army and the British Second Army, and as such it was a delicate position. This particular island, if held by German forces, could have disrupted communications between the armies. The movement of the cavalry allowed the 30th ID to secure this critical location while pushing their infantry forward to expand the bridgehead and further protecting their boundary.

On 27 March, elements of the 75th ID relieved the 15th CRS from their positions south of Wesel. The squadron then joined the rest of the group in an assembly area generally centered in the corps bridgehead. On 29 March, parts of the 15th CRS conducted area security in support of elements of the 79th ID, who were clearing German resistance from the vicinity of Hamborn, just north of the Lippe River.[114] This security allowed the infantry to focus on the immediate mission while the cavalry took care of the cordon, preventing Germans from escaping.

As the XVI Corps bridgehead slowly expanded, the Ninth Army began filtering across the Rhine. McLain's XIX Corps would take over the main effort on the southern edge of the army (the Lippe River), passing through the XVI Corps and continuing the attack toward Hamm and Paderborn. Gillem's XIII Corps would pass through the XVI Corps as well and move to the north of the XIX Corps, protecting the army's flank while attempting to maintain contact with the British Second Army. Simpson ordered the XVI Corps to maintain the bridgehead and participate in operations south into the developing Ruhr Pocket.[115]

The attack of the XIX Corps began on 30 March 1945, as elements of the 2nd AD drove toward Lippstadt and a link with the First Army attacking from the south. The next day, the Ninth Army shifted the 15th MCG to this corps to protect its open right (southern) flank. On 1 April, the cavalry took over an approximately twenty-two-mile screen from the Dortmund-Ems Canal to Hamm along the Lippe River.[116] This security mission served two purposes. The first was to protect the flank of the 2nd AD as it attacked east, allowing it to push all of its combat power forward. The second was to prevent German forces from escaping north out of the Ruhr.

The XIII Corps initiated its crossing of the Rhine on 31 March, with the 5th AD followed closely by the 11th MCG. The 102nd ID (also of XIII Corps) would hold the cavalry's positions along the river until it could be relieved by the newly arrived XXII Corps of the Fifteenth Army. The first objective for the corps would be Münster, then just to the east of the corps' forward positions. The 5th AD would lead, backed by the 84th ID and 17th Airborne. The XIII Corps assigned the 11th MCG, reinforced with a TD battalion (equipped with M36 Jacksons), the responsibility for protecting the corps' left (northern) flank as it moved east, toward the Elbe. The group also was to maintain contact with the southern edge of the British Second Army as it advanced to the left of the XIII Corps and Ninth Army.[117] This connection would prove important as the British advanced at a different rate than the Americans (faster and slower, depending on the day), and the Blackhorse prevented either side from receiving unpleasant surprises from the flanks.

The XIX Corps' 113th MCG, which had started the offensive in reserve, crossed the Rhine on 1 April, rejoining the forward elements of the corps eight miles south of Münster. McLain, the corps commander, presented the Redhorse with two contradictory missions. The first was to advance along the northern flank of the corps, maintaining contact between the XIII Corps' 5th AD and the XIX Corps' 2nd AD. The other task was to protect the assembly areas of the 30th and 95th IDs over a nine-mile-wide area around the Davensberg as they gathered for combat after crossing the Rhine. Biddle stretched his group as best as possible, although the combination of being tied to a fixed point in the west while trying to maintain contact with a rapidly moving force to the east meant that the cavalry soon lost contact with the 2nd AD. Confronted with this problem, McLain relieved the cavalry of their fixed area security mission so that they could concentrate on the left flank guard of the 2nd AD in conjunction with the 15th MCG, who were holding the division's right flank.[118]

The 113th MCG continued their mission of protecting the northern flank of the XIX Corps until 2 April. At that point, the XIX Corps experienced a significant shift in its plan. McLain had planned to attack with two armored divisions abreast, the 2nd AD in the north and the 8th AD in the south. However, Simpson had ordered the 8th AD to participate in the destruction of the Ruhr Pocket. McLain still wished to launch a two-pronged assault to the east. Therefore, he ordered the 113th MCG to join the 83rd ID in the south and lead that division in the assault to the east. He detached the 125th CRS from the group and attached it to the 30th ID in the northern prong to give that division additional mobility as it followed the 2nd AD. To assist the 113th MCG and the 113th CRS in their role as a replacement for an armored division, the 83rd ID attached to the cavalry a battalion of motorized infantry, a battalion of towed 105mm artillery, a TD company, most of the 736th Tank Battalion, and an engineer company. Together, this force became known as Task Force Biddle.[119]

On the northern end of the Ninth Army line, Gillem's XIII Corps began its advance on 1 April, with the 5th AD moving rapidly toward the Weser River and the corps infantry trailing behind. The 11th MCG established a thirty-seven-mile screen along the corps' left (north) flank. Due to the need to keep up with the rapidly advancing armor, the Blackhorse was moving through territory completely untouched by any other Allied formations. This meant that the flank guard took on the risks and hazards more commonly associated with an advance guard.[120] By 3 April 1945, the 5th AD was closing on the Weser River, sixty miles to the east of Münster, but the infantry divisions were advancing much more slowly, with fighting still occurring at Münster as the 17th Airborne Division cleared the city. Moreover, due to the speed of the American advance and the northeasterly direction of attack of the British Second Army, several unmolested German formations existed north of the corps.[121] Therefore, the importance of the cavalry's guard grew every day of the advance. Without their efforts, the supply columns keeping the 5th AD moving would have suffered unacceptable casualties.

On 3 April the 11th MCG found itself in a demanding tactical situation. The group's elements near Ostbevern, nine miles northeast of Münster, found themselves directly in the path of Germans attempting to withdraw from the fighting. This positioning led to several sharp and violent fights as the cavalry held their ground. The most serious occurred on the morning of 4 April, when a force of two hundred Germans supported by six assault guns attacked Ostbevern from the south as they tried to escape from the XIII Corps. The Blackhorse held their positions, destroying all of the assault guns and killing or capturing the rest of the German force.[122]

In addition to blocking escaping Germans, the 11th MCG also had to keep pace with the overall advance of the XIII Corps, so on 4 April the screen was extended to Melle, an additional fifteen miles northeast of the previous easternmost point. However, this extension was mitigated somewhat by the advance of friendly elements, relieving the cavalry of some of their responsibilities on the western end of the screen. In fact, by 5 April the group had shifted to the east, with the screen now stretching over forty-eight miles to the Weser River.[123]

To the south of the XIII Corps, McLain's XIX Corps launched its attack on 4 April. TF Biddle quickly moved out on a five-mile front, seizing a number of towns around Bad Driburg twelve miles east of Paderborn. German resistance proved scattered and disjointed but still determined, requiring the cavalry to fight for every town. The next day the task force advanced another nine miles against the same type of resistance. On 6 April the cavalry broke through to the Weser River.[124]

The 83rd ID and TF Biddle crossed the Weser and continued their attack toward the Leine River. German resistance was flagging, and the cavalry reached the Leine on 8 April, seizing a bridge fourteen miles northwest of Osterode. On 9 April, the XIX Corps underwent another reorganization, as those formations still in the vicinity of the Ruhr Pocket fell underneath the XVI Corps while the formations in the east rearranged themselves to attack three divisions abreast. The 30th ID would attack in the north, with the 125th CRS attached to protect its northern flank. The 2nd AD would attack in the center, while the 83rd ID advanced in the south with the remainder of the 113th MCG.[125]

On the southern end of the army drive, Gillem (XIII Corps) ordered the 11th MCG on 7 April off its screen to the west of the Weser River, directing it to emplace a screen from the Weser east to the Leine River, a distance of over twenty-five miles. This screen would support the corps' advance to and seizure of the city of Hannover. The Blackhorse crossed the Weser and began their new mission, establishing half of the required screen that same day. The next day, the 44th CRS seized a bridge over the Leine River ten miles northwest of Hannover. Although the Germans had made concerted efforts to destroy most of the Leine bridges, the cavalry were able to use a combination of their mobility, firepower, and a substantial dose of luck to seize the bridge. This seizure allowed the 84th ID to cross the Leine on 8 April (the same day as the cavalry took the bridge) and prepare for an attack on Hannover from the north.[126] Although crossing this river would not have been a major issue for the infantry, the cavalry's actions allowed for a more rapid attack on the city, preventing the German defenders from establishing themselves more.

As the 84th ID moved into the attack against Hannover on 9 April, the 11th MCG protected the flank and rear of the division, which otherwise would have been exposed, as the British Second Army's movement to the north had opened a nearly ten-mile gap between the American and British forces.[127] With the division able to concentrate solely on its primary task, the 84th ID cleared the city by 10 April.[128]

McLain's XIX Corps resumed its offensive from the Leine on 10 April, with three divisions abreast. The 83rd ID struck the northern edge of the Harz Mountains to the north of Osterode and shifted along the boundary of the range. On 11 April, the division ordered the 113th MCG (minus the 125th CRS) to seize a series of towns on the northern side of the Harz Mountains. With the seizure of these towns, the Redhorse would block German egress from the Harz region as well as protect the flank of the 83rd ID as it attacked to the east. The task force seized all four of its initial objectives that day, though each town required progressively more effort. The next day, the 113th MCG continued its attack but was stopped by intense German fire halfway. After several attempts stretching over two days failed to seize the town, the commander of the 83rd ID ordered the group to stop their attacks and concentrate on the mission of protecting the flank of the division against any attacks from the Harz Mountains. The cavalry's efforts allowed the division to focus its attention forward, seizing a small bridgehead across the Elbe fifteen miles southeast of Magdeburg on 13 April.[129]

After the capture of Hannover, the XIII Corps turned to the east once more on 10 April, with the 11th MCG following three days later. From 13 to 14 April, the group would leapfrog its squadrons forward from Hannover to the Elbe River, protecting the exposed flank of the 5th AD and the rest of the XIII Corps. Along the way the group would liberate over one thousand Allied prisoners near the town of Salzwedel. By 14 April the group screen stretched an incredible fifty miles.[130] The screen would soon shrink as the XIII Corps consolidated along the Elbe.

On 14 April, the 8th AD, newly returned to the XIX Corps, relieved the 113th MCG of its blocking positions along the Harz Mountains on the southern flank of the corps. As most of the corps had already closed to the Elbe, the cavalry moved to an assembly area seventeen miles south of Magdeburg. Then the cavalry moved forward slowly, relieving elements of the 83rd ID as it cleared the region between the Saale and Elbe Rivers, all while protecting the southern flank of the corps. On 21 April, as the VII Corps met the XIX Corps at the Elbe, the Redhorse transitioned to holding a section of the front along the river, maintaining contact between the 83rd ID and the VII Corps. The cavalry would maintain their positions along the Elbe until 29 April, when McLain ordered the 125th CRS to patrol east of the Elbe to make contact with Russian forces. The cavalry's mix of speed and mounted firepower made them perfect for such a precision dash behind enemy lines.

Despite meeting occasionally strong resistance, the squadron accomplished their linking mission on 30 April. Following this last reconnaissance mission for the corps, the entire 113th MCG was withdrawn from the line and prepared for military government duty in north-central Germany.[131]

The rapid advance of the XIII Corps, coupled with a northward shift in the boundary of the British Second Army, left a large pocket of German resistance to the north of the corps' formations. These German forces raided deep into the rear of the corps, striking supply columns as they moved forward. Most of these depredations occurred to the west of the 11th MCG's cavalry screen that, until mid-April, had been focused on the flanks of the combat formations.[132] However, with the corps having traversed over ninety miles in two days, its flanks were simply too long to guard effectively.

In order to deal with this threat, Gillem planned an attack north with elements of the 5th AD, as well as the 84th and 29th IDs. However, before that attack could begin, on 19 April, a German counterattack by portions of the Von Clausewitz Division penetrated the corps' flank and drove eighteen miles south to the vicinity of Klötze. The Germans were reported to be at regimental strength, with eight hundred soldiers, thirty-six half-tracks, eight assault guns, four Panzer IV tanks, and artillery.[133] This attack effectively cut most of the supply lines for the corps. The 11th MCG, along with a battalion of the 102nd ID, responded and succeeded in containing the Germans in a wooded lot southeast of the town. A combined force of a regiment of the 29th ID, the 11th MCG (reinforced with tank destroyers), and the corps artillery made plans to annihilate the marauders on the morning of 21 April. Until that time, the 11th MCG and its tank destroyers cordoned off the wood lot containing the German force, defeating several small attempts to break out.[134]

Early on the morning of 21 April, the German force staged a breakout attempt, smashing through the cavalry's pickets. Despite losing several vehicles, the desperate attackers broke through and made it to another wooded lot. However, the 11th MCG quickly responded in force, using a combination of light tanks, armored cars, and tank destroyers to regain containment of the Germans. The cavalry then called for the corps artillery, comprised of 8-inch and 155mm artillery pieces, to place a "heavy concentration" of fire on the enemy position. Although the Germans began surrendering in droves as soon as the artillery started, the group ordered the bombardment to continue for thirty minutes in order to ensure no resistance remained.[135] A subsequent sweep of the woods by the infantry would find twenty-nine half-tracks, three Panzer IV tanks, two assault guns, and four towed anti-aircraft guns.[136] The cavalry's mobility and firepower played a large role in the rapid destruction of the marauding Germans. Although by April 1945 there was no chance of this force actually doing lasting harm to the XIII Corps as an organization, it could have inflicted more casualties if it had not been stopped as quickly as it had.

After the destruction of the German incursion at Klötze, the 11th MCG transitioned to convoy escort, protecting the corps' supply lines from random attacks by other fugitive German soldiers. This mission would continue until 26 April, when the corps felt that the supply routes were sufficiently secure that convoys did not need additional security. The Blackhorse would end the war conducting area security in the XIII Corps zone.[137]

While the rest of the Ninth Army attacked to the Elbe River, the 15th MCG held their positions along the Lippe River on the north side of the Ruhr Pocket for two weeks. On 9 April 1945, as the XIX Corps passed farther to the east, the group came back under the control of the XVI Corps, which was responsible for the Ninth Army's portion of the Ruhr Pocket. On 10 April, the 95th ID and 8th AD attacked southeast across the front of the cavalry's western positions, closing the 17th CRS out of the line by the next day. The group then maintained contact between the 95th ID and elements of the First Army's III Corps as it fought to reduce its portion of the Ruhr Pocket.

On 15 April, after major combat operations in the Ruhr had ceased, the XVI Corps moved the 15th MCG to Bad Prymont, twenty-eight miles northeast of Paderborn, to serve in a military government capacity. The group also protected bridges across the Weser River, ensuring that a steady flow of supplies reached the XIX and XIII Corps as they operated along the Elbe River.[138] The group would end the war in this area security mission.

The Ninth Army would witness the end of hostilities in positions along the Elbe, holding the northernmost posts in the American sector. Its cavalry had played a major role in its operational success in reaching this river. The groups had conducted security operations protecting the flanks of the army's Rhine beachhead, allowing the corps to concentrate combat power forward against the diminishing German resistance. Additionally, the cavalry participated in containing the northern portion of the Ruhr Pocket, preventing enemy escape from that direction. Finally, the 11th MCG's participation in the destruction of the Clausewitz Division stands as a textbook example of area security. Without the cavalry's actions, the Ninth Army would have struggled to move as fast as it did, as infantry and armor formations would have had to have been pulled off the line to do these missions. Additionally, the infantry formations would not have been as effective, as they lacked the speed and flexibility of the cavalry. Armored combat commands had the speed and flexibility, but they were too valuable to spend on security missions.

Finally, just like their brethren in the other American field armies, the cavalry of the Ninth Army stitched that formation together and tied it into adjacent armies through coordination and liaison duties. This duty proved particularly vital, as Simpson's formation served as the glue between the British 21st Army Group and the American 12th Army Group. The army would serve in both formations at various points in the campaign as priorities shifted. The cavalry helped coordinate and smooth the transition zones between the armies. This duty was even more vital along the boundary between the 12th and 21st Army Groups, as Montgomery had a tendency to move according to his own wishes rather than the wishes of SHAEF. Once again, the mobility and flexibility of the cavalry along the flank helped allow the Allies to overcome the difficulties caused by two different national formations maneuvering alongside one another. Thus, the cavalry of the Ninth Army proved essential to the overall success of that army as well as its parent army groups.

The corps cavalry of the U.S. Army proved essential to the character of the Allied victory in the Germany campaign. By this point in the war, victory was nearly assured. However, the Germans still had a significant amount of fighting spirit left and could still be dangerous, as evidenced by the fierce fighting encountered from the Harz Mountains all the way to Württemberg and Bavaria. The cavalry's actions in security, reconnaissance, and liaison duties helped the army win more cheaply and more quickly than might otherwise have been the case.

The highly mobile nature of this particular campaign meant that units could easily move too fast and impale themselves upon a determined group of defenders. The cavalry helped prevent such incidents from occurring—or at the least took the damage themselves, thus protecting larger units from harm. While perhaps insignificant on an individual basis, an accumulation of these incidents can build to the point where the difference is hundreds or thousands of additional casualties.

In addition to their security tasks, the cavalry's actions in liaison duties helped stitch together one of the largest ground offensives in American military history. This campaign included army groups conducting operational maneuvers in support of each other, as witnessed by the interaction between the 12th and 6th Army Groups as they moved to assault through southern Germany. Within these huge formations, field armies and corps maneuvered and shifted directions of attack on a nearly daily basis. With so many units moving so quickly in close proximity, Clausewitzian friction is guaranteed to cause problems, including traffic jams, snarled logistics, and fratricide. While the corps cavalry did not eliminate these issues, they did mitigate some of the worst effects, particularly at unit boundaries.

Considering all of the contributions of the corps cavalry in this campaign, it is evident that these formations were among the most valuable in the U.S. Army. They had the mobility, flexibility, and firepower to quickly move across the battlefield and make a difference when they arrived. Armored combat commands also had this ability, but they were needed to spearhead attacks. Infantry regiments, even when truck mounted, could not hope to keep pace while still maintaining security, particularly in such an ambiguous threat environment. Therefore, the cavalry proved to be the perfect fit for a number of operational requirements as the U.S. Army drove across Germany to end the war.

9

Conclusions

On 19 May 1945, the 3rd MCG celebrated the ninety-ninth anniversary of the regiment.[1] In a letter addressed to the officers and men of the group, Lieutenant General Walton Walker praised the cavalrymen: "The 'crossed sabers' you wear bear a new luster due to your deeds in the present campaign. When the history of the present War in Europe is written, no narrative could be complete, no account could be either adequate or accurate unless it told, and told at some length, of your achievements."[2]

Although Walker specifically addressed only the 3rd MCG, the same could be said for all of the cavalry groups that had served in the ETO. These groups had served with distinction in almost every theater of combat in which the U.S. Army had fought, from Normandy to Germany. The only campaign in the entire ETO that involved American forces at the corps level that the cavalry missed was Operation MARKET-GARDEN. Designed and trained primarily for a reconnaissance role, the cavalry had conducted that mission in addition to offensive and defensive security operations, economy of force missions, and coordination and liaison duties.

Corps cavalry had proven their worth in reconnaissance beginning on the first day of combat in the ETO. The 4th MCG's actions confirming the lack of enemy presence at the Îles Saint Marcouf and at Utah Beach materially aided the success of the VII Corps on D-Day. Corps cavalry led the Third Army on its massive end run through France and identified stiffening German resistance along the Moselle. The 113th MCG rode through Belgium in less than a week, marking the route for the XIX Corps to follow. The 117th CRS led Task Force Butler north into the French Alps, determining the fitness of routes and aiding that unit's rapid advance. Cavalry probed the Siegfried Line throughout the fall and winter, determining its strengths and weaknesses. Finally, after the brutal fighting to advance to and across the Rhine, cavalry once more led the way, scouting routes and bridges for the advancing American columns. Beyond these missions, thousands of individual cavalry patrols had ascertained German positions and the possibilities of terrain, aiding the army throughout the war. These actions occurred during many periods labeled as "quiet," but they provided information that proved critical when large-scale actions resumed.

Intimately and inextricably linked with reconnaissance, security missions also proved a vital component of the corps cavalry lexicon. The cavalry screened divisional, corps, and army flanks, fronts, and rears with regularity in both offensive and defensive roles. The 113th MCG protected the flank of the XIX Corps in heavy fighting through the hedgerows. The 2nd MCG fought through a German security zone in front of the Moselle in early September, and followed it with a grueling example of a defensive guard around Lunéville. The 4th MCG covered the flank of the VII Corps as it fought in the Mons area, allowing the corps to participate in a major victory. The 106th MCG guarded the flank of the XV Corps as it attacked through the Saverne Gap, identifying and slowing the German attack prior to handing off the battle to the infantry. Finally, throughout the drives to the Rhine and beyond, corps cavalry protected the main bodies of their corps from German ambushes and flank attacks. Beyond all of these high-profile missions, the cavalry groups provided area security in corps and army zones, preventing significant losses to vital supply echelons. Additionally, cavalry troops could also be found securing corps- and army-level headquarters due to their firepower and mobility.

Economy of force operations proved another key mission of the corps cavalry. The 4th MCG covered such vast distances for the VII Corps that it had to be relieved by an entire corps twice in nearly a month. The 3rd MCG covered half of the XX Corps' sector in the fall of 1944, allowing for massed combat power in the November crossing of the Moselle. The 2nd MCG covered a corps' worth of front along the Moselle in the winter of 1944–1945, allowing the XII Corps to concentrate its infantry divisions on much smaller fronts. The 11th, 15th, and 113th MCGs helped the Ninth Army stretch its limited resources over a large front during the Ardennes offensive. American forces gained success on the attack by massing combat power, attacking with regiments or even divisions in column. Yet operational requirements so stretched American units that they became used to attacking with no reserve.[3] These two facts should have been mutually exclusive. However, the presence of the cavalry helped corps and army commanders meet that need by allowing them to mass combat power at the decisive point. Without the important capabilities offered by these formations, it is doubtful that the Americans could have succeeded, given the already stretched nature of the line formations.

The cavalry groups' coordination and liaison duties, long overlooked in the historical record, also proved of immense value to the corps and armies of the U.S. forces. Included in nearly every flank security mission, these tasks proved essential to cross-boundary cooperation, particularly at the army and army group level. The unique configuration and equipment of the cavalry particularly suited them to this role, as radio detachments could reside at adjacent headquarters to provide an additional radio net exclusively committed to lateral communications. In situations where the next unit over might not only be from a different army group, but also a different nation (as in the case with the 113th MCG, the 117th CRS, the 11th MCG, etc.), anything that could enhance communications between units was a good thing. Finally, the cavalry had the mobility to quickly move to and establish contact points, the physical meeting of adjacent units. These points complemented radio coordination with face-to-face contact, weaving the two formations together.

Finally, the cavalry often participated in direct combat, both offensive and defensive. However, combat is not by itself a mission, but instead a state of being. It simply means fighting, and does not refer to any particular goal or objective. The cavalry fought in order to accomplish the other missions listed above. Unfortunately, the specific definitions used in the Mechanized Cavalry General Board Report have confused the issue. For example, it claims that corps cavalry spent a little over 3 percent of their days in action conducting reconnaissance. While true, a more thorough reading of the General Board Report comes to a very different conclusion. Included in the same table as the finding on reconnaissance is a note stating that "the accomplishment of reconnaissance missions normally involved offensive combat." A similar modifier is appended to the description of security operations.[4] Thus, the doctrinal definitions of these missions in the General Board Report are highly particular and overly specific. The authors of the board, understanding that the doctrinal definitions did not match the realities of combat, added these comments to clarify their meanings and move beyond overly narrow terminology. Therefore, nearly every action the cavalry undertook against the enemy could be considered either offensive or defensive combat.

Through the accomplishment of security, reconnaissance, coordination and liaison, and economy of force operations, the corps cavalry proved themselves critical members of the U.S. Army team in Europe. The tasks that the cavalry conducted were essential to the overall success of the field armies and corps committed to this theater of operations. While not decisive by themselves, these missions enabled the army to conduct the critical moves to win the war. The supportive nature of these shaping operations meant that they rarely received much attention, but they were still absolute prerequisites to success in the main effort. Imagine if the 90th ID had had to secure the Moselle in September 1944 in addition to preparing for its assault crossing. The division may have succeeded, but the actions of the 3rd MCG in its guard along the river helped transfer the odds of success from maybe to probably (there is always room for chance in military operations). The assault crossing of the XX Corps on the Moselle is just one example, but this work is literally filled with similar instances.

Although the missions the cavalry performed may have been essential, did that necessarily make the corps cavalry essential themselves? In other words, could another unit have accomplished the same tasks? The answer is a qualified yes. Basically, the tasks conducted by the cavalry for their corps could have been conducted by any infantry, combat engineer, or armor formation. Other units, like tank destroyer or artillery units, were simply not suited to independent combat and would not have been as successful. However, the fact that any infantry (engineers can be considered infantry simply if they are performing a role outside of their specialty) or armor unit could accomplish cavalry tasks does not mean that they should do them, or that they will be as good at them as the cavalry.

The army is designed to be a team. Each unit is built with specific abilities to accomplish its share of the army's tasks. For instance, an infantry battalion is better at clearing woods than an armor battalion, but it leaves engaging enemy tanks in open terrain to their tracked brethren. Thus, the army needs a mix of unit types to accomplish as wide a variety of tasks as possible. While other units would occasionally conduct cavalry-like missions, such as the commitment of an infantry division to stiffen the right flank of the Third Army in late August 1944, this was not the most efficient use of combat power. However, cavalry could only stay in one place so long before being left so far behind that they were no longer relevant to their parent corps. Additionally, the cavalry did have weaknesses that needed to be backstopped, particularly in high-risk situations. However, the fact remains that in most cases the cavalry were the most cost-effective and appropriate units to conduct cavalry missions.

The cavalry groups were much more mobile than any infantry formation in the U.S. Army in 1944 or 1945. Even when the infantry were motorized in trucks, they were more vulnerable to enemy action than the cavalry, which could fight mounted. Many cavalry missions called for speed, and the infantry simply were not as fast. Additionally, infantry regiments needed to be massed to maximize their effect on the enemy, whereas cavalry missions often called for dispersal. Thus, using infantry to perform cavalry missions was not a good use of assets.

On the other hand, armor combat commands had similar speed to the cavalry, but their medium tanks were often too large to fit down roads or across bridges that the lighter cavalry could negotiate. Moreover, armor divisions were valued for their mix of armor, mechanized infantry, organic cavalry, and self-propelled artillery. The army only produced sixteen armored divisions, several of which arrived very late in the war. To use large portions of these formations for supporting efforts meant that they could not be on hand to spearhead important drives.

Thus, the mechanized cavalry groups filled an important niche in the operational design of the army. They had the requisite speed, mobility, and firepower to perform missions that did not make sense for the infantry or armor, or actions for which these formations were not well suited. The cavalry groups were often reinforced by tank destroyers, artillery, engineers, and even infantry or tank battalions. However, this is simply another earmark of the army in the Second World War rather than a particular failing of the unit design. Almost all combat multipliers, such as artillery and tank destroyers, were held at the corps or army level, then disseminated down to those units that required them. Therefore, to qualify the accomplishments of the cavalry because they were reinforced with various attachments is to qualify the success of the entire army in the war.

While the absolute inadequacy of the army's cavalry doctrine of pure reconnaissance has been well established by such excellent authors as Matthew Morton, Louis DiMarco, and George Hofmann, it is essentially a moot point. This work has demonstrated that no one, from the army commanders to cavalry lieutenants, ever seriously attempted to follow it. Although this doctrine would influence the organization and equipment of the cavalry groups, experience showed that these tools and formations would work, albeit not ideally. Furthermore, as any tanker in any World War II U.S. armor division would argue, the cavalry did not have a monopoly on less-than-ideal equipment. Yet the cavalry, just like every unit faced with adversity, found ways to adapt and overcome.

What makes the mechanized cavalry groups so special is that their impact on the battlefield proved consistently larger than that of any other equivalently sized unit. As noted earlier, cavalry groups often held frontages better suited for divisions or even corps. No other type of unit in the army routinely did this. Moreover, even in cases where the cavalry relieved a single regiment, numbers speak loudly. A regular infantry regiment had an authorized strength of approximately thirty-two hundred personnel. A cavalry group with both squadrons would muster less than half of that, coming in below fifteen hundred. More often than not, a single squadron of just over seven hundred would relieve an infantry regiment, meaning that the cavalry would be relieving a formation over four times its size.[5] Even assuming a higher attrition rate in the infantry, the cavalry were routinely expected to do more with less.

The cavalry groups also acted as independent commands reporting directly to the corps commander, and they were managed and maneuvered as such. A corps would typically only have one mechanized cavalry group. These groups filled an important niche and were routinely committed to ensure the success of the overall corps. Infantry regiments, though important, did not have the same significance to the corps. Although the infantry regiments and armored combat commands of the corps were the building blocks to unit success, the corps cavalry made it possible by allowing the main line forces to concentrate their efforts.

The corps cavalry was not always successful. This work has recorded numerous times where German resistance proved too strong, or the cavalry were too weak to resist an attack. The worst single incidence of the failure of corps cavalry was the 14th MCG at the Losheim Gap. However, significant failures were generally the exception and should not be taken as an indictment of the concept or the entirety of corps cavalry. The ETO was the scene of often brutal fighting. In such a situation, an army does not always win, for a legion of different reasons. Thus, for a true assessment of the value of corps cavalry, the full body of work should be assessed.

When considering the entire combat history of American corps cavalry in the ETO, the evidence is clear. These smallest regimental-size formations in the U.S. Army made an outsized impact. Their contributions are noted repeatedly in corps after action reports. Of the thirteen groups and one squadron to see combat in the ETO, one group (the 6th MCG) and one squadron (the 38th CRS of the 102nd MCG) received Presidential Unit Citations.

In the end, corps cavalry proved incredibly important to the success of the army in the Second World War. They played their part well, contributing to the victory of the divisions and corps of the four field armies committed to the ETO. That the cavalry did so while being the smallest operational formations on the battlefield speaks to their versatility, bravery, and skill. Their actions, long relegated to footnotes, now stand as General Walker intended.

Acknowledgments

I would like to gratefully acknowledge the help of some people without whom I could never have finished this project:

My wife, Mariann, who endured countless hours of lecture on cavalry doctrine and operations, and also for her invaluable assistance in making the maps seen in the text.

My battle buddy, David Musick, who provided good counsel and better friendship.

Colonel Christopher Prigge, the man who initially set me on the path to study mechanized cavalry.

Lieutenant Colonel (ret) Louis DiMarco, for his kind advice and suggestions to a young captain who called him out of the blue.

The professors of the University of North Texas Military History Center, especially my major professor, Robert Citino, as well as Professors Michael Leggiere, Geoffery Wawro, Richard McCaslin, and Richard Lowe, who helped turn a tanker into a scholar.

Colonel (ret) Dennis Dougherty, Philip Notestine, the 117th Cavalry Association, and 1/102 Cavalry for their hospitality and generosity in sharing the history of New Jersey cavalry.

Scott Hamric, the curator of the Third Cavalry Regiment Museum, and Chris McKeever of the Sixth Cavalry Museum, for their support in providing me with historical materials not generally available.

Bill Heidner, Dave Gettman, and Chris Golden of the Second Cavalry Association for their comments, support, and providing historical materials.

Finally, to the Omar N. Bradley Foundation and the University of North Texas Military History Center, whose kind financial support made possible two critical research trips to the National Archives in College Park, Maryland.

Notes

1. Introduction

1. While the term "operational art" can be fraught with different meanings for different military professionals, in this work it refers to the planning, synchronization, movement, and combat actions of corps and field armies. These were the base units of maneuver in Europe during the Second World War.

2. Department of the Army, *FM 1-02: Operational Terms and Graphics* (Washington, D.C.: Government Printing Office, 2004), 1–158.

3. Ibid., 1–168.

4. Ibid., 1–67.

5. There were examples of corps-level maneuvers in the Philippines and Okinawa. However, as they were fairly limited and no cavalry groups participated in these actions, they are left out of the study.

6. John N. Tully, "Doctrine, Organization and Employment of the 4th Cavalry Group during World War II" (Master's thesis, U.S. Army Command and General Staff College, 1994); Dean A Nowowiejski, "Adaptation to Change: U.S. Army Cavalry Doctrine and Mechanization, 1938–1945" (Monograph, U.S. Army School of Advanced Military Studies, 1994); Louis A. DiMarco, "The U.S. Army's Mechanized Cavalry Doctrine in WW II" (Master's thesis, U.S. Army Command and General Staff College, 1995); Matthew A. Dooley, "Ignoring History: The Flawed Effort to Divorce Reconnaissance from Security in Modern Cavalry Transformation" (Master's thesis, U.S. Army Command and General Staff College, 2006).

7. Christopher N. Prigge, "Tradition and Transformation: The Origins of the U.S. Armored Cavalry Regiments" (Ph.D. diss., Harvard University, 2011); George Hofmann, *Through Mobility We Conquer: The Mechanization of U.S. Cavalry* (Lexington: Univ. Press of Kentucky, 2006); Harry Yeide, *Steeds of Steel: A History of U.S. Mechanized Cavalry* (Minneapolis: Zenith Press, 2008); Matthew Darlington Morton, *Men on Iron Ponies: The Death and Rebirth of the Modern U.S. Cavalry* (DeKalb: Northern Illinois Univ. Press, 2009); Robert S. Cameron, *To Fight or Not to Fight? Organizational and Doctrinal Trends in Mounted Maneu-*

ver Reconnaissance from the Interwar Years to Operation IRAQI FREEDOM (Fort Leavenworth, Kans.: Combat Studies Institute Press, 2010); Gary W. Palmer, *The United States Cavalry: Time of Transition, 1938–1944, Horses to Mechanization* (San Diego, Calif.: Voyak Publications, 2013).

8. Louis DiMarco, "The American Mechanized Cavalry's Critical Contribution to Allied Victory in Europe, 1944–1945," *Global War Studies* 9, no. 2 (2012): 39–66.

2. Background

1. Portions of this chapter have appeared previously in William S. Nance, "Lost Sabers: Why We Need Operational Cavalry and How to Get It Back," *Armor* 123, no. 4 (October–December 2014): 51–55; and William S. Nance, "The Armored Reconnaissance Squadron and the Mechanized Cavalry Group," *Armor* 115, no. 1 (January–February 2006): 7–11.

2. Matthew Darlington Morton, *Men on Iron Ponies: The Death and Rebirth of the Modern U.S. Cavalry* (DeKalb: Northern Illinois Univ. Press, 2009), 200, 218.

3. Robert S. Cameron's *To Fight or Not to Fight,* provides a superb outline of this progression and the tension between reconnaissance and security missions.

4. Mary Lee Stubb and Stanley Connor, *Army Lineage Series: Armor-Cavalry Part I: Regular Army and Army Reserve* (Washington, D.C.: Office of the Chief of Military History, 1969), 8.

5. James A. Sawicki, *Cavalry Regiments of the U.S. Army* (Dumfries, Va.: Wyvern Publications, 1985), 151–153.

6. Ibid., 155.

7. Edward G. Longacre, *The Cavalry at Gettysburg: A Tactical Study of Mounted Operations during the Civil War's Pivotal Campaign, 9 June–14 July 1863* (Lincoln: Univ. of Nebraska Press, 1986), 57.

8. Although in this particular case, the lack of horses had more to do with logistical ineptitude than operational decision making.

9. U.S. War Department, *Drill Regulations for Cavalry, Amended 1909, Corrected to January 1, 1911* (Washington, D.C.: GPO, 1911), 3.

10. Ibid., paragraphs 130–169.

11. Ibid., paragraph 282.

12. Ibid., paragraph 340. Foragers refers to attack in open order.

13. However, the romantic idea of massed cavalry charges did indeed remain fixed in the imaginations of many American cavalry officers. Patton himself even designed a saber for use in American cavalry regiments. Raised on stories of Marshals Ney and Murat, and the example of the Lord Cardigan and the Light Brigade, some officers still yearned for Napoleonic glory, despite the fact that almost

every massed cavalry charge on the American continent had failed. The doctrinal manuals of the turn of the twentieth century clearly show that these dangerous impulses were generally contained, though comments such as this paragraph were clearly left as a sop to those hewing to traditionalist European views.

14. U.S. War Department, *Drill Regulations for Cavalry, Amended 1909, Corrected to January 1, 1911*, paragraph 855.

15. Ibid., paragraph 847.

16. U.S. War Department, *Field Service Regulations 1913, Corrected to May 21, 1913* (Washington, D.C.: GPO, 1913), paragraphs 260–264.

17. American cavalry professional writing during the First World War is fascinating for its critiques of different nations' techniques for cavalry utilization. The British, with their experiences in the Boer War fresh in mind, generally come in for high praise, while the Germans and French are often taken to task for unrealistic expectations.

18. William O. Odom, *After the Trenches: The Transformation of U.S. Army Doctrine, 1918–1939* (College Station: Texas A&M Univ. Press, 1999), 25.

19. U.S. War Department, *Field Service Regulations 1923* (Washington, D.C.: GPO, 1924), paragraph 80.

20. Ibid., paragraph 81.

21. Ibid., paragraph 82.

22. Robert S. Cameron, *Mobility, Shock, and Firepower—The Emergence of the U.S. Army's Armor Branch, 1917–1945* (Washington, D.C.: Center of Military History, U.S. Army, 2008), 21.

23. Ibid., 26.

24. George F. Hofmann, "The Demise of the U.S. Tank Corps and Medium Tank Development Program," *Military Affairs* 37, no. 1 (February 1973): 23.

25. George F. Hofmann, "A Yankee Inventor and the Military Establishment: The Christie Tank Controversy," *Military Affairs* 39, no. 1 (February 1975): 17.

26. As an interesting aside, Christie would have great success selling his designs to the Soviets, who used his suspension in a number of their tanks, including the famous T34.

27. George F. Hofmann, *Through Mobility We Conquer: The Mechanization of U.S. Cavalry* (Lexington: Univ. of Kentucky Press, 2006), 124.

28. Cameron, *Mobility, Shock, and Firepower*, 36.

29. John J. Reardon, "The Evolution of Transportation," *Cavalry Journal* 44, no. 187 (January–February 1935): 46.

30. Bernard Lentz, "A Justification of Cavalry," *Cavalry Journal* 44, no. 187 (January–February 1935): 10.

31. Morton, *Men on Iron Ponies*, 9.

32. Cameron, *Mobility, Shock, and Firepower,* 60.

33. Motorized refers to vehicles with wheels, while mechanized relates to those with tracks. However, in the confused early stages of the introduction of vehicles to the military, the entire process became known as mechanization, regardless of propulsion type.

34. Cameron, *Mobility, Shock, and Firepower,* 168.

35. Hayden A. Sears, "Mobility—Firepower and Shock," *Cavalry Journal* 48, no. 4 (July–August 1939): 288.

36. Ibid., 288.

37. Cameron, *Mobility, Shock, and Firepower,* 230.

38. U.S. War Department, *FM 100-5: Field Service Regulations: Operations, 1941* (Washington, D.C.: GPO, 1941), paragraph 38.

39. Ibid., paragraph 1061.

40. Morton, *Men on Iron Ponies,* 51.

41. Robert W. Grow, "New Developments in the Organization and Equipment of Cavalry," *Cavalry Journal* 48, no. 3 (May–June 1939): 205.

42. Hofmann, *Through Mobility We Conquer,* 235.

43. Cameron, *Mobility, Shock, and Firepower,* 238.

44. Morton, *Men on Iron Ponies,* 70.

45. Hofmann, *Through Mobility We Conquer,* 266.

46. Odom, *After the Trenches,* 8.

47. U.S. War Department, *FM 2-10: Cavalry Field Manual: Mechanized Elements, 1941* (Washington, D.C.: GPO, 1941), paragraph 135.

48. U.S. War Department, *FM 100-5: Field Service Regulations: Operations, 1941,* paragraph 1072.

49. Ibid., paragraphs 1057–1069.

50. The horse-*portee* system involved assigning a horse cavalry regiment a set of horse trailers and trucks to give it greater operational mobility. In practice, the system proved cumbersome, combining the worst elements of motorized vehicles and horses.

51. Hofmann, *Through Mobility We Conquer,* 287.

52. U.S. War Department, *Training Circular 107: Employment of Mechanized Cavalry Units* (Washington, D.C.: GPO, 23 September, 1943), 1.

53. Ibid., 3.

54. U.S. War Department, *FM 100-5: Field Service Regulations: Operations, 1944* (Washington, D.C.: GPO, 1944), paragraph 38.

55. Robert R. Palmer, Bell I. Wiley and William R. Keast, *United States Army in World War II: The Army Ground Forces: The Procurement and Training of Ground Combat Troops* (Washington, D.C.: Historical Division of the Army, 1948), 522.

56. In some formations, at least the 38th Cavalry Reconnaissance Squadron, the jeeps were augmented by half-tracks. (Colonel Alfred Shehab, interview by William S. Nance, 26 May 2013.)

57. Headquarters V Corps, "Operation of Corps Cavalry on Terrain of Normandy," operations memorandum from Headquarters V Corps, U.S. Army, 26 June 1944, 1.

58. U.S. Forces Europe, the General Board, *Mechanized Cavalry Units,* Study Number 49, 1945 (Washington, D.C.: GPO, 1945), appendix 8, 2.

59. Headquarters V Corps, "Operation of Corps Cavalry on Terrain of Normandy," 1.

60. The 117th Squadron at least was able to upgrade their 75mm M8s for 105mm variants. According to tradition in the 117th Cavalry Association, some nonstandard requisitioning and dealing involving at least one captured German Luger pistol was required to make this transaction. (Dennis Dougherty, interview by William S. Nance, 14 June 2013.)

61. "History of the 113th Cavalry Reconnaissance Squadron 1 Jan 1944–31 Dec 1944," CAVS113, Entry 427, Record Group 407, National Archives II, College Park, Md., 1.

62. Note that the troop had significantly more than twenty-seven men, but the demands of placing soldiers as drivers of vehicles and manning all vehicle-mounted machine guns reduced the number of available troopers that could be "on the ground." In actual combat operations, units would improvise to put more troops on foot.

63. This is the "light" model, the standard after 1943, and to which all but two American armored divisions (the 2nd and 3rd ADs) converted by the time of the D-Day invasion. The "heavy" armor divisions each consisted of two armor regiments and one armored infantry regiment—thus, approximately six battalions of tanks and three battalions of infantry.

64. Shelby L. Stanton, *World War II Order of Battle U.S. Army (Ground Force Units)* (Mechanicsburg, Pa.: Stackpole Books, 2006), 13, 19.

65. James H. Polk, "Interview by Jesse Stiller and Rebecca Craver, November 1987–April 1988," 3rd Armored Cavalry Regiment Museum, Fort Hood, Texas, 24. Apparently, according to General Polk, because of the particular ethnic makeup of the group, Germans who were slow to surrender to the 3rd Cavalry rarely got a second chance, and in some cases not even a first one.

66. James H. Polk interview, 23.

67. Sawicki, *Cavalry Regiments of the U.S. Army.*

68. William H. Collier, *The 106th Cavalry's Story* (Bloomington, Ind.: Trafford Publishing, 2012), 18, 62.

69. Robert Lutz, "117th Cavalry Reconnaissance Squadron (MECZ) in World War II," 117th Cavalry Association, http://www.117th-cav.org, 3.

70. Charles E. Rousek, "A Short History of the 38th Cavalry Reconnaissance Squadron (Mechanized)" (Prestice, Czechoslovakia, 1945), available via 117th Cavalry Association, www.117th-cav.org, 2. One of the final remaining cavalry regiments in the army, the 112th Cavalry Regiment, a formation of the Texas National Guard, retained its cavalry designation and organization but fought as a specialized dismounted regimental combat team in the Pacific. Its actions, while not chronicled here, are well documented in the excellent work *Learning under Fire: The 112th Cavalry Regiment in World War II.*

71. James H. Polk interview, 18.

72. U.S. War Department, *FM 2-20: Cavalry Reconnaissance Troop: Mechanized, 1944* (Washington, D.C.: GPO, 1944), paragraph 3.

73. U.S. War Department, *FM 100-5, Operations, 1944,* paragraph 1040.

74. Ibid., paragraph 1026.

75. Christopher N. Prigge, "Tradition and Transformation: The Origins of the U.S. Armored Cavalry Regiments" (Ph.D. diss., Harvard University, 2011), 191–196.

76. Matthew A. Dooley, "Ignoring History: The Flawed Effort to Divorce Reconnaissance from Security in Modern Cavalry Transformation" (Master's thesis, U.S. Army Command and General Staff College, 2006), 30.

77. Ibid., 33.

78. Ibid., 35.

3. Cavalry in the Bocage

1. Richard Hargreaves, *The Germans in Normandy* (Mechanicsburg, Pa.: Stackpole Books, 2008), 26.

2. John N. Tully, "Doctrine, Organization and Employment of the 4th Cavalry Group during World War II" (Master's thesis, U.S. Army Command and General Staff College, 1994), 42.

3. "4th Mechanized Cavalry Group After Action Report, June 1944," CAVG4, Entry 427, Record Group 407, National Archives II, College Park, Md., 1–2.

4. "Annex No. 1 to Unit History, 4th Cavalry Reconnaissance Squadron, June 1944," CAVG4, Entry 427, RG 407, National Archives II, 1.

5. Robert R. Tincher, "Reconnaissance in Normandy," *Cavalry Journal* (January–February 1945): 13; "Annex No. 1 to Unit History, 4th Cavalry Reconnaissance Squadron, June 1944," CAVG4, Entry 427, RG 407, National Archives II, 1–3.

6. "102nd Mechanized Cavalry Group After Action Report, June 1944," CAVG102, Entry 427, RG 407, National Archives II, 3–4; Harold J. Samsel, *Operational History of the 102nd Cavalry Regiment "Essex Troop" World War II* (N.p.: self-published, 1983), chapter 6.

7. "102nd Mechanized Cavalry Group After Action Report, June 1944," 4; *History, V Corps* (U.S. Army, circa 1945), 82.

8. "102nd Mechanized Cavalry Group After Action Report, June 1944," 4.

9. Ibid., 5; *History, V Corps,* 92–93.

10. Tully, "Doctrine, Organization and Employment of the 4th Cavalry Group during World War II" 45.

11. Gordon A. Harrison, *United States Army in World War II: The European Theater of Operations: Cross Channel Attack* (Washington, D.C.: Center of Military History, U.S. Army, 1989), 416–417.

12. "4th Mechanized Cavalry Group After Action Report, June 1944," 3.

13. Tully, "Doctrine, Organization and Employment of the 4th Cavalry Group during World War II" 49–50.

14. "4th Mechanized Cavalry Group After Action Report, June 1944," 6.

15. Tully, "Doctrine, Organization and Employment of the 4th Cavalry Group during World War II" 49.

16. Ibid., 51.

17. "VIII Corps After Action Report, July 1944," Record 208, Entry 427, RG 407, National Archives II, 4–5.

18. Martin Blumenson, *United States Army in World War II: The European Theater of Operations: Breakout and Pursuit* (Washington, D.C.: Historical Division of the Army, 1961), 93.

19. "113th Mechanized Cavalry Group After Action Report, July 1944," CAVG113, Entry 427, RG 407, National Archives II, 3.

20. Blumenson, *Breakout and Pursuit,* 113–114.

21. "113th Mechanized Cavalry Group After Action Report, July 1944," 3. As far as the author can determine, the highway in question is now the D89.

22. Ibid.

23. Blumenson, *Breakout and Pursuit,* 139; Mark J. Reardon, ed., *Defending Fortress Europe: The War Diary of the German 7th Army in Normandy, 6 June to 26 July 1944* (Bedford, Pa.: Aberjona Press, 2012), 174.

24. Matthew Darlington Morton, *Men on Iron Ponies: The Death and Rebirth of the Modern U.S. Cavalry* (DeKalb: Northern Illinois Univ. Press, 2009), 151.

25. "113th Mechanized Cavalry Group After Action Report, July 1944," 3.

26. Morton, *Men on Iron Ponies,* 151.

27. "113th Mechanized Cavalry Group After Action Report, July 1944," 4.

28. Frederick E. Pamp Jr., *Normandy to the Elbe, XIX Corps* (N.p.: 62nd Engineer TOPO Company, circa 1945), 12.

29. "VII Corps After Action Report, July 1944," Record 207, Entry 427, RG 407, National Archives II, 26; Tully, "Doctrine, Organization and Employment of the 4th Cavalry Group During World War II," 54. The assignments are

matters of historical record. The reasoning behind them is the conjecture of the author.

30. Tully, "Doctrine, Organization and Employment of the 4th Cavalry Group During World War II," 53.

31. Ibid., 56.

32. *History, V Corps,* 121; Michael D. Doubler, *Closing with the Enemy: How the GIs Fought the War in Europe, 1944–1945* (Lawrence: Univ. Press of Kansas, 1994), 46.

33. *History, V Corps,* 121.

34. Blumenson, *Breakout and Pursuit,* 283. The term "pinch out" refers to a situation where a unit becomes left behind the front line due to the movement of formations to either flank across its front.

35. "102nd Mechanized Cavalry Group After Action Report, July 1944," CAVG102, Entry 427, RG 407, National Archives II, 5; Blumenson, *Breakout and Pursuit,* Map V.

36. Charles E. Rousek, "A Short History of the 38th Cavalry Reconnaissance Squadron (Mechanized)" (Prestice, Czechoslovakia, 1945), available via 117th Cavalry Association, www.117th-cav.org, 3.

37. Blumenson, *Breakout and Pursuit,* 285.

38. Samsel, *Operational History of the 102nd Cavalry Regiment "Essex Troop" World War II,* chapter 6.

39. Ibid.

40. Ibid., 286.

41. As an interesting note, the official history notes that Staff Sergeant Edward V. Maloney and Private Clifford L. Curry of the 38th CRS earned the Distinguished Service Cross (DFC) for heroism during this action. The DFC is the second highest medal in the U.S. Army, directly behind the Medal of Honor (ibid., 285).

42. "113th Mechanized Cavalry Group After Action Report, July 1944," 11–15.

4. Race to Glory

1. Louis DiMarco, "The American Mechanized Cavalry's Critical Contribution to Allied Victory in Europe, 1944–1945," *Global War Studies* 9, no. 2 (2012): 49.

2. Martin Blumenson, *United States Army in World War II: The European Theater of Operations: Breakout and Pursuit* (Washington, D.C.: Historical Division of the Army, 1961), map 7.

3. "4th Mechanized Cavalry Group After Action Report, August 1944," CAVG4, Entry 427, Record Group 407, National Archives II, College Park, Md., 1.

4. "VII Corps After Action Report, August 1944," Record 207, Entry 427, RG 407, National Archives II, 1.

5. "4th Mechanized Cavalry Group After Action Report, August 1944," 2–3.

6. Ibid., 2–3.

7. Alan Levine, *From the Normandy Beaches to the Baltic Sea: The Northwest Europe Campaign, 1944–1945* (Westport, Conn.: Praeger, 2000), 79.

8. Ibid., 80.

9. "4th Mechanized Cavalry Group After Action Report, August 1944," 3–5.

10. "113th Mechanized Cavalry Group After Action Report, August 1944," CAVG113, Entry 427, RG 407, National Archives II, 7–8.

11. Ibid., 11.

12. "4th Mechanized Cavalry Group After Action Report, August 1944," 10; "113th Mechanized Cavalry Group After Action Report, August 1944," 11.

13. Martin Blumenson, *The Battle of the Generals: The Untold Story of the Falaise Pocket—The Campaign That Should Have Won World War II* (New York: William Morrow, 1993), 246.

14. Joachim Ludewig and David Zabecki, ed. *Rückzug: The German Retreat from France, 1944* (Lexington: Univ. Press of Kentucky, 2012), 125.

15. "113th Mechanized Cavalry Group After Action Report, August 1944," 13–15.

16. David M. Russen, "Combat History: 102nd Cavalry Reconnaissance Squadron (MECZ): World War II," available via 117th Cavalry Association, www.117th-cav.org, 5.

17. Charles E. Rousek, "A Short History of the 38th Cavalry Reconnaissance Squadron (Mechanized)" (Prestice, Czechoslovakia, 1945), available via 117th Cavalry Association, www.117th-cav.org, 3.

18. Russen, "Combat History," 5; Blumenson, *Breakout and Pursuit,* map 11.

19. Harold J. Samsel, *Operational History of the 102nd Cavalry Regiment "Essex Troop" World War II* (N.p.: self-published, 1983), chapter 7.

20. Ibid.

21. Russen, "Combat History," 6.

22. Ibid., 5. Interestingly, the iconic photo of an M8 Greyhound in front of the Arc de Triomphe used on the paperback cover of Richard Overy's *Why the Allies Won* is an image of one of B/102nd MCG's vehicles.

23. "113th Mechanized Cavalry Group After Action Report, September 1944," 1.

24. Blumenson, *Breakout and Pursuit,* 679–680.

25. "113th Mechanized Cavalry Group After Action Report, September 1944," 2.

26. Ibid., 3.

27. Ben Rose, ed., *The Saga of the Red Horse* (Nijmegen, Holland: N.V. Drukkerij G.J. Thieme, 1945), 16–17.

28. "4th Mechanized Cavalry Group After Action Report, August 1944," CAVG4, Entry 427, RG 407, National Archives II, 14.

29. Ibid., 16.

30. Ibid., 17.

31. Blumenson, *Breakout and Pursuit,* 684.

32. J. Lawton Collins, *Lightning Joe: An Autobiography* (Baton Rouge: Louisiana State Univ. Press, 1979), 261–263.

33. "4th Mechanized Cavalry Group After Action Report, September 1944," 1–2.

34. "VII Corps After Action Report, September 1944," Record 207, Entry 427, RG 407, National Archives II, 5.

35. "4th Mechanized Cavalry Group After Action Report, September 1944," 2–3.

36. Collins, *Lightning Joe,* 264.

37. Rousek, "A Short History of the 38th Cavalry Reconnaissance Squadron (Mechanized)," 5; *History, V Corps* (U.S. Army, circa 1945), 214.

38. *History, V Corps,* 233.

39. Russen, "Combat History," 6. Although the unit history claims it was a Tiger, in reality it probably was another model. Tigers were rather few and far between, but had such a reputation that any German tank quickly became labeled a Tiger. However, as no evidence to the contrary exists, this study will repeat the claims of the unit history.

40. *History, V Corps,* 240.

41. Russen, "Combat History," 7. This action was more political and for propaganda purposes than anything else. Significant fighting still had to occur in Luxembourg, and Prince Felix was a serving member of the British Army. However, the triumphal return of a political leader to his capital always makes for good newspaper copy, as well as maintaining civilian morale.

42. Ibid.

43. John Rickard, *Patton at Bay: The Lorraine Campaign, 1944* (Washington, D.C.: Brassey's, 2004), 9.

44. This order of events is extrapolated from analysis of maps from the following sources: Thomas E. Griess, ed., *West Point Atlas for the Second World War: Europe and the Mediterranean* (Wayne, N.J.: Avery Publishing Group, 1998), and Blumenson, *Breakout and Pursuit.*

45. Blumenson, *Breakout and Pursuit,* 389.

46. "VIII Corps After Action Report August," Record 208, Entry 427, RG 407, National Archives II, 4.

47. 2nd Cavalry Association, *The Ghosts of Patton's Third Army: A History of the Second U.S. Cavalry* (Munich, Germany: Münchner Graphische, 1946), 91.

48. "2nd Cavalry Group After Action Report, August 1944," CAVG2, Entry 427, RG 407, National Archives II, 3–7 August.

49. 2nd Cavalry Association, *The Ghosts of Patton's Third Army,* 93–102.

50. "VIII Corps After Action Report, August 1944," 4.

51. "XV Corps After Action Report, August 1944," Record 215, Entry 427, RG 407, National Archives II, 2.

52. Blumenson, *Breakout and Pursuit,* 370.

53. "VIII Corps After Action Report, August 1944," 4.

54. "15th Cavalry Reconnaissance Squadron After Action Report August 1944," CAVS15, Entry 427, RG 407, National Archives II, August 3.

55. Matthew Darlington Morton, *Men on Iron Ponies: The Death and Rebirth of the Modern U.S. Cavalry* (DeKalb: Northern Illinois Univ. Press, 2009), 153; "15th Cavalry Reconnaissance Squadron After Action Report August 1944," 3 August. Colonel Reybold resurfaced at the conclusion of the war in a German prison camp on the Channel Island of Jersey.

56. "15th Mechanized Cavalry Group After Action Report 1944," CAVG15, RG 407, National Archives II, 3.

57. Blumenson, *Breakout and Pursuit,* 391.

58. Zone reconnaissance is reconnaissance in a given zone, defined by a higher headquarters.

59. "XV Corps After Action Report, August 1944," 3.

60. Ibid., 4.

61. "15th Mechanized Cavalry Group After Action Report 1944," 3.

62. Ibid., 4; Blumenson, *Breakout and Pursuit,* 391.

63. "15th Mechanized Cavalry Group After Action Report 1944," 4.

64. Blumenson, *Breakout and Pursuit,* 392.

65. "15th Mechanized Cavalry Group After Action Report 1944," 5.

66. The location in question was the Foret de Perseigne. "XV Corps After Action Review, August 1944," 5–6.

67. "15th Mechanized Cavalry Group After Action Report 1944," 5; Blumenson, *Breakout and Pursuit,* 393.

68. *"Patton's Ghost Troops"—After Action Report 9 August 1944–9 May 1945* (Phoenix: 3rd Cavalry Veteran's Association, 1974), 49.

69. "XX Corps After Action Report, August 1944," Record 220, Entry 427, RG 407, National Archives II, 5.

70. *"Patton's Ghost Troops,"* 49.

71. "XX Corps After Action Report, August 1944," 5; William Breuer's work *Death of a Nazi Army* provides an excellent description of the impact of XV Corps' attack during the middle of August.

72. *"Patton's Ghost Troops,"* 49–50.

73. "121st Cavalry Reconnaissance Squadron After Action Review, August," CAVS121, Entry 427, RG 407, National Archives II, 3.

74. "XV Corps After Action Report, August 1944," 8.

75. 2nd Cavalry Association, *The Ghosts of Patton's Third Army,* 103.

76. "2nd Cavalry Group After Action Report, August 1944," 13 August; Morton, *Men on Iron Ponies,* 152.

77. "2nd Cavalry Group After Action Report, August 1944," 17 August.

78. *"Patton's Ghost Troops,"* 49–50.

79. *The XX Corps: Its History and Service in World War II* (Osaka, Japan: XX Corps Association, 1951), 79.

80. *"Patton's Ghost Troops,"* 50.

81. Ibid.

82. "2nd Cavalry Group After Action Report, August 1944," 23 August.

83. "XII Corps Report of Operations August 1944," Record 212, Entry 427, RG 407, National Archives II, 24 August.

84. "2nd Cavalry Group After Action Report, August 1944," 26 August.

85. *The XX Corps: Its History and Service in World War II,* 91.

86. The 3rd Squadron had been relieved by the 2nd Cavalry Group, who had been released from their mission along the Nantes–Angers region. Incidentally, the records of the XII Corps show this unit to be the 43rd Squadron, at least for a while, but the records of the 3rd Group, the 3rd Squadron, and XX Corps show the detached unit to have been the 3rd Squadron. There seems to be no explanation for this discrepancy other than an error in the XII Corps' records. Also of interest, the 3rd Group AAR records the 3rd Squadron as being attached to XXX Corps, an obvious error. (*"Patton's Ghost Troops,"* 50.)

87. U.S. War Department, *FM 100-5: Field Service Regulations: Operations, 1944* (Washington, D.C.: GPO, 1944), paragraph 39; "2nd Cavalry Group After Action Report, August 1944," 28 August.

88. "2nd Cavalry Group After Action Report, August 1944," 28 August.

89. "History of the 106th Cavalry Group," CAVG106, Entry 427, RG 407, National Archives II, 2.

90. "15th Mechanized Cavalry Group After Action Report 1944," 5.

91. Blumenson, *Breakout and Pursuit,* 393.

92. These divisions had originally belonged to V Corps.

93. "15th Mechanized Cavalry Group After Action Report 1944," 5–6.

94. Ibid., 6.

95. Ibid.

96. A hung bomb is a situation in which the pilot attempts to drop a bomb, but the catches holding it to the plane fail to function properly. This is extremely dangerous, as the bomb can fall off at any time, and it almost always seems to fall off at the worst possible moment.

97. "15th Mechanized Cavalry Group After Action Report 1944," 6.

98. *The Lion Rampant* (N.p.: U.S. Army, circa 1945), 14–17.

99. "2nd Cavalry Group After Action Report, August 1944," 30 August.

100. "2nd Cavalry Group After Action Report, September 1944," CAVG2, Entry 427, RG 407, National Archives II, 2 September.

101. "XII Corps Report of Operations September 1944," Record 212, Entry 427, RG 407, Nation Archives II, 7.

102. Hugh M. Cole, *United States Army in World War II: The European Theater of Operations: The Lorraine Campaign* (Washington, D.C.: Historical Division of the Army, 1950), 58–60. The other crossing point was the town of Toul.

103. Ibid., 65.

104. Ibid., 62.

105. "XII Corps Report of Operations September 1944," 7.

106. Rickard, *Patton at Bay,* 78.

107. "2nd Cavalry Group After Action Report, September 1944," 7 September.

108. The Madon River is a small tributary of the Moselle running from south to north, intersecting the main river four miles southwest of Nancy; "2nd Cavalry Group After Action Report, September 1944," September 4–10.

109. Ibid., 4 September.

110. A cavalry troop consisted of approximately 140 officers and men.

111. "XX Corps After Action Report, August 1944," 13–14.

112. *"Patton's Ghost Troops,"* 51. For those keeping track, this was the second cavalry group commander to be captured in action. This is particularly interesting considering that in September 1944 only seven cavalry groups were in the European theater.

113. Ibid., 50–52.

114. Ibid., 52; Rickard, *Patton at Bay,* 80.

115. *"Patton's Ghost Troops,"* 52–53.

116. Martin Blumenson, *The Patton Papers, 1940–1945* (Boston: Da Capo Press, 1974), 485.

117. *"Patton's Ghost Troops,"* 53.

118. "XV Corps After Action Report, September 1944," Record 215, Entry 427, RG 407, National Archives II, 2.

119. Ibid., 3–5; Rickard, *Patton at Bay,* 93.

120. "XV Corps After Action Report, September 1944," 6.

121. Ibid., 7.

122. William Collier, *The 106th Cavalry's Story* (Bloomington, Ind.: Trafford Publishing, 2012), 36.

123. *Unicorn Rampant: History of the Sixth Cavalry Regiment/Group at Home and Abroad* (N.p.: Sixth Cavalry Regiment Association, 1945), 41.

124. Ibid., 63. The term "hip pocket reserve" is an informal military term that implies a formation that a senior commander retains for use in missions he deems important. It is different from an operational or tactical reserve in that it is generally smaller and figures less into subordinate unit planning. It also not normally designated as a reserve in operations orders.

125. Ibid., 65.

126. Ibid., 64.

127. "Third Army Operations Diary, August," Record 103, Entry 427, RG 407, National Archives II, 1 August.

128. *Unicorn Rampant,* 64.

129. Blumenson, *Breakout and Pursuit,* 350.

130. *Unicorn Rampant,* 63; Blumenson, *Breakout and Pursuit,* 352.

131. *Unicorn Rampant,* 63–64.

132. Blumenson, *Breakout and Pursuit,* 352. The phrase "stepped on" refers to a condition wherein two stations on a radio frequency are broadcasting simultaneously. The stronger signal will override the weaker, so that the intended recipient will only hear the stronger message. Although divisions had similar radio equipment, stations that were closer to the corps headquarters would have had a stronger signal at the corps command post. When large distances are involved, this problem is exacerbated as neither the station being "stepped on" nor the other station might realize what is going on, as they may not hear the other party, but only the higher powered corps signal.

133. Blumenson, *Breakout and Pursuit,* 353.

134. "6th Mechanized Cavalry Group AAR August 1944," CAVG6, Entry 427, RG 407, National Archives II, 27 August.

135. Don M. Fox, *Patton's Vanguard: The United States Army Fourth Armored Division* (Jefferson, N.C.: McFarland, 2003), 83; *Unicorn Rampant,* 66.

136. Robert S. Allen, *Patton's Third U.S. Army: Lucky Forward* (New York: Manor Books, 1947), 104.

137. *Unicorn Rampant,* 67. An interesting aside is that Polk had been the executive officer for the 106th Cavalry at Fort Hood as it mobilized, then deployed with them to England, and then onto Normandy, where he had been given temporary command of the 6th Cavalry. Thus, Polk would have been a key participant in four of the six cavalry groups assigned to the Third Army—in order:

106th, 6th, 15th, 3rd. A confusing note is that Polk in both his published wartime letters and oral history in 1988 describes taking command of the 14th MCG around Brest, and not the 15th MCG. In a conversation with General Polk's children on this topic, they referred back to the original letters, which also state that Polk went to the 14th MCG. There does not seem to be an explanation for this discrepancy. The history of the 6th Cavalry Group states that Polk went to the 15th MCG, so that is what is used in this narrative.

138. *"Patton's Ghost Troops,"* 53–56.

139. "XV Corps After Action Report September 1944," Record 215, Entry 427, RG 407, National Archives II, September, 17.

140. "History of the AIS October 1944," CAVG6, Entry 427, RG 407, National Archives II, 3.

141. The 117th began life as a squadron of the 102nd MCG, a New Jersey Army National Guard formation. In 1942 it was separated from its parent regiment and sent overseas to participate in TORCH.

142. Robert Lutz, "117th Cavalry Reconnaissance Squadron (MECZ) in World War II," 117th Cavalry Association, http://www.117th-cav.org, 2–15.

143. "VI Corps After Action Report August 1944," Record 206, Entry 427, RG 407, National Archives II, 2.

144. Harold Samsel, *Operational History of the 117th Cavalry Reconnaissance Squadron (MECZ) World War II,* 2nd printing (N.p.: self-published, 1983), "Shades of JEB Stuart," 1–2.

145. Lutz, "117th Cavalry Reconnaissance Squadron (MECZ) in World War II," 16.

146. Charles Hodge, untitled memoir (N.p., n.d.), 117th Cavalry Association, Westfield Armory, New Jersey, 113–115.

147. Ibid., 116–119.

148. "VI Corps After Action Report August 1944," 9.

149. Samsel, *Operational History of the 117th Cavalry Reconnaissance Squadron (MECZ) World War II,* "Shades of JEB Stuart," 6.

150. "117th Cavalry Reconnaissance Squadron After Action Report August 1944," CAVS117, Entry 427, RG 407, National Archives II, 8–9.

151. Ibid., 8–9; "VI Corps After Action Report August 1944," 16.

152. Lutz, "117th Cavalry Reconnaissance Squadron (MECZ) in World War II," 21.

153. Jeffrey J. Clarke and Robert R. Smith, *United States Army in World War II: The European Theater of Operations: Riviera to the Rhine* (Washington, D.C.: Center of Military History, U.S. Army, 1993), 160–161.

154. Lutz, "117th Cavalry Reconnaissance Squadron (MECZ) in World War II," 23.

155. Clarke and Smith, *Riviera to the Rhine,* 175–177.

156. Ibid., 180.

157. Ibid., 187.

158. "117th Cavalry Reconnaissance Squadron After Action Report September 1944," CAVS117, Entry 427, RG 407, National Archives II, 3–4; "VI Corps After Action Report September 1944," Record 206, Entry 427, RG 407, National Archives II, 5.

159. "117th Cavalry Reconnaissance Squadron After Action Report September 1944," 4.

160. "VI Corps After Action Report September 1944," 9.

161. "117th CRS After Action Report September 1944," 5.

162. "VI Corps After Action Report September 1944," 12–13.

163. Harry Yeide and Mark Stout, *First to the Rhine: The 6th Army Group in World War II* (Saint Paul, Minn.: Zenith Press, 2007), 175.

164. Lutz, "117th Cavalry Reconnaissance Squadron (MECZ) in World War II," 29.

165. "VI Corps After Action Report September 1944," 20.

5. The Bitter Fall

1. Keith E. Bonn, *When the Odds Were Even* (Novato, Calif.: Presidio Press, 1994), 14.

2. Charles B. MacDonald, *United States Army in World War II: The European Theater of Operations: The Siegfried Line Campaign* (Washington, D.C.: Center of Military History, U.S. Army, 1990), 37–38.

3. J. Lawton Collins, *Lightning Joe: An Autobiography* (Baton Rouge: Louisiana State Univ. Press, 1979), 267.

4. "4th Mechanized Cavalry Group After Action Report September 1944," CAVG4, Entry 427, Record Group 407, National Archives II, College Park, Md., 6.

5. Ibid., 7.

6. MacDonald, *The Siegfried Line Campaign,* map 3.

7. "113th Mechanized Cavalry Group After Action Report September 1944," CAVG113, Entry 427, RG 407, National Archives II, 10–11.

8. William Eagen, *The Man on the Red Horse* (Portland, Oreg.: Metropolitan Printing, 1975), 117. Interestingly, Corlett seems to have been making a point with the commander of the 30th ID by making him support the operation whose success he was betting against.

9. "113th Mechanized Cavalry Group After Action Report September 1944," 13–14.

10. Joseph Balkoski, *From Brittany to the Reich: The 29th Infantry Division*

in Germany, September–November 1944 (Mechanicsburg, Pa.: Stackpole Books, 2012), 123–124.

11. "113th Mechanized Cavalry Group After Action Report September 1944," 16–17.

12. Eagen, *The Man on the Red Horse,* 123.

13. Charles E. Rousek, "A Short History of the 38th Cavalry Reconnaissance Squadron (Mechanized)" (Prestice, Czechoslovakia, 1945), available via 117th Cavalry Association, www.117th-cav.org, 9; David M. Russen, "Combat History: 102nd Cavalry Reconnaissance Squadron (MECZ): World War II," available via 117th Cavalry Association, www.117th-cav.org, 7.

14. "4th Mechanized Cavalry Group After Action Report September 1944," 9–12.

15. Ibid., 12.

16. David Higgins, *The Roer River Battles: Germany's Stand at the Westwall, 1944–45* (Philadelphia: Casemate Publishers, 2010), 47–48.

17. U.S. Forces Europe, the General Board, *Mechanized Cavalry Units,* Study Number 49, 1945 (Washington, D.C.: GPO, 1945), appendix 6, page 8; MacDonald, *The Siegfried Line Campaign,* 251–252.

18. *History, V Corps* (U.S. Army, circa 1945), 272–273.

19. Ibid., 277.

20. John N. Tully, "Doctrine, Organization and Employment of the 4th Cavalry Group during World War II" (Master's thesis, U.S. Army Command and General Staff College, 1994), 71.

21. MacDonald, *The Siegfried Line Campaign,* 328.

22. Ibid., 340; Edward Miller, *A Dark and Bloody Ground: The Hürtgen Forest and the Roer River Dams, 1944–1945* (College Station: Texas A&M Univ. Press, 1995), 41–46.

23. "113th Mechanized Cavalry Group After Action Report October 1944," CAVG113, Entry 427, RG 407, National Archives II, 6–9. A significantly more detailed account of this battle can be found in Joseph Balkoski's *From Brittany to the Reich.*

24. "XIX Corps After Action Report October 1944," Record 219, Entry 427, RG 407, National Archives II, 6–7.

25. *Conquer: The Story of the Ninth Army* (Washington, D.C.: Infantry Journal Press, 1947), 69.

26. *The Lion Rampant* (N.p.: U.S. Army, circa 1945), 14.

27. "XIII Corps After Action Report November 1944," Record 213, Entry 427, RG 407, National Archives II, 8.

28. Charles MacDonald, *The Battle of the Huertgen Forest* (Philadelphia: Univ. of Pennsylvania Press, 2002), 89.

29. MacDonald, *The Siegfried Line Campaign,* 374.

30. Miller, *A Dark and Bloody Ground,* 141.

31. "4th Mechanized Cavalry Group After Action Report November 1944," Record CAVG4, Entry 427, RG 407, National Archives II, 3.

32. Tully, "Doctrine, Organization and Employment of the 4th Cavalry Group during World War II," 73; "4th Mechanized Cavalry Group After Action Report November 1944," 3.

33. Tully, "Doctrine, Organization and Employment of the 4th Cavalry Group during World War II," 73; "4th Mechanized Cavalry Group After Action Report December 1944," CAVG4, Entry 427, RG 407, National Archives II, 1.

34. "4th Mechanized Cavalry Group After Action Report December 1944," 2.

35. Ibid., 2–3.

36. *The Lion Rampant,* 15.

37. "XIII Corps After Action Report November 1944," 38–43.

38. Eagen, *The Man on the Red Horse,* 142.

39. "XIII Corps After Action Report December 1944," Record 213, Entry 427, RG 407, National Archives II, 4.

40. MacDonald, *The Siegfried Line Campaign,* map 7.

41. "2nd Cavalry Group After Action Report, September 1944," 7 September.

42. "XII Corps Report of Operations September 1944," 9.

43. This fort was found to be held by members of the 3rd Fallschirmjäger Division, considered an elite German formation; 2nd Cavalry Association, *The Ghosts of Patton's Third Army: A History of the Second U.S. Cavalry* (Munich, Germany: Münchner Graphische, 1946), 137; "2nd Cavalry Group After Action Report, September 1944," 8 September.

44. "XII Corps Report of Operations September 1944," 12.

45. Hugh M. Cole, *United States Army in World War II: The European Theater of Operations: The Lorraine Campaign* (Washington, D.C.: Historical Division of the Army, 1950), 71.

46. "2nd Cavalry Group After Action Report, September 1944," 11 September.

47. Cole, *The Lorraine Campaign,* 220.

48. "2nd Cavalry Group After Action Report, September 1944," 15 September.

49. "XII Corps Report of Operations 1 September 1944–30 September 1944," 16.

50. The number of tanks present in the attack varies from the number quoted here in the unit after action report (six tanks) to over forty in the group's official history. Additional confusion over the number of enemy is also created by the unit's only identifying the full force of the leading edge of the attack,

and not the full assault. Furthermore, the group's history reports the tanks as Tigers. However, later scholarship has challenged this assumption, as most German tanks were called Tigers regardless of the actual type. The determination that these were Panther tanks comes from Cole, *The Lorraine Campaign,* 221. A cavalry instructor might admonish the troopers of the 42nd that day for inaccurate reporting, a cardinal sin for reconnaissance soldiers. Still, perhaps the troopers might be forgiven for exaggerations in what was surely a traumatic day. "2nd Cavalry Group After Action Report, September 1944," 18 September.

51. The corps truly called in the fire brigade, with elements from three combat commands and a tank destroyer battalion arriving to stem the attack.

52. Cole, *The Lorraine Campaign,* 221–223.

53. 2nd Cavalry Association, *Ghosts of Patton's Third Army,* 152.

54. Cole, *The Lorraine Campaign,* 223.

55. Ibid., 224.

56. John Nelson Rickard, *Patton at Bay: The Lorraine Campaign, 1944* (Washington, D.C.: Brassey's, 2004), 111.

57. Ibid., 138–145.

58. Ibid., 53–54.

59. *"Patton's Ghost Troops"—After Action Report 9 August 1944–9 May 1945* (Phoenix: 3rd Cavalry Veteran's Association, 1974), 54.

60. Ibid., 56. The Free French of the Paris Division were notoriously short of crew-served and anti-tank weapons, as evidenced by one battalion having a strength of 320 soldiers with 190 rifles, 12 heavy machine guns, and 13 Browning Automatic Rifles. The battalion possessed two trucks and did not have uniforms for of all its soldiers. (*"Patton's Ghost Troops,"* 59.)

61. *"Patton's Ghost Troops,"* 62.

62. Cole, *The Lorraine Campaign,* 290.

63. 2nd Cavalry Association, *The Ghosts of Patton's Third Army,* 166–173.

64. Cole, *The Lorraine Campaign,* 380–382.

65. *"Patton's Ghost Troops,"* 69; Cole, *The Lorraine Campaign,* 375.

66. *"Patton's Ghost Troops,"* 69–70.

67. "XX Corps After Action Report, November 1944," Record 220, Entry 427, RG 407, National Archives II, 12.

68. Preston Utterback, ed., *The 150 Year Saga of the 3rd U.S. Cavalry* (Phoenix: 3rd Cavalry Veterans Association, 1996), 145.

69. *"Patton's Ghost Troops,"* 69.

70. Ibid., 71; "XX Corps After Action Report, November 1944," 5.

71. Michael Doubler, *Closing with the Enemy: How GIs Fought the War in Europe 1944–1945* (Lawrence: Univ. Press of Kansas, 1994), 155.

72. *"Patton's Ghost Troops,"* 71–72.

73. "2nd Cavalry Group After Action Report, November 1944," CAVG2, Entry 427, RG 407, National Archives II, 8 November.

74. "XII Corps Report of Operations November 1944," Record 212, Entry 427, RG 407, National Archives II, 14–16.

75. *"Patton's Ghost Troops,"* 72–74.

76. Ibid.; "XX Corps After Action Report, 1 November 1944–30 November 1944," 14–21.

77. *"Patton's Ghost Troops,"* 72.

78. "XX Corps After Action Report, November 1944," 21.

79. "XX Corps After Action Report, December 1944," Record 220, Entry 427, RG 407, National Archives II, 13.

80. "2nd Cavalry Group After Action Report, November 1944," 22 November.

81. "2nd Cavalry Group After Action Report, December 1944," CAVG2, Entry 427, RG 407, National Archives II, 8–14 December.

82. "XII Corps Report of Operations December 1944," Record 212, Entry 427, RG 407, Nation Archives II, 19–21.

83. *Unicorn Rampant: History of the Sixth Cavalry Regiment/Group at Home and Abroad* (N.p.: Sixth Cavalry Regiment Association, 1945), 71.

84. Ibid., 73.

85. Ibid., 74.

86. Ibid., 76.

87. Saarlautern is now known as Saarlouis. The name changed around 1945.

88. "XX Corps After Action Report, December 1944," Record 220, Entry 427, RG 407, National Archives II, 10 December.

89. Jeffrey Clarke and Robert Smith, *United States Army in World War II: The European Theater of Operations: Riviera to the Rhine* (Washington, D.C.: Center of Military History, U.S. Army, 1993), 272–276.

90. Robert Lutz, "117th Cavalry Reconnaissance Squadron (MECZ) in World War II," 117th Cavalry Association, http://www.117th-cav.org, 32.

91. William H. Collier, *The 106th Cavalry's Story* (Bloomington, Ind.: Trafford Publishing, 2012), 36; "XV Corps After Action Report September 1944," Record 215, Entry 427, RG 407, National Archives II, 15; Harry Yeide and Mark Stout, *First to the Rhine: The 6th Army Group in World War II* (Saint Paul, Minn.: Zenith Press, 2007), 202.

92. "XV Corps After Action Report September 1944," 17.

93. Ibid., 18.

94. 106th Mechanized Cavalry Group, *The 106th Cavalry in Europe: 1944–1945* (Augsburg, Germany: J.P. Himmer KG, 1945), 60–61.

95. "106th Mechanized Cavalry Group After Action Report October 1944," CAVG106, Entry 427, RG 407, National Archives II, 2.

96. Collier, *The 106th Cavalry's Story,* 38.

97. Ibid.

98. Lutz, "117th Cavalry Reconnaissance Squadron (MECZ) in World War II," 40.

99. Clarke and Smith, *Riviera to the Rhine,* 342.

100. Ibid., 365.

101. "XV Corps After Action Report November 1944," Record 215, Entry 427, RG 407, National Archives II, 14–15.

102. Ibid., 20; Collier, *The 106th Cavalry's Story,* 39.

103. "XV Corps After Action Report November 1944," 27.

104. Alan J. Levine, *From the Normandy Beaches to the Baltic Sea: The Northwest Europe Campaign, 1944–1945* (Westport, Conn.: Praeger, 2000), 141.

105. Lutz, "117th Cavalry Reconnaissance Squadron (MECZ) in World War II," 41–42.

106. Clarke and Smith, *Riviera to the Rhine,* map 26; Yeide and Stout, *First to the Rhine,* 242–243.

107. Clarke and Smith, *Riviera to the Rhine,* map 27.

108. "106th Mechanized Cavalry Group After Action Report November 1944," CAVG106, Entry 427, RG 407, National Archives II, 16–18.

109. Clarke and Smith, *Riviera to the Rhine,* 386.

110. Lutz, "117th Cavalry Reconnaissance Squadron (MECZ) in World War II," 43.

111. Clarke and Smith, *Riviera to the Rhine,* map 30.

112. "VI Corps After Action Report December 1944," Record 206, Entry 427, RG 407, National Archives II, 1.

113. Collier, *The 106th Cavalry's Story,* 41.

114. "VI Corps After Action Report December 1944," 12.

115. Lutz, "117th Cavalry Reconnaissance Squadron (MECZ) in World War II," 45.

116. "117th Cavalry Reconnaissance Squadron After Action Report December 1944," CAVS117, Entry 427, RG 407, National Archives II, 7–8.

117. "XV Corps After Action Report December 1944," Record 215, Entry 427, RG 407, National Archives II, 30.

118. Ibid., 38.

6. A Desperate Winter

1. "VIII Corps After Action Report October 1944," Record 208, Entry 427, Record Group 407, National Archives II, College Park, Md., 4.

2. Ibid.

3. Hugh Cole, *United States Army in World War II: The European Theater of*

Operations: The Ardennes: Battle of the Bulge (Washington, D.C.: Center of Military History, U.S. Army, 1965), map 3.

4. "14th Mechanized Cavalry Group After Action Report November 1944," CAVG14, Entry 427, Record Group 407, National Archives II, College Park, Md.; "14th Mechanized Cavalry Group After Action Report December 1944," CAVG14, Entry 427, RG 407, National Archives II, 1.

5. "VIII Corps After Action Report November 1944," Record 208, Entry 427, RG 407, National Archives II, 3.

6. Cole, *Battle of the Bulge,* 138.

7. John S. D. Eisenhower, *The Bitter Woods: The Battle of the Bulge* (New York: Da Capo Press, 1995), 195.

8. Cole, *Battle of the Bulge,* 138.

9. Ibid., 139.

10. Ibid.

11. Peter Mansoor, *The GI Offensive in Europe: The Triumph of American Infantry Divisions, 1941–1945* (Lawrence: Univ. Press of Kansas, 1999), 217–218.

12. Eisenhower, *Bitter Woods,* 100–101.

13. Cole, *Battle of the Bulge,* maps 2 and 3.

14. Ibid., 147.

15. "14th Mechanized Cavalry Group After Action Report December 1944," CAVG14, Entry 427, RG 407, National Archives II, 1.

16. Ibid., map titled "dispositions 2300 16 December."

17. Ibid., 2.

18. Cole, *Battle of the Bulge,* 163; "14th Mechanized Cavalry Group After Action Report December 1944," 2.

19. "14th Mechanized Cavalry Group After Action Report December 1944," 2.

20. Ibid., 3–4.

21. Cole, *Battle of the Bulge,* 145.

22. Alan J. Levine, *From the Normandy Beaches to the Baltic Sea: The Northwest Europe Campaign, 1944–1945* (Westport, Conn.: Praeger, 2000), 151–152.

23. Cole, *Battle of the Bulge,* 81–87.

24. Alfred Shehab, "Cavalry on the Shoulder: The 38th CRS and the Defense of Monschau," ed. Philip Notestine, available via 117th Cavalry Association, www.117th-cav.org, 2.

25. Charles E. Rousek, "A Short History of the 38th Cavalry Reconnaissance Squadron (Mechanized)" (Prestice, Czechoslovakia, 1945), available via 117th Cavalry Association, www.117th-cav.org, 14; Shehab, "Cavalry on the Shoulder," 1.

26. Cole, *Battle of the Bulge,* 87.

27. Ibid., 89.

28. "102nd Mechanized Cavalry Group After Action Report December 1944," CAVG102, Entry 427, RG 407, National Archives II, 3–4.

29. Cole, *Battle of the Bulge,* 120.

30. Eisenhower, *Bitter Woods,* 349–350.

31. For its efforts, the 38th CRS would receive a Presidential Unit Citation, evidence of how much V Corps valued its contributions during these critical days.

32. "4th Mechanized Cavalry Group After Action Report December 1944," CAVG4, Entry 427, RG 407, National Archives II, 3.

33. Ibid., 4.

34. John N. Tully, "Doctrine, Organization and Employment of the 4th Cavalry Group during World War II" (Master's thesis, U.S. Army Command and General Staff College, 1994), 75.

35. "4th Mechanized Cavalry Group After Action Report December 1944," 4.

36. *Mission Accomplished: The Story of the Campaigns of the VII Corps, United States Army, in the War against Germany, 1944–1945,* ed. Ray Merriam (Leipzig, Germany: J. J. Weber, 1945; reprint, Bennington, Vt.: Merriam Press, 1998), 36.

37. Levine, *From the Normandy Beaches to the Baltic Sea,* 157.

38. "4th Mechanized Cavalry Group After Action Report December 1944," 5.

39. Ibid., 6; Eisenhower, *Bitter Woods,* 367.

40. "4th Mechanized Cavalry Group After Action Report December 1944," 6.

41. Ibid., 7; "VII Corps After Action Report December 1944," Record 207, Entry 427, RG 407, National Archives II, 87.

42. "4th Mechanized Cavalry Group After Action Report December 1944," 8.

43. Mansoor, *The GI Offensive in Europe,* 228.

44. "VII Corps After Action Report December 1944," 101; "4th Mechanized Cavalry Group After Action Report December 1944," 8.

45. "VII Corps After Action Report January 1945," Record 207, Entry 427, RG 407, National Archives II, 5; Eisenhower, *Bitter Woods,* 413.

46. "4th Mechanized Cavalry Group After Action Report January 1945," CAVG4, Entry 427, RG 407, National Archives II, 1; "VII Corps After Action Report January 1945," compilation of reports from VII Corps After Action Report January.

47. "4th Mechanized Cavalry Group After Action Report January 1945," 1–3.

48. "VII Corps After Action Report January 1945," 31.

49. "4th Mechanized Cavalry Group After Action Report January 1945," 5.

50. Ibid., 5–6. An interesting note is that the Corps after action report of this same period makes no mention of the confusion over the date of the

attack, merely stating that the cavalry conducted a reconnaissance in force and met heavy resistance. So, either the corps or the cavalry mixed up the date, or the corps did not pass along updated information. One can imagine that such a mistake would be very embarrassing regardless of who made it.

51. Ibid., 6–8.

52. John Nelson Rickard, *Advance and Destroy: Patton as Commander in the Bulge* (Lexington: Univ. Press of Kentucky, 2011), 311. This work is just one of many that praise Patton's actions in the Bulge. In fact, Rickard is often one of the most critical authors in regard to Patton, but he still finds time to call his attacks "bold" and views Patton as the best Allied army commander in the field.

53. "III Corps After Action Report, December 1944," Record 203, Entry 427, RG 407, National Archives II, 4.

54. *Unicorn Rampant: History of the Sixth Cavalry Regiment/Group at Home and Abroad* (N.p.: Sixth Cavalry Regiment Association, 1945) 79.

55. "2nd Cavalry Group After Action Report, December 1944," 22 December.

56. General Support (GS) Engineer Regiments were generally expected to perform construction as well as build obstacles, in essence nonspecialized engineers. 2nd Cavalry Association, *The Ghosts of Patton's Third Army: A History of the Second U.S. Cavalry* (Munich, Germany: Münchner Graphische, 1946), 211.

57. Direct support differs from assignment in that the group has priority access to the fires of that unit, but does not dictate their positioning, and fires from that unit can be pulled to other units if the direct support unit does not have a competing demand. (2nd Cavalry Association, *The Ghosts of Patton's Third Army,* 211.)

58. The actual frontage would be significantly more. Twenty-five miles is simply the straight line distance between these two points, not accounting for bends and curves in the river and front line. "XII Corps Report of Operations December 1944," Ops Map #8; Rickard, *Advance and Destroy,* 171.

59. "III Corps After Action Report, December 1944," 12; "6th Mechanized Cavalry Group AAR December 1944," CAVG6, Entry 427, RG 407, National Archives II; Eisenhower, 342.

60. Mansoor, *The GI Offensive in Europe,* 229.

61. "III Corps After Action Report, December 1944," 12.

62. Cole, *Battle of the Bulge,* 621.

63. "2nd Cavalry Group After Action Report, January 1945," CAVG2, Entry 427, RG 407, National Archives II, 11 January.

64. This information was gathered from Google Earth.

65. Charles B. MacDonald, *United States Army in World War II: The European Theater of Operations: The Last Offensive* (Washington, D.C.: Historical Division of the Army, 1973), map 2.

66. "Presidential Unit Citation, 6th Cavalry Group," found in *Unicorn Rampant.*

67. "III Corps After Action Report, January 1945," Record 203, Entry 427, RG 407, National Archives II, 10; Rickard, *Advance and Destroy,* 267.

68. *Unicorn Rampant,* 87–88.

69. German strengths are an assumption of the author based on the following: three hundred Germans captured indicates approximately a battalion strength (three hundred is more than one company, and could be as many as two to three full-strength companies). Assuming that there were more Germans who were killed or escaped, this puts the number over one battalion, possibly a second. Then, the inclusion of as much artillery present indicates support assets more commonly seen at the regimental level.

70. A unit must have performed in such a manner that if an individual had done those actions, he would have received the Medal of Honor.

71. "III Corps After Action Report, January 1945," 18. Interestingly, the group recounts the story with a little more passion, including how the "brass" from the 80th ID "ranked" the cavalrymen out of the warm houses they had procured for the night.

72. "2nd Cavalry Group After Action Report, January 1945," 20 January.

73. Ibid., 22 January.

74. "XX Corps After Action Report, December 1944," 1–26. *"Patton's Ghost Troops"—After Action Report 9 August 1944–9 May 1945* (Phoenix: 3rd Cavalry Veteran's Association, 1974), 80–83.

75. "XX Corps After Action Report, January 1945," Record 220, Entry 427, RG 407, National Archives II; *"Patton's Ghost Troops,"* 84–92.

76. *Conquer: The Story of the Ninth Army* (Washington, D.C.: Infantry Journal Press, 1947), 117–118. The 78th and 8th IDs were transplants from the V Corps that retained their positions during the massive reorganization of the line.

77. Note that the flooding of the Roer at this point was natural and more a product of the wet fall and winter than German actions. Although the thought of German forces unleashing a flood on the Roer during an Allied crossing normally terrified American commanders, during this period the high water levels proved a comfort.

78. *Eleventh Cavalry from the Roer to the Elbe, 1944–1945* (Eleventh Cavalry Group, circa 1945; reprint, N.p.: Bibliogov Project, print on demand, 2013), 35.

79. "XIX Corps After Action Report December 1944," Record 219, Entry 427, RG 407, National Archives II, map, Incl 2 to Section III, 31 December 1944; William Eagen, *The Man on the Red Horse* (Portland, Oreg.: Metropolitan Printing, 1975), 151.

80. *Eleventh Cavalry from the Roer to the Elbe,* 36.

81. David Higgins, *The Roer River Battles: Germany's Stand at the Westwall, 1944–45* (Philadelphia: Casemate Publishers, 2010), 212.

82. *Conquer: The Story of the Ninth Army,* 142; *Eleventh Cavalry from the Roer to the Elbe,* 39.

83. *Eleventh Cavalry from the Roer to the Elbe,* 40.

84. Eagen, *The Man on the Red Horse,* 156; *Conquer: The Story of the Ninth Army,* 129–130; It should be also noted that the cavalry performed another useful task in this mission: keeping the commander happy. Although not found in any tactical task list, keeping a higher commander content can mean the difference between a happy unit and one that is not.

85. Jeffrey Clarke and Robert Ross Smith, *United States Army in World War II: The European Theater of Operations: Riviera to the Rhine* (Washington, D.C.: Center of Military History, U.S. Army, 1993), 491.

86. Ibid., 501–507.

87. Robert Lutz, "117th Cavalry Reconnaissance Squadron (MECZ) in World War II," 117th Cavalry Association, http://www.117th-cav.org, 45.

88. Richard E. Engler Jr., *The Final Crisis: Combat in Northern Alsace, January 1945* (Bedford, Pa.: Aberjona Press, 1999), 98.

89. Keith E. Bonn, *When the Odds Were Even* (Novato, Calif.: Presidio Press, 1994), 193.

90. Lutz, "117th Cavalry Reconnaissance Squadron (MECZ) in World War II," 47–51.

91. Harold J. Samsel, *Operational History of the 117th Cavalry Reconnaissance Squadron (MECZ) World War II,* 2nd printing (N.p.: self-published, 1983), part 2, "Bitche Action," 11. While acknowledging the fact that this narrative is taken from the unit or from recollections of the unit, the time lines provided by XV and VI Corps do not substantially differ from these reports.

92. "XV Corps After Action Report January 1945," Record 215, Entry 427, RG 407, National Archives II, 2.

93. Bonn, *When the Odds Were Even,* 200.

94. Clarke and Smith, *Riviera to the Rhine,* 506.

95. "XV Corps After Action Report January 1945," 4; Clarke and Smith, *Riviera to the Rhine,* 505.

96. "XV Corps After Action Report January 1945," 4–14.

97. Lutz, "117th Cavalry Reconnaissance Squadron (MECZ) in World War II," 55–57. An interesting discrepancy in the records is an action that occurred on 31 January 1945, when the squadron seized a wood to its front. The new squadron commander recounts in his memoir, written after the war, a rather dramatic battle that inflicted hundreds of German casualties and resulted in 250 enemy prisoners. The squadron after action report makes almost no mention of

these seemingly very significant events. Instead, it mentions the woods as mined but generally empty. Even including fighting throughout this area in early February, a comparison of the commander's story to the squadron journal reveals significant exaggeration. This is most likely explained by the fact that the memoir was written postwar, while the after action report recorded the event very shortly after its occurrence. War stories have a way of growing over time.

98. William H. Collier, *The 106th Cavalry's Story* (Bloomington, Ind.: Trafford Publishing, 2012), 45.

7. To the Rhine

1. "III Corps After Action Report, January 1945," Record 203, Entry 427, RG 407, National Archives II, College Park, Md., maps labeled annex 1e–1h.

2. *Unicorn Rampant: History of the Sixth Cavalry Regiment/Group at Home and Abroad* (N.p.: Sixth Cavalry Regiment Association, 1945), 93.

3. "III Corps After Action Report, February 1945," Record 203, Entry 427, RG 407, National Archives II, 2.

4. Ibid., 8.

5. Martin Blumeson, *The Patton Papers, 1940–1945* (Boston: Da Capo Press, 1974), 638.

6. Ibid., 10.

7. "2nd Cavalry Group After Action Report, February 1945," CAVG2, Entry 427, RG 407, National Archives II, 3 February.

8. "XII Corps Report of Operations February 1945," Record 212, Entry 427, RG 407, National Archives II, Ops map #3.

9. "2nd Cavalry Group After Action Report, February 1945," 8 February.

10. "XII Corps Report of Operations February 1945," 11–19.

11. For more on this particular region, read about the 3rd MCG's actions from November to February.

12. "2nd Cavalry Group After Action Report, February 1945," 19 February.

13. "2nd Cavalry Reconnaissance Squadron After Action Report, February 1945," CAVS2, Entry 427, RG 407, National Archives II, 14–15.

14. Ibid., 23 February.

15. *Unicorn Rampant,* 98.

16. Ibid., 98.

17. "VIII Corps After Action Report, February 1945," Record 208, Entry 427, RG 407, National Archives II, 10.

18. *Unicorn Rampant,* 101.

19. "VIII Corps After Action Report, 1 February 1945–28 February 1945," 12.

20. *Unicorn Rampant,* 101.

21. "XX Corps After Action Report, 1 February 1945–28 February 1945," Record 220, Entry 427, RG 407, National Archives II, 26–27.

22. *"Patton's Ghost Troops"—After Action Report 9 August 1944–9 May 1945* (Phoenix: 3rd Cavalry Veteran's Association, 1974), 99–100.

23. Tony Le Tisser, *Patton's Pawns: The 94th US Infantry Division at the Siegfried Line* (Tuscaloosa: Univ. of Alabama Press, 2007).

24. Alan J. Levine, *From the Normandy Beaches to the Baltic Sea: The Northwest Europe Campaign, 1944–1945* (Westport, Conn.: Praeger, 2000), 174.

25. *Unicorn Rampant,* 102.

26. The issue of quality in Volksgrenadier divisions, particularly at this stage of the war, is somewhat problematic. Some divisions were relatively well equipped and decently trained, while others were not. Considering the ferocity encountered by the 6th MCG in late February, the formations in front of them possessed, if nothing else, significant fighting spirit matched with sufficient firepower. For an excellent analysis of the entire Volksgrenadier issue, Douglas Nash's *Victory Was beyond Their Grasp: With the 272nd Volks-Grenadier Division from the Hürtgen Forest to the Heart of the Reich* (Bedford, Pa.: Aberjona Press, [2008]) is perhaps one of the best works on the subject.

27. "VIII Corps After Action Report, March 1945," Record 208, Entry 427, RG 407, National Archives II, 6.

28. *Unicorn Rampant,* 104.

29. Ibid., 105.

30. "VIII Corps After Action Report, March 1945," 18.

31. 2nd Cavalry Association, *The Ghosts of Patton's Third Army: A History of the Second U.S. Cavalry* (Munich, Germany: Münchner Graphische, 1946), 249.

32. "2nd Cavalry Reconnaissance Squadron After Action Report, March 1945," CAVS2, Entry 427, RG 407, National Archives II, 2.

33. "42nd Cavalry Reconnaissance Squadron After Action Report, March 1945," CAVS42, Entry 427, RG 407, National Archives II, 11.

34. 2nd Cavalry Association, *Ghosts of Patton's Third Army,* 259.

35. "XX Corps After Action Report, March 1945," Record 220, Entry 427, RG 407, National Archives II, 14–15.

36. Ibid., 17–18.

37. Charles B. MacDonald, *United States Army in World War II: The European Theater of Operations: The Last Offensive* (Washington, D.C.: Historical Division of the Army, 1973), 244.

38. *"Patton's Ghost Troops,"* 114.

39. "16th Cavalry Group History, 1 November 1944–31 January 1946," CAVG16, Entry 427, RG 407, National Archives II, 13 March.

40. Ibid., 14–15 March.

41. *"Patton's Ghost Troops,"* 115.

42. Incidentally, this realization had long been an assumption of American horse cavalry doctrine, a point that is often forgotten in the denigration of the horse cavalry advocates of the 1930s.

43. Though the numbers are left out of the after action report, a typical tank platoon of the time possessed five tanks—in this particular case, M24 Chaffees.

44. *"Patton's Ghost Troops,"* 116.

45. *The XX Corps: Its History and Service in World War II* (Osaka, Japan: XX Corps Association, 1951), 296.

46. Ibid., 21 March.

47. Ibid., 23 March.

48. *"Patton's Ghost Troops,"* 118–119.

49. Levine, *From the Normandy Beaches to the Baltic Sea,* 182.

50. MacDonald, *The Last Offensive,* 135.

51. Ibid., map 6.

52. Levine, *From the Normandy Beaches to the Baltic Sea,* 176.

53. "113th Mechanized Cavalry Group After Action Report February 1945," CAVG113, Entry 427, RG 407, National Archives II, 1–13.

54. Ibid., 19; "XIX Corps After Action Report March 1945," Record 219, Entry 427, RG 407, National Archives II, 5.

55. "113th Mechanized Cavalry Group After Action Report February 1945," 21.

56. David R. Higgins, *The Roer River Battles: Germany's Stand at the Westwall, 1944–45* (Philadelphia: Casemate Publishers, 2010), 222.

57. *Eleventh Cavalry from the Roer to the Elbe, 1944–1945* (Eleventh Cavalry Group, circa 1945; reprint, N.p.: Bibliogov Project, print on demand, 2013), 46; "XIII Corps After Action Report February 1945," Record 213, Entry 427, RG 407, National Archives II, 9–10.

58. *Eleventh Cavalry from the Roer to the Elbe,* 46–47.

59. Ibid., 47; "XIII Corps After Action Report March 1945," Record 213, Entry 427, RG 407, National Archives II, 1–3.

60. "11th Mechanized Cavalry Group After Action Report March 1945," CAVG11, Entry 427, RG 407, National Archives II, 1.

61. *Eleventh Cavalry from the Roer to the Elbe,* 48–49; "11th Mechanized Cavalry Group After Action Report March 1945," March, 2.

62. "XIII Corps After Action Report March 1945," 6.

63. *Eleventh Cavalry from the Roer to the Elbe,* 50–54; "11th Mechanized Cavalry Group After Action Report March 1945," 4.

64. *The Lion Rampant* (N.p.: U.S. Army, circa 1945), 14–15; *History of the XVI Corps: From Its Activation to the End of the War in Europe* (Washington, D.C.: Infantry Journal Press, circa 1945), 22–23.

65. *History of the XVI Corps,* 27–28.

66. *The Lion Rampant,* 16.

67. Ibid., 15.

68. *History of the XVI Corps,* 32–33.

69. Ibid., 35.

70. *History, V Corps* (U.S. Army, circa 1945), 372–373.

71. Charles E. Rousek, "A Short History of the 38th Cavalry Reconnaissance Squadron (Mechanized)" (Prestice, Czechoslovakia, 1945), available via 117th Cavalry Association, www.117th-cav.org, 15; David M. Russen, "Combat History: 102nd Cavalry Reconnaissance Squadron (MECZ): World War II," available via 117th Cavalry Association, www.117th-cav.org, 9.

72. MacDonald, *The Last Offensive,* 67–68.

73. Levine, *From the Normandy Beaches to the Baltic Sea,* 173.

74. MacDonald, *The Last Offensive,* 75–83; Russen, "Combat History," 9; Edward G. Miller, *A Dark and Bloody Ground: The Hürtgen Forest and the Roer River Dams, 1944–1945* (College Station: Texas A&M Univ. Press, 1995), 200.

75. "4th Mechanized Cavalry Group After Action Report February 1945," CAVG4, Entry 427, RG 407, National Archives II, 2; J. Lawton Collins, *Lightning Joe: An Autobiography* (Baton Rouge: Louisiana State Univ. Press, 1979), 298–299; "VII Corps After Action Report February 1945," Record 207, Entry 427, RG 407, National Archives II, 22.

76. "4th Mechanized Cavalry Group After Action Report February 1945," 2; "VII Corps After Action Report February 1945," 33.

77. "4th Mechanized Cavalry Group After Action Report February 1945," 3.

78. "VII Corps After Action Report February 1945," 45.

79. "4th Mechanized Cavalry Group After Action Report February 1945," 2. As a point of comparison, this distance is the frontage for a typical infantry division, a formation over four times the size of the cavalry group.

80. "VII Corps After Action Report February 1945," 53; "4th Mechanized Cavalry Group After Action Report March 1945," CAVG4, Entry 427, RG 407, National Archives II, 1.

81. "VII Corps After Action Report March 1945," Record 207, Entry 427, RG 407, National Archives II, 6–7.

82. "4th Mechanized Cavalry Group After Action Report March 1945," 2.

83. Ibid., 4.

84. Levine, *From the Normandy Beaches to the Baltic Sea,* 178.

85. "4th Mechanized Cavalry Group After Action Report March 1945," 4; "VII Corps After Action Report March 1945," 48.

86. "14th Mechanized Cavalry Group After Action Report February 1945," CAVG14, Entry 427, RG 407, National Archives II, 2; "III Corps After Action

Report February 1945," Record 203, Entry 427, RG 407, National Archives II, 19–20.

87. "14th Mechanized Cavalry Group After Action Report February 1945," 2; "III Corps After Action Report February 1945," 21.

88. "14th Mechanized Cavalry Group After Action Report March 1945," CAVG14, Entry 427, RG 407, National Archives II, 2; "III Corps After Action Report March 1945," Record 203, Entry 427, RG 407, National Archives II, 8.

89. "14th Mechanized Cavalry Group After Action Report March 1945," 3; "III Corps After Action Report March 1945," 11.

90. "14th Mechanized Cavalry Group After Action Report March 1945," 3.

91. Levine, *From the Normandy Beaches to the Baltic Sea,* 178–179.

92. "14th Mechanized Cavalry Group After Action Report March 1945," 4; "III Corps After Action Report March 1945," 20.

93. Rousek, "A Short History of the 38th Cavalry Reconnaissance Squadron (Mechanized)," 15.

94. *History, V Corps,* 390; "102nd Mechanized Cavalry Group After Action Report March 1945," record CAVG102, Entry 427, RG 407, National Archives II, March, 5.

95. *History, V Corps,* 394–396; "102nd Mechanized Cavalry Group After Action Report March 1945," 6.

96. Russen, "Combat History," 10.

97. "VI Corps After Action Report February 1945," Record 206, Entry 427, RG 407, National Archives II, 15; Robert Lutz, "117th Cavalry Reconnaissance Squadron (MECZ) in World War II," 117th Cavalry Association, http://www.117th-cav.org, 59–60.

98. Harry Yeide and Mark Stout, *First to the Rhine: The 6th Army Group in World War II* (Saint Paul, Minn.: Zenith Press, 2007), 342.

99. MacDonald, *The Last Offensive,* map 9; John Frayn Turner and Robert Jackson, *Destination Berchtesgaden: The Story of the United States Seventh Army in World War II* (New York: Charles Scribner's Sons, 1975), 133–140.

100. *Wingfoot: Rhineland and Central Europe Campaigns: Official History of the 101st Cavalry Group Mechanized* (Weinheim, Germany: Hugo Diesbach, 1945), 21.

101. For those who have never seen a corps staff planning process, the time savings might not seem apparent. However, cutting off a full phase of combat operations easily saved several hundred man-hours.

102. "XXI Corps After Action Report March 1945," Record 221, Entry 427, RG 407, National Archives II, 2; *Wingfoot: Rhineland and Central Europe Campaigns,* 23.

103. *Wingfoot: Rhineland and Central Europe Campaigns,* 23.

104. Turner and Jackson, *Destination Berchtesgaden,* 145.

105. Yeide and Stout, *First to the Rhine,* 344.

106. "XV Corps After Action Report March 1945," Record 215, Entry 427, RG 407, National Archives II, 31–34; MacDonald, *The Last Offensive,* map 9.

107. Turner and Jackson, *Destination Berchtesgaden,* 136.

108. Yeide and Stout, *First to the Rhine,* 346.

109. "106th Mechanized Cavalry Group After Action Report March 1945," Record CAVG106, Entry 427, RG 407, National Archives II, 8–9; William H. Collier, *The 106th Cavalry's Story* (Bloomington, Ind.: Trafford Publishing, 2012), 48.

110. "106th Mechanized Cavalry Group After Action Report March 1945," 9–10.

111. *Wingfoot: Rhineland and Central Europe Campaigns,* 25–26.

112. "XV Corps After Action Report March 1945," Record 215, Entry 427, RG 407, National Archives II, 12; Lutz, "117th Cavalry Reconnaissance Squadron (MECZ) in World War II," 69.

113. Lutz, "117th Cavalry Reconnaissance Squadron (MECZ) in World War II," 73–74.

114. Ibid., 75–76.

8. Sabers through the Reich

1. Charles B. MacDonald, *United States Army in World War II: The European Theater of Operations: The Last Offensive* (Washington, D.C.: Historical Division of the Army, 1973), 223, 232.

2. J. Lawton Collins, *Lighting Joe: An Autobiography* (Baton Rouge: Louisiana State Univ. Press, 1979), 305.

3. "III Corps After Action Report March 1945," Record 203, Entry 427, RG 407, National Archives II, College Park, Md., 22.

4. "14th Mechanized Cavalry Group After Action Report March 1945," CAVG14, Entry 427, RG 407, National Archives II, 4–5; "III Corps After Action Report March 1945," 50.

5. "4th Mechanized Cavalry Group After Action Report March 1945," CAVG4, Entry 427, RG 407, National Archives II, 4.

6. "VII Corps After Action Report March 1945," Record 207, Entry 427, RG 407, National Archives II, 92.

7. "102nd Mechanized Cavalry Group After Action Report March 1945," CAVG102, Entry 427, RG 407, National Archives II, 7; Charles E. Rousek, "A Short History of the 38th Cavalry Reconnaissance Squadron (Mechanized)" (Prestice, Czechoslovakia, 1945), available via 117th Cavalry Association, www.117th-cav.org, 16.

8. General Omar Bradley had relieved Major General John Millikin as commander of the III Corps shortly after the successful crossing of the Rhine. Although Millikin had achieved something no other corps commander in any Allied army would do—capture an intact Rhine bridge, Bradley had not been satisfied with his performance exploiting this opportunity and fired him. (MacDonald, *The Last Offensive,* 229.)

9. MacDonald, *The Last Offensive,* map 13; "III Corps After Action Report March 1945," 60.

10. "VII Corps After Action Report March 1945," 102; Collins, *Lightning Joe,* 311.

11. "4th Mechanized Cavalry Group After Action Report March 1945," 5.

12. "VII Corps After Action Report March 1945," 127.

13. "4th Mechanized Cavalry Group After Action Report March 1945," 6; "VII Corps After Action Report March 1945," 134.

14. "4th Mechanized Cavalry Group After Action Report March 1945," 6.

15. "4th Mechanized Cavalry Group After Action Report April 1945," CAVG4, Entry 427, RG 407, National Archives II, 2–3.

16. "14th Mechanized Cavalry Group After Action Report March 1945," 5–6.

17. "III Corps After Action Report April 1945," Record 203, Entry 427, RG 407, National Archives, 5.

18. *History, V Corps* (U.S. Army, circa 1945), 408.

19. Ibid., 411–412; David M. Russen, "Combat History: 102nd Cavalry Reconnaissance Squadron (MECZ): World War II," available via 117th Cavalry Association, www.117th-cav.org, 10.

20. *History, V Corps,* 414.

21. Ibid., 416.

22. Derek Zumbro's *Battle for the Ruhr: The German Army's Final Defeat in the West* (Lawrence: Univ. Press of Kansas, 2006) presents a stunning image of the utter devastation wrought by this battle. Told from the perspective of civilians and participants, this work truly conveys the humanity of this tragedy.

23. "III Corps After Action Report April 1945," 10; "14th Mechanized Cavalry Group After Action Report April 1945," CAVG14, Entry 427, RG 407, National Archives II, 2.

24. "III Corps After Action Report April 1945," 15–17.

25. Ibid., 21–22; MacDonald, *The Last Offensive,* 372.

26. *History, V Corps,* 429.

27. Ibid., 432.

28. Ibid., 438–440; Rousek, "A Short History of the 38th Cavalry Reconnaissance Squadron (Mechanized)," 17.

29. *History, V Corps,* 438.

30. MacDonald, *The Last Offensive,* 466.

31. "102nd Mechanized Cavalry Group After Action Report April 1945," CAVG102, Entry 427, RG 407, National Archives II, 3.

32. "14th Mechanized Cavalry Group After Action Report April 1945," Record 14, Entry 427, RG 407, National Archives II, 2. See the Third Army Section for the final details of the 14th MCG.

33. Alan J. Levine, *From the Normandy Beaches to the Baltic Sea: The Northwest Europe Campaign, 1944–1945* (Westport, Conn.: Praeger, 2000), 192.

34. An eight-mile front could be considered a large to very large division frontage in an attack, depending on the type of terrain. The 4th MCG, albeit reinforced, covered this same ground with a force one-third the size of a division.

35. "4th Mechanized Cavalry Group After Action Report April 1945," 3.

36. Ibid., 4–5.

37. Ibid., 5.

38. Ibid.

39. Ibid., 6.

40. *Mission Accomplished: The Story of the Campaigns of the VII Corps, United States Army, in the War against Germany, 1944–1945,* ed. Ray Merriam (Leipzig, Germany: J. J. Weber, 1945; reprint, Bennington, Vt.: Merriam Press, 1998), 55; Collins, *Lightning Joe,* 321.

41. "4th Mechanized Cavalry Group After Action Report April 1945," 6.

42. Collins, *Lightning Joe,* 322.

43. "4th Mechanized Cavalry Group After Action Report April 1945," 7.

44. Ibid., 8.

45. Levine, *From the Normandy Beaches to the Baltic Sea,* 184.

46. *Unicorn Rampant: History of the Sixth Cavalry Regiment/Group at Home and Abroad* (N.p.: Sixth Cavalry Regiment Association, 1945), 105–107.

47. "VIII Corps After Action Report, March 1945," 25.

48. "6th Mechanized Cavalry Group AAR March 1945," CAVG6, Entry 427, RG 407, National Archives II, 8.

49. "VIII Corps After Action Report, March 1945," 26–28.

50. *Unicorn Rampant,* 111.

51. "16th Cavalry Group History, 1 November 1944–31 January 1946," CAVG16, Entry 427, RG 407, National Archives II, 25 March.

52. "42nd Cavalry Reconnaissance Squadron After Action Report, March 1945," 15–16.

53. MacDonald, *The Last Offensive,* map 10.

54. Ibid., 31 March.

55. *The XX Corps: Its History and Service in World War II* (Osaka, Japan: XX

Corps Association, 1951), 330–331; *"Patton's Ghost Troops"—After Action Report 9 August 1944–9 May 1945* (Phoenix: 3rd Cavalry Veteran's Association, 1974), 120.

56. MacDonald, *The Last Offensive,* 351.

57. *"Patton's Ghost Troops,"* 123.

58. Preston Utterback, ed., *The 150 Year Saga of the 3rd U.S. Cavalry* (Phoenix: 3rd Cavalry Veterans Association, 1996), 230.

59. "XII Corps Report of Operations April 1945," Record 212, Entry 427, RG 407, National Archives II, 10.

60. Ibid., 12.

61. *Unicorn Rampant,* 112.

62. *"Patton's Ghost Troops,"* 128.

63. Ibid., 112–113.

64. "6th Mechanized Cavalry Group AAR April 1945," CAVG6, Entry 427, RG 407, National Archives II, 4.

65. *The XX Corps,* 374; *"Patton's Ghost Troops,"* 140.

66. "6th Mechanized Cavalry Group AAR, April 1945," 5.

67. *Unicorn Rampant,* 114.

68. "VIII Corps After Action Report, 1 April 1945–30 April 1945," Record 208, Entry 427, RG 407, National Archives II, 14.

69. "XII Corps Report of Operations April 1945," Record 212, Entry 427, RG 407, National Archives II, 16; "42nd Cavalry Reconnaissance Squadron After Action Report, April 1945," CAVS42, Entry 427, RG 407, National Archives II, 13.

70. "42nd Cavalry Reconnaissance Squadron After Action Report, April 1945," 14.

71. Ibid., 16.

72. *Unicorn Rampant,* 115.

73. "14th Mechanized Cavalry Group After Action Report April 1945," CAVG14, Entry 427, RG 407, National Archives II, 3; "III Corps After Action Report April 1945," Record 203, Entry 427, RG 407, National Archives II, 27.

74. "14th Mechanized Cavalry Group After Action Report April 1945," 4.

75. Ibid., 5.

76. "14th Mechanized Cavalry Group After Action Report May 1945," CAVG14, Entry 427, RG 407, National Archives II, 2.

77. *The XX Corps,* 374.

78. *"Patton's Ghost Troops,"* 140.

79. Ibid. Of particular note, with the exception of the ranger company, this task organization bears a striking resemblance to a modern heavy cavalry troop.

80. *"Patton's Ghost Troops,"* 142.

81. Ibid., 116–119.

82. 2nd Cavalry Association, *The Ghosts of Patton's Third Army: A History of the Second U.S. Cavalry* (Munich, Germany: Münchner Graphische, 1946), 294.

83. This is a very well-documented operation. Disney even made a movie about it. This amount of attention seems strange, considering the importance and weight of other activities during this time. Perhaps this rescue receives so much attention because not only was it unusual, but it is also a hopeful and good story amid the backdrop of so much horror.

84. Harry Yeide and Mark Stout, *First to the Rhine: The 6th Army Group in World War II* (Saint Paul, Minn.: Zenith Press, 2007), 351.

85. "106th Mechanized Cavalry Group After Action Report March 1945," CAVG106, Entry 427, RG 407, National Archives II, 2; "XV Corps After Action Report March 1945," Record 215, Entry 427, RG 407, National Archives II, 76–78.

86. Charles Whiting, *America's Forgotten Army: The True Story of the U.S. Seventh Army in WW II—and an Unknown Battle that Changed History* (New York: St. Martin's Press, 1999), 190.

87. "106th Mechanized Cavalry Group After Action Report March 1945," 2.

88. *Wingfoot: Rhineland and Central Europe Campaigns: Official History of the 101st Cavalry Group Mechanized* (Weinheim, Germany: Hugo Diesbach, 1945), 28.

89. Robert Lutz, "117th Cavalry Reconnaissance Squadron (MECZ) in World War II," 117th Cavalry Association, http://www.117th-cav.org, 76–77.

90. *Wingfoot: Rhineland and Central Europe Campaigns,* 45–47.

91. Sadly, the home of cavalry and armor has moved to Fort Benning, perhaps the original home of the infantry tank, but not the soul of the mechanized force. Fort Knox will keep that distinction for a long time, at least in this author's heart.

92. "VI Corps After Action Report April 1945," Record 206, Entry 427, RG 407, National Archives II, 1; Lutz, "117th Cavalry Reconnaissance Squadron (MECZ) in World War II," 78–80.

93. "XV Corps After Action Report April 1945," Record 215, Entry 427, RG 407, National Archives, 19.

94. William H. Collier, *The 106th Cavalry's Story* (Bloomington, Ind.: Trafford Publishing, 2012), 53.

95. "XXI Corps After Action Report April 1945," Record 221, Entry 427, RG 407, National Archives II, 1; *Wingfoot: Rhineland and Central Europe Campaigns,* 47–49.

96. *Wingfoot: Rhineland and Central Europe Campaigns,* 47–51.

97. Ibid., 57.

98. "VI Corps After Action Report April 1945," 35.

99. Lutz, "117th Cavalry Reconnaissance Squadron (MECZ) in World War II," 83.

100. Collier, *The 106th Cavalry's Story,* 53.

101. *Wingfoot: Rhineland and Central Europe Campaigns,* 57–62.

102. "106th Mechanized Cavalry Group After Action Report April 1945," CAVG106, Entry 427, RG 407, National Archives II, 1; Collier, *The 106th Cavalry's Story,* 54.

103. "XXI Corps After Action Report April 1945," 17–23.

104. "VI Corps After Action Report April 1945," 49.

105. "VI Corps After Action Report May 1945," Record 206, Entry 427, RG 407, National Archives II, 1–11.

106. *Wingfoot: Rhineland and Central Europe Campaigns,* 77–79.

107. "XV Corps After Action Report May 1945," Record 215, Entry 427, RG 407, National Archives II, 5.

108. Collier, *The 106th Cavalry's Story,* 55.

109. Heads of state tend to become irritable when kept waiting, particularly while in captivity.

110. MacDonald, *The Last Offensive,* map 11.

111. Levine, *From the Normandy Beaches to the Baltic Sea,* 182.

112. *Conquer: The Story of the Ninth Army* (Washington, D.C.: Infantry Journal Press, 1947), 204–205.

113. "15th Mechanized Cavalry Group After Action Report March 1945," CAVG15, Entry 427, RG 407, National Archives II, 2; "15th Cavalry Reconnaissance Squadron After Action Report March 1945," CAVS15, Entry 427, RG 407, National Archives II, 2.

114. "15th Cavalry Reconnaissance Squadron After Action Report March 1945," 2.

115. MacDonald, *The Last Offensive,* 35, map 13.

116. "XIX Corps After Action Report April 1945," Record 219, Entry 427, RG 407, National Archives II, 1; "15th Mechanized Cavalry Group After Action Report 1944," 1.

117. "11th Mechanized Cavalry Group After Action Report April 1945," CAVG11, Entry 427, RG 407, National Archives II, 1; "XIII Corps After Action Report April 1945," Record 213, Entry 427, RG 407, National Archives II, 1–2.

118. "113th Mechanized Cavalry Group After Action Report April 1945," CAVG113, Entry 427, RG 407, National Archives II, 1.

119. "113th Mechanized Cavalry Group After Action Report April 1945," 6.

120. *Eleventh Cavalry from the Roer to the Elbe, 1944–1945* (Eleventh Cavalry Group, circa 1945; reprint, Bibliogov Project, print on demand, 2013), 60.

121. "XIII Corps After Action Report April 1945," 2.

122. "11th Mechanized Cavalry Group After Action Report April 1945," 2; "XIII Corps After Action Report April 1945," 2. The XIII Corps report notes the fighting happening on 2 April and from a different axis of advance. The group after action report is used, as the cavalry were actually involved in the action, whereas the corps report was attempting to summarize a very busy and confusing couple of days.

123. "11th Mechanized Cavalry Group After Action Report April 1945," 2–3; *Eleventh Cavalry from the Roer to the Elbe,* 62.

124. "XIX Corps After Action Report April 1945," 3.

125. Ibid., 4.

126. "XIII Corps After Action Report April 1945," 3; "11th Mechanized Cavalry Group After Action Report April 1945," 3.

127. *Eleventh Cavalry from the Roer to the Elbe,* 65.

128. "XIII Corps After Action Report April 1945," 3.

129. "113th Mechanized Cavalry Group After Action Report April 1945," 18–22.

130. *Eleventh Cavalry from the Roer to the Elbe,* 67.

131. "113th Mechanized Cavalry Group After Action Report April 1945,"24–33.

132. *Eleventh Cavalry from the Roer to the Elbe,* 69; "XIII Corps After Action Report April 1945," 5.

133. *Eleventh Cavalry from the Roer to the Elbe,* 70.

134. "XIII Corps After Action Report April 1945," 6; "11th Mechanized Cavalry Group After Action Report April 1945," 8.

135. *Eleventh Cavalry from the Roer to the Elbe,* 73. Considering that corps artillery routinely contained the heaviest calibers in the American arsenal, this must have been an awe-inspiring sight.

136. "11th Mechanized Cavalry Group After Action Report April 1945," 9.

137. *Eleventh Cavalry from the Roer to the Elbe,* 75.

138. *The Lion Rampant* (N.p.: U.S. Army, circa 1945), 17.

9. Conclusions

1. Portions of this chapter have appeared previously in William S. Nance, "Lost Sabers: Why We Need Operational Cavalry and How to Get It Back," *Armor* 123, no. 4 (October–December 2014): 51–55; William S. Nance, "The Armored Reconnaissance Squadron and the Mechanized Cavalry Group," *Armor* 115, no. 1 (January–February 2006): 7–11.

2. Preston Utterback, ed., *The 150 Year Saga of the 3rd U.S. Cavalry* (Phoenix: 3rd Cavalry Veterans Association, 1996), 229.

3. Michael D. Doubler, *Closing with the Enemy: How GIs Fought the War in Europe, 1944–1945* (Lawrence: Univ. Press of Kansas, 1994), 229–235.

4. U.S. Forces Europe, the General Board, *Mechanized Cavalry Units,* Study Number 49, 1945 (Washington, D.C.: GPO, 1945), appendix 3, 2.

5. Shelby L. Stanton, *World War II Order of Battle U.S. Army (Ground Force Units)* (Mechanicsburg, Pa.: Stackpole Books, 2006), 15, 23.

Bibliography

Primary Sources

National Archives II, College Park, Maryland

2nd Cavalry Reconnaissance Squadron, "Report of Operations," CAVS2, Record Group 407.

2nd Mechanized Cavalry Group, "Combat Interviews," C. I., Record Group 407.

2nd Mechanized Cavalry Group, "Report of Operations," CAVG2, Record Group 407.

Third Army, "Report of Operations," Record 103, Record Group 407.

III Corps, "Report of Operations," Record 203, Record Group 407.

3rd Mechanized Cavalry Group, "Combat Interviews," C. I., Record Group 407.

4th Mechanized Cavalry Group, "Report of Operations," CAVG4, Record Group 407.

V Corps, "Report of Operations," Record 205, Record Group 407.

6th Cavalry Reconnaissance Squadron, "Report of Operations," CAVS6, Record Group 407.

VI Corps, "Report of Operations," Record 206, Record Group 407.

6th Mechanized Cavalry Group, "Combat Interviews," C. I., Record Group 407.

6th Mechanized Cavalry Group, "Report of Operations," CAVG6, Record Group 407.

VII Corps, "Report of Operations," Record 207, Record Group 407.

VIII Corps, "Report of Operations," Record 208, Record Group 407.

11th Mechanized Cavalry Group, "Report of Operations," CAVG11, Record Group 407.

XII Corps, "Report of Operations," Record 212, Record Group 407.

XIII Corps, "Report of Operations," Record 213, Record Group 407.

14th Mechanized Cavalry Group, "Report of Operations," CAVG14, Record Group 407.

15th Cavalry Reconnaissance Squadron, "Report of Operations," CAVS15, Record Group 407.

XV Corps, "Report of Operations," Record 215, Record Group 407.

15th Mechanized Cavalry Group "Combat Interviews," C. I., Record Group 407.

15th Mechanized Cavalry Group, "Report of Operations," CAVG15, Record Group 407.

16th Cavalry Reconnaissance Squadron, "Report of Operations," CAVS16, Record Group 407.

16th Mechanized Cavalry Group, "Report of Operations," CAVG16, Record Group 407.

17th Cavalry Reconnaissance Squadron, "Report of Operations," CAVS17, Record Group 407.

XVIII Corps, "Report of Operations," Record 218, Record Group 407.

19th Cavalry Reconnaissance Squadron, "Report of Operations," CAVS2, Record Group 407.

XIX Corps, "Report of Operations," Record 219, Record Group 407.

XX Corps, "Report of Operations," Record 220, Record Group 407.

XXI Corps, "Report of Operations," Record 221, Record Group 407.

XXII Corps, "Report of Operations," Record, 222, Record Group 407.

28th Cavalry Reconnaissance Squadron, "Report of Operations," CAVS28, Record Group 407.

42nd Cavalry Reconnaissance Squadron, "Report of Operations," CAVS42, Record Group 407.

101st Mechanized Cavalry Group, "Report of Operations," CAVG101, Record Group 407.

102nd Mechanized Cavalry Group, "Report of Operations," CAVG102, Record Group 407.

106th Cavalry Reconnaissance Squadron, "Report of Operations," CAVS106, Record Group 407.

106th Mechanized Cavalry Group, "Report of Operations," CAVG106, Record Group 407.

113th Mechanized Cavalry Group, "Report of Operations," CAVG113, Record Group 407.

115th Mechanized Cavalry Group, "Report of Operations," CAVG115, Record Group 407.

117th Cavalry Reconnaissance Squadron, "Report of Operations," CAVS117, Record Group 407.

121st Cavalry Reconnaissance Squadron, "Report of Operations," CAVS121, Record Group 407.

Other Archives

Hodge, Charles. Untitled memoir. Manuscript, no date. In the possession of 117th Cavalry Association, Westfield Armory, New Jersey.

Headquarters V Corps. "Operation of Corps Cavalry on Terrain of Normandy." Operations memorandum from Headquarters V Corps, U.S. Army, 26 June 1944.

Polk, James H. "Interview by Jesse Stiller and Rebecca Craver, November 1987–April 1988." 3rd Armored Cavalry Regiment Museum, Fort Hood, Texas.

Schwarz, Jody, and James Polk III. E-mail interview by William S. Nance, 11–12 January 2011. Notes in the possession of the author.

Government Documents

U.S. Department of the Army. *General Order No. 13—General James Hilliard Polk.* Washington, D.C.: GPO, 3 April 1992.

U.S. Forces Europe, the General Board. *Mechanized Cavalry Units.* Study Number 49, 1945. Washington, D.C.: GPO, 1945.

U.S. War Department. *Cavalry Drill Regulations 1916.* Washington, D.C.: GPO, 1917.

———. *Cavalry Drill Regulations 1916, corrected to December 31, 1917.* Washington, D.C.: GPO, 1918.

———. *Cavalry Service Regulations (Experimental) 1914.* Washington, D.C.: GPO, 1914.

———. *Drill Regulations for Cavalry, Amended 1909, Corrected to January 1, 1911.* Washington, D.C.: GPO, 1911.

———. *Field Service Regulations 1913, Corrected to May 21, 1913.* Washington, D.C.: GPO, 1913.

———. *Field Service Regulations 1914, Corrected to April 15, 1917.* Washington, D.C.: GPO, 1917.

———. *Field Service Regulations 1923.* Washington, D.C.: GPO, 1924.

———. *FM 1-02: Operational Terms and Graphics.* Washington, D.C.: Government Printing Office, 2004.

———. *FM 2-10: Cavalry Field Manual: Mechanized Elements, 1941.* Washington, D.C.: GPO, 1941.

———. *FM 2-15: Cavalry Field Manual: Employment of Cavalry.* Washington, D.C.: GPO, 1941.

———. *FM 2-20: Cavalry Reconnaissance Troop: Mechanized, 1944.* Washington, D.C.: GPO, 1944.

———. *FM 2-30: Cavalry Mechanized Reconnaissance Squadron.* Washington, D.C.: GPO, 1943.

———. *FM 2-30: Cavalry Mechanized Reconnaissance Squadron.* Washington, D.C.: GPO, 1944.

———. *FM 17-10: Armored Force Field Manual: Tactics and Techniques.* Washington, D.C.: GPO, 1942.

———. *FM 17-20: Armored Force Field Manual: Employment of Armored Units; Reconnaissance Platoon and Company.* Washington, D.C.: GPO, 1942.

———. *FM 17-22: Armored Force Field Manual: Reconnaissance Battalion.* Washington, D.C.: GPO 1942.

———. *FM 17-30: Armored Force Field Manual: Tank Platoon.* Washington, D.C.: GPO, 1942.

———. *FM 100-5: Field Service Regulations: Operations, 1941.* Washington, D.C.: GPO, 1941.

———. *FM 100-5: Field Service Regulations: Operations, 1944.* Washington, D.C.: GPO, 1944.

———. *Superior Board Report.* Washington, D.C.: GPO, 1919.

———. *Training Circular 107: Employment of Mechanized Cavalry Units.* Washington, D.C.: GPO, 23 September 1943.

Articles

"The 2nd Cavalry Group: Defense of the West Bank of the Moselle River, in the Mountfort Area, Luxembourg, December 24, 1944–March 3, 1945." *Cavalry Journal* 55, no. 3 (May–June 1946): 9–10.

"The 3rd Cavalry Group: Pursuit from Leinburg to Regensburg, Preceding the XX Corps, to Seize Crossings over the Danube River, April 22–24, 1945." *Cavalry Journal* 55, no. 3 (May–June 1946): 10–11.

"The 6th Cavalry Group: Attack to Seize L'Hôpital and Clear Karlsbrunn Forest, December 2–5, 1944." *Cavalry Journal* 55, no. 3 (May–June 1946): 12–13.

"15th Cavalry Group Part 1: An Ambush in Brittany." *Cavalry Journal* 54, no. 5 (September–October 1945): 2–3.

"The 316th Provisional Mechanized Cavalry Brigade in Combat." *Cavalry Journal* 55, no. 3 (May–June 1946): 8–9.

Allen, Terry. "Cavalry Maneuvers—Southwest of Alexandria, LA, August 17, 1940." *Cavalry Journal* 49, no. 6 (November–December 1940): 528–531.

Allison, J. B. "Has the Army Too Much Radio?" *Cavalry Journal* 45, no. 6 (November–December 1936): 485–488.

Anderson, John D. "Drama at Headquarters." *Cavalry Journal* 54, no. 6 (November–December 1945): 37–38.

"The Armored Force." *Cavalry Journal* 50, no. 1 (January–February 1941): 22–23.

Auger, Wayland B. "Eleventh Cavalry in Fourth Army Maneuvers." *Cavalry Journal* 49, no. 5 (September–October 1940): 444–447.

Baldwin, Hanson W. "Maneuvers Reveal Deficiencies." *Cavalry Journal* 48, no. 5 (September–October 1939): 390–391.

Batchelor, Vance W., and Charles H. Noble. "The First Cavalry Division in the

Third Army Maneuvers." *Cavalry Journal* 49, no. 4 (July–August 1940): 336–337.

Batley, Robert M. "Mechanized Cavalry Group in Defense." *Cavalry Journal* 54, no. 5 (September–October 1945): 10–12.

Bibb, E. "Commercial Truck Portage." *Cavalry Journal* 49, no. 1 (January–February 1940): 54–56.

Bierman, Delfred. "Comments from Combat: Patrol across the Rhine." *Cavalry Journal* 54, no. 6 (November–December 1945): 32–33.

Bixel, C. P. "Cavalry Motorcycle Troop." *Cavalry Journal* 50, no. 1 (January–February 1941): 52–55.

Black, Percy G. "The Armored Force and Its Development." *Cavalry Journal* 49, no. 6 (November–December 1940): 484–488.

———. "The U.S. Armored Force: The Possibilities of Its Strategical and Tactical Employment." *Cavalry Journal* 49, no. 5 (September–October 1940): 400–403.

Brandt, G. "Modern Cavalry: A Discussion of Employment, Troop Leading, Organization, and Training (part I)." *Cavalry Journal* 44, no. 187 (January–February 1935): 25–36.

———. "Modern Cavalry: A Discussion of Employment, Troop Leading, Organization, and Training (part II)." *Cavalry Journal* 44, no. 188 (March–April 1935): 14–24.

———. "Modern Cavalry: A Discussion of Employment, Troop Leading, Organization, and Training (part III)." *Cavalry Journal* 44, no. 189 (May–June 1935): 41–45.

———. "Modern Cavalry: A Discussion of Employment, Troop Leading, Organization, and Training (part IV)." *Cavalry Journal* 45, no. 190 (July–August 1935): 35–46.

Brett, Thomas J. "Harassing." *Cavalry Journal* 55, no. 2 (March–April 1946): 22–23.

———. "Little Cannae." *Cavalry Journal* 54, no. 6 (November–December 1945): 18–21.

———. "The U.S. North Flank." *Cavalry Journal* 54, no. 5 (September–October 1945): 24–26.

Britton, First Lieutenant Frank H. "Cavalry Reconnaissance Detachments on Reconnaissance." *Cavalry Journal* 45, no. 5 (September–October 1936): 409–412.

Burke, Paul L. "A Cavalry Mechanized Squadron in Defense." *Cavalry Journal* 55, no. 2 (March–April 1946): 18–21.

Burke, Paul L., and Lyman C. Anderson. "Patrolling the Siegfried." *Cavalry Journal* 54, no. 3 (May–June 1945): 12–15.

"Cavalry Affairs in Congress." *Cavalry Journal* 49, no. 3 (May–June 1940): 201–206.

"Cavalry in Poland." *Cavalry Journal* 48, no. 4 (July–August 1939): 315.

"Cavalry in the Foreign Press." *Cavalry Journal* 46, no. 5 (September–October 1937): 476–480.

"Cavalry in the Foreign Press." *Cavalry Journal* 46, no. 6 (November–December 1937): 563–567.

"Cavalry in the Foreign Press." *Cavalry Journal* 47, no. 1 (January–February 1938): 76–79.

"The Cavalry School." *Cavalry Journal* 49, no. 5 (September–October 1940): 404.

"The Cavalry School Digest of Information." *Cavalry Journal* 44, no. 192 (November–December 1935): 37–47.

"The Cavalry School Digest of Information." *Cavalry Journal* 45, no. 1 (January–February 1936): 31–41.

"The Cavalry School Digest of Information." *Cavalry Journal* 45, no. 2 (March–April 1936): 106–113.

"The Cavalry School Digest of Information." *Cavalry Journal* 46, no. 2 (March–April 1937): 145–149.

"The Cavalry School Visits Fort Knox." *Cavalry Journal* 46, no. 4 (July–August 1937): 336–341.

Chaffee, Adna R. "The Army of the United States." *Cavalry Journal* 47, no. 2 (March–April 1938): 110–113.

Chaffee, Adna R. "The Seventh Cavalry Brigade in the First Army Maneuvers." *Cavalry Journal* 48, no. 6 (November–December 1939): 450–461.

———. "The 7th Cavalry Brigade in the Third Army Maneuvers." *Cavalry Journal* 49, no. 4 (July–August 1940): 318–319.

Chamberlin, Harry D. "Cavalry Training." *Cavalry Journal* 49, no. 5 (September–October 1940): 405–409.

Chase, William C. "Fourth Army Maneuvers—1937: The Fort Riley Phase: August 15–29." *Cavalry Journal* 46, no. 5 (September–October 1937): 427–436.

Cocke, James W. "Battle Reconnaissance." *Cavalry Journal* 54, no. 3 (May–June 1945): 18–23.

———. "A Cavalry Group in Delaying Action." *Cavalry Journal* 54, no. 6 (November–December 1945): 39–44.

———. "Comments from Combat—Light Tanks in Pursuit." *Cavalry Journal* 54, no. 5 (September–October 1945): 18–20.

Cohn, Aaron. "A Cavalry Tank Force in the Defense of a River Line." *Cavalry Journal* 54, no. 4 (July–August 1945): 28–30.

"Comments from Combat: Zeiko Falls." *Cavalry Journal* 54, no. 6 (November–December 1945): 33–34.

"Corps Reconnaissance Regiment." *Cavalry Journal* 48, no. 6 (November–December 1939): 498–499.

Cramer, L. W. "Portee Cavalry: An Experiment with Commercial Trucks." *Cavalry Journal* 49, no. 3 (May–June 1940): 254–255.

Crittenberger, Willis D. "Cavalry Maneuvers at Fort Knox." *Cavalry Journal* 46, no. 5 (September–October 1937): 420–426.

Crockett, Cary I. "Five Days at Fort Knox." *Cavalry Journal* 46, no. 6 (November–December 1937): 527–529.

Dalton, James L. "Field Exercises of the 1st Squadron, 3rd Cavalry." *Cavalry Journal* 44, no. 191 (September–October 1935): 43–46.

Daniels, Robert W. "New Ordnance with the Cavalry Division." *Cavalry Journal* 49, no. 6 (November–December 1940): 503–506.

Deaderick, Captain Richard O. "From the Book." *Cavalry Journal* 54, no. 6 (November–December 1945): 22–27.

Dobbins, Garret J. "15th Cavalry Group Part 2: Mopping up an Enemy Pocket." *Cavalry Journal* 54, no. 6 (November–December 1945): 17.

Dobbins, Garret J., and Thomas Fiori. "15th Cavalry Group Part 2: Cavalry and Infantry at Saint Malo." *Cavalry Journal* 54, no. 6 (November–December 1945): 15–16.

Du Faur, Faber. "Strategic Reconnaissance in War of the Future." *Cavalry Journal* 46, no. 1 (January–February 1937): 61–66.

Edmunds, Kinzie. "6th Cavalry at the Maneuvers of the 8th Brigade (part I)." *Cavalry Journal* 44, no. 190 (July–August 1935): 6–9.

Edmunds, Kinzie, and Rufus S. Ramey. "6th Cavalry at the Maneuvers of the 8th Brigade (part II)." *Cavalry Journal* 44, no. 191 (September–October 1935): 21–29.

Eliot, George Fielding. "The Future of U.S. Cavalry." *Cavalry Journal* 48, no. 3 (May–June 1939): 194–199.

"Expansion of the 7th Cavalry Brigade." *Cavalry Journal* 49, no. 3 (May–June 1940): 207.

Flynn, Henry L. "The Part Played by the 6th Cavalry in the Infantry School Maneuvers." *Cavalry Journal* 45, no. 5 (September–October 1936): 365–376.

"Fourth Cavalry (H-Mecz) in Fourth Army Maneuvers." *Cavalry Journal* 49, no. 5 (September–October 1940): 441–444.

Gerhardt, C. H. "Fourth Army Maneuvers—1937: The San Luis Obispo Phase: August 10–12." *Cavalry Journal* 46, no. 5 (September–October 1937): 436–438.

"German Cavalry Doctrine." *Cavalry Journal* 50, no. 1 (January–February 1941): 49–51.

"German Maneuvers Lesson." *Cavalry Journal* 47, no. 2 (March–April 1938): 113.

Grimes, William M. "The 1940 Spring Maneuvers." *Cavalry Journal* 49, no. 2 (March–April 1940): 98–114.

Grow, Robert W. "Mechanized Cavalry." *Cavalry Journal* 47, no. 1 (January–February 1938): 30–31.

———. "Military Characteristics of Combat Vehicles." *Cavalry Journal* 45, no. 6 (November–December 1936): 508–511.

———. "New Developments in the Organization and Equipment of Cavalry." *Cavalry Journal* 48, no. 3 (May–June 1939): 204–207.

———. "Twenty Years of Evolution in U.S. Cavalry Equipment." *Cavalry Journal* 46, no. 2 (March–April 1937): 127–129.

Hamilton, H. G. "A Light Cross-Country Car." *Cavalry Journal* 44, no. 189 (May–June 1935): 30.

Hargreaves, Reginald. "Dress Rehearsal for the Next World War." *Cavalry Journal* 48, no. 4 (July–August 1939): 274–280.

Harvey, F. M. "Use of Cavalry under Modernization." *Cavalry Journal* 44, no. 192 (November–December 1935): 35–36.

Hawkins, Hamilton S. "Advance Guard or Covering Detachment." *Cavalry Journal* 44, no. 189 (May–June 1935): 22–23.

———. "The Composition of Army Covering Forces and the Employment of Mechanized Force in this Role." *Cavalry Journal* 46, no. 6 (November–December 1937): 517–520.

———. "General Hawkins' Notes." *Cavalry Journal* 47, no. 2 (March–April 1938): 173–174.

———. "General Hawkins' Notes." *Cavalry Journal* 48, no. 5 (September–October 1939): 424–427.

———. "General Hawkins' Notes." *Cavalry Journal* 48, no. 6 (November–December 1939): 516–518.

———. "General Hawkins' Notes." *Cavalry Journal* 49, no. 1 (January–February 1940): 74–76.

———. "General Hawkins' Notes." *Cavalry Journal* 49, no. 2 (March–April 1940): 163–165.

———. "General Hawkins' Notes." *Cavalry Journal* 49, no. 3 (May–June 1940): 268–269.

———. "General Hawkins' Notes." *Cavalry Journal* 49, no. 4 (July–August 1940): 340–343.

———. "General Hawkins' Notes." *Cavalry Journal* 49, no. 5 (September–October 1940): 434–435.

———. "General Hawkins' Notes" *Cavalry Journal* 50, no. 1 (January–February 1941): 30–33.

———. "We Must Have Cavalry." *Cavalry Journal* 46, no. 5 (September–October 1937): 405–409.

Hayden, Sears A. "Mobility—Firepower and Shock." *Cavalry Journal* 48, no. 4 (July–August 1939): 284–289.

Heavey, Thomas J. "Demonstration of Scout Cars at the Field Artillery School." *Cavalry Journal* 44, no. 189 (May–June 1935): 26–28.

———. "The Horse-Mechanized Regiment." *Cavalry Journal* 49, no. 5 (September–October 1940): 424–428.

———. "An Observer at the First Army Maneuvers." *Cavalry Journal* 48, no. 6 (November–December 1939): 461–463.

Herr, John K. "Notes from the Chief of Cavalry." *Cavalry Journal* 49, no. 4 (July–August 1940): 322–323.

———. "A Survey of Our Cavalry." *Cavalry Journal* 49, no. 6 (November–December 1940): 482–483.

"Horse and Mechanized Cavalry Maneuvers at Fort Knox, Kentucky." *Cavalry Journal* 46, no. 4 (July–August 1937): 382.

"Horse for Defense." *Cavalry Journal* 48, no. 4 (July–August 1939): 306–312.

Hudson, W. E. "Cavalry Holds a River Line." *Cavalry Journal* 55, no. 1 (January–February 1946): 9–10.

Jones, Carleton P., Jr. "Mounted Attack, Mechanized." *Cavalry Journal* 54, no. 3 (May–June 1945): 31–33.

Jones, Morton McD. "15th Cavalry Group Part 2—Seizing and Holding a River Line." *Cavalry Journal* 54, no. 6 (November–December 1945): 14–15.

Kraft, William R. "15th Cavalry Group Part 2—Cavalry in Dismounted Action." *Cavalry Journal* 54, no. 6 (November–December 1945): 11–12.

Kramer, Thomas. "An Incident and an Experiment." *Cavalry Journal* 45, no. 5 (September–October 1936): 376–378.

Lentz, Bernard. "A Justification of Cavalry." *Cavalry Journal* 44, no. 187 (January–February 1935): 10.

Lininger, Clarence. "Random Impressions at Fort Knox." *Cavalry Journal* 47, no. 1 (January–February 1938): 32–33.

Marlow, Herman M. "15th Cavalry Group—The Relief of an Armored Division." *Cavalry Journal* 55, no. 1 (January–February 1946): 9.

Martin, Charles F. "A Horse Cavalry Night March to Combat against Mechanized Cavalry." *Cavalry Journal* 44, no. 192 (November–December 1935): 8–14.

———. "Influences of Mechanization, Motorization and Machine Guns on the Horse Cavalry Regiment's Tactics, Organization and Supply Methods (part I)." *Cavalry Journal* 44, no. 188 (March–April 1935): 5–10.

———. "Influences of Mechanization, Motorization and Machine Guns on the

Horse Cavalry Regiment's Tactics, Organization and Supply Methods (part II)." *Cavalry Journal* 44, no. 189 (May–June 1935): 15–21.

———. "Influences of Mechanization, Motorization and Machine Guns on the Horse Cavalry Regiment's Tactics, Organization and Supply Methods (part III)." *Cavalry Journal* 44, no. 190 (July–August 1935): 28–34.

Martin, Thomas L. "Cavalry in Beach Defense." *Cavalry Journal* 49, no. 2 (March–April 1940): 130–131.

Matlack, Tom E. "Reconnaissance Troop Officer's Diary." *Cavalry Journal* 49, no. 6 (November–December 1940): 532–535.

McAnsh, A. T. "The New German Army Showing Organization of Panzer Divisions." *Cavalry Journal* 49, no. 4 (July–August 1940): 307–314.

McGuire, James M. "15th Cavalry Group Part 2—Reconnoitering an Enemy Position." *Cavalry Journal* 54, no. 6 (November–December 1945): 13–14.

Merten, F. W. "Cavalry in the Foreign Military Press." *Cavalry Journal* 46, no. 1 (January–February 1937): 79–81.

———. "Cavalry in the Foreign Military Press." *Cavalry Journal* 46, no. 2 (March–April 1937): 175–177.

———. "Cavalry in the Foreign Military Press." *Cavalry Journal* 46, no. 3 (May–June 1937): 290–291.

———. "Cavalry in the Foreign Military Press." *Cavalry Journal* 46, no. 4 (July–August 1937): 385–387.

Millholland, George B. "The Third Cavalry at Indiantown Gap." *Cavalry Journal* 46, no. 6 (November–December 1937): 533–534.

Millikin, John. "The Fall Maneuvers of the Cavalry School—1934." *Cavalry Journal* 44, no. 188 (March–April 1935): 45–52.

Nance, William S. "The Armored Reconnaissance Squadron and the Mechanized Cavalry Group" *Armor* 115, no. 1 (January–February 2006): 7–11.

———. "Lost Sabers: Why We Need Operational Cavalry and How to Get It Back" *Armor* 123, no. 4 (October–December 2014): 51–55.

"Necessity for Horse Cavalry under Modern Conditions: Extract from Recent Hearings Before the Subcommittee of the Committee on Appropriations, House of Representatives, on the War Department Appropriation Bill, 1938." *Cavalry Journal* 46, no. 3 (May–June 1937): 251.

"The Nine Troop Regiment." *Cavalry Journal* 48, no. 6 (November–December 1939): 496–497.

"Organization of New U.S. Armored Corps." *Cavalry Journal* 49, no. 4 (July–August 1940): 317.

Palmer, Bruce. "Mechanized Cavalry in the Second Army Maneuvers." *Cavalry Journal* 45, no. 6 (November–December 1936): 461–478.

Probst, Alan R. "A Cavalry Group with an Armored Division." *Cavalry Journal* 55, no. 3 (May–June 1946): 2–7.

Randolph, James R. "Defense against Tanks." *Cavalry Journal* 49, no. 3 (May–June 1940): 231–236.

Reardon, John J. "The Evolution of Transportation." *Cavalry Journal* 44, no. 187 (January–February 1935): 46.

Reilly, Henry J. "Horse Cavalry and the Gas Engine's Children." *Cavalry Journal* 49, no. 1 (January–February 1940): 2–9.

Reynolds, William G. "Screen for Infantry." *Cavalry Journal* 54, no. 3 (May–June 1945): 16.

Richardson, Robert C., Jr. "The Wider Role of Cavalry." *Cavalry Journal* 50, no. 1 (January–February 1941): 2–8.

Riordan, Forrest H., Jr. "A Mechanized Night Ride." *Cavalry Journal* 48, no. 4 (July–August 1939): 313–315.

Rodney, Dorsey R. "Fourth Army Maneuvers—1937." *Cavalry Journal* 46, no. 6 (November–December 1937): 530–532.

Rowan-Robinson, H. "Lessons of a Blitzkrieg." *Cavalry Journal* 49, no. 3 (May–June 1940): 208–218.

Schwien, E. E. "Cavalry Division Maneuvers, October 1939." *Cavalry Journal* 48, no. 6 (November–December 1939): 464–468.

———. "Intensive Training of the First Cavalry Division." *Cavalry Journal* 49, no. 2 (March–April 1940): 115–119.

Scott, Charles L. "Are More Changes Needed in Our Horsed Cavalry Regiments Now?" *Cavalry Journal* 44, no. 191 (September–October 1935): 42.

———. "Progress in Cavalry Mechanization: Scout Car Developments." *Cavalry Journal* 45, no. 4 (July–August 1936): 281–284.

Seborer, Stuart J. "From Escherhausen to Einbeck." *Cavalry Journal* 54, no. 5 (September–October 1945): 16–17.

"Second Cavalry in the Fourth Army Maneuvers." *Cavalry Journal* 49, no. 5 (September–October 1940): 440.

Sherburne, Thomas L. "A Tribute to the Mechanized from an Old-Timer." *Cavalry Journal* 45, no. 6 (November–December 1936): 479–480.

"The Sixth Cavalry in the Fourth Corps Maneuvers." *Cavalry Journal* 49, no. 3 (May–June 1940): 194–200.

Stackpole, Edward J., Jr. "22nd Cavalry Division in First Army Maneuvers." *Cavalry Journal* 49, no. 5 (September–October 1940): 448–449.

Steward, Hal D. "Cavalry in World War II." *Cavalry Journal* 55, no. 3 (May–June 1946): 27.

Stewart, H. S. "Mechanization and Motorization: The Final Chapter Has Not Been Written." *Cavalry Journal* 49, no. 1 (January–February 1940): 35–44.

Stockton, Marcellus L. "Reconnaissance and Attack Problems." *Cavalry Journal* 46, no. 3 (May–June 1937): 234–238.

Stolze, Richard B., and Donald J. Dupree. "Comments from Combat: Berg, France—A Recon Troop in Dismounted Action and Berg, France—A Tank Company in Support." *Cavalry Journal* 54, no. 1 (January–February 1945): 24–26.

Surles, Alexander D. "The Cavalry and Mechanization." *Cavalry Journal* 45, no. 1 (January–February 1936): 6–7.

Taylor, William J. "The 305th Cavalry Command Post Exercise." *Cavalry Journal* 44, no. 189 (May–June 1935): 24–25.

"Time to Wake Up." *Cavalry Journal* 48, no. 6 (November–December 1939): 507–509.

Tincher, Robert R. "Reconnaissance in Normandy." *Cavalry Journal* (January–February 1945): 13.

"Training of Modern Cavalry for War: Polish Cavalry Doctrine." *Cavalry Journal* 48, no. 4 (July–August 1939): 298–305.

"U.S. Cavalry in the ETO" (chart). *Cavalry Journal* 55, no. 3 (May–June 1946): 15.

Voorhies, Don W. "Comments from Combat—Help Wanted: A Cavalry Rifle Troop." *Cavalry Journal* 54, no. 5 (September–October 1945): 18.

Wainwright, Jonathan. "Mobility." *Cavalry Journal* 44, no. 191 (September–October 1935): 20.

Williams, Robert Willoughby. "With the Unicorn West of Bastogne." *Cavalry Journal* 54, no. 2 (March–April 1945): 6–11.

Williams, Robert Willoughby, and Lyman C. Anderson. "Third Army Reconnaissance." *Cavalry Journal* 54, no. 1 (January–February 1945): 20–23.

Williamson M. S. "6th Cavalry Participates in Eighth Brigade Maneuvers." *Cavalry Journal* 46, no. 4 (July–August 1937): 354–356.

Wilson, Arthur R. "A Cavalry Reconnaissance Squadron for an Infantry Division." *Cavalry Journal* 45, no. 1 (January–February 1936): 51–54.

"With the Mechanized Cavalry." *Cavalry Journal* 47, no. 2 (March–April 1938): 175–176.

Yale, Wesley W. "The 1936 Maneuvers of the 1st Cavalry Division." *Cavalry Journal* 45, no. 3 (May–June 1936): 174–195.

———. "Training in Attack Methods for Cavalry." *Cavalry Journal* 44, no. 191 (September–October 1935): 30–32.

Zeller, Henry M. "Cavalry in the Army Maneuvers." *Cavalry Journal* 50, no. 1 (January–February 1941): 59.

Books

2nd Cavalry Association. *The Ghosts of Patton's Third Army: A History of the Second U.S. Cavalry.* Munich, Germany: Münchner Graphische, 1946.

The 90th: A History of the 90th Division in World War II. N.p.: 90th Infantry Division, circa 1945. Reprint, Nashville, Tenn.: Battery Press, 1999.

106th Mechanized Cavalry Group. *The 106th Cavalry Group in Europe, 1944–1945.* Augsburg, Germany: J. P. Himmer KG, 1945.

Blumenson, Martin. *The Patton Papers, 1940–1945.* Boston: Da Capo Press, 1974.

Collier, William H. *The 106th Cavalry's Story.* Bloomington, Ind.: Trafford Publishing, 2012.

Collins, J. Lawton. *Lightning Joe: An Autobiography.* Baton Rouge: Louisiana State Univ. Press, 1979.

Conquer: The Story of the Ninth Army. Washington, D.C.: Infantry Journal Press, 1947.

Eleventh Cavalry from the Roer to the Elbe, 1944–1945. Eleventh Cavalry Group, circa 1945. Reprint, N.p.: Bibliogov Project, print on demand, 2013.

The Ghost Corps through Hell and High Water: A Short History of the XX Corps, U.S. Army. Washington, D.C.: U.S. Army, 1945.

Greenwood, John, ed. *Normandy to Victory: The War Diary of General Courtney H. Hodges and the First U.S. Army.* Lexington: Univ. Press of Kentucky, 2008.

History of the XVI Corps: From Its Activation to the End of the War in Europe. Washington, D.C.: Infantry Journal Press, circa 1945.

The Lion Rampant. N.p.: U.S. Army, circa 1945.

Mission Accomplished: The Story of the Campaigns of the VII Corps, United States Army, in the War against Germany, 1944–1945. Edited by Ray Merriam. Leipzig, Germany: J. J. Weber, 1945. Reprint, Bennington, Vt.: Merriam Press, 1998.

Mission Accomplished: A Summary of Military Operations of the XVIII Corps (Airborne) in the European Theater of Operations 1944–1945. Schwerin, Germany: XVIII Corps (Airborne), 1945.

Pamp, Frederick E., Jr. *Normandy to the Elbe, XIX Corps.* N.p.: 62nd Engineer TOPO Company, circa 1945.

"Patton's Ghost Troops"—After Action Report 9 August 1944–9 May 1945. Phoenix: 3rd Cavalry Veteran's Association, 1974.

Polk, James H., III, ed. *World War II Letters and Notes of Colonel James H. Polk.* Oakland, Oreg.: Red Anvil Press, 2005.

Province, Charles M., ed. *Military Essays and Articles by George S. Patton.* San Diego: George S. Patton, Jr. Historical Society, 2002.

Reardon, Mark J., ed. *Defending Fortress Europe: The War Diary of the German 7th Army in Normandy, 6 June to 26 July 1944.* Bedford, Pa.: Aberjona Press, 2012.

Rose, Ben, ed. *The Saga of the Red Horse.* Nijmegen, Holland: N.V. Drukkerij G.J. Thieme, 1945.

Samsel, Harold J. *Operational History of the 102nd Cavalry Regiment "Essex Troop" World War II.* N.p.: self-published, 1983.

———. *Operational History of the 117th Cavalry Reconnaissance Squadron (MECZ) World War II,* 2nd printing. N.p.: self-published, 1983.

Spearhead in the West: The Third Armored Division 1941–1945. N.p.: Third Armored Division, circa 1945. Reprint, Nashville, Tenn.: Battery Press, 1980.

The XX Corps: Its History and Service in World War II. Osaka, Japan: XX Corps Association, 1951.

Unicorn Rampant: History of the Sixth Cavalry Regiment/Group at Home and Abroad. N.p.: Sixth Cavalry Regiment Association, 1945.

United States Cavalry Association. *Cavalry Combat.* Harrisburg, Pa.: Telegraph Press, 1937.

Utterback, Preston, ed. *The 150 Year Saga of the 3rd U.S. Cavalry.* Phoenix: 3rd Cavalry Veterans Association, 1996.

Wingfoot: Rhineland and Central Europe Campaigns: Official History of the 101st Cavalry Group Mechanized. Weinheim, Germany: Hugo Diesbach, 1945.

Wood, James A., ed. *Army of the West: The Weekly Reports of German Army Group B from Normandy to the West Wall.* Mechanicsburg, Pa.: Stackpole Press, 2007.

Secondary Sources

Journal Articles

DiMarco, Louis. "The American Mechanized Cavalry's Critical Contribution to Allied Victory in Europe, 1944–1945." *Global War Studies* 9, no. 2 (2012): 39–66.

Hofmann, George F. "The Demise of the U.S. Tank Corps and Medium Tank Development Program." *Military Affairs* 37, no. 1 (February 1973): 20–25.

———. "The Tactical and Strategic Use of Attaché Intelligence: The Spanish Civil War and the U.S. Army's Misguided Quest for a Modern Tank Doctrine." *Journal of Military History* 62, no. 1 (January 1998): 101–134.

———. "A Yankee Inventor and the Military Establishment: The Christie Tank Controversy." *Military Affairs* 39, no. 1 (February 1975): 12–18.

Books

Adams, John A. *The Battle for Western Europe, Fall 1944: An Operational Assessment.* Bloomington: Indiana Univ. Press, 2010.

Allen, Robert S. *Patton's Third U.S. Army: Lucky Forward.* New York: Manor Books, 1947.

Balkoski, Joseph. *From Brittany to the Reich: The 29th Infantry Division in Germany, September–November 1944.* Mechanicsburg, Pa.: Stackpole Books, 2012.

———. *Our Tortured Souls: The 29th Infantry Division in the Rhineland, November–December 1944.* Mechanicsburg, Pa.: Stackpole Books, 2013.

Barron, Leo. *Patton at the Battle of the Bulge: How the General's Tanks Turned the Tide at Bastogne.* New York: NAL Caliber, 2014.

Baumer, Robert W. *Aachen: The U.S. Army's Battle for Charlemagne's City in World War II.* Mechanicsburg, Pa.: Stackpole Books, 2015.

Blackhorse: The History of the 11th U.S. Cavalry, 1901–1991. Bad Kissingen, Germany: T. A. Schachenmayer, 1991.

Blumenson, Martin. *The Battle of the Generals: The Untold Story of the Falaise Pocket—The Campaign That Should Have Won World War II.* New York: William Morrow, 1993.

———. *United States Army in World War II: The European Theater of Operations: Breakout and Pursuit.* Washington, D.C.: Historical Division of the Army, 1961.

Bonn, Keith E. *When the Odds Were Even.* Novato, Calif.: Presidio Press, 1994.

Bradham, Randolph. *To the Last Man: The Battle for Normandy's Cotentin Peninsula and Brittany.* Westport, Conn.: Praeger Security International, 2008.

Cameron, Robert S. *Mobility, Shock, and Firepower: The Emergence of the U.S. Army's Armor Branch, 1917–1945.* Washington, D.C.: Center of Military History, U.S. Army, 2008.

———. *To Fight or Not to Fight? Organizational and Doctrinal Trends in Mounted Maneuver Reconnaissance from the Interwar Years to Operation* IRAQI FREEDOM. Fort Leavenworth, Kans.: Combat Studies Institute Press, 2010.

Cirillo, Roger. *Ardennes-Alsace.* Washington, D.C.: GPO, 1995.

Clarke, Jeffrey J., and Robert Ross Smith. *United States Army in World War II: The European Theater of Operations: Riviera to the Rhine.* Washington, D.C.: Center of Military History, U.S. Army, 1993.

Cole, Hugh M. *United States Army in World War II: The European Theater of Operations: The Ardennes: Battle of the Bulge.* Washington, D.C.: Historical Division of the Army, 1965.

———. *United States Army in World War II: The European Theater of Operations: The Lorraine Campaign.* Washington, D.C.: Historical Division of the Army, 1950.

Doherty, Richard. *The British Reconnaissance Corps in World War II.* New York: Osprey Publishing, 2007.

———. *Only the Enemy in Front (Every Other Beggar Behind . . .): The Recce Corps at War, 1940–1946.* London: Tom Donovan Publishing, 1994.

Dorondo, David R. *Riders of the Apocalypse: German Cavalry and Modern Warfare, 1870–1945.* Annapolis, Md.: Naval Institute Press, 2012.

Doubler, Michael D. *Closing with the Enemy: How GIs Fought the War in Europe, 1944–1945.* Lawrence: Univ. Press of Kansas, 1994.

Eagen, William. *The Man on the Red Horse.* Portland, Oreg.: Metropolitan Printing, 1975.

Eisenhower, John S. D. *The Bitter Woods: The Battle of the Bulge.* New York: Da Capo Press, 1995.

Ellis, John. *Cavalry: The History of Mounted Warfare.* Barnsley, U.K.: Pen and Sword Military Classics, 2004.

Engler, Richard E., Jr. *The Final Crisis: Combat in Northern Alsace, January 1945.* Bedford, Pa.: Aberjona Press, 1999.

Fox, Don M. *Patton's Vanguard: The United States Army Fourth Armored Division.* Jefferson, N.C.: McFarland, 2003.

Gabel, Christopher R. *The Lorraine Campaign: An Overview, September–December 1944.* Fort Leavenworth, Kans.: Combat Studies Institute, 1985.

———. *The US Army GHQ Maneuvers of 1941.* Washington, D.C.: Center of Military History, U.S. Army, 1992.

Golden, Chris. *History, Customs and Traditions of the "Second Dragoons."* Newton, Mass.: 2d Cavalry Association, 2010.

Griess, Thomas E., ed. *West Point Atlas for the Second World War: Europe and the Mediterranean.* Wayne, N.J.: Avery Publishing Group, 1998.

Guderian, Heinz Günther. *From Normandy to the Ruhr: With the 116th Panzer Division in World War II.* Translated by Ulrich Abele, Esther Abele, and Keith E. Bonn. Bedford, Pa.: Aberjona Press, 2001.

Haasler, Timm. *Hold the Westwall: The History of Panzer Brigade 105, September 1944.* Mechanicsburg, Pa.: Stackpole Books, 2011.

Hargreaves, Richard. *The Germans in Normandy.* Mechanicsburg, Pa.: Stackpole Books, 2008.

Harrison, Gordon A. *United States Army in World War II: The European Theater of Operations: Cross Channel Attack.* Washington, D.C.: Center of Military History, U.S. Army, 1989.

Higgins, David R. *The Roer River Battles: Germany's Stand at the Westwall, 1944–45.* Philadelphia: Casemate Publishers, 2010.

Hofmann, George F. *Through Mobility We Conquer: The Mechanization of U.S. Cavalry.* Lexington: Univ. Press of Kentucky, 2006.

Hofmann, George F., and Donn A. Starry, eds. *Camp Colt to Desert Storm: The History of U.S. Armored Forces.* Lawrence: Univ. Press of Kansas, 1999.

House, Jonathan M. *Toward Combined Arms Warfare: A Survey of Tactics, Doctrine, and Organization in the 20th Century.* Fort Leavenworth, Kans.: Combat Studies Institute, 1984.

Jarymowycz, Roman. *Cavalry from Hoof to Track.* Mechanicsburg, Pa.: Stackpole Press, 2008.

Johnson, David E. *Fast Tanks and Heavy Bombers: Innovation in the U.S. Army, 1917–1945.* Ithaca: Cornell Univ. Press, 1998.

Keegan, John. *Six Armies in Normandy.* New York: Penguin Press, 1994.

Le Tisser, Tony. *Patton's Pawns: The 94th US Infantry Division at the Siegfried Line.* Tuscaloosa: Univ. of Alabama Press, 2007.

Levine, Alan J. *From the Normandy Beaches to the Baltic Sea: The Northwest Europe Campaign, 1944–1945.* Westport, Conn.: Praeger, 2000.

Longacre, Edward G. *The Cavalry at Gettysburg: A Tactical Study of Mounted Operations during the Civil War's Pivotal Campaign, 9 June–14 July 1863.* Lincoln: Univ. of Nebraska Press, 1986.

Ludewig, Joachim, and David Zabecki, ed. *Rückzug: The German Retreat from France, 1944.* Lexington: Univ. Press of Kentucky, 2012.

MacDonald, Charles B. *The Battle of the Huertgen Forest.* Philadelphia: Univ. of Pennsylvania Press, 2002.

———. *United States Army in World War II: The European Theater of Operations: The Last Offensive.* Washington, D.C.: Historical Division of the Army, 1973.

———. *United States Army in World War II: The European Theater of Operations: The Siegfried Line Campaign.* Washington, D.C.: Center of Military History, U.S. Army, 1990.

Mansoor, Peter. *The GI Offensive in Europe: The Triumph of American Infantry Divisions, 1941–1945.* Lawrence: Univ. Press of Kansas, 1999.

McGrath, John J. *Scouts Out! The Development of Reconnaissance Units in Modern Armies.* Fort Leavenworth, Kans.: Combat Studies Institute, 2007.

Miller, Edward G. *A Dark and Bloody Ground: The Hürtgen Forest and the Roer River Dams, 1944–1945.* College Station: Texas A&M Univ. Press, 1995.

Mitcham, Samuel W., Jr. *Retreat to the Reich: The German Defeat in France, 1944.* Mechanicsburg, Pa.: Stackpole Books, 2007.

———. *The Siegfried Line: The German Defense of the West Wall, September–December 1944.* Mechanicsburg, Pa.: Stackpole Books, 2009.

Morton, Matthew Darlington. *Men on Iron Ponies: The Death and Rebirth of the Modern U.S. Cavalry.* DeKalb: Northern Illinois Univ. Press, 2009.

Moisan, Melaney Welch. *Tracking the 101st Cavalry: A Reconnaissance Mission to Discover What Our Fathers Did in World War II.* Keizer, Oreg.: Wheat Field Press, 2008.

Nash, Douglas E. *Victory Was beyond Their Grasp: With the 272nd Volks-Grenadier Division from the Hürtgen Forest to the Heart of the Reich.* Bedford, Pa.: Aberjona Press, 2008.

Odom, William O. *After the Trenches: The Transformation of U.S. Army Doctrine, 1918–1939.* College Station: Texas A&M Univ. Press, 1999.

Palmer, Gary W. *The United States Cavalry: Time of Transition, 1938–1944: Horses to Mechanization.* San Diego, Calif.: Voyak Publications, 2013.

Palmer, Robert A., Kent Roberts Greenfield, and Bell I. Wiley. *United States Army in World War II: The Army Ground Forces: The Organization of Ground Combat Troops.* Washington, D.C.: Historical Division of the Army, 1947.

Palmer, Robert A., Bell I. Wiley, and William R. Keast. *United States Army in World War II: The Army Ground Forces: The Procurement and Training of Ground Combat Troops.* Washington, D.C.: Historical Division of the Army, 1948.

Piekalkiewicz, Janusz. *The Cavalry of World War II.* New York: Stein and Day, 1980.

Prefer, Nathan N. *Cracking the Siegfried Line: Patton's Ghost Corps.* New York: iBooks, 2003.

Richter, Klaus Christian. *Cavalry of the Wehrmacht: 1941–1945.* Translated by David Johnston. Atglen, Pa.: Schiffer Military History, 1995.

Rickard, John Nelson. *Advance and Destroy: Patton as Commander in the Bulge.* Lexington: Univ. Press of Kentucky, 2011.

———. *Patton at Bay: The Lorraine Campaign, 1944.* Washington, D.C.: Brassey's, 2004.

Rottman, Gordon L. *World War II Combat Reconnaissance Tactics.* New York: Osprey Publishing, 2007.

———. *World War II US Cavalry Groups: European Theater.* New York: Osprey Publishing, 2012.

Rusiecki, Stephen M. *In Final Defense of the Reich: The Destruction of the 6th SS Mountain Division "Nord."* Annapolis, Md.: Naval Institute Press, 2010.

———. *The Key to the Bulge: The Battle for Losheimergraben.* Mechanicsburg, Pa.: Stackpole Books, 2009.

Salter, Fred H. *Recon Scout.* New York: Ballantine Books, 1994.

Sawicki, James A. *Cavalry Regiments of the U.S. Army.* Dumfries, Va.: Wyvern Publications, 1985.

Stanton, Shelby L. *World War II Order of Battle U.S. Army (Ground Force Units).* Mechanicsburg, Pa.: Stackpole Books, 2006.

Stubb, Mary Lee, and Stanley Connor. *Army Lineage Series: Armor-Cavalry Part I: Regular Army and Army Reserve.* Washington, D.C.: Office of the Chief of Military History, 1969.

Thompson, Reginald W. *The Battle for the Rhineland.* Yardley, Pa.: Westholme Publishing, 2012.

Turner, John Frayn, and Robert Jackson. *Destination Berchtesgaden: The Story of the United States Seventh Army in World War II.* New York: Charles Scribner's Sons, 1975.

Whiting, Charles. *America's Forgotten Army: The True Story of the U.S. Seventh Army in WW II—and an Unknown Battle that Changed History.* New York: St. Martin's Press, 1999.

———. *Battle of the Ruhr Pocket.* London: Ballantine Books, 1970.

Yeide, Harry, *The Longest Battle, September 1944 to February 1945: From Aachen to the Roer and Across.* Saint Paul, Minn.: Zenith Press, 2005.

———. *Steeds of Steel: A History of U.S. Mechanized Cavalry.* Minneapolis: Zenith Press, 2008.

Yeide, Harry, and Mark Stout. *First to the Rhine: The 6th Army Group in World War II.* Saint Paul, Minn.: Zenith Press, 2007.

Zoepf, Wolf T. *Seven Days in January: With the 6th SS-Mountain Division in Operation* NORDWIND. Bedford, Pa.: Aberjona Press, 2001.

Zumbro, Derek S. *Battle for the Ruhr: The German Army's Final Defeat in the West.* Lawrence: Univ. Press of Kansas, 2006.

Theses, Dissertations, and Monographs

DiMarco, Louis A. "The U.S. Army's Mechanized Cavalry Doctrine in WW II." Master's thesis, U.S. Army Command and General Staff College, 1995.

Dooley, Matthew A. "Ignoring History: The Flawed Effort to Divorce Reconnaissance from Security in Modern Cavalry Transformation." Master's thesis, U.S. Army Command and General Staff College, 2006.

Nowowiejski, Dean A. "Adaptation to Change: U.S. Army Cavalry Doctrine and Mechanization, 1938–1945." Monograph, U.S. Army School of Advanced Military Studies, 1994.

Prigge, Christopher N. "Tradition and Transformation: The Origins of the U.S. Armored Cavalry Regiments." Ph.D. diss., Harvard University, 2011.

Tully, John N. "Doctrine, Organization and Employment of the 4th Cavalry Group during World War II." Master's thesis, U.S. Army Command and General Staff College, 1994.

Volpe, Michael J. "Task Force Butler: A Case Study in the Employment of an Ad Hoc Unit in Combat Operations during Operation Dragoon, 1–30 August 1944." Master's thesis, U.S. Army Command and General Staff College, 2007.

Watson, Andrew J. "The U.S. Cavalry: Still Relevant in Full Spectrum Operations?" Monograph, U.S. Army School of Advanced Military Studies, 2010.

Online Articles and Resources

Lutz, Robert. "117th Cavalry Reconnaissance Squadron (MECZ) in World War II." 117th Cavalry Association, http://www.117th-cav.org. Accessed May 2013.

"History of the Third Cavalry Regiment." 3rd Armored Cavalry Regiment, http://www.hood.army.mil/3d_acr/Unit%20Lineage/Regimental%20History.aspx. Accessed 11 January 2011.

Rousek, Charles E. "A Short History of the 38th Cavalry Reconnaissance Squadron (Mechanized)." Prestice, Czechoslovakia, 1945. Available via 117th Cavalry Association, www.117th-cav.org. Accessed May 2013.

Russen, David M. "Combat History: 102nd Cavalry Reconnaissance Squadron (MECZ): World War II." 117th Cavalry Association, www.117th-cav.org. Accessed May 2013.

Shehab, Alfred H. M. "The Ardennes Offensive: My Experiences in the 38th Cavalry Squadron's Defense of Monschau during the Battle of the Bulge." 117th Cavalry Association, www.117th-cav.org. Accessed May 2013.

———. "Cavalry on the Shoulder: The 38th CRS and the Defense of Monschau." Edited by Philip Notestine. 117th Cavalry Association, www.117th-cav.org. Accessed May 2013.

"World War II 1942–1945." 2d Dragoons, http://history.dragoons.org/category/world-war-ii/. Accessed 5 August 2010.

Index

Italic page numbers refer to illustrations.